OXFORD ... ... JR LAW

General Editors: PAUL DAVIES, KEITH EWING, MARK FREEDLAND

Towards a Flexible Labour Market

Labour Legislation and Regulation since the 1990s

OXFORD MONOGRAPHS ON LABOUR LAW

General Editors: Paul Davies, Cassel Professor of Commercial Law in the London School of Economics; Keith Ewing, Professor of Public Law at King's College, London; and Mark Freedland, Fellow of St John's College, and Professor of Employment Law in the University of Oxford.

This series has come to represent a significant contribution to the literature of British, European and international labour law. The series recognises the arrival not only of a renewed interest in labour law generally, but also the need for fresh approaches to the study of labour law following a period of momentous change in the UK and Europe. The series is concerned with all aspects of labour law, including traditional subjects of study such as collective labour law and individual employment law, but it also includes works which concentrate on the growing role of human rights and the combating of discrimination in employment, and others which examine the law and economics of the labour market and the impact of social security law and of national and supranational employment policies upon patterns of employment and the employment contract. Two of the authors contributing to the series, Lucy Vickers and Diamond Ashiagbor, have received awards from the Society of Legal Scholars in respect of their books.

Titles already published in this series

The Right to Strike
KEITH EWING

Legislating for Conflict
SIMON AUERBACH

Justice in Dismissal
HUGH COLLINS

Pensions, Employment, and the Law
RICHARD NOBLES

Just Wages for Women
AILEEN McCOLGAN

Women and the Law
SANDRA FREEDMAN

Freedom of Speech and Employment
LUCY VICKERS

International and European Protection of the Right to Strike
TONIA NOVITZ

The Law of the Labour Market
SIMON DEAKIN AND FRANK WILKINSON

The Personal Employment Contract
MARK FREEDLAND

The European Employment Strategy
DIAMOND ASHIAGBOR

Towards a Flexible Labour Market

Labour Legislation and Regulation
since the 1990s

PAUL DAVIES FBA, QC (Hon)

Cassel Professor of Commercial Law
in the London School of Economics

and

MARK FREEDLAND FBA

Professor of Employment Law
in the University of Oxford

OXFORD
UNIVERSITY PRESS

OXFORD
UNIVERSITY PRESS

Great Clarendon Street, Oxford OX2 6DP

Oxford University Press is a department of the University of Oxford.
It furthers the University's objective of excellence in research, scholarship,
and education by publishing worldwide in

Oxford New York

Auckland Cape Town Dar es Salaam Hong Kong
Karachi Kuala Lumpur Madrid Melbourne Mexico City Nairobi
New Delhi Shanghai Taipei Toronto

With offices in

Argentina Austria Brazil Chile Czech Republic France Greece
Guatemala Hungary Italy Japan Poland Portugal Singapore South Korea
Switzerland Thailand Turkey Ukraine Vietnam

Oxford is a registered trade mark of Oxford University Press
in the UK and in certain other countries

Published in the United States
by Oxford University Press Inc., New York

© P. Davies and M. Freedland, 2007

British Library Cataloguing in Publication Data

Data available

Library of Congress Cataloging in Publication Data

Davies, P. L. (Paul Lyndon)
Towards a flexible labour market : labour legislation and regulation since the 1990s /
Paul Davies and Mark Freedland.
p. cm. — (Oxford monographs on labour law)
ISBN-13: 978–0–19–921787–8 (hbk. : acid-free paper)
ISBN-13: 978–0–19–921788–5 (pbk. : acid-free paper)
1. Labor laws and legislation—Great Britain—History. I. Freedland, M. R. (Mark Robert) II. Title.
KD3009.D386 2007
344.4101—dc22

2007003840

Typeset by Newgen Imaging Systems (P) Ltd., Chennai, India
Printed in Great Britain
on acid-free paper by
Biddles Ltd, King's Lynn

ISBN 978–0–19–921787–8 (Hbk.) 978–0–19–921788–5 (Pbk.)

1 3 5 7 9 10 8 6 4 2

General Editor's Preface

Labour Legislation and Public Policy by Paul Davies and Mark Freedland was published in 1993. It quickly came to be regarded as one of the most important books on labour law, with a breadth of vision combined successfully with a great depth of analysis. In that seminal study, the authors emphasised the role and importance of collective laissez-faire as a distinctive regulatory stance, and traced the unfolding drama of labour law from the relatively quiet decade of the 1950s, to the troubled 1960s and 1970s, and to the turbulent years of the Thatcher regime. But history marches on, and in *Towards a Flexible Labour Market* the authors return to their task with an equally important, fully informed and predictably authoritative account of developments since 1993. Although the short period of the Major government is covered, the account in this volume is based mainly on the period of the Labour government from 1997 to 2006, a period which, as the authors point out, almost coincides with the anticipated extent of Mr Blair's tenure as Prime Minister. It is an account with a typically broad span, stretching from personal work relations, to collective labour law, and to initiatives designed to ensure full labour market participation.

It is a great pleasure to welcome this book as an Oxford Monograph on Labour Law, and most warmly to thank the authors for agreeing to publish it in the series. In this one volume, the authors add greatly to our understanding of the changes that have taken place since 1997, and deal most effectively with the shifting nature of the discipline once called Labour Law. Although associated with the Conservative governments preceding it, this is a process that has continued under New Labour, with the authors setting out to demonstrate that modern governments of both parties have subsumed labour legislation into 'a larger activity or pursuit of labour market regulation in the interests of a free and competitive economy'. Developing this theme in the final chapter of the book, the authors provide what is calculated to be an influential framework of 'methodologies of labour market regulation', and at the same time highlight that the contemporary focus of labour legislation on social inclusion, and the expansion of a productive economy, presents important new challenges for labour law scholars. In the years ahead, admirers of this work will look forward to a third volume on labour legislation from Paul Davies and Mark Freedland, for their wise insights on how these challenges have been met.

Keith Ewing
London
September 2006

Preface

The writing project from which this book has emerged was initially a less ambitious one than it eventually became; our original intention was simply to produce a second, up-dated edition of our work on *Labour Legislation and Public Policy* which had been published in the Clarendon Law Series in 1993. As we sought to implement that intention, several difficulties presented themselves; there had been a prodigious amount of legislation and regulatory activity since that time, which both defied compression into the space notionally available at the end of the existing volume and, equally important, was not amenable to being coerced into the analytical framework of that work, which we were anxious to preserve if not intact then at least in a recognisable and coherent form. It is those factors which brought about the decision to write this book; it was integral to our intentions that *Labour Legislation and Public Policy* would remain in existence as the companion to it, and we are grateful to our publishers for having agreed to re-print and re-issue that work on that basis.

A similar set of factors has in a sense determined the temporal coverage of this work; we have sought a compromise between on the one hand simply starting where the earlier work left off in 1992 and getting as near up-to-date to the publication of the new work as possible, and on the other hand providing a chronicle of the doings of the first two New Labour governments from 1997 to 2005. It seemed analytically satisfactory to regard that latter period as the focal one, but where appropriate to extend both backwards into the 1990s—the regulatory or deregulatory activities of Mr Major's Conservative governments were of no small interest and relevance—and forwards from May 2005 into the not insignificant developments of Mr Blair's third New Labour government, until the time of final revision of our manuscript in October 2006.

One result of the particular history of this book is that, although the production of a new edition of the original work had been under contemplation for some time, the time for researching and writing this new work has been relatively short, and so has the time for discussion about it with a wider group of colleagues; their influence will, however, be apparent, we hope, from our citations of secondary sources. That said, we wish specifically to acknowledge the benefits of discussions between Mark Freedland and Alain Supiot in the course of an academic visit to Nantes in March 2006, of continuing encouragement from Keith Ewing as the other Series Editor of Oxford Labour Law Monographs, of research input or assistance from Nicola Countouris and Astrid Sanders, of productive interaction with the Academic Division of Oxford University Press in the persons of John Louth, Gwen Booth, and Kate Bailey, and, as ever, of the indispensable background support of Sue Ashtiany and Geraldine Freedland.

Paul Davies
Mark Freedland
Oxford
Michaelmas Day 29 September 2006

Contents

Table of Cases

Table of Legislation

Abbreviations

ACAS	Advisory, Conciliation and Arbitration Service
ADR	Alternative Dispute Resolution
BJIR	British Journal of Industrial Relations
CAC	Central Arbitration Committee
CBI	Confederation of British Industry
CEEP	European Centre of Enterprises with Public Participation and of Enterprises of General Economic Interest
CF	Competitive flexibility
CIBP	Correction of inequality of bargaining power
CTC	Child Tax Credit
DDA	Disability Discrimination Act
DEFRA	Department for Environment Food and Rural Affairs
DfEE	Department of Education and Employment
DfES	Department for Education and Skills
DG	Directorate General
DRC	Disability Rights Commission
DTI	Department of Trade and Industry
DWP	Department for Work and Pensions
EAT	Employment Appeal Tribunal
EC	European Community
ECHR	European Convention on Human Rights
ECJ	European Court of Justice
ECR	European Court Reports
ECT	European Community Treaty
ECtHR	European Court of Human Rights
EEA	European Economic Area
EEC	European Economic Community
EERBR	Employment Equality (Religion or Belief) Regulations
EES	European Employment Strategy
EESOR	Employment Equality (Sexual Orientation) Regulations
EHRR	European Human Rights Reports
EMU	Economic and Monetary Union
EOC	Equal Opportunities Commission
EPA 1975	Employment Protection Act 1975
EPCA	Employment Protection (Consolidation) Act
ERA 1996	Employment Rights Act 1996
ERA 1999	Employment Relations Act 1999
ERA 2004	Employment Relations Act 2004
ESA	Employment and Support Allowance
ESCR	Electronic Social Care Record
ETUC	European Trade Union Confederation

EU	European Union
EWC	European Works Council
GDP	Gross Domestic Product
HMRC	Her Majesty's Revenue and Customs
HMSO	Her Majesty's Stationery Office
HSMP	Highly Skilled Migrant Programme
ICE	Information and Consultation of Employees
ICJ	International Court of Justice
ICR	Industrial Cases Reports
ILJ	Industrial Law Journal
ILO	International Labour Organisation
IRA	Industrial Relations Act
IRLR	Industrial Relations Law Reports
ITB	Industrial Training Board
JCHR	Joint Committee on Human Rights
JCMS	Journal of Common Market Studies
JSA	Jobseeker's Allowance
KSF	Knowledge and Skills Framework
LLPP	*Labour Legislation and Public Policy*
LMR	Labour market regulation
MLR	Modern Law Review
MPC	Monetary Policy Committee
MSC	Manpower Services Commission
NAP	National Action Plan
NEDC	National Economic Development Council
NHS	National Health Service
NMW	National Minimum Wage
NMWA	National Minimum Wage Act
NRP	National Reform Plan
ODPM	Office of the Deputy Prime Minister
OECD	Organisation for Economic Cooperation and Development
OED	*Oxford English Dictionary*
OEEC	Organisation for European Economic Co-operation
OJ	Official Journal
OJLS	Oxford Journal of Legal Studies
OPRA	Occupational Pensions Regulatory Authority
OPSR	Office of Public Services Reform
PA	Pensions Act
PCA	Personal Capability Assessment
PFI	Private Finance Initiative
RER	Regulation of employment relations

RRA	Race Relations Act
SDA	Sex Discrimination Act
SE	European Public Company
SI	Statutory Instrument
SMP	Statutory Maternity Pay
SNB	Special Negotiation Body
SSA	Sector Skills Agreement
SSAC	Social Security Advisory Committee
SSC	Sector Skills Council
SSDA	Sector Skills Development Agency
SSP	Statutory Sick Pay
TICE	Transnational Information and Consultation of Employees
TUC	Trades Union Congress
TULRECA	Trade Union and Labour Relations (Consolidation) Act
TUPE	Transfer of Undertakings Protection of Employment
TURERA	Trade Union Reform and Employment Rights Act
ULR	Union Learning Representative
UN	United Nations
UNICE	Union of Industrial and Employers' Confederations of Europe
WERS	Workplace Employment Relations Survey
WFTC	Working Families Tax Credit
WTC	Working Tax Credit

1

Introduction

House of Commons Debates, 14 January 2004
Employment Relations Bill: *Order for Second Reading read.*
The Secretary of State for Trade and Industry (Ms Patricia Hewitt): I beg to move, That the Bill be now read a Second time. *[Interruption.]*
Mr Speaker: Order. May I ask hon. Members to leave the Chamber quietly?[1]

There may of course have been entirely circumstantial reasons why the House of Commons seems to have emptied when the Employment Relations Bill of 2004 was presented by Ms Patricia Hewitt; it was, for instance, at lunch-time that this debate began, and this debate had been preceded by a session of Questions to the Prime Minister in which his veracity about the events leading to war in Iraq had been much in question; many MPs may have attended the House only for that discussion. However, it is still of some symbolical significance that, in the later part of the period which will be under review in this work, the opening of the Second Reading debate about a major government proposal for labour legislation should appear to command so little interest. Twenty or thirty years before, the presentation of a set-piece government Bill on labour law would have produced a mass movement of MPs into the chamber rather than out of it. In this Introduction, we present some preliminary suggestions about the ways in which labour legislation and the associated body of public policy have developed in Britain since the 1990s, and in particular under the New Labour administration in power from 1997 onwards, which might explain why such a change occurred.

1.1 From collective laissez-faire to labour market regulation

It should not be thought, however, that our purpose in this work is to spin out, from this parliamentary anecdote, a story of decline of British labour law, or of any general loss of political interest in that subject, since our work on *Labour Legislation and Public Policy* was completed in 1992 and published in 1993. That work, taking its historical starting point in 1945, described a transition from a period of studied legislative restraint in the sphere of employment relations to one

---

[1] *Hansard*, HC (series 6) vol 416, col 819 (14 January 2004).

of high legislative activism from the mid-1960s onwards. That activism continued to manifest itself, in one form or another, from the 1970s to the 1990s; but since the New Labour administration came to power in 1997 under the Prime Ministership of Mr Tony Blair that activity has if anything been intensified, so that the volume of legislation and of policy documents reviewed in this second work is a very considerable one, both in absolute terms and in proportion to that of the earlier period as a whole. So if our anecdotal opening hints at some kind or degree of marginalisation of labour law in recent and current British public policy, it would be misleading so far as it suggested any decline of legislative activity; and it would also be misleading about the direction that the inquiry and argument of this work will follow. Our concern in this analysis is not with the rate of flow along the pipe of British labour legislation, but rather with the taste and quality of the stream which issues forth, and, even more importantly, with the path of the river of public policy into which it is channelled.

This was, of course, no less the case for our earlier work upon which this book seeks to build. It is important to point that out, because a contrary view might be possible of what we were trying to achieve in our work on *Labour Legislation and Public Policy*. It might be thought that, when we chose in that book to depict and trace the fortunes of the doctrine of 'collective laissez-faire', we were primarily concerned with the movement from low, even minimal, legislative regulation of employment relations to a state of intense juridification of those relations, and then towards partial legislative de-regulation. That, however, would be to miss our initial purpose, which was to show how the collective laissez-faire approach of the early to middle post-Second World War period was, in aspiration at least, not so much a rationale or excuse for refusal or failure to legislate in the sphere of employment relations, as instead a distinctive regulatory stance in which it was sought to achieve a particular set of positive normative outcomes primarily by reliance on the capacity and potential of the system of voluntary collective bargaining.

The history which was related in *Labour Legislation and Public Policy* was one of change around and then away from the collective laissez-faire approach. But for the reasons which we have just given, that process of change should not be viewed as a movement from an absence of regulation towards the presence of regulation of employment relations, or even necessarily as an intensification of regulation of employment relations. It is instead a change or series of changes in the regulatory stance of the lawmakers and formulators of policy in the sphere of employment relations—most obviously, for our purposes, legislators and government policy-makers. Our analysis contemplates and concentrates upon two kinds or dimensions of change of regulatory stance, one concerned with ends, and the other with means.

The changes of the latter kind, that is to say in the means of regulation, are perhaps more familiar and easier to identify. They consist not so much of absolute changes in the means of regulation, but rather in partial changes in the composition of a mixture of regulatory means or techniques. Thus in *Labour Legislation and Public Policy*, and especially in the middle part of that work, we were concerned with a movement away from collective laissez-faire which consisted essentially in the shift from the 'method' or regulatory technique of collective bargaining towards the method or regulatory technique of legislation. But this was not, of course, a complete shift; there was always some legislative regulation under the regime of collective laissez-faire, and some collective bargaining survived the change away from that regime; it was the balance or preponderance between the two normative techniques which altered, generally speaking in favour of legislation and against collective bargaining.

Even with that qualification, the statement that there was a re-constituting of the balance between collective bargaining and legislation is an over-simplified one, if only because there were associated changes in the nature both of legislation and of collective bargaining. In the early post-war years, labour legislation moved away from its war-time format of governmental or ministerial ordering towards a pattern in which it consisted mainly of Acts of Parliament; but by the end of the period which was reviewed in *Labour Legislation and Public Policy* there was a renewed fashion for secondary legislation, and for the supplementation of legislation by codes of practice or guidance, such as those issued by the Advisory Conciliation and Arbitration Service (ACAS), and other mechanisms of informal legislation. An important part of the shift to secondary legislation was that it became, under the provisions of the European Communities Act 1972, the preferred method of honouring obligations on the part of the government of the UK to give effect to European Community Directives; and that was also a major element in the changes in the sources of labour legislation which resulted from UK accession to the Community in 1972.

If, during the period under review in *Labour Legislation and Public Policy*, labour legislation changed in its techniques as well as in its relative preponderance, so, even more radically, did collective bargaining. Among many such changes, the most significant was the progressive transformation from the 1960s onwards of a dual system of collective bargaining, consisting mainly of formal national or industry-wide multi-employer collective bargaining combined with informal workplace bargaining, into a system or practice increasingly dominated by single-employer and increasingly formalised enterprise-level bargaining. The beginnings of this transformation were identified by the Donovan Commission in 1968, and were welcomed and encouraged in their Report as a basis for maintaining the vitality and viability of voluntary collective bargaining as the preferred method of regulation of employment relations.

However, although that transformation did continue during the 1970s and gathered pace in the 1980s and early 1990s, it did not operate to preserve the voluntary collective bargaining system of the early and middle post-war period in the way that its protagonists in the Donovan Commission had hoped. Not only did it fail to stem the demand or assuage the appetite for legislative regulation of employment relations from all quarters of the political territory, but it also generally marked a shift in the previously existing equilibrium between management and trade unions, in favour of the former. The converging of collective bargaining upon the individual enterprise consisted of or brought about a concentration of managerial bargaining power at the point where it was most effective. Ironically enough, the very development of enterprise bargaining which had been sought after by those who wished to protect the collective character of employment relations in the 1960s and 1970s became one of the main factors of their individualisation in the 1980s and early 1990s.

Those observations about changes in the means or techniques of regulation of employment relations during the period under review in *Labour Legislation and Public Policy* lead us on to identify more subtle, but even more important, changes in the ends or purposes of that regulation which began to occur towards the end of that period. In that work, our analysis was to a considerable extent focused upon the destiny of the doctrine of collective laissez-faire; we framed the introduction to, and to a considerable extent the conclusions from, that work around it. But, as we have indicated earlier, collective laissez-faire was much more than an attitude of negativity towards the legislative regulation of employment relations; it was a positive approach to their regulation primarily by collective bargaining.

Moreover, there was a particular rationale for that positive approach, which identified a certain role and purpose for the regulation of employment relations; in that sense, the discussion about collective laissez-faire was about the ends and not just the means of regulation of employment relations, and that is why we regarded it as the most useful starting point for the analysis of labour legislation and public policy in the period under review, even if the collective laissez-faire approach, as a technique of regulation, was largely abandoned in the course of that period. The underlying rationale for the collective laissez-faire approach consisted in its capacity to achieve a certain degree or kind of correction of inequality of bargaining power between employers, or management, and workers; our observation was that, during the period under review in *Labour Legislation and Public Policy*, there were profound changes both within and around that conception of the ends or the purpose of regulation of employment relations, and therefore of the role of labour legislation and the associated body of public policy.

The starting point for that evolution in and from the collective laissez-faire approach, with regard to the ends rather than the means of regulation of employment relations, was of course the belief, on the part of its theorists such as Kahn-Freund, that it was the essential role and purpose of that regulation to correct what amounted to an inherent inequality of bargaining power in favour of employers and against workers, at least as long as the latter power was an individuated and not a collective one. Even in that radically worker-protective formulation, the collective laissez-faire approach recognised the necessity for the collectivised power of organised labour to be contained within a framework of legal regulation, but at the outset of the period under review in *Labour Legislation and Public Policy* the political as well as the theoretical perception was that this framework could afford to be a strongly permissive one. The story of labour legislation and public policy from the 1960s onwards, as we related it in that work, was one of changing political judgments as to what was a desirable or sustainable balance of that bargaining power, and a generally increasing resort to legislative intervention in order to reflect those changes in outlook.

Those shifts of perception, especially as they occurred from the mid-1960s onwards, generated what could be regarded as different ways of correcting inequality of power in employment relations. An erratic but underlyingly persistent movement began to occur between two modes of doing so; one of them consisted of using labour legislation to moderate the collective bargaining power of trade unions, while supplementing the protections of individual workers; the other consisted more straightforwardly of re-balancing the equilibrium of power in employment relations in favour of management. The policy of Labour governments in the later 1960s and 1970s was to operate in the former mode. While the contemporary assessment of the Conservative administration of 1970 to 1974 was that it had moved decisively into the latter mode, a retrospective view would rather regard it as poised between the two modes. It was generally agreed at the time, and is still perceived with hindsight to be the case, that the Conservative governments of the 1980s opted decisively for the second mode; for them, the correction of inequality of bargaining power in employment relations consisted unequivocally of reducing the power of trade unions.

However, the re-conceiving of the ends or purposes of labour law which occurred during the 1980s went further than this, in a sense transcending the ups and downs of the see-saw of correction of inequalities of bargaining power between management and workers, and amounting to a more fundamental re-casting of the function of labour legislation and its role in the public policy of governments. In effect, labour law began to move out of the zone of 'social law' and worker protection, and became part of a larger and rather different vision of labour market regulation in the interests of a free market economy. From that perspective, labour law and the regulation of employment relations were viewed, in a much more pronounced and overt way than they had previously been, as instrumental to the securing and maintaining of a political equilibrium constructed around the key notions of full employment, carefully controlled inflation, taxation and social security expenditure, and financially efficient provision of public services.

1.2 The labour policy of New Labour

As we neared the end of the preparations for the present work, having formulated some tentative ideas about the ways in which labour legislation and public policy had been developed by the Labour administration since 1997 (or 'New Labour', as it was soon re-styled), we re-considered what our corresponding assessments had been at the end of our analysis of the period down to the beginning of the 1990s in *Labour Legislation and Public Policy*. The effect of so doing was to be reminded that, although we had concluded that work with a retrospective upon collective laissez-faire which traced the fate of that doctrine and approach right through the period under consideration, we were already casting our presentation of the 1980s in these quite radically different terms of labour market regulation in the interests of a free market economy. Thus we emphasised that, while the reduction of the power of trade unions was undoubtedly an important pre-occupation of governments in the 1980s, that formed only part of a larger political enterprise of 'restructuring the labour economy' which, as we put it, 'gradually focused upon the notion of a market economy as the ideal for industrial society'.[2]

In the development of that theme, we considered a number of elements of regulation of employment relations and of the labour market which we suggested were no less important parts of the picture than the reduction of trade union power. Such elements included a re-structuring of pay bargaining, and of the individual employment relationship, in such a way as to recognise and establish a functional relationship between the 'removal of rigidities' and the promotion of full employment. We also noted the beginning of the assertion of a greater than previous degree of resistance to European Community social policy and labour legislation, the re-designing of the governmental approach to occupational pension provision and social security and vocational training provision more generally, and finally what we identified as 'the restructuring of the public employment sector in the 1980s', which we regarded as part and parcel of the creation of a new and marketised approach to the provision of public services and the discharge of the functions and responsibilities of government.

It is that theme or strand of our work on *Labour Legislation and Public Policy* which forms the most appropriate starting point for our present work, and the best point of reference for comparison and contrast with the ways of regulation of employment relations and the labour market under the New Labour administration from 1997 onwards. It should be explained at this point that, although the present work, as its title claims, follows on chronologically from the earlier work, picking up the story of British labour legislation from the early 1990s where the earlier work left off, nevertheless our analysis, as our title also slightly implies, is centrally focused upon the labour legislation and associated public policy of the New Labour governments which were in power after May 1997 and down to the time of writing in 2006—thus in effect during the Prime Ministership of Mr Tony Blair. At various points in the work we consider the labour legislation and associated public policy of the Conservative administration of Mr John Major which was in power between 1990 and 1997, and sometimes this is the subject of quite extensive discussion; but such discussion is motivated less by the intrinsic interest

---

[2] *Labour Legislation and Public Policy* (hereafter, LLPP), 526.

of the developments of that period (though that is not negligible) than by its contribution to the understanding of the developments which followed after the General Election of May 1997.

Perhaps, moreover, the main reason for regarding the developments in labour legislation and the associated body of public policy of the Major administration as being of real but nevertheless subordinate importance in the present work, is that they appear (sometimes deceptively) to be the work of a government which was relatively quiescent in policy terms, bridging the gap between the undoubtedly radical and ground-breakingly innovative politics of the administration of Mrs Margaret Thatcher, and the new era which the New Labour administration claimed to have ushered in after 1997. By deciding to structure our discussion according to those factors, we deliberately focus attention on the relationship between the labour legislation and public policy of the post 1997 period and that of the period under review in *Labour Legislation and Public Policy*, especially its concluding decades. This is specially appropriate insofar as the New Labour administration regarded itself as representing a new way, or Third Way, of conducting the regulation of employment relations which was different not only from that of its immediate predecessor but, even more significantly, from those of the governments of the preceding decades, both Conservative and Labour.

Perhaps the most important and therefore central question in the analysis which follows is whether that self-perception, or projection of itself, on the part of the Blair administration was an accurate or justified one—that is to say, whether a new way of governing in general, and of regulating employment relations in particular, really had been invented and could be put into effect from 1997 onwards. So comparison and contrast with the preceding administrations, not least that of Mrs Thatcher, recur throughout this work. It is important for us not to anticipate the outcomes of that process of comparison and contrast before examining the evidence in detail; but one very significant initial comparison may be tentatively drawn with the conclusions which we reached in *Labour Legislation and Public Policy* about the developments which had occurred in the 1980s, as we have recalled them in the preceding pages.

The suggestion we make, as a tentative hypothesis at this stage which will be explored in the course of the substantive chapters which follow, is that it is as accurate and appropriate to regard the Blair administration as it was to regard the Thatcher administration as having subsumed labour legislation and its associated body of social policy into a larger activity or pursuit of labour market regulation in the interests of a free and competitive market economy. Many—though, we hasten to emphasise, by no means all—of our observations of this kind with regard to the politics of the later 1980s, as rehearsed above, find loud and clear echoes in the years after 1997, even if the precise policy formulations are different ones.

However tentatively it is expressed, if the hypothesis which we have thus proposed is to command any attention and respect, we have in some way to make good two propositions which it implies: first, a negative one that New Labour governments moved away from the enclosed frame of reference in which labour legislation is regarded as solely or overwhelmingly concerned with correction of inequality of bargaining power between management and workers, and secondly that they moved towards labour market regulation in the interests of a wider set of policies for a competitive market-oriented economy and society. The first of those two propositions is relatively easy to sustain; we shall see at various points in the ensuing chapters how it proclaims itself from the principal policy document of the New Labour administration for the regulation of employment relations, the White Paper of May 1998, *Fairness at Work*.[3]

The second proposition is a harder one to substantiate, and it will be for our readers to judge how far it is borne out in the course of the succeeding chapters; but some features and sources of the grand design of the New Labour administration for labour market regulation may usefully be sketched in at this point. As we submit in detail later on, an important part of that articulation was carried out by Hugh Collins when he identified a distinctively New Labour conception of 'regulating for competitiveness' and identified its major source as the DTI while that department was in the charge of Mr Peter Mandelson.[4] However, we perhaps need to dig even more deeply in search of the roots of the New Labour approach to labour market regulation; in the course of doing so we may further strengthen the analogy with the policy framework of the later 1980s and early 1990s as we identified it in *Labour Legislation and Public Policy*, though not without remarking upon some very important points of contrast.

A good starting point for that further investigation is *Fairness at Work* itself. It is of no small significance that the presentation in that White Paper of the main proposals of the New Labour government for legislation relating both to individual rights at work and to collective representation at work are framed in a discourse not only, as we have indicated, of settling the old or traditional conflicts surrounding labour law, but also of active engagement in a more broadly based kind of labour market regulation. It is declared that 'Britain needs a flexible and efficient labour market in which enterprise can flourish, companies can grow and wealth can be created';[5] the pursuit of this objective is identified strongly with the combating of high unemployment and extensive social exclusion;[6] and it is asserted that 'For those in work, the Government has two key objectives for the labour market: efficiency and fairness', these being seen as 'wholly compatible' objectives in the sense that 'It is perfectly possible to have a modern, flexible and efficient labour market which is both a vital engine for economic growth and business output and a means for people to find well-paid and satisfying jobs.'[7]

---

[3] Cm 3968, 1998; see below, 43–44, 45–46.
[4] H Collins, 'Regulating the Employment Relation for Competitiveness' (2001) 30 ILJ 17; see below, 44.   [5] Para 2.10.
[6] Para 2.11.   [7] Para 2.12.

The White Paper further elaborates the ways in which that reconciliation can be achieved in the following terms:

The keys to securing efficiency and fairness are employability and flexibility. Employability means ensuring that people are well prepared, trained and supported, both initially as they enter the labour market, and throughout their working lives. Flexibility means businesses being able to adapt quickly to changing demand, technology and competition. By enabling business success, flexibility promotes employment and prosperity.[8]

And it goes on from there to confirm its objectives of embodying the regulation of employment relations within a larger ideology and practice of labour market regulation:

To support both employability and flexibility we need a labour market culture and a legislative framework which together promote economic growth, enhance competitiveness, encourage entrepreneurship and foster job creation.[9]

We shall see in subsequent chapters how strongly these notions of labour market regulation conditioned and informed the legislation and policy of the New Labour administration in the spheres of individual and collective labour law.

Our hypothesis that the roots of New Labour policy for labour legislation are to be found buried in the soil of labour market regulation might seem no more than an acceptance of the rhetorical spin which the framers of that policy chose to put upon it; but we think that it acquires more substance when we observe the various ways in which that approach to labour legislation was linked up with a similar set of approaches to a number of other kinds of social and economic regulation bearing upon employment relations and the functioning of the labour market. This is very well illustrated by the way in which, in the sphere of taxation and social security provision, a review initiated by the Treasury and published at the end of 1997 announced, in a manner very comparable with that of *Fairness at Work*, the institution of a new agenda which was essentially one of active labour market regulation:

The old approach to full employment relied heavily on the levers of macroeconomic management. But that was because active welfare to work policies were less important when a high proportion of the unemployed were only out of work for a short time. Skills mattered less when unskilled workers had access to good job opportunities. The interaction of tax and benefits for the low paid was less relevant when most jobs paid a wage which took people well above the levels of benefits. Flexible working practices were less important when fewer people needed to balance work and family responsibilities. And the focus on the claimant unemployed was valid when those outside the labour market were there from personal choice, rather than lack of opportunity. But now the old policy agenda has become out of date.[10]

---

[8] Para 2.13.   [9] Ibid.
[10] *The Modernisation of Britain's Tax and Benefit System—Number One: Employment Opportunity in a Changing Labour Market*, foreword by the Chancellor of The Exchequer and the Secretary of

The great significance of these shifts in priorities will become fully apparent later, especially in our substantive chapter on 'Promoting Work' (chapter 4).

This digging below the surface of the politics of New Labour after 1997 always throws up reminders that it was, right from the outset, an administration directed from the 'twin peaks' of the Cabinet Office and the Treasury by both the Prime Minster and the Chancellor, Mr Gordon Brown. Probably the most important and over-arching policy initiative of the first New Labour government was the Comprehensive Spending Review which was initiated by the Treasury and launched within a month of the government's coming into power.[11] This Review was to lay the policy foundations for a whole governmental programme of control of public spending and of inflation and taxation, intended to provide the basis for full employment and economic prosperity, and generally regarded as conspicuously successful in achieving those ends over the space of a number of years.

There were evident resonances between this programmatic approach and the enterprise of re-structuring the economy which, in *Labour Legislation and Public Policy*, we identified as the backdrop to the labour market regulation of Conservative governments in late 1980s and at the beginning of the 1990s. Also recognisable in the policy discourse of that time, though now even more strongly articulated, was the notion of a chain of political or social contracts which would secure the necessary set of commitments to this programme, culminating in an overtly contractual and consumerist vision of the relations between citizens, government, and the agencies of public service provision. This notion is clearly visible in the new design for social security provision which was generated by the Comprehensive Spending Review, and which was proposed by the Green Paper of March 1998, *A New Ambition for Our Country–A New Contract for Welfare*[12]—a policy document which we consider more fully later in this work.[13]

It should be stressed that, by contrast with the approach to economic re-structuring which was taken in the later 1980s, this policy framework was a design for increasing social investment in public services and the relief of poverty rather than reducing it; but the political contract which both approaches had more or less in common could not have been more clearly spelt out than by the Prime Minister in his Foreword to the Comprehensive Spending Review White Paper of July 1998 when, speaking of the government's intentions to increase expenditure on key public services, he declared that:

... because money for education and health has been so hard won, there is an obligation on those spending that money to do so wisely in pursuit of agreed and ambitious targets. That is why we insist on a new principle for funding public services: 'money for

---

State for Education and Employment: see <http://www.hm-treasury.gov.uk/documents/taxation_work_and_welfare/work_and_welfare/tax_workwel_index.cfm>.

[11] By Mr Alistair Darling as Chief Secretary to the Treasury in a Statement to the House of Commons on 12 June 1997; *Hansard*, HC (series 6) vol 295, col 1423 et seq (12 June 1997).

[12] Cm 3805, 1998.   [13] See below ch 4 section 4.1.

modernisation'. 'Money for modernisation' is a contract. It says we will invest more money but that money comes with strings attached. In return for investment there must be reform.[14]

There is a further sense in which, from these various starting points, we can observe that the New Labour administration created a particular policy framework which it is meaningful to analyse in terms of labour market regulation. This administration was as strongly convinced as its immediate predecessors that its main task in the employment sphere was to ensure and maintain the existence of a flexible and adaptable labour market; it had a vision about how that could best be achieved which was not very dissimilar from that of those immediate predecessors, but was perhaps a somewhat more sophisticated one. This involved a recognition that 'the labour market' was an entity or a conception which was both complex and undergoing various mutations, largely associated with the transitions from a predominantly manufacturing economy to an economy predominantly producing services, and from an economy in which the public and private sectors were quite strongly separated to one in which they were elaborately inter-twined.

The New Labour administration seems especially to have realised that new divisions or aspects or formations of the labour market were identifying themselves, so that the securing of a flexible and adaptable labour market required regulatory reinforcement at rather different points and in rather different ways from those of earlier regulatory practice in the employment sphere. In earlier phases, it had been appropriate to regard employing enterprises as creating or operating within two quite sharply differentiated kinds of labour market, one being internal and the other external. An employing enterprise would operate an 'internal labour market' when it drew primarily on its own workforce to meet demands for enhancement of technical and managerial capacity, and would tend to limit its recourse to the 'external labour market' to special situations of occasional demand. In the recent and current phase, employing enterprises have mixed and mingled their drawings upon internal and external labour markets to the point where there is no sharp distinction between the two typologies.

A principal form or manifestation of this elision between internal and external labour markets consisted in an exponential expansion, during the period under review, of various patterns of outsourcing or contracting out of labour provision; and this increasingly often extended to the core functions and the management of the employing enterprise itself. We can discern here the emergence of a kind of market in the management and 'packaging' of labour provision. The New Labour administration perceived it as a matter of the utmost importance to maximise the ability of employing enterprises to shift into and out of intermediate and external labour markets, and to have free recourse to this emerging market in

[14] Foreword to White Paper, *Modern Public Services for Britain: Investing in Reform—Comprehensive Spending Review: New Public Spending Plans 1999–2002* (Cm 4011, 1998).

the management of labour. We shall see that many of their regulatory decisions or interventions in the employment sphere were specifically directed to protecting these particular and often novel forms of labour market freedom and adaptability for employing enterprises.

1.3 The scope of the book

If the foregoing paragraphs succeed to any extent in establishing an understanding of the policy foundations of the New Labour administration from 1997 onwards, and in indicating some analogies with the policy frameworks of governments in the 1980s and earlier in the 1990s, they must, however, leave the reader wondering in what ways we suppose that those foundations gave shape to the superstructure of labour market regulation which we argue was built upon them. It is one of the tasks and purposes of the ensuing chapters to answer that question. This we seek to do in three stages. First, a chapter on individual employment law, or, as we prefer to conceptualise it, the regulation of personal work relations, considers how governments since the 1990s have constructed notions of managerial adaptability and 'light regulation'; and we argue that there have been specially strong interconnections between those normative constructions and the programmes of reform of public services which successive governments have pursued during this period, a central example being the project of public service 'modernisation' to which the Prime Minister was referring in the preceding extract.

Secondly, a chapter on the collective labour legislation and associated public policy of the period since the 1990s will show in particular how New Labour governments sought, with greater success than might have been anticipated, to find a workable compromise for long-standing conflicts about the appropriate mode and level of statutory support for the recognition of trade unions in collective bargaining with employing enterprises, and how they moved on to try to put in place rather different approaches to collective representation in the workplace based upon looser notions of 'partnership' between employers or managements and workers. Finally, in a third stage of the development of the argument of the work as a whole, and one which is crucial to the establishment of the concept of labour market regulation which we have proposed in this Introduction, we move beyond the sphere traditionally comprehended within the terminology of 'labour legislation' (though in this respect only pursuing further a path which we opened up in our work on *Labour Legislation and Public Policy*), and we discuss a wide range of measures and policies which are concerned primarily with the promotion of work or employment rather than with the terms and conditions upon which it takes place.

Before embarking upon that detailed substantive analysis, a further word is appropriate about one other aspect of our methodology. We are conscious of a danger that a study of this kind may become an insular one, overly-concentrated upon continuity and change in labour legislation and labour market regulation within the United Kingdom. No less interesting and important than those internal continuities and changes is the development of the comparisons and contrasts between that national evolution and the corresponding national evolutions occurring elsewhere in Europe, and between the policy directions taken by governments of the UK and those taken by the European Community as a whole. In the ensuing chapters we seek to develop an awareness of that set of relationships between normative systems as an important dimension of our discussion. While it is not practical within the compass of this work to engage in direct comparison between the evolution of labour legislation and public policy in particular Member States, it is on the other hand feasible and useful to regard the evolution of European Community legislation and policy both as a lens through which to obtain a synoptic view of developments in the various Member States and also as a free-standing and very important paradigm of the emergence of a particular kind of framework of labour market regulation.

The particular significance, for the present work, of that framework of EU labour market regulation consists in the way that it first became intertwined with, and has eventually become an enveloping discourse for, EU labour legislation and social policy. This is a development which has occurred since the 1990s, and it is especially interesting to relate that chronology to the evolution towards labour market regulation in British public policy which we have identified in outline and will describe in detail in the ensuing chapters. It was, of course, the case that in certain senses the European Community had been engaged in labour market regulation well before the 1990s, indeed from its very inception, since we could regard as forms of labour market regulation both the whole Community apparatus for securing the freedom of movement of workers between Member States, and the Structural Funds for regional economic development, and there is no doubt that the regime of control upon State Aids to industry and commerce has had an important function of labour market regulation.

However, it would be almost equally uncontroversial to assert that before the 1990s these kinds of Community labour market regulation were conceived of as being quite distinct from the mechanisms by which the Community engaged in the regulation of employment relations, and from the framework of Community Social Policy which determined the ways in which those mechanisms were devised and operated. It was that distinction which was progressively dissolved in the 1990s, in fact from the time of the Maastricht Treaty of 1992 onwards. The ground-breaking work in this respect was accomplished by the European Commission during the Presidency of M Jacques Delors, at whose initiative there was produced in 1993 and 1994 a crucial set of Green and White Papers which between them[15] had the aim and effect of yoking together the Social

---

[15] The crucial integrative policy document was *Growth, Competitiveness, Employment: The Challenges and Ways Forward into the 21st Century—A White Paper* (COM(93) 700, December 1993); it was followed by *European Social Policy—A Way Forward for the Union—A White Paper* (COM(94) 333, July 1994).

Policy and the Economic Policy of the Community with regard to the labour market and subordinating them to an overriding concern with growth, competitiveness, and full employment.

This became a history, which we need not recount in detail in this work, of conscious development of Community Employment Policy and the co-ordination of the employment policy of Member States from the Essen European Council of 1994, leading to agreement in 1997 upon the new employment provisions of the Treaty of Amsterdam and the launching of the European Employment Strategy by the Luxembourg Jobs Summit of November 1997, a set of initiatives heightened and intensified by the Lisbon European Council of March 2000. That history has been regarded as of increasing intrinsic and general interest to labour lawyers; but its special significance for the present work, as we have indicated, consists in the way that Community labour legislation and its associated body of social policy came increasingly to be debated and rationalised in the terms and objectives of that set of employment strategies. It is in that sense that labour market regulation came increasingly to subsume the regulation of employment relations at Community level, both in the ideological and in the practical institutional dimensions.

There are, as we have also indicated, very significant parallels and even some important mutualities between those developments at Community level and the emergence of a new pattern of labour market regulation as the paradigm for British labour legislation and public policy which it is the principal purpose of the ensuing chapters to explore. However, we suggest that it is at the same time very important, while observing those mutual influences, not to expect or impose any simple correlation between the evolution in the UK which is the main subject of our inquiry and the evolution at Community level which forms the back-drop to it. On the contrary, we prefer to think of the evolution at Community level as demonstrating a range and diversity of approaches to labour market regulation, and therefore indicating the extent to which the particular patterns of labour market regulation which have emerged in the UK during and since the 1990s may be contingent and path-dependent ones rather than inevitable or universal ones. That, in fact, is the essence of the hypothesis which we will explore in the ensuing substantive chapters and try to evaluate in the Conclusion to this work.

2

Personal Work Relations and Managerial Adaptability

2.1 The law and management of personal work relations—context and policy

This chapter shows how the main policy dynamic of legislation and regulation concerning personal work relations during this period was, during the initial part of the period, that of the Conservative administration of Mr John Major,[1] fairly straightforwardly one of de-regulation. But during the subsequent New Labour governments of Mr Tony Blair,[2] that dynamic was transmuted into a more complex one of maximising the freedom and flexibility of the forms and structures of personal work relations, while maintaining and cautiously enhancing a set of protections for workers conceptualised around notions of fairness, equality, and work-life balance. It emerges how that equilibrium often had to be sought by means of difficult inter-actions with the norms and policies of EU employment law. Largely, though by no means entirely, as a result of those inter-actions, the period was one of considerable legislative activity affecting personal work relationships, and also of very extensive governmental normative activity in a wider sense, for example, as we shall see, in the reform of public services. The main challenge in providing an account of that legislation and normative activity is to understand the nature of the changes or evolutions of public policy which occurred from 1997 onwards. In this introductory section we identify some salient contextual features of the development of the management of personal work relations during the period in question, and we introduce a set of arguments about the way in which those contextual features were linked to, indeed almost in a sense created, the framework of public policy in this particular area after 1997.

It will not have escaped the notice of our readers that we have introduced this discussion of this chapter under a novel and unfamiliar category, that of 'personal

---

[1] Mr Major's administration ran from November1990 when Margaret Thatcher resigned from being Prime Minster, through the General Election of May 1992 until the General Election of May 1997. Our main concern is with the period from the 1992 Election.

[2] From May 1997 to May 2001, from May 2001 to May 2005, and from May 2005 to the time of writing.

work relations', and that we are thereby invoking a notion of 'the law of personal work relations'. This is intended to identify, by its subject-matter, a particular sub-set or sub-division of labour or employment law; we distinguish or separate it from the other sub-divisions of, on the one hand, collective labour law and, on the other hand, the wider kind of labour market regulation which in this work we have designated under the heading of 'promoting work'. It corresponds to the sub-set of labour or employment law usually known as 'individual employment law'. The concept or terminology of 'the law of personal work relations' seems to us to have the following advantages over the concept or terminology of 'individual employment law'. First, the identification of its subject-matter as 'personal work relations' rather than 'employment' more clearly extends to semi-dependent or independent work relationships (while still, by its confinement to those work relations which are 'personal', excluding inter-firm or commercial work relations).

Secondly, and even more importantly, the description of its subject-matter as 'personal' rather than as 'individual' maintains its distinction from 'collective' labour or employment law, but in a more satisfactory way than by making a sharp and clean contrast between 'individual' and 'collective' labour or employment law. This is more satisfactory because it better accommodates the perception that work relations which are not 'collective' are not necessarily 'individual', so that labour or employment law which is not 'collective' may not be appropriately conceived of as 'individual'. By 'collective labour or employment law' we usually mean the labour or employment law which concerns relations between, on the one hand, employing enterprises and, on the other hand, workers in collective organisations or the representatives of workers. But the work relations which are not between those collective parties or which are not mediated through workers' representatives may well be best understood as relations with groups of workers in the sense of types or classes or cohorts of workers, such as 'the part-time workers in or for the firm' or 'the women workers in or for the firm'. An important message from this chapter will be that work relations which are 'de-collectivised' are not thereby 'individu-alised' in any straightforward or clearly understood sense, and that we need to understand more clearly than we do the transformations which have been wrought by a partial de-collectivisation of work relations.

Another useful feature of the organising concept or terminology of 'the law of personal work relations' is that it is conducive to the identification of a cor-responding body of social and economic activity or practice, and of social and economic science which examines that activity or practice—much more so than the relatively isolated concept of 'individual employment law'. This is not to say that there is a corresponding science or recognised discipline of 'personal work relations'. The taxonomical reality is a more complex one in which the study of 'industrial relations', traditionally heavily concentrated upon collective employ-ment relations,[3] has tended to spread beyond that collective sphere, often being

---

[3] As in the classical text, A Flanders and H A Clegg (eds), *The System of Industrial Relations in Great Britain* (Oxford: Blackwell Publishing, 1954), containing O Kahn-Freund's famous chapter on

re-named 'employment relations'[4] or 'employee relations'.[5] In the course of doing so, it has to some extent absorbed the study of 'personnel management', itself transmuted into 'human resources management' in the course of the 1980s and 1990s. The notion of 'personal work relations' usefully focuses upon the non-collective aspect of the area of study which has emerged from those transformations.

The question, therefore, is what have been the trends in the evolution of personal work relations during the period under consideration which have been influential upon the formation and implementation of public policy with regard to labour legislation. This is a rather specific and evaluative question, predicated upon the notion that only certain particular trends, among all those which could be identified as significant, will actually be important factors in the shaping of public policy, whether this is at a theoretical or rhetorical or practical level. There is general agreement that the most obvious general trends in the evolution of personal work relations during this period consisted in the continued progression towards, first, 'non-standard' forms of employment, and, secondly, at least until the end of the 1990s, de-collectivisation in the sense of the reduction of the significance of collective bargaining and, to that extent, the individualisation of work relations. We shall suggest, however, that in the case of each of these two general trends, it is useful to identify particular versions which were especially influential upon public policy. This will involve a partial shift of emphasis, as compared with the conclusions which have been drawn by theorists both of employment relations and of employment law, from the analysis of empirical data concerning employment patterns and their evolution. That shift of emphasis will be towards a particular analysis of the changing approaches to systems of organisation and management of personal work relations; that analysis characterises those changing approaches as the pursuit of 'managerial flexibility' in personal work relations.

We begin by re-examining, from that perspective, the significance for public policy of a progression towards non-standard forms of employment during the period under review. There is widespread agreement among both social science analysts and legal analysts that there were important shifts in that direction during this period; the views of legal analysts are important here because the categories of 'non-standard forms of employment' are to quite some extent in their custody.[6] There is a general consensus that there was during this period growth in the size of

---

the 'Legal Framework', which formed the point of departure for the modern theory of the incorporation of norms derived from collective bargaining into the 'individual' contract of employment.

[4] As in N Millward, A Bryson, and J Forth, *All Change at Work?* (London: Routledge, 2000) (hereafter, '*All Change?*'). This work was sub-titled, '*British employment relations 1980–1998, as portrayed by the Workplace Industrial Relations Survey series*'. Whereas the surveys of 1980, 1984, and 1990 were styled as Surveys of Industrial Relations, that of 1998 was styled as a Survey of Employment Relations.

[5] P Blyton and P Turnbull, *The Dynamics of Employee Relations* (3rd edn, Basingstoke: Palgrave Macmillan, 2004).

[6] Cf, for instance *All Change?*, n 4 above, at 43–48 ('Changing composition of the workforce'); S Fredman, 'Labour Law in Flux: The Changing Composition of the Workforce' (1997) 26 ILJ 337–352.

the sections of the workforce, and the proportions of the total workforce, who were engaged in part-time, temporary, agency, and casual employment.[7]

However, there is considerable uncertainty, and even disagreement, about the nature and extent of those shifts, and as to how far they amount to an inexorable and overwhelming transformation of employment practice and structures; earlier depictions to the latter effect have been the subject of recent scepticism.[8] There does in particular seem to be good reason for doubting the transcendent import-ance of a trend, earlier regarded as a central one, away from individual employ-ment relationships towards those of self-employment, though precise statistical assessment is rather controversial.[9] More generally, the debate as to whether and how far these evolutions represent the systemic erosion of standard forms of employment remains a difficult and unsatisfactory work of assessment, if only because of the extent to which those phenomena occur in complex patterns of coincidence with each other. Personal work relations might be constituted in, or converted to, any or all of those non-standard forms, or any combination of them; there is in short no simple contrast between 'standard' and 'non-standard' per-sonal work relations, nor any single point at which de-standardisation of personal work relations can be said to have occurred.

Even more fundamentally, in a sense we may miss the point and central signifi-cance of those phenomena by placing them within an analytical framework of de-standardisation of employment or work relationships. That analysis may have come to form a distorting lens in more than one respect. On the one hand, it may over-unify or unduly homogenise a set of phenomena which may be very dis-parate ones, occurring in very varied economic and occupational contexts. The situation of a senior managerial employee who becomes a part-time consultant to his or her employing enterprise may be a world away from that of a manual employee working on an 'on-demand' basis; the descriptive unification of the two situations as ones of de-standardised employment may well be a misleading one. On the other hand, and perhaps less obviously, the idea of de-standardisation of personal work relations may exaggerate the distinctiveness of the phenomena of

---

[7] See *All Change?*, n 4 above, at 47–48; *The Dynamics of Employee Relations*, n 5 above, at 67–69, 72–73, 81–82.

[8] See, for instance, P Nolan and S Wood, 'Mapping the Future of Work' (2003) 41 BJIR 165–174.

[9] Cf the following assessment from the ESRC Future of Work Research Programme in 2003: 'in the UK, findings from recent national surveys show . . . there is no rapid increase in self-employment. Self-employment grew rapidly from 5 to 11 per cent of total employment between 1979 and 1984, but at present it stands at 7 per cent' (<http://www.esrcsocietytoday.ac.uk/ESRCInfoCentre/PO/releases/2003/june/top.aspx?ComponentId=2050&SourcePageId=1404>). However, a dif-ferent statistical assessment of 11% for 2001 is given in a fact-sheet issued from the same source (<http://www.esrcsocietytoday.ac.uk/ESRCInfoCentre/facts/index36.aspx?ComponentId=7109&SourcePageId=7091>). That discrepancy may of course be attributable to the notorious difficulty of drawing that particular category distinction; cf S Deakin and F Wilkinson, *The Law of the Labour Market—Industrialisation, Employment and Legal Evolution* (Oxford: OUP, 2005) at 310–311 for discussion of confusion in the Labour Force Survey data between self-employment and casual employment.

'de-standardisation' from other parallel shifts and changes occurring *within* the supposedly 'standard' employment relationship.

Our suggestion for an analysis which corrects those distortions is to view the phenomena of 'de-standardisation' as being aspects of a larger, looser category of ways in which personal work relations may undergo re-structuring, typically on the initiative of the employing enterprise. According to this analysis, there has been a strong and somewhat accelerating general dynamic of re-structuring of personal work relations during the period under review. The phenomena of 'de-standardisation' constitute aspects of this dynamic, but they are certainly not the only aspects and may not even be the most important ones. Other major kinds of re-structuring of personal work relations may occur even fully within the compass of the full-time, long-term employment relationship. An employment relationship or a set of employment relationships may be re-structured and fully re-specified without necessarily being de-standardised.

This will become clearer if we identify a set of ways in which employing enterprises have often, during the period under review, been seeking to re-organise their employment structures or systems. The general goal of cost-efficiency has been pursued by means of a very wide variety of strategies and tactics in the organisation of forms and structures of production and of use of manpower.[10] De-standardisation of personal work relations, in its various forms, is an important part of the arsenal, but two other main parts of the arsenal may usefully be mentioned. One has to do with the re-organising of working-time, job specification, and payment systems within 'standard' employment relationships. The other concerns the re-organisation of employing enterprises, which might consist of either external re-structuring or internal re-structuring. External re-structuring consists of the re-arrangement of ownership or control of the employing enterprise or the total or, more usually, partial contracting out, contractual sharing, or delegation to agencies, of its employing functions. Internal re-structuring consists of re-distributing or re-grouping managerial responsibility for employment functions within the employing enterprise. We may refer to these two sets of strategies as, respectively, institutional re-organisation and job re-organisation.

We do not suggest that either of these sets of strategies is a new one, or a novelty to the period under review; there are many forerunners of them in earlier periods; indeed, they could be seen as having a continuous history at least from the 1960s onwards, if not before. However, each of these two sets of strategies seems to have been deployed more intensively and extensively, and in increasingly elaborate forms, in the course of the period under review. So far as job re-organisation is concerned, more and more sophisticated systems of performance management, appraisal, pecuniary and non-pecuniary incentives, and methods of arranging and

---

[10] A useful set of theoretical perspectives upon this set of strategies is provided by Part I of R S Schuler and S E Jackson, *Strategic Human Resource Management* (Oxford: Blackwell Publishing, 1999).

remunerating working time have been introduced.[11] With regard to institutional re-organisation, the evolution of external re-structuring has been usefully summarised in these terms:

The development of more complex organisational forms—such as cross-organisation networking, partnerships, alliances, use of external agencies for core as well as peripheral activities, multi-employer sites and the blurring of the public/private sector divide—has implications for both the legal and the socially constituted nature of the employment relationship.[12]

There is also evidence of similar elaboration of internal employment structures within many employing enterprises and corporate groups, involving many variants on a theme of creation and re-organisation of internal agencies or profit centres or units or divisions of accounting and accountability.[13]

A somewhat parallel set of observations may be made in respect of the other apparently simple but actually very complex and easily misinterpreted trend in personal work relations during the period under review, that of de-collectivisation or de-unionisation. As with de-standardisation, there is a danger that this trend may be misinterpreted, or at least not sufficiently clearly related to a larger set of evolutions which concerns system re-organisation[14] and managerial flexibility. The trend of de-collectivisation in the 1980s, its continuation in the 1990s, and its halting or even partial reversal from the end of the 1990s, has been well-documented and carefully analysed; but the analysis has been significantly shaped by its commitment to a concept or paradigm of 'individualisation' as the counterpart or outcome of de-collectivisation.[15] Even in the hands of analysts, such as those cited, who are not for a moment beguiled into the perception that gaps left by the decline of collective bargaining are filled by a corresponding rise of individual bargaining, the paradigm of 'individualisation' inevitably induces a consciousness that the purpose and effect of de-unionisation is to make way for personal work relations which are more than previously varied as between one worker and another even within a single employing enterprise.

---

[11] A good general sense of these developments is given by the papers in G White and J Druker (eds), *Reward Management—A Critical Text* (London and New York: Routledge, 2000).

[12] J Rubery, J Earnshaw, M Marchington, F L Cooke, and S Vincent, 'Changing Organisational Forms and the Employment Relationship' (2002) 39 Journal of Management Studies 645–672 at 645.

[13] See, generally, M Marchington, D Grimshaw, J Rubery, and H Willmott, *Fragmenting Work—Blurring Organisational Boundaries and Disordering Hierarchies* (Oxford: OUP, 2005).

[14] This terminology alludes to David Marsden's notion of 'employment systems', without necessarily assigning the same meaning to 'employment system' as he does; cf D Marsden, *A Theory of Employment Systems: Micro-Foundations of Societal Diversity* (Oxford: OUP, 1999) especially at 3–5.

[15] Compare, for instance, W Brown, S Deakin, M Hudson, C Pratten, and P Ryan, *The Individualisation of the Employment Contract in Britain* (London: DTI Employment Relations Research Series, 1998); T Colling, 'Managing without Unions: The Sources and Limitations of Individualism', chapter 14 of P Edwards (ed), *Industrial Relations Theory and Practice* (2nd edn, Oxford: Blackwell Publishing, 2003).

A corrective thesis is advanced by some analysts which makes the point that de-collectivisation is certainly not inimical, and may even be conducive, to the evolution of contracts of employment as standard form contracts, in the sense of *contrats d'adhésion*, that is to say, highly specified and formalised contracts proposed by management which workers may accept or reject, but the terms of which are not open to negotiation.[16] Our own analysis, however, has a different emphasis; we are of the view that the centrally significant effect of de-collectivisation is to increase the freedom of the employing enterprise, both in a procedural and a substantive sense, to engage in re-organisation of personal work relations—that is to say, according to the distinction which we made earlier, to engage in either job re-structuring or institutional re-structuring or both. The overall effect of de-collectivisation is to facilitate and contribute to a trend towards frequent and often fundamental re-contracting of personal work relations—a dynamic which we might identify as that of 'managerial flexibility' or 'managerial adaptability', those terms being used interchangeably in this work.

Let us recapitulate this theme and develop it somewhat further. Our suggestion is that both de-standardisation and de-collectivisation of personal work relations can usefully be seen as aspects of, or contributors to, the state of managerial flexibility.[17] The concept of managerial flexibility describes the capacity of, and the propensity for, employing enterprises to engage in job re-structuring and institutional re-structuring. Where employing enterprises assert managerial flexibility, they engage in processes of evolution which amount to the re-contracting of personal work relations. The pursuit or exercise of managerial flexibility may take the form of, or result in, frequent or even continuous re-contracting of those relationships. The processes of re-contracting will take place at the initiative of the controllers and managers of employing enterprises, and will be conducted by their managers. In a state of managerial flexibility, the articulation and introduction of new contractual structures or frameworks will tend to be a unilateral management activity, even though the settling of detailed tariffs of terms and conditions within those frameworks may be a matter for collective bargaining or consultation, and the locating of particular workers within those structures or frameworks may be a matter for individual negotiation or discussion.[18] In short, this re-contracting may be partly on a uniform basis across a whole group of workers, but partly individuated; it could be considered as the re constituting of the internal labour

---

[16] See for instance H Collins, 'Legal Responses to the Standard Form Contract of Employment' publication due in (2007) 36 ILJ March issue.

[17] The idea of managerial flexibility or adaptability as here articulated has some similarity to, and is in some measure inspired by, the notion of 'flexible employment' as outlined in H Collins, 'Regulating the Employment Relation for Competitiveness' (2001) 30 ILJ 17–47 especially at 25–31, though it will also be apparent that there are differences in emphasis and focus.

[18] Cf W Brown, P Marginson, and J Walsh, 'The Management of Pay as the Influence of Collective Bargaining Diminishes', chapter 8 of *Industrial Relations Theory and Practice*, n 15 above.

market and the re-locating of it with regard to the external labour market.[19] Managerial flexibility is the capacity to make those adaptations.

It is of course another difficult matter of assessment how far this state of managerial flexibility was realised during the period under review.[20] And it is to be stressed that, to the extent that managerial flexibility became predominant or paradigmatic during this period, this was no sudden or totally novel development; the pursuit of managerial flexibility can be seen as an underlying goal of managements in the conduct of industrial relations or employment relations over a long period of time. Indeed, in its most general sense it is an inherent and perpetual pursuit in the management of employing enterprises. However, there were important factors which were especially conducive to the development and deployment of managerial flexibility during the period under review. We have considered the ways in which de-standardisation and de-unionisation contributed to, indeed formed central parts of, this evolution. Another such factor was the strong tendency of the economy to evolve towards service industries and occupations, away from manufacturing industries and occupations;[21] for the processes and mechanisms of service provision seem generally to be more susceptible to, and dependent upon, rapid adaptability of personal work relations than those of the production of physical goods. A further important factor has been the intensification and increasing professionalisation of personnel management, re-conceptualised as human resource management, during the period under review.[22]

Nevertheless, even if one accepts the foregoing account of factors conducing towards a maximisation and deployment of managerial flexibility, there is still much scope for debate as to how far there was a change of kind in favour of managerial flexibility as a mode of, or approach to, the conduct of personal work relations during the period under review. However, the importance of managerial flexibility to our argument in this chapter does not ultimately reside in the extent of its growth, actual or supposed, during the period under review. Its central importance to our present argument consists, instead, in the way that managerial flexibility became, we suggest, a guiding ideal for public policy during this period, perhaps for labour legislation in general but certainly for the aspects of legislation and regulation of personal work relations with which we are concerned in this chapter.

During the Major administration this ideal was a discernible one, but only in a rather general and negative sense; it dictated a continuation of the policies of de-regulation of the previous Thatcher administration, and an increasingly

---

[19] A useful introduction to the way in which the distinction between external and internal labour markets might be drawn, in the analysis of personal work relations in the period under review, is provided by P Nolan and G Slater in 'The Labour Market: History, Structure and Prospects', chapter 3 of *Industrial Relations Theory and Practice*, n 15 above, at 66–70.

[20] Some support for the view that this had become a dominant paradigm for British personal work relations by the mid-1990s is provided by D Gallie, *Restructuring the employment relationship* (Oxford: Clarendon Press, 1998), especially at 5–9 on 'New Forms of Management'.

[21] Some useful detail of the extent of this shift is provided by *All Change?*, n 4 above, at 18–23.

[22] Ibid, 50–59, 61–82; *The Dynamics of Employee Relations*, n 5 above, at 111–121.

recalcitrant resistance to European Community social policy legislation. After the election of 1997, however, the Blair administration was to pursue the goal of managerial flexibility in personal work relations in a somewhat more positive and nuanced way. In the early years after 1997 this promised to be a strongly programmatic policy pursuit, both at rhetorical and practical levels, and both in the manner of engagement with EU social law and policy and in the development of domestic legislative policy. In subsequent years the progressive edge of this policy pursuit became blunted, and an initial New Labour consensus around the public policy of personal work relations tended to dissolve. That erosion of consensus was very significant with regard to the politics of personal work relations in the public sector, for whereas the goal of managerial flexibility could be pursued without a great deal of legislative or normative activity with regard to the private sector, it required a great deal of positive governmental reformist activity to pursue it in relation to the public sector. By the close of the period under review it was this normative activity, in the form of a programme of 'modernisation' of public services, which was the most significant location of public policy development with regard to personal work relations, and of the pursuit of managerial flexibility.

These evolutions are traced in detail in the subsequent sections of this chapter. The legal subject-matter of this chapter, which corresponds to the notion of personal work relations as expounded in this introduction, is, roughly speaking, that which is often referred to as 'individual employment law'. That is to say, the chapter deals with the legislation and governmental measures which concern the rights and protections and obligations accorded to or imposed upon workers as individuals, their term and conditions of employment or work, and their work arrangements in a general sense, but as distinct from the arrangements for their collective representation, organisation, or action. But, consonantly with the focus upon structural flexibility which has been developed in this introduction, our focus broadens to include a rather wider range of legislation and governmental measures than might be included within a conventional understanding of 'individual employment law'. Our survey extends rather further into measures which have to do with the re-structuring, in various senses, of employing enterprises and of work arrangements within and between those enterprises in ways which bear upon workers as individuals.

The method of organisation of the discussion will be to divide it into four *areas*, though it should be emphasised that these are overlapping areas, between which no rigid separation is asserted. The four areas are those of:

1 adjustments to basic labour standards and general worker protection;
2 recognition of human and equality rights at work;
3 adaptation to non-standard employment patterns; and
4 re-structuring of public sector work relations.

Across those areas, three sets of *policy concerns* are identified, which in varying degrees and combinations interplay with each other to shape the patterns and priorities of the relevant legislation and measures. Those policy concerns, which again are not presented as fully distinct from each other, are those of:

(a) de-regulation and the alleviation of rigidities;
(b) moderating European Community law making (in the sense of tempering it with local policy considerations, whether by influencing its formulation, or by the timing and manner of its implementation); and
(c) the positive construction of managerial flexibility.

Those areas and policy concerns will be explained and expounded in the course of the following sections of the chapter. In the next section, that discussion will be initiated with a survey of developments during the Major administration. It will then be pursued more comprehensively in the subsequent sections, in relation to the New Labour administration, that is to say with respect to developments between 1997 and the time of writing in 2006.

2.2 Regulation of personal work relations under the Major administration, 1990–97

The administration of Mr John Major began with the resignation of Mrs Margaret Thatcher as Prime Minister in November 1990. It was renewed by his victory in the General Election of 1992, and lasted until his defeat by New Labour in 1997. In the evaluation of the significance of this administration for the law of personal work relations, it is all too easy to fix one's attention on the activities of the governments which preceded and which followed it, regarding this adminis-tration as merely an interval between the two. This would be a mistake, for the legislation and measures in the field of personal work relations, and the politics surrounding them, form in a more positive and significant sense a bridge between Thatcherism and Blairism, and are of no small importance in and of themselves.

We begin our account of them by suggesting what was the relative importance during this period of the three analytical themes which were identified in the previous section. The theme which dominated the rhetoric of government policy in this area was that of de-regulation. During this period, that pursuit became intimately bound up with the tempering of EC legislation. In fact, the policy of de-regulation became largely identified with the politics of resistance to EC social legislation, and with the minimal implementation of such EC social legislation as could not be completely resisted. Behind that very prominent set of policies and pre-occupations, quite a lot was happening with regard to the positive re-structuring of personal work relations, especially in the public sector. In this respect, we shall argue that the Citizen's Charter initiative was of no small significance.

A curious result of this particular set of priorities was that this period of development of the law of personal work relations is more distinguished for the measures that were not taken, or were resisted, than for those which were taken. The politics of de-regulation were concentrated upon standing still in the face of the onward march of EC social policy. The narrative of the previous volume of this work concluded[23] with the refusal of the UK government to participate in the adoption, in December 1989, of the European Community Charter of Fundamental Social Rights of Workers, and the negotiation, completed in December 1991, of an agreement upon the terms of the Treaty of Maastricht. This agreement was for an arrangement whereby the UK would not be bound by the provisions which had been proposed as the so-called Social Chapter of that Treaty, but which, by reason of the British opt-out from those provisions, would take the form of a Protocol agreed between and applying between the remaining eleven Member States.[24]

The making of the latter agreement was arguably the crucial event of the Major administration so far as the law of personal work relations was concerned, both because it represented the moment at which the Prime Minister decisively took up his stance with regard to that body of law, and because of the practical outcomes which resulted from it. The enactment which would have been made by all twelve Member States had the Social Chapter been embodied in the Treaty itself, and which was in fact made by the other eleven in the Social Policy Protocol, was to create a new and expanded framework or set of competences for social policy legislation to be approved by qualified majority voting rather than by unanimous voting in the Council of Ministers, and was also to commit the Community to giving effect by means of Directives to agreements made between the European Social Partners, that is to say, the organisations representing employers and workers at European level, under the EC Social Dialogue arrangements.[25]

Mr Major clearly regarded it as an achievement of the first importance to have ensured that the United Kingdom would not be subject to Community legislation enacted under this process. Speaking in the House of Commons to the rather self-laudatory motion which he had proposed,[26] he said of these Social Dialogue provisions that:

The Opposition cannot credibly claim that such extraordinary provisions would not recreate precisely the kind of national bargaining—but now at a Community level—which

---

[23] *Labour Legislation and Public Policy* (LLPP) at 594–598.

[24] The full details are set out in 1992/93 Cm 1934 Foreign and Commonwealth Office: *Treaty on European Union including the Protocols and Final Act with Declarations* (Maastricht, 1992).

[25] See, for a full explanation and critique: Barry Fitzpatrick, 'Community Social Law after Maastricht' (1992) 21 ILJ 199; Catherine Barnard, *EC Employment Law* (Chichester: John Wiley, 1995) 2.28–2.26 (the original edition of that work providing an important contemporary account of a situation which had changed by the time of the later editions).

[26] 'I beg to move, That this House congratulates the Prime Minister on achieving all the negotiating objectives set out in the motion that was supported by the House on 21st November: and warmly endorses the agreement secured by the Government at Maastricht.' *Hansard*, HC (series 6) vol 201, col 275 (18 December 1991).

created what was called the 'British disease' of the 1960s and 1970s, so I rejected those proposals.[27]

and, of the Protocol as a whole, that:

It will not impose damaging costs on British industry and workers. I feel, as so many employers in this country and abroad feel, that it will give a competitive advantage to this country, not a competitive disadvantage.[28]

It is important to understand precisely of what that negative achievement consisted, that is to say what EC social policy legislation the UK was spared by reason of this opt-out. This is of course in part a hypothetical inquiry, since the whole course of development of EC social policy might have been different if that opt-out had not been agreed. If, accepting that limitation, one nevertheless seeks to answer the question by considering how much social policy legislation was enacted under the Social Dialogue process which was instituted by the Protocol, therefore affecting the other eleven member states but not the UK, the answer is not a great deal—the only such legislation during the period of the Major administration was the Parental Leave Directive of 1996.[29]

This, however, would represent an incomplete calculus of the effect of the British opt-out. A more important respect in which that opt-out seems to have affected the course of legislative history is in relation to the regulation of working time. By the time of the negotiation of the Maastricht Treaty, the UK government was already leading a long struggle either to resist or to water down proposals for a Directive on working time.[30] It seems highly likely that, if the Treaty had included the Social Chapter, the European Commission would strongly have wished to invoke the enhanced legislative competence, which it would have conferred, to secure the enactment by qualified majority voting of such a Directive in a way which would have been binding upon all the Member States.

Supportive of that hypothesis is the fact that the European Commission, in the very different legislative environment of the British opt-out, rather than settling for a Working Time Directive enacted under the Protocol and therefore not applying to the UK, chose instead to pursue the more contentious and insecure route of reliance on the capacity to legislate by qualified majority voting which had been created by the Single European Act of 1986 for 'measures relating to the improvement in particular of the working environment to protect the health and safety of workers'.[31] The purpose was thus to secure legislation which would bind all the Member States including the UK, and no doubt the Commission hoped to have

---

[27] Ibid, col 282.   [28] Ibid, col 281.

[29] Council Directive 96/34/EC (OJ L145/4, 19 June 1996), implementing the Framework Agreement on Parental Leave of 1995.

[30] A useful account is provided by Gwyneth Pitt and John Fairhurst, *Blackstone's Guide to Working Time* (London: Blackstone Press, 1998) at 1–8.

[31] The Single European Act added new article 118a to the EC Treaty, which later became part of article 137 in the Treaty as re-numbered.

achieved this both with the Working Time Directive of 1993[32] and the Young Workers Directive of 1994.[33] The response of the UK government was triply intransigent; having first sought to water down the proposals for the Working Time Directive, it brought an action before the European Court of Justice for the annulment of the Directive, arguing that the legal base for it was defective, and when that action failed[34] it conducted a desultory and grudging implementation exercise,[35] letting the implementation date[36] pass without having legislated, and maintaining a negative stance which became associated with the rhetoric of 'no gold-plating'. So matters continued until, and stood at, the time the government went out of office in 1997.[37]

If those attitudes on the part of Mr Major and his government serve to explain the legislation which was resisted, they also characterise the legislation which was enacted during this administration. Generally speaking, when legislation was enacted in this field during this period, it occurred by way of reluctant response to external pressures; the legislative exercises were carried out in a fairly minimalist way, and requirements to enhance the protections accorded to workers were subjected to a process of liberalising dilution. The exception which proves this rule is that, where the government did see the opportunity to pursue a positive agenda of re-structuring personal work relations, especially in the public sector, it did so with real enthusiasm. We proceed to examine this legislative history in slightly greater detail, following the order of subject-matter which was specified earlier in this section.

2.2.1 Basic labour standards and general worker protection

In the field of basic labour standards and general worker protection, there were two major sets of measures, one contained in the Trade Union Reform and Employment Rights Act 1993 (TURERA 1993) and the other in the Pensions Act 1995 (PA 1995). Each of them in its own way exemplifies the analysis put forward in the previous paragraph. TURERA 1993 is now best remembered for its various provisions, in Part I, in the field of collective labour law, which gave effect to various policies which the government strongly wished to pursue,[38] and for Part III which administered the final quietus to the system of sectoral minimum wage arrangements administered by Wages Councils,[39] already

---

[32] Council Directive 93/104/EC (OJ 1993 L307/18) ('Working Time Directive').

[33] Council Directive 94/33/EC (OJ 1994 L216/12).

[34] *UK* v *Council of the European Union* (Case C-84/94) [1996] ECR I-5755.

[35] Compare the *Consultation Document on Measures to Implement Provisions of the EC Directive on the Organisation of Working Time* (DTI, December 1996).   [36] 23 November 1996.

[37] The sequence of events is very usefully described by Pitt and Fairhurst in their *Blackstone's Guide*, n 30 above.   [38] Compare below, 2.2.4, 3.2.1.

[39] Leaving behind only the Agricultural Wages Board, still extant at the time of writing: see <http://www.defra.gov.uk/news/awb/awb0503.htm>.

greatly depleted by various abolitions or curtailments of powers during the previous administration.[40] Less well-remembered, perhaps because discordant with
general recollections as to the policy directions taken by the government, is Part
II of the Act, which represented a significant set of enhancements of worker
protections.

The explanation for this apparent incongruence consisted in the fact that,
despite the British opt-out from the Social Chapter which was detailed earlier,
there was a significant accumulation of obligations to complete or repair the
implementation of EC Directives which were binding upon the UK.[41] Although
it was not always very apparent from the terms in which the Secretary of State for
Employment, Gillian Shepherd, presented this part of the Bill,[42] it represented an
implementation, and in fact on the whole a fairly minimal implementation, of a
number of such Directives,[43] rather than a set of initiatives for worker protection
on the part of the UK government.

Thus the Pregnant Workers Directive of 1992[44] was implemented to the
extent that a right to a minimum of fourteen weeks' maternity leave was introduced, irrespective of the hours and length of service of the worker;[45] but no provision requiring that to be paid leave was made at that stage, although progressive
best practice might by then have been to make such provision. Somewhat similarly, the Information about Conditions of Employment Directive of 1991[46] was
implemented by enhancement of existing provision for employment particulars
and for itemised pay statements;[47] but the opportunity was not taken to adopt a
comprehensively transparent approach to information about terms and conditions of employment.[48]

Among various other measures taken by TURERA 1993 which had the objective of responding to obligations to complete or repair the implementation of EC
Directives, it is useful to single out a couple of such measures which, although
fairly complete and positive so far as individual worker protection is concerned,
were conspicuously cautious at the collective level. Thus the implementation of
the Health and Safety Framework Directive of 1989[49] was taken further[50] by the
provision of special employment protection, in terms both of unfair dismissal
rights and rights not to suffer detriment, for workers who in various senses raise or

---

[40] See LLPP, 542–545.

[41] As was pointed out and detailed by Keith Ewing, in 'Swimming with the Tide: Employment
Protection and the Implementation of European Labour Law' (1993) 22 ILJ 165.

[42] *Hansard*, HC (series 6) vol 214, cols 168ff (17 November 1992).

[43] Keith Ewing, loc cit (n 41 above) at 165, points out that seven Directives were involved.

[44] Council Directive 92/85/EEC (OJ 1992 L348/1).   [45] TURERA 1993, ss 23–25.

[46] Council Directive 91/533/EEC (OJ 1991 L288/32). (See J Clark and M Hall, 'The Cinderella
Directive?' (1992) 21 ILJ 106.)   [47] TURERA 1993, ss 26–27.

[48] Compare Keith Ewing, loc cit (n 41 above) at 168–169.

[49] Council Directive 89/391/EEC (OJ 1989 L183/1).

[50] Much of the implementation in the UK had been effected by the Management of Health and
Safety at Work Regulations 1992, SI 1992/2051.

pursue health and safety concerns in the workplace.[51] Indeed, at the same time a general unfair dismissal protection was conferred, from the beginning of their employment, upon employees dismissed for asserting any of an extensive list of statutory employment rights.[52] But it was arguable that the Directive remained less than fully implemented at the collective level in that the health and safety consultation rights which were required by the Directive remained confined to representatives appointed by recognised trade unions.[53]

This issue of single channel versus dual channel collective consultation rights was, of course, due to present itself as a major one in other contexts.[54] Rather as with the Health and Safety Framework Directive, the government was willing to use the opportunity to repair its implementation of the Acquired Rights Directive of 1977[55] in some important respects in which individual worker protection was enhanced, but was not prepared to take on that collective issue. The compliance measures taken in TURERA 1993 did, however, include the crucially important removal, from the TUPE Regulations 1981,[56] of the exclusion, from the scope of the Regulations, of undertakings not in the nature of commercial ventures.[57] That was a measure which the government brought forward apparently only in the face of the clearest indications that it was dangerously out of compliance with the Directive,[58] and with considerable misgivings as to its impact upon its ambitions for further privatisations and contracting out of public sector enterprises and activities—a set of issues to which we revert later.[59]

If the provisions of TURERA 1993 which we have just described seem to typ-ify the approach of a government strongly committed to minimising the impact of worker-protective legislation upon managerial flexibility, that impression is reinforced by the other main item of such legislation enacted during the Major administration, namely the Pensions Act 1995. A preliminary word about the nature and role of legal regulation of occupational pension schemes is needed here, before continuing with a discussion which presumes to regard the Pensions Act 1995 as falling, even partly, under the rubric of worker-protective employ-ment legislation. A re-reading of the previous volume of the present work[60] reminds us that it was not until the 1970s that the law regulating occupational pension schemes even began to move out of the domains of social security law, trust law, and income tax law into that of employment law;[61] and the measure

---

[51] TURERA 1993, s 28 and Sch 5. [52] TURERA 1993, s 29.
[53] Compare Keith Ewing, loc cit (n 41 above) at 170–171.
[54] See below, 147–148.
[55] Council Directive 77/187/EEC (OJ 1977 L61/26). [56] SI 1981/1794.
[57] TURERA 1993, s 33(1)–(2).
[58] The inconsistency had been confirmed by the decision of the ECJ in *Sophie Redmond Stichtung* v *Bartol* Case C-6/90 [1992] IRLR 366. See Keith Ewing, loc cit (n 41 above) at p 174.
[59] See below, 38–42. [60] Where the subject of pensions is treated at 569–574.
[61] This was a way of regarding pensions law which was common to both practical and academic legal discourse; a very useful corrective in this respect was R Nobles, *Pensions, Employment and the Law* (Oxford: OUP, 1994).

which was critical in that respect, the Social Security Pensions Act 1975, was still paraded under the old social security banner.[62]

So, equally, were the relevant parts of the Social Security Acts 1986 and 1990, the very differently toned set of measures by which the Thatcher administration diverted the legal regulation of occupational pension schemes into a very novel direction, that of the market liberalisation of occupational pension provision so that the worker began to receive greater consumer choice in saving for retirement, but lower levels of guaranteed provision from the welfare state and as against the employing enterprise.[63] So the location of the legal regulation of occupational pension schemes within the realm of worker protection and labour law had never been historically secure; and when the Major administration found itself impelled to bring forward such legislation, it did so with a typical reluctance, and tempered the steel of worker protection with the cold waters of market liberalisation and the prospective downgrading of state welfare provision for retirement.

To be more precise, the Pensions Act 1995 represented the product, or the attempted reconciliation, of a number of different pressures which exerted themselves upon the Major administration with regard to the regulation of occupational pension schemes. First, there was the pressure exerted by public outrage at the raiding of the funds of the Mirror Group occupational pension scheme by the proprietor of the Mirror Group corporation, the notorious Robert Maxwell; this was a pressure to improve the legal protection of the entitlements and expectations of occupational pension scheme members against fraudulent or dishonest management of such schemes. Secondly, there was the pressure exerted by EC law to equalise the terms and conditions of occupational pension schemes as between men and women, which had resulted from the fundamentally important decision of the European Court of Justice in the *Barber*[64] case that the equal pay principle of EC law[65] extended prospectively to occupational pension scheme provision.[66] Thirdly, there was a more general medium-term political pressure to equalise the age of entitlement to the state-provided or social security retirement pension as between women and men. Finally, there was a longer-term need to enable both state and private occupational pension provision to cope with the enhanced demand resulting from the accelerating increase in life expectancy.[67]

As in many similar sets of circumstances, it was the first of these pressures, the one generated by a particular outrageous incident, which exerted itself most

---

[62] See LLPP at 569–570.   [63] See LLPP at 571–574.

[64] *Barber* v *Guardian Royal Exchange Assurance Group* Case C-262/88 [1990] IRLR 240.

[65] As enacted in ECT art 119 (now art 141).

[66] This is a very simplified summary of a complex position of which a very useful fuller discussion is provided by S Deakin and G Morris, *Labour Law* (4th edn, Oxford: Hart Publishing, 2005) at s 6.96.

[67] Some interesting detail of, and comparative background to, these policy pressures is provided by G Bonoli, *The Politics of Pension Reform: Institutions and Policy Change in Western Europe* (Cambridge: Cambridge University Press, 2000) at 81–83.

strongly upon the government. This resulted in the remitting of the whole set of issues about the protection of occupational pension scheme members to a review committee under the chairmanship of Professor Roy Goode, a pre-eminent expert in commercial law and insolvency law. That committee produced a report[68] which proposed robust measures to strengthen the protection of the entitlements and specific legitimate expectations of pension scheme members, but which did not seek to reform occupational pension scheme provision in any more fundamental respect, no doubt regarding such reform as a matter of high policy for the government rather than for them.[69]

From that starting point, the government produced a White Paper[70] and brought forward legislation which, as ultimately enacted in the shape of the Pensions Act 1995, combined a cautious implementation of the scheme-member-protective regime proposed by the Review Committee, and a response to immediate and longer-term pressures for equalisation of pension provision between men and women, with various moves which would enable state provision to be gradually limited while continuing the underlying liberalisation of the regime for private occupational pension provision. Important though the measures for member protection[71] and gender equalisation[72] in the management of occupational pension schemes were, it is the tendencies towards de-regulation, liberalisation, and the general downgrading or relaxation of pension expectations which command attention for their continuing significance. Thus, the downgrading[73] of the previous requirements for guaranteed minimum pension provision as a condition for contracting out of the State Earnings-Related Pension Scheme represented a kicking away of one of the props which supported the structure of final-salary-related fixed pension benefits, and the introduction[74] of the new Guaranteed Minimum Funding Requirement for occupational pension schemes did not in any real sense provide an equivalent guarantee. Thus again, and quite crucially, the gender equalisation of the state pension age[75] consisted of a downward adjustment to women's state pension entitlement—the staged postponement of that entitlement from the age of 60 to that of 65—rather than an upward adjustment of women's pension age to that of men, or a convergence

---

[68] *Pension Law Reform: The Report of the Pension Law Review Committee* Cm 2342-1 (London: HMSO 1993). See R Nobles, 'Occupational Pensions' (1994) 23 ILJ 69.

[69] See R Nobles (1994) 23 ILJ 69–72.

[70] *Security, Equality, Choice: the Future for Pensions* Cm 2594 (London: HMSO, June 1994).

[71] Part I of the Act, the main effect of which was to provide for a new Occupational Pensions Regulatory Authority and to endow it with extensive supervisory powers over the management and conduct of occupational pension schemes.

[72] Sections 62–66 of the Act instituted a new Equal Treatment Rule for, and detailed its application to, occupational pensions schemes.

[73] Section 136; for a full explanation see R Nobles, 'Pensions Act 1995' (1996) 59 MLR 241 at 247–249.

[74] Under the provisions of section 56 of the Act—see R Nobles, loc cit (n 73 above), at 252–254.

[75] Under the provisions of section 126 of the Act.

upwards and downwards of women's and men's state pension ages. Finally, there were measures which further encouraged saving for retirement via personal pension provision on the more speculative and less protective money-purchase basis rather than via occupational scheme-based provision on the basis of defined benefits related to final salary.[76]

Richard Nobles drew from all this the perceptive and prescient conclusion that:

This is an Act in which pension policy is structured by the government's perceptions of what cannot be afforded; taxpayers in the next century cannot afford the levels of state pensions previously promised and private pension providers (especially employers) cannot afford to pay significantly more towards private pensions than they do at present. These perceptions represent a severe constraint on pensions policy. *The State is not only unable to offer adequate state pensions, but it cannot coerce the private sector into offering secure and adequate private provision* [emphasis added].[77]

So behind a rhetorical façade of enhancement of protection, fairness, and freedom of choice for workers with regard to the provision of retirement pensions, this legislation actually continued the gradual resiliation of the state from the direct and indirect responsibilities for pension provision assumed by earlier administrations, upon which the government had commenced in the 1980s. We shall see in a later section[78] that there were to be significant echoes of this theme in the approaches and actions of the following administration.

2.2.2 Recognition of human and equality rights in personal work relations

Just as we have seen that the Major administration approached demands for the development of basic labour standards with marked caution, so it was also suspicious of negative effects upon managerial flexibility so far as the recognition of human and equality rights was concerned. The main illustration of this tendency is to be found in the history and content of the Disability Discrimination Act 1995. Coming under intense political pressure following a sequence of abortive Private Member's Bills culminating in the 'talking-out' of the Civil Rights (Disabled Persons) Bill in 1994, the government moved to bring forward its own legislation,[79] which although representing a very important advance in the recognition of equality rights, was limited in several significant respects by comparison with what the campaigners had hoped to achieve.[80]

---

[76] Under the provisions of section 138 of the Act—see R Nobles, loc cit (n 73 above), at 249–250.

[77] R Nobles, loc cit (n 73 above), at 259–260.

[78] See below, text at n 300.

[79] A more than previously positive stance was taken up in the White Paper, *Ending Discrimination against Disabled People* Cm 2729 (London: HMSO, January 1995).

[80] Very useful historical detail, upon which this passage draws, is provided by G Thomas's Annotations to the Disability Discrimination Act 1995, Current Law Statutes 1995/50 especially at 50-3–50-5.

In the employment field, the Act made it unlawful for employers to discriminate against disabled persons employed by them or against applicants for employment with them,[81] and also introduced a duty upon employers to make reasonable adjustment to their arrangements or their premises to prevent substantial disadvantage to disabled persons.[82] These were very significant innovations, exceptional in the history of the Major administration in having been introduced without or ahead of requirements to legislate imposed by or under EC law.[83] However, that testifies more to the strength of domestic political agitation for such a measure than to positive enthusiasm on the part of the government.

Thus governmental resistance to that pressure did manage to secure a narrower approach to the definition of disability discrimination than had been sought by the activists, one which confined the concept to the more restrictive medical construction of disability rather than the more broadly based social construction of that concept.[84] Moreover, the employment provisions of the Act were not to apply to those working in the police force, the prison service, or in the military or fire-fighting services,[85] or, most crucially, to those working for small businesses employing fewer than twenty employees.[86] This latter exclusion, highly controversial at the time, was justified by spokesmen for the government partly by the general rhetoric of minimising burdens upon businesses, especially small ones, and partly by drawing a spurious analogy with the corresponding exemption from the quota system for disabled workers which had been instituted by the Disabled Persons (Employment) Act 1944.[87]

A further criticism levelled[88] against the government's approach concentrates on the fact that the 1995 Act replaced the 1944 Act rather than building upon it, though the strategy of the earlier Act had not proved successful[89] and one might doubt whether it was fully consonant with the approach of the new Act. Other

---

[81] Sections 4–5 of the 1995 Act.

[82] Section 6 of the 1995 Act. This provision is linked to those of sections 4–5; as B Doyle neatly put it, 'Section 6 is the keystone to the employment provisions in the DDA. It attempts to create a virtuous circle. An employer discriminates if it unjustifiably fails to comply with the duty to make reasonable adjustments (s 5(2)). Such a failure can only be justified for a reason which is material and substantial (s 5(4)).' B Doyle, 'Disabled Workers' Rights, the Disability Discrimination Act and the UN Standard Rules' (1996) 25 ILJ 1 at 8.

[83] S Deakin and G Morris, in *Labour Law* (4th edn, Oxford: Hart Publishing 2005) at 714, go so far as to credit the 1995 Act with providing inspiration for the incorporation of a prohibition upon disability discrimination into the EC Framework Directive on Discrimination in Employment 2000/78/EC (see below, ch 4, n 155).

[84] This contrast is explained by B Doyle, loc cit n 82 above, at 11–12.

[85] Section 64(5)–(8) of the 1995 Act.

[86] Section 7 of the 1995 Act. This exclusion was reduced from twenty to fifteen, then entirely repealed from October 2004 by SI 2003/1673 in compliance with Directive 2000/78/EC.

[87] See G Thomas, loc cit n 80 above, at 50–21; the analogy is spurious in the sense that a quota of 5% or less does not work numerically for a group of fewer than twenty workers, whereas there would be (and now is) no such problem in applying the provisions of the 1995 Act among a small group of workers.   [88] By B Doyle, loc cit n 82 above at 10.

[89] See B Doyle, loc cit n 82 above at 1 and documentary evidence cited ibid at fn 4.

negative features were also identified in the same contemporary critique, which pointed to the failure of the 1995 Act fully to give effect to the then recently adopted UN Standard Rules on Equalisation of Opportunities for Persons with Disabilities.[90] Even if that is regarded as too aspirational a standard of evaluation to be appropriate in the present context, it might nevertheless still be agreed that there was considerable evidence of foot-dragging on the part of the government in the course of this episode in the development of human and equality rights in the workplace.

2.2.3 Modifying legislation to non-standard employment

For a government engaged upon the pursuit of managerial adaptability in personal work relations, a complex set of questions presents itself about how far and how to modify employment legislation to non-standard employment. There is of course the usual set of balances to be struck between, on the one hand, impulses to enhance the protection of workers and the recognition of human and civil rights in the workplace and, on the other hand, impulses to minimise regulatory burdens upon employing enterprises. But there is in addition a special set of considerations about the widening of participation in the labour market and about social inclusion, which are considered in a later chapter, and about how the situation of the extended workforce, engaged in non-standard employment, is to be aligned with that of the workforce as previously constituted, the members of which were the original subjects of much of the existing body of worker-protective legislation. Just as we have seen with regard to other aspects of worker-protective and human and civil rights related legislation, the position of governments during the Major administration was generally speaking a defensive and reactive rather than a protective one.

Illustrative of that approach was the single episode of legislative adaptation to non-standard employment which took place during that administration, that is to say, the enactment in 1995 of regulations[91] to abolish the total or partial exclusions of part-time workers from a wide range of statutory employment rights. Many of the central statutory rights of employees, such as those relating to redundancy payments and to unfair dismissal, had been subject to a total exclusion of those working for less than 8 hours per week, and to a partial exclusion of those working for between 8 and 16 hours per week whereby their qualifying period of continuous contractual employment was five years, whereas the qualifying period for those working for 16 hours or more per week was at that time two years. The government having been unwilling to respond to the demands for abolition of these differentiations between part-time and full-time work as being discriminatory against women—demands made because women constituted an overwhelming majority of the part-time work force—the Equal Opportunities Commission

---

[90] See B Doyle, loc cit n 82 above, especially at 13–14.
[91] The Employment Protection (Part-time Employees) Regulations 1995, SI 1995/31.

challenged this regime in litigation, alleging that it involved violation of Article 119 (now Article 141) of the EC Treaty or the Equal Treatment Directive.[92]

When that challenge was upheld in the House of Lords[93] the initial reaction of the government was nevertheless to refuse, or to at least to postpone, alteration of the legislation. When the government did eventually decide to bring forward legislation, the measure that was taken went further than had been immediately necessitated by the judgment in the *EOC* case, in that it abolished both the total exclusion of under-8-hour employees and the partial exclusion of 8–16-hour employees, when it was only the latter partial exclusion which had been the subject of the challenge and the decision of the court.[94] This, however, should not be viewed as evincing any impetus on the part of the government to go beyond the requirements of EU law in a worker-protective direction. More probably, it represents a pragmatic view that it was not worth fighting a further battle when this campaign was, from the government's point of view, a lost cause. They were probably concentrating their energy on their continuing and successful resistance to the enactment of further EU legislation about the equalisation of the situation of part-time workers with that of full-time workers.

2.2.4 The positive construction of managerial adaptability and public service reform

Thus far we have been considering those areas or aspects of legislative activity, in the sphere of personal work relations, in which the Major administration sought to secure managerial adaptability by the essentially negative means of total or partial resistance to various pressures, both external European and domestic, for the enhancement of the rights and protections of workers. We now conclude this section with a consideration of the different aspects of this legislative activity in which the Major administration was engaged in a more positive construction of managerial adaptability. In that connection we start to develop the thesis that a central location for that process of construction was that of public service reform.

This more positive construction began in various ways to emerge from behind the visible façade of de-collectivisation and de-regulation. A good example is afforded by the famous 'Ullswater amendment' which was added to the provisions of TURERA 1993 at a late stage of its passage through Parliament[95] in order, as we

---

[92] 76/2007/EC (since amended and re-cast as the Equal Opportunities and Equal Treatment Directive 2006/54/EC (OJ 2006 L204/23, 26 July 2006)).

[93] In *R v Secretary of State for Employment ex parte Equal Opportunities Commission* [1994] IRLR 176.

[94] Compare A McColgan, 'The Employment Protection (Part-time Employees) Regulations 1995 SI 1995 No. 31' (1996) 25 ILJ 43; C Kilpatrick and M R Freedland, 'The United Kingdom: How is EU Governance Transformative?' in S Sciarra, P L Davies, and M R Freedland (eds), *Employment Policy and the Regulation of Part-time Work in the European Union* (Cambridge: Cambridge University Press, 2004) at 315–316.

[95] Useful detail of the unusual process of enactment is provided by G Thomas, 'Annotations to Trade Union Reform and Employment Rights Act 1993' [1993] Current Law Statutes 19 at 19–31.

explain in the context of our discussion of the collective labour law of the period,[96] to fend off an apparent illegality which the Court of Appeal seemed to have attached[97] to the then very current and growing practice of offering inducements to workers to move out of the protection of collective bargaining in the determination of their terms and conditions of employment and into what would be, in that particular sense, 'individual' or 'personal' contracts of employment.

It is very significant for the present discussion to observe the way in which the resulting measure was framed, namely, in the form of an imposed presumption that action taken by an employer which could be regarded as having the purpose of 'furthering a change in his relationship with all or any class of his employees' as well as the purpose of discouraging trade union membership or activity must be regarded as having the former purpose and not the latter purpose (unless the action was judged to be such as no reasonable employer would take having regard to that purpose).[98] This seems to go beyond what was needed in order simply to ensure the legality of the particular practice referred to above,[99] and it seems likely that this measure was deliberately asserting and legitimating a more widely conceived managerial freedom—namely, in fact, the freedom to change and adapt personal work relations in any way which commended itself to the employer. We can see in this the emergence of a particular disposition to esteem and protect managerial adaptation and adaptability as a good thing in and of itself.

In a more subtle sense, the same is true of the Deregulation and Contracting Out Act 1994. Part I of the Act, on Deregulation, is not at all subtle. Its aim and effect was to pursue further the programme of deregulation of the Thatcher administration,[100] invoking the same[101] often crude rhetoric of 'reducing burdens on business' and 'cutting red tape',[102] even making the former terminology into a legislative term of art. The principal aim and effect of Part I was to enable deregulatory repeals or amendments of primary legislation to be effected by ministerial orders, a transfer of legislative power from Parliament to government often characterised as a 'Henry VIII clause'.[103] It was clearly intended that this power might

---

[96] See below, 3.3.1.

[97] By their later overturned decision in *Associated Newspapers Ltd* v *Wilson: Associated British Ports* v *Palmer* [1994] ICR 97.

[98] TURERA, s 13 inserting a new s 148(3) into the Trade Union and Labour Relations (Consolidation) Act 1992.

[99] Compare G Thomas, loc cit n 95 above, drawing attention to the greater width of this formulation as compared with the government's declared rationale of protecting action taken with the more specifically *procedural* purpose of bringing about a change in 'the way [the employer] conducts his relationship with his employees'.   [100] See LLPP at 587–589.

[101] The rhetoric harked back to the Deregulation Initiative which had been taken in 1985, the subject of the policy document *Burdens on Business* (1985), and the White Papers *Lifting the Burden* Cmnd 9571 (1985) and *Building Businesses... not Barriers* Cmnd 9794 (1986).

[102] In January 1994 the Deregulation Unit of the DTI (while Mr Michael Heseltine was the Secretary of State) issued a policy document under the title *Deregulation: Cutting Red Tape*, and a more general set of *Proposals for Reform* was issued by the seven Deregulation Task Forces.

[103] The House of Lords Select Committee on the Scrutiny of Delegated Powers defined a Henry VIII clause as, 'a provision in a bill which enables primary legislation to be amended or repealed by

be used with regard to employment legislation (though in the event this seems to have happened in only one[104] of about fifty instances in which this power was invoked). But although that power was scarcely used in the employment area, Part I itself contained some significant deregulatory measures affecting employment, of which the most important was the conferment of a specific power to repeal certain occupational health and safety legislation,[105] the curtailment of existing legislation concerning unfair dismissal consisting of selection for redundancy,[106] and the replacement of the system of licensing for employment agencies by a less intense regulation by prohibition orders.[107]

It is, however, Part II of the Act, on Contracting Out, which instantiates the more subtle sense in which the government, in bringing forward this legislation, was engaged not simply in deregulation but also in the construction of a particular version of, or approach to, managerial freedom and adaptability in personal work relations. The immediate purpose and effect of Part II was to facilitate the contracting out of central government functions, essentially by ensuring that a broad set of such functions could be delegated to private contractors by ministerial order.[108] In order to demonstrate why this particular piece of facilitation of public sector re-organisation was important to the development of the law and public policy of personal work relations, we proceed to consider more generally the important evolutions in the continuing saga of public sector reform which occurred during the Major administration.

At this stage in the discussion, it will be useful to re-capitulate upon the theme which was introduced in the first section of this chapter and to develop it slightly further in the particular context of the politics of public sector reform in the early 1990s. In that first section, it was argued that the legislative policy of British governments in the sphere of personal work relations has, since the early 1990s, been, in varying degrees but nevertheless fairly consistently, shaped by a goal or priority of maximising managerial adaptability. The ways in which that goal has been formulated or specified have varied over time, within and between successive governments, but there has been some underlying continuity of thinking around

subordinate legislation with or without further Parliamentary scrutiny' (HLP 57 1992/93). The clauses were so named from the Statute of Proclamations 1539, which gave Henry VIII power to legislate by proclamation.

[104] The Deregulation (Employment in Bars) Order 1997 (SI 1997/957) permitted people aged under 18 on approved apprenticeship schemes to serve in bars.

[105] Section 37 of the Act, the subject of a very critical note by K Williams, 'Deregulating Occupational Health and Safety' (1995) 24 ILJ 133.

[106] Section 36—significantly, this removed the right to complain of selection for dismissal as unfair on the ground of contravention of 'customary arrangement or agreed procedure'—which referred in practice to collectively bargained arrangements or procedures.

[107] Section 35. See LLPP at 344–345 for the introduction of this licensing system by the Employment Agencies Act 1973.

[108] The technicalities of public law which were involved are the subject of a note by M R Freedland, 'Privatising *Carltona*: Part II of the Deregulation and Contracting Out Act 1994' [1995] Public Law 21.

it. It was suggested that notions of de-collectivisation and de-standardisation of personal work relations play a contributory part in the idea of managerial adaptability, but do not provide the whole content or thrust of that idea. A further, and indeed central, element in the idea of managerial adaptability was identified as consisting of a well-developed capacity and readiness for the frequent re-structuring of personal work relations, whether with regard to the institutional structure of the employing enterprise, or with regard to the contractual and managerial framework of relations with particular workers.

At this point it is useful to draw a contrast between the ways in which governments during and since the 1990s have pursued that goal, in whatever form they have precisely conceived of it, in the different contexts of, on the one hand, private sector personal work relations, and, on the other hand, those in the public sector. This is a differentiation both in terms of need and of opportunity. With regard to personal work relations in the private sector, governments did not, broadly speaking, perceive the need positively to impose their notion of managerial adaptability; on the contrary, they generally took the view that the best examples of managerial adaptability were being generated spontaneously from within the private sector of personal work relations, so that the role of government was to encourage and facilitate that best practice rather than to exact it in any coercive way.

On the other hand, so far as personal work relations in the public sector were concerned, governments strongly perceived the necessity to engender and insist upon the maximising of managerial adaptability, and were increasingly intent upon using their power of organisation of public sector activity in order to impose their own particular constructs of managerial adaptability. It is that which lies at the heart of the many programmes and initiatives of reform of public services which successive governments have undertaken during this period. So, by examining in what ways those various programmes and initiatives were oriented and directed, we obtain valuable insights into the particular visions of managerial adaptability which those governments were trying to realise and effectuate.

In this respect the Major administration received a very specific inheritance from the previous Thatcher administration, which in turn it was to develop and build upon. The previous volume of the present work recounts how, in the course of the 1980s, there was an extensive re-structuring of the public employment sector.[109] A very important aspect of that re-structuring consisted, of course, in transferring the provision of many services, both primary or ancillary, into the private sector, whether by means of privatisation of enterprises or by means of contracting out of activities through processes of competitive tendering. The Major administration continued that process; during its course the most ambitious of privatisations was undertaken, that of British Rail;[110] and the Private Finance Initiative began to foster a new practice of long-term contracting out to the private sector

[109] LLPP 10.6, at 615–635.
[110] This privatisation was effected by and under the provisions of the Railways Act 1993.

the building and running of various public service facilities such as hospitals, prisons, and road bridges.[111]

Although that process of transfer of public service activity to the private sector had no small impact upon public sector personal work relations, of even greater relevance to our present discussion were various organisational evolutions within the public sector which were initiated during the Thatcher administration and continued into the Major administration. For it was especially through those evolutions that we can observe the particular form or pattern of organisational re-structuring through which those successive governments most greatly hoped to realise and put into effect an ideal of managerial adaptability. That is to say, they believed that managerial adaptability, and therefore the continuing efficiency of use of public resources in providing public services, could best be achieved by means of reforms which were in the nature of controlled de-centralisation, or partial disintegration, of managerial organisation into a hierarchy or network of units of service provision, between which contract-like and market-like relations would prevail.

It was, we suggest, a premise or assumption of these initiatives that these wholly or partly contractualised and marketised organisational patterns would also imprint themselves upon personal work relations with individual workers and managers within those units and at the points of contact between those units. Towards the end of the previous volume of this work, we showed[112] how a process of reform towards these ends began in the latter years of the Thatcher administration; it was perhaps best instantiated by the programme of breaking up the departmental organisation of the Civil Service into a complex of departments on the one hand and, on the other hand, distinct agencies of public service which stood in contract-like relations with their parent departments,[113] accorded some degree of managerial autonomy but constrained by objectives, targets, and procedures which were set and pursued and varied as necessary by the departments. This programme, known as the Next Steps programme from the title of the policy document by which it was launched,[114] continued into the Major administration; in 1991, the Prime Minister's Adviser on Efficiency reported to him that:

In the quest for public services which achieve the highest quality within the finance available, it has been the expressed policy of the Government to give Next Steps Agencies the managerial freedoms and incentives necessary to deliver the improved performance which is the initiative's raison d'être.[115]

---

[111] For an account of the origins and history of this initiative in the early 1990s, see M R Freedland, 'Public Law and Private Finance' [1998] Public Law 288 at 290–291.

[112] LLPP at 628–630.

[113] These relations were mediated through 'Framework Agreements'; for a discussion of their status and significance, see M R Freedland, 'Government by Contract and Public Law' [1994] Public Law 86 at 88–90.

[114] Efficiency Unit, *Improving Management in Government: the Next Steps—Report to the Prime Minister* (London: HMSO, May 1988).

[115] Efficiency Unit, *Making the Most of Next Steps: The Management of Ministers' Departments and their Executive Agencies—Report to the Prime Minister* (London: HMSO, May 1991) Foreword.

The significant evolution in this programme of reform during the Major administration, indeed the stamp which Mr Major personally put upon it, consisted in its transformation into the form and discourse of the 'Citizen's Charter', an initiative launched by the Prime Minister in the Citizen's Charter White Paper of July 1991.[116] In essence, this was an exercise in the intensification of the existing public service reform programme, mounted in the discourse of enhancement of the rights and expectations of citizens as the users of public services. It is easy to fall into the assumption that this represented no more than a presentational shift into a symbolism which was at once grandiose and populist, but which was of little practical consequence. In fact, the implications and effects for the law and governance of personal work relations in public service provision were quite considerable.[117]

One important legislative outcome of the Citizen's Charter, in the field of the law relating to industrial action, was the introduction of a new 'citizen's right of action' for an individual to seek an order restraining industrial action, which, as originally proposed in the Citizen's Charter White Paper, would have been directed at unlawful industrial action 'affecting the services covered by the Citizen's Charter' but was, as eventually enacted in 1993,[118] capable of being sought against a wider range of industrial action threatening to prevent or delay the supply of or reduce the quality of goods or services supplied to the individual making the claim. However, by focusing upon that one specific legislative outcome in the field of collective labour law, one would miss the main normative impact of the Citizen's Charter initiative upon the development of personal work relations in the field of public service provision, and perhaps even, by extension, in the whole field of personal work relations during the Major administration.

That more far-reaching, if less immediately tangible, impact consisted in the, not inconsiderable, capacity of the Citizen's Charter initiative to concentrate the programme of reform of public services upon the local delivery of those services, and thus upon the organisation of personal work relations between the public service workers immediately engaged upon interaction with the users of public services, and those who managed their work. The demand for managerial adaptability, although in a sense addressed to the whole organisation of public services, was thereby focused upon the partly de-centralised management and conduct of units of service delivery. Moreover, that powerfully focused demand was expressed through the imposition, upon the work of local service delivery, of objectives and standards through which those at the higher levels of government

---

[116]   *The Citizen's Charter—Raising the Standard* Cm 1599 (London: HMSO, July 1991).

[117]   For a discussion of the implications, for the law and practice of personal work relations, of the appeal at that period to the rights and expectations of citizens in relation to public services in Europe at large, see M R Freedland and S Sciarra (eds), *Public Services and Citizenship in European Law—Public and Labour Law Perspectives* (Oxford: Clarendon Press, 1998), especially M R Freedland at 23–26 on 'Labour Law, the Public-service sector, and Citizenship'.

[118]   By Section 22 of TURERA 1993, inserting new s 235A into TULRECA 1992.

and management could claim to be reflecting and vindicating the expectations of the citizen-users of the services and thus the citizenry in general.

Furthermore, this discourse of vindication of the interests of citizens also legitimated an emphasis upon the incentivisation of workers and managers to serve those interests, and upon the importance of rewarding them as individuals, and as units of organisation, according to the degree of success with which they did so. The Citizen's Charter White Paper was imbued with this approach; it was especially identifiable in the section on 'Delivering Quality' and, more particularly, in the passage on 'Pay and Performance', where it was said that 'Pay systems in the public sector need to make a regular and direct link between a person's contribution to the standards of service provided and his or her reward.'[119] With this as a significant priority, the whole programme of reform of public services which this administration had inherited was progressively re-cast in the discourse and institutional framework of the Citizen's Charter. In this badge and livery, the Treasury issued early in 1992 the highly significant White Paper *Competing for Quality*,[120] which made proposals for the extension of competition in the public sector by means of further contracting out and market testing. It emphasised the role of public service managers in buying in services from either the private or public sectors, and recommended the use of performance pay for them.[121] By 1994 the Next Steps process of development of executive agencies had been brought within the Citizen's Charter programme, and a White Paper reviewing its progress could claim that 'Agencies have . . . led the way in developing pay and grading arrangements tailored to their specific needs which enable them to improve value for money from their paybill.'[122]

However, the Citizen's Charter initiative was then to progress even beyond its co-optation of the Next Steps programme, and to take its particular approach to the organisation and running of public services right into the heart of the Civil Service. This was accomplished by the White Paper *The Civil Service: Continuity and Change*,[123] in which it was announced that "The Government believes that delegation of further management flexibility is the key to improved performance, within the framework of clear standards of service and output targets under the Citizen's Charter and continued tight control of the costs of running the Civil Service.'[124] The main practical outcome of this White Paper was a set of moves towards placing members of the Senior Civil Service on formal written contracts of employment, and into a more flexible pay system with pay ranges within which progress of individuals would be linked to their performance.[125]

---

[119] *The Citizen's Charter*, n 116 above, at 35.
[120] *Competing for Quality: buying better public services* Cm 1730 (London: HMSO, November 1991).
[121] Ibid, 5.
[122] *Next Steps: Agencies in Government: Review 1994* Cm 2750 (London: HMSO, December 1994).
[123] *The Civil Service: Continuity and Change* Cm 2627 (London: HMSO, July 1994).
[124] At para 1.4.
[125] As announced at para 1.5. For details of the process of introduction to the Senior Civil Service of formal written contracts, with provision in some cases for performance related-pay, see

This particular sequence of development so exactly typifies the way in which, during the Major administration, governments sought to pursue their particular vision of managerial flexibility, and to impose it upon the processes and institutions of provision of public services, that it provides an appropriate point at which to conclude our consideration of the development of legislation and public policy with regard to personal work relations at this period. The succeeding sections are concerned with the directions which were taken within this field during the Blair administration from May 1997 onwards. In the course of that discussion it will become apparent why we have judged it appropriate to consider the developments of the period of the Major administration in quite considerable detail.

2.3 The first phase of the Blair administration, 1997–2001

In this and the next section we consider the developments in legislation and public policy with regard to personal work relations during the first two terms in government of the Blair administration, that is to say, from 1997 to 2001 and from 2001 to 2005. We begin by explaining our proposed method of presentation, which has the following two particular features; first, that it treats those two periods as identifying two distinct phases in the evolution of legislation and public policy in this area, and, secondly, that it proceeds by comparison and contrast of the development in each of those two phases with those of the Major administration as analysed in the previous section. Our intention in so doing is to explore as effectively as possible the variants which are encountered, as between those three periods, upon what we identified at the beginning of this chapter as the continuing theme or common objective of maximising managerial adaptability.

The notion of 'managerial adaptability' or 'managerial flexibility' was put forward in the introductory section of this chapter as one which, while avoiding the terminology preferred by any one recent government during and since the 1990s, nevertheless identified a discourse about objectives for the regulation of personal work relations which was, in broad terms, common to all those governments. The interesting inquiry is as to precisely how far that discourse was in fact a shared one, and how far the community of objectives extended. Given the extent to which the Labour opposition during the early and middle 1990s, and the New Labour government from May 1997 onwards, proclaimed a capacity and an intention to pursue very different paths from those taken by the Major administration, it is particularly important to consider how much re-convergence of objectives there had turned out to be by the end of the period under review in this work.

In this and the next section we shall therefore offer an account of the governmental conceptualisation and pursuit of an objective or ideal of managerial

M R Freedland, 'Contracting the Senior Civil Service—a Transparent Exercise?' [1995] Public Law 225.

adaptability in personal work relations, and we shall be using that as our method of testing the claim or assertion that the New Labour administration had found a new way, or 'Third Way', to approach the regulation of personal work relations (among many other fields in relation to which that claim was made).[126] This method of proceeding is not motivated by any deep-rooted or unshakeable scepticism about that claim. Our analysis will suggest that there was at least a partial sense in which a new way was found, though perhaps more at the level of methodology than at that of underlying objectives. The detailed carrying out of this analysis is, we suggest, best effected by following the four-part division of subject-matter which was used in the previous section, and by continuing to give prominence to governmental reforms of personal work relations in the provision of public services.

The other main option or choice which we have made in the carrying out of this analysis is, as we have indicated, the decision to divide our discussion of this period into two phases loosely separated by the General Election of 2001. The separation is a loose one both in a chronological and a substantive sense, because we do not believe or suggest that there was any sudden or categorical change of political direction or objective in this field of the regulation of personal work regulations at the point at which the first Blair government was replaced by the second one. Nevertheless, we hope to show that, with regard both to legislative regulation of personal work relations in general and to reform of public service work relations in particular, some real shifts of priority and some alterations of pace are, in retrospect, clearly perceptible. Although our division of the period into two phases is in no sense instrumentally designed to prove the point, we shall eventually suggest that those shifts do serve to bring out and demonstrate a real degree of re-convergence upon the earlier approaches of the Major administration to the underlying goal of managerial adaptability.

Pursuing that plan and methodology of analysis, we begin our discussion, of the developments in the legislation and public policy of personal work relations during the first Blair government, by examining the governmental policy discourse which was evolved to present, to rationalise, and to legitimate the practical measures which were taken or planned. The starting point, and in many ways the focal point, for the identification of that policy discourse is the White Paper *Fairness at Work*, presented by the Department of Trade and Industry in

---

126 A useful characterisation of 'Third Way' politics was at the time of writing offered in the relevant Wikipedia entry in the following terms: 'The Third Way (centrism), an economic and political idea that positions itself between democratic socialism and laissez-faire capitalism, combining the ordoliberal "social market" with neo-liberalism. In the late 1990s, several groups independently began using the term "radical centre" to refer to this kind of third way thinking. Former US President Bill Clinton, former German Chancellor Gerhard Schröder and current British Prime Minister Tony Blair have been prominent advocates of Third Way politics. Among the most prominent social theorists of that field have been Anthony Giddens, author of *The Third Way, The Renewal of Social Democracy, The Third Way and Its Critics* and *The Global Third Way Debate*.' <http://en.wikipedia.org>.

May 1998,[127] in which the government set out its approach to, and programme for, employment law in the ensuing years. It is that policy document which will largely frame our discussion of the particular measures which were taken or debated during that period of government. However, before proceeding to a discussion organised in that way, we need to make the point that the policy discourse in this area is not fully captured or localised by concentrating solely upon that one policy document.

There are in fact two other policy documents which should be regarded as representing significant components in the policy framework for the regulation of personal work relations during this period, albeit that neither of them figured as centrally or prominently in the public policy discussion in this area as *Fairness at Work* did. One of these, the Department of Trade and Industry White Paper, *Our Competitive Future: Building the Knowledge Driven Economy*,[128] provides some significant insights into the objectives of the government of the day for the direction of the development of personal work relations in general, while the other, the Prime Minister's White Paper, *Modernising Government*,[129] gives some further indications of the government's ambitions for their development in the particular sphere of public service provision. We revert to the latter policy document in our discussion of reform of public services later in this section, but expand at this stage on the importance of the former document.

The particular importance of the *Competitive Future* White Paper consists in the fact that it articulates, more fully and extensively than *Fairness at Work* did, the government's ideal or objective for the development of personal work relations. This was realised by Hugh Collins and expounded by him in a highly perceptive article published in 2001,[130] in which he explains how the government had embarked upon an enterprise of 'regulating the employment relation for competitiveness' and sought to carry out that function by fostering 'flexible work relations'—a notion closely corresponding to the objective which we have here identified as that of 'managerial adaptability'. Collins' main concern—and considerable achievement—was to offer, from that starting point, a normative exposition of a coherent theory of 'regulation for competitiveness' and of 'flexible work relations', rather than to identify in full detail the government's own notion of its regulatory aims.

Our concern here being more of the latter kind, we remark upon the fact that, while this White Paper bore quite some similarity to the one which the previous government had presented on the same subject in June 1996,[131] this new policy

---

[127] Cm 3968 (London: TSO, May 1998).   [128] Cm 4176 (London: TSO, December 1998).

[129] Cm 4310 (London: TSO, March 1999).

[130] H Collins, 'Regulating the Employment Relation for Competitiveness' (2001) 30 ILJ 17. Compare also his 'Is there a Third Way in Labour Law?' in J Conaghan, R Fischl, and K Klare, *Labour Law in an Era of Globalisation* (Oxford: OUP, 2001).

[131] *Competitiveness: Creating the enterprise centre of Europe* Cm 3300 (London: HMSO, June 1996).

document, bearing the imprint of Mr Peter Mandelson as Secretary of State for Trade and Industry, presents a rather more specific model of managerial adaptability in personal work relations than the previous government's presentation had done. In particular, the associated Analytical Report,[132] which forms part of the whole statement of position, fleshes out the idea of a highly entrepreneurial, but at the same time intensively managed, approach to personal work relations, as indeed to the running of corporate enterprises in general. This approach especially emphasised factors such as the importance of the development of information technology as an instrument of management of personal work relations as well as of production, and the need for the construction of workers as managers, highly incentivised on an individual basis and attuned to rapid and constant innovation.[133]

We need, however, to revert to the *Fairness at Work* White Paper in order to understand the way in which the New Labour government perceived and presented itself as having mapped out fresh ground upon which to pursue that ideal in practical terms. At an ideological level, the White Paper set out a model of 'flexible' work relations within 'modern companies'[134] driven by notions of 'competitiveness' and 'partnership' of which further development was anticipated, the former by means, as we have seen, of the then forthcoming White Paper on competitiveness,[135] and the latter by the funding of research and the training of managers and employee representatives.[136] It cannot have been entirely a coincidence that this rhetoric was very similar to that of the Green Paper, *Partnership for a new organisation of work*, which had been presented by the European Commission in 1997,[137] and which served as a following-on from the Commission's White Paper of 1993 on growth, competitiveness, and employment,[138] so far as the microeconomic regulation of work relations within employing enterprises (as opposed to the macro-economic management of the labour market) was concerned.

Within that ideological framework, at a more immediately practical level, there emerges from *Fairness at Work* a design for the law of personal work relations in the UK in which, rather adeptly, a space was created and cleared for legislative action. The Prime Minister's Foreword was a tour de force of draftsmanship in this respect. It sketched out, in effect, a path between two extremes of excessive regulation and insufficient regulation, the former being represented by the collective labour legislation of the 1970s by which industrial action and trade union restrictive practices were over-protected, and the latter by the withdrawal or absence of even minimal protections for workers in some areas as the result of the policies of

---

[132] Published by the DTI as a supporting document to the White Paper; see <http://www.dti.gov.uk/comp/competitive/>.

[133] See especially paras 1.15–1.18 and 4.11–4.14 (Enterprise and Innovation).

[134] *Fairness at Work*, paras 2.1–2.8   [135] Ibid, para 1.6.   [136] Ibid, para 2.7.

[137] European Commission, Bulletin of the European Union Supplement 4/97.

[138] European Commission, *Growth, competitiveness, employment: The challenges and ways forward into the 21st century*, Bulletin of the European Communities Supplement 6/93.

governments towards individual employment legislation in the 1980s and 1990s. In pithy summary, the Prime Minister declared that:

The White Paper steers a way between the absence of minimum standards of protection at the workplace, and a return to the laws of the past. It is based on the rights of the individual, whether exercised on their own or with others, as a matter of their choice. It matches rights and responsibilities. It seeks to draw a line under the issue of industrial relations law.[139]

During its first term of office the Blair administration thus perceived itself as having real freedom of manoeuvre in its development of the legislation and public policy of personal work relations. That freedom of manoeuvre would be exercised in four overlapping ways: first, to introduce a new body of minimum standards for some basic terms and conditions of employment;[140] secondly, to accept and give effect to an obligation to move back into the mainstream of European Union social and employment policy formation and to implement the relevant Directives;[141] thirdly, to introduce family-friendly provisions conferring greater rights upon workers in favour of their fuller engagement with the responsibilities of parenthood and family life;[142] and, fourthly and finally, to respond to certain other specific domestic demands for the enhancement of workers' rights and protections, as for example in relation to 'whistle blowing' by them.[143]

As well as detailing that set of directions in which the new government intended to move within their perceived space for manoeuvre, *Fairness at Work* also indicated the spirit in which that freedom would be used. Indeed, this defined the sense which was assigned to the notion of 'fairness' in the White Paper; that notion of fairness was closely linked to that of maintaining the competitiveness of British commerce and industry;[144] it meant that the legislative programme for personal work relations should be carried out with an overriding carefulness not to jeopardise the gains in managerial flexibility which had been achieved by Conservative governments since 1979. In the rest of this section, we consider, according to the scheme used in the previous section, how that balance was envisaged in detail and maintained in practice between 1997 and 2001.

2.3.1 Basic labour standards and general worker protection

During the first New Labour government, there were three principal legislative episodes which were in the nature of enhancement of basic labour standards and workers' protections, namely the national minimum wage legislation of 1998–99, the working time legislation also of 1998–99, and the individual employment legislation of 1999, mainly contained in the Employment Relations Act of that year. These measures between them represented the high-water mark of New Labour

---

[139] *Fairness at Work*, Foreword, para 2.   [140] Ibid, para 3.2.   [141] Ibid, para 1.10.
[142] Ibid, chapter 5.   [143] Ibid, para 3.3–3.13.   [144] Ibid, para 1.11.

progressiveness in the partial re-regulation of personal work relations, but in each case that progressiveness was tempered by cautiousness in the close texture of the legislation. We begin with the National Minimum Wage legislation, which was and has remained in a real sense the flagship of the *Fairness at Work* armada, and perfectly instantiates the delicate regulatory equilibrium which the government sought to establish.

The National Minimum Wage legislation has to be considered as a package composed of the 1998 Act and two sets of Regulations enacted in 1999[145]—this incidentally displaying a fondness on the part of the Blair administration at least as marked as that of the preceding administration for delegating important substantive lawmaking in the employment field from Parliament to governmental departments. The area of national minimum wages was one of those in which the government could most convincingly claim to be taking a very different and more progressive approach to the development of basic labour standards than its predecessors.[146] For whereas the Major administration had, as we have seen,[147] completed the dismantling of the system for setting minimum wages on an industrial sectoral basis by Wages Councils, the new government was bringing in a minimum wage which would be uniform and nearly universal throughout the labour market, and indeed would extend beyond the category of 'employees' to the wider category of 'workers',[148] an extension which is discussed further below.[149]

Hence it was that Bob Simpson, who has produced the most authoritative academic commentaries upon the National Minimum Wage legislation,[150] could offer the preliminary assessment in 1999 that:

Whatever form the political compromise over the government's proposals for changes to British labour law put forward in the White Paper *Fairness at Work* ultimately takes, it is arguable that the most radical and far-reaching reform of employment rights made by the 1997 Labour government will prove to be the introduction of the national minimum wage.[151]

The government had been prepared, unforced by European Union obligations because this was an area in which the EU had (and has) no legislative competence,[152] to take the risk that a real underpinning of basic labour standards could

---

[145] The National Minimum Wage Act (Amendment) Regulations 1999, SI 1999/583, and the National Minimum Wage Regulations 1999, SI 1999/584.

[146] As Mrs Margaret Beckett, then Secretary of State for Trade and Industry, was not slow to do in the Second Reading Debate on the Bill in the House of Commons: *Hansard*, HC (series 6) vol 303, col 162 et seq (16 December 1997). [147] Above, 2.2.1.

[148] Section 1 of the Act, workers to be paid at least the national minimum wage, section 54 defining the term 'worker'. [149] Below, 2.3.3.

[150] B Simpson, 'A Milestone in the Legal Regulation of Pay: The National Minimum Wage Act 1998' (1999) 28 ILJ 1; 'Implementing the National Minimum Wage—The 1999 Regulations' (1999) 28 ILJ 171; 'The National Minimum Wage Five Years On: Reflections on Some General Issues' (2004) 33 ILJ 22. [151] B Simpson (1999) 28 ILJ 1 (see n 150) at 1.

[152] This is by reason of the exclusion by EC Treaty Article 137(5) of 'pay' from the application of the legislative competencies in the area of social policy otherwise conferred by Article 137.

be accomplished without serious adverse effects upon levels of employment and unemployment, a judgment which seems in the event to have been a well-founded one.[153] Perhaps that was because the almost complete universality of this intervention into the labour market was in a real sense counter-balanced by its relatively low intensity, denoted in particular by the cautious approach to the actual setting of the National Minimum Wage[154] which was arrived at between the government and the Low Pay Commission, and by the decisions to apply a lower 'development' wage to workers between the ages of 18 and 22 and certain other workers between 22 and 26 and to impose no minimum wage for workers below the age of 18.[155]

In fact, it is arguable that the level at which the National Minimum Wage legislation intervened in the whole wage-setting process was such a low one as to demonstrate that the government's concern in introducing this mechanism was, not so much to make an onslaught on a problem perceived as one of unconscionably low pay at the lowest existing grades of personal work relations, as rather to encourage the development of a more inclusive labour market without thereby enormously increasing the cost, to the state social security system, of guaranteeing subsistence wages for the workers newly drawn into that market.[156] Those labour market aspects are considered later in this work;[157] it suffices at this point to observe that, by the time that the legislative package had been completed by the enactment of the two sets of accompanying Regulations, which cast some doubt on the likely robustness of the enforcement mechanism,[158] and by the time the initial rate-setting had occurred, this innovation seemed somewhat less radical than it had originally been projected to be.

The balance between the competing political pressures upon the New Labour government for re-regulation on the one hand and, on the other hand, for the preservation of the strong version of managerial adaptability which had been hard-won by the previous administration, was held rather differently, as compared with the way in which minimum wages were re-introduced, when it came to the

---

[153] Compare B Simpson (2004), n 150 above, at 23–24.

[154] The initial main rate, from April 1999, was £3.60 per hour; that had risen to £5.35 by October 2006. Successive Reports of the Low Pay Commission provide evidence of the parameters of discussion within which, and the considerations with reference to which, those rates were set.

[155] Provisions to impose or enable these exclusions or modifications of the main National Minimum Wage were made in general terms by the 1998 Act and specifically by the 1999 Regulations; see for full details B Simpson (1999) 28 ILJ 171 (see n 150 above) at 172–175. The rate initially set for workers between 18 and 22 was £3, which had risen to £4.45 by October 2006. (The requirement to set minimum wage rates for young workers was extended to workers of 16 or more by Regulations made in 2004 (SI 2004/1930), at which point an hourly minimum of £3 was set for workers between 16 and 18.)

[156] Compare B Simpson, (1999) 28 ILJ 1 (see n 150 above) at 2–3.

[157] See below, 4.3.1.

[158] (1999) 28 ILJ 171 (see n 150 above) at 180–181. Simpson was specially concerned about the dropping of proposals for a right for workers to be given a national minimum wage statement, concluding at 182 that 'the desire to minimise the cost to employers has undermined the goal of the NMW as a largely self-enforcing right'.

other main area in which progressive intentions were announced by *Fairness at Work* with regard to individual employment law, that of the regulation of working time. In this case, we suggest, despite appearances to the contrary, the balance was tilted rather further towards managerial adaptability and away from re-regulation. In order to explain this, we need to recapitulate and expand upon the account given in the previous section of the evolution of relations between British governments and the European Community in the matter of the regulation of personal work relations.

In 1997 the incoming government immediately exercised the electoral mandate which it had acquired to re-engage with European Union social policy, by accepting the enlargement of Community competence in that area which had been effected, for the other eleven Member States, by the Social Policy Protocol accompanying the Maastricht Treaty in 1991, and which was now extended to the United Kingdom in the very slightly modified form[159] in which it emerged from the Treaty of Amsterdam in 1997.[160] As we have indicated earlier,[161] the resulting obligations to catch up with Directives made under those enlarged powers since 1991 were not specially onerous; of much more general consequence was the fact that this re-engagement with Community social policy connoted an intention to abandon further resistance[162] to the implementation of the Working Time Directive of 1993 and the Young Workers Directive of 1994.[163]

One might say that in this respect the government rather skillfully made a virtue of necessity, claiming,[164] no doubt sincerely enough, that implementation of the Directive chimed in well with its own aspirations for a family-friendly regime for personal work relations, in which the need for good work/life balance was fully vindicated. The government's credentials for progressiveness in this respect were further enhanced by the fierceness with which the Conservative opposition maintained the attack upon this legislation.[165] Within that particular environment, the government was well-placed to take advantage of the softening of the Working Time Directive which the previous government had helped to effect as that Directive went through the Community's political process, so that the version of the Directive which was enacted in the Working Time Regulations of 1998[166] was one which carefully took up all the opportunities which the

---

[159] See C Barnard, 'The United Kingdom, the "Social Chapter", and the Amsterdam Treaty' (1998) 27 ILJ 275–282.

[160] Forming Title XI, Chapter 1, Articles 136–141 of the post-Amsterdam EC Treaty.

[161] See above text at n 29—and also see below text at n 189.

[162] Though not necessarily to proceed with the utmost swiftness; the new government's *Consultation Document on implementation of the Working Time Directive* (DTI, URN 98/645) was not issued until April 1998, and the final implementation was nearly two years after the deadline of 23 November 1996.   [163] See above, respectively n 32 and n 33.

[164] For example in *Fairness at Work*, para 5.7.

[165] Especially in the debate on Working Time in the House of Commons on 27 October 1998 (*Hansard*, HC (series 6) vol 318, cols 213 et seq).

[166] SI 1998/1833 ('Working Time Regulations'; a full analysis was provided by C Barnard, 'The Working Time Regulations 1998' (1999) 28 ILJ 61, and G Pitt and J Fairhurst, op cit n 30 above.

Directive afforded for derogation by collective agreement,[167] or individual agreement,[168] from the basic labour standards which it imposed.

The decision to invoke all possible opportunities for derogation by agreement was of the utmost practical importance. Of the two central labour standards[169] which the Directive required of Member States—the weekly working time limit for an average of 48 hours, and the entitlement to a minimum period of paid annual leave—while the latter was not derogable by agreement of any kind, the former was allowed by the Directive to be the subject of derogation by individual agreement.[170] By taking up,[171] in particular, the option for derogation from the 48 hours standard by individual agreement, the Regulations espoused what might have been predicted to be, and certainly turned out to be, a relatively[172] lightly prescriptive regulation of weekly working time, mainly because of the ease with which employing enterprises are in practice able to obtain waivers of the 48 hours maximum from individual workers or applicants to become workers. A major empirical study, the results of which were published in 2003, concluded that the use of individual opt-outs was a principal reason for the failure of the Directive thus far to have had much impact on an ingrained culture of working long hours in the UK.[173] The sense that the government was seeking a light regulatory touch was heightened by the amending Regulations of 1999,[174] which in particular reduced the record-keeping obligations upon employing enterprises in respect of individual opt-outs, and took a broad approach to the defining of the category of workers who could be treated as outside the 48 hours rule because they were deemed to be working on 'unmeasured time'.[175]

With the enactment of the National Minimum Wage and Working Time legislation, the first Blair government had put in place the main planks of its platform

---

[167] Working Time Directive, Art 17.

[168] Working Time Directive, Art 18(1)(b)(i), with respect to the maximum weekly working time (the 48-hour week) provision of Art 6; conditions and safeguards are thereby placed upon this capacity for derogation, including that Member States invoking it shall take the necessary measures to ensure that no worker is subjected to any detriment by his employer because he is not willing to give his agreement to work for more than 48 hours per week.

[169] Further very important provisions were made for limits and controls on night work (Working Time Directive, Arts 8–11; Working Time Regulations, Regs 6–7) and for daily rest and rest breaks and weekly rest periods (Working Time Directive, Arts 3–5; Working Time Regulations, Regs 10–12).　　　　　　　　　　　　　　　　　　　　　　　　　　　[170] See above, n 168.

[171] Working Time Regulations, Reg 5. Reg 31 confers a right upon workers not to suffer detriment for refusal to make such an agreement; but it is notable that this protection does not extend to *applicants* for work, and possibly arguable that Working Time Directive, Art 18, properly interpreted, requires applicants for work to be included in the protection.

[172] Only the UK opted for a generalised introduction of individual opt-outs under Art 18 of the Directive. France, Spain, and Germany introduced individual opt-outs in the health sectors, Luxembourg in the hotel sector.

[173] C Barnard, S Deakin, and R Hobbs, 'Opting Out of the 48-hour Week: Employer Necessity or Individual Choice? An Empirical Study of the Operation of Article 18(1)(b) of the Working Time Directive in the UK' (2003) 32 ILJ 223.

[174] SI 1999/3372. See, for a detailed critique, C Barnard (2000) 29 ILJ 167.

[175] By including, pro tanto, those working *partly* on unmeasured working time—new Reg 20(2). Barnard, ibid, at 169–171 shows how undermining of the 48 hours standard this was.

of measured re-regulation of personal work relations. A number of measures taken in the course of 1999 and grouped around the Employment Relations Act of that year constituted what it was hoped would be sufficient to complete the carpentry of that platform. Thus Mr Stephen Byers, as Secretary of State for Trade and Industry, declared roundly when introducing the Employment Relations Bill that 'There will not be a continuous drip, drip of employment legislation throughout this Parliament. We have no plans to bring forward further measures.'[176] Among this set of 'end of the beginning' measures, we need to refer at this juncture to two particular sub-sets, one concerned with the extension or improvement of unfair dismissal rights, and the other with the extension or improvement of the maternity and parental rights of workers. In each case, we find much the same combination of progressiveness with caution, and of re-engagement with EC social policy with deference to Euro-sceptic sensibilities, as we encountered in the context of the ground-breaking legislation of 1998.

The sub-set of measures concerned with the law of unfair dismissal can be easily summarised, but is a little bit more difficult to characterise, or to locate in the spectrum of re-regulatory enthusiasm which we have identified. There were three such measures; the first consisted in the reduction of the qualifying period for general[177] unfair dismissal rights from two years to one year;[178] the second of the abolition of the possibility of waiver of unfair dismissal rights by employees in respect of the expiry of fixed-term employments for one year or more;[179] and the third of the substantial raising of the upper limit upon compensation for unfair dismissal.[180] None of these measures was a response to an immediate legislative obligation resulting from EC law; yet all could in various ways be seen as essentially cautious pre-emptive measures in the face of anticipated future development towards such obligations.

Thus, at the time when the intention to reduce the qualifying period for unfair dismissal rights to one year was announced in *Fair Deal at Work*,[181] the existing two-year period was under attack in the *Seymour-Smith* litigation[182] as being unlawfully discriminatory against women and so in violation of EC equality obligations, in much the same way that the total or partial exclusion of part-time workers had been attacked in the *EOC* case.[183] Although by the time the reduction was effected in 1999 it was already clear that the litigation was unlikely to

---

[176] *Hansard*, HC (series 6) vol 325, col 134 (9 February 1999). This exemption for partly unmeasured working time was eventually revoked by the Working Time (Amendment) Regulations 2006, SI 2006/99 laid before Parliament just before infringement proceedings by the European Commission were due to be heard by the ECJ.

[177] There being no qualifying period for a series of particular unfair dismissal rights, which themselves reinforce certain human, civil, or equality rights which it is felt should be protected without time qualification.

[178] The Unfair Dismissal and Statement of Reasons for Dismissal (Variation of Qualifying Period) Order 1999, SI 1999/1436.   [179] ERA 1999, s 44 and Sch 9, Pt 3.

[180] ERA 1999, s 34(4).   [181] Paras 3.9–3.10.

[182] The matter had by then been referred to the ECJ by the House of Lords: *R v Secretary of State ex parte Seymour-Smith* [1997] IRLR 315.   [183] See above, n 93.

succeed,[184] it might well have been thought prudent partially to reduce the limit to avoid a greater forced reduction at some time in the future. The possibility of waiver of unfair dismissal rights must, rather similarly, have seemed vulnerable in the face of the 1997 agreement between the Social Partners which had led to the Fixed-term Work Directive;[185] again, perhaps it was thought that to move straight to legislation against such waivers might help to maintain the possibility of similar waivers of redundancy payment on the expiry of fixed-term contracts.[186]

Yet again, although there was no immediate direct pressure from EC law upon the existing limit, in the region of £12,000, upon the compensatory award for unfair dismissal, those formulating *Fairness at Work* might have had it in mind that EC law had required the removal of the upper limit of compensation for sex discrimination,[187] and that the law of unfair dismissal was increasingly being used as one of the means of giving effect to a number of emerging rights which were within, or were likely to come within, the ambit of EC law or European human rights law. Moreover it may then have seemed most appropriate to increase the upper limit considerably—to £50,000—without altogether abandoning it as had been at first proposed.[188]

If all this serves to create an impression of a government which by 1999 was still intent on a progressive approach to the development of basic labour standards and workers' protections, but was becoming increasingly concerned to ensure that this would be a cautious and tightly controlled advance, that impression is heightened by a consideration of the manner in which a concrete obligation to legislate—to implement the Parental Leave Directive of 1996[189]—was discharged by the enactment of the Maternity and Parental Leave etc Regulations 1999.[190] Progressive and 'family-friendly' though this measure was, when taken together with the provisions on the same subject in the ERA 1999 itself,[191] both in improving the existing maternity leave regime and in introducing parental leave for the first time, it caused disappointment among the proponents of family-friendly policies[192] by

---

[184] The ECJ had rejected the challenge to the two-year qualifying period: Case C-167/97 [1999] IRLR 253.   [185] Council Directive 99/70/EC (OJ L175/ 43, 10 July 1999).

[186] That provision for waiver was in fact later repealed by way of compliance with the Fixed-term Work Directive, by the Fixed-term Employees (Prevention of Less Favourable Treatment) Regulations 2002, SI 2002/2034.

[187] Following the successful challenge to that upper limit in the *Marshall (No 2)* case, Case C-271/91 [1993] IRLR 445.   [188] See above, n 180.

[189] See above, n 29   [190] SI 1999/3312.

[191] Section 7 and Part I of Schedule 4 provided a new framework for maternity and parental leave, within which the Regulations enacted detailed provisions. In addition, in what is generally regarded as a straightforward, or marginally generous to employees, implementation of the relevant provisions of the Directive, section 8 and Schedule 4 Part II (creating new ERA, s 57A) introduced a new right variously referred to as 'time off for domestic reasons' or 'time off for dependants', entitling employees to take a reasonable amount of time off during working hours to deal with incidents affecting their dependants.

[192] Compare the detailed critique offered by A McColgan, 'Family Friendly Frolics? The Maternity and Parental Leave etc Regulations 1999' (2000) 29 ILJ 125.

setting the period of leave at the minimum allowed by the Directive,[193] and by failing to require that any part of the leave should be paid leave. We shall in the succeeding parts of this section observe a similar increasing restrictiveness of approach in other areas of regulation of personal work relations.

2.3.2 Recognition of human and equality rights in personal work relations

The tendency of the first Blair government to pursue an ostensibly progressive but nevertheless increasingly cautious approach to the expansion of workers' protections was also discernible with regard to the recognition of human and equality rights in personal work relations. It is useful, for the purpose of developing this analysis, to group the relevant measures of the period into three divisions: first, the Human Rights Act 1998 in general; secondly, the Public Interest Disclosure Act 1998; and thirdly, a group of measures specifically affecting privacy in, and in relation to, the workplace. We proceed to consider those measures in those groupings.

Although the proposal for a Human Rights Act, which would render the principal Articles of the European Convention of Human Rights directly justiciable in the British courts, was of considerable potential significance for the law of personal work relations,[194] there is little sign that the government wished to maximise that impact either in substantive or presentational terms; neither *Fairness at Work* nor the Home Office White Paper *Rights Brought Home*,[195] which introduced and consulted about the Human Rights Bill, expressed any such aspiration; the two political discourses were not visibly overlapping ones. Moreover, it seems not unfair to assert that part of the agenda of 'bringing rights home' was to ensure that those rights could be developed by the British judiciary in a more controlled and locally contextual way than by the European Court of Human Rights, and that the government would have welcomed that prospect of judicial moderation and self-restraint not least in the sphere of personal work relations.[196]

If the government was not especially anxious to depict its initiative for a Human Rights Act as part of a progressive approach to human and civil rights in the sphere of personal work relations, they had the contrary concern to present in exactly those terms[197] their support for the Private Member's Bill which was enacted as the Public Interest Disclosure Act 1998.[198] However, this legislation,

---

[193] The minimum period of maternity leave for which the Regulations provided was eighteen weeks, also the minimum stipulated by the Directive.

[194] The potential was explored by B Hepple, 'The Impact on Labour Law' in B Markesinis (ed), *The Impact of the Human Rights Bill on English Law* (Oxford: OUP, 1998); K Ewing, 'The Human Rights Act and Labour Law' (1998) 27 ILJ 275.

[195] *Rights Brought Home: The Human Rights Bill* Cm 3782 (London: TSO, October 1997).

[196] If so, they might have regarded their aspirations as having been realised by the relatively cautious way in which the Convention rights were admitted into the law of unfair dismissal by the Court of Appeal in *X* v *Y* [2004] IRLR 625.   [197] Compare *Fairness at Work*, para 3.3.

[198] A detailed analysis of its provisions is provided by D Lewis, 'The Public Interest Disclosure Act 1998' (1998) 27 ILJ 325.

which protects 'whistle blowers', that is to say, workers who denounce illegality or malpractice in their employing enterprises, was not motivated by any simple or general impulse to enhance the fundamental rights of workers, but rather by the sense that it was necessary to do so in this particular respect in order that workers would be incentivised to act, or at least not be deterred from acting, in pursuit of a general public interest in the disclosure of corporate misconduct.

So there were those rather special reasons for, and a rather unusual alliance of interests around,[199] the creation of this specially protected category within the law of unfair dismissal and of detriment inflicted upon workers by those employing them. For the government, this legislation was, for those special reasons, relatively readily reconcilable with its underlying aspiration of maintaining managerial adaptability; this measure could be viewed as making an especially positive contribution to the quality and efficiency of enterprise management which justified the rigidity which it might be seen as imposing upon managerial disciplinary powers to protect corporate confidentiality.[200] The balance of interests was rather differently perceived by the government in the matter of legislative protection of the privacy of workers in the workplace and in relation to their employment more generally; in that context, the concern to maintain managerial adaptability in an untrammelled state was a more single-minded one.

That conclusion emerges if we disentangle a complex set of threads of legislation bearing upon worker privacy which was woven at this period, the most prominent strands in which were the incorporation of ECHR Article 8 (on respect for private and family life) into UK law by the Human Rights Act 1998, and the implementation in the UK of the Data Protection Directive of 1993[201] by the Data Protection Act of 1998. Specialist commentators such as John Craig were initially optimistic about the likely impact of such measures; he wrote in 1999 that: '... the incorporation of the European Convention on Human Rights and the implementation of the European Directive on Data Protection [by the Data Protection Act 1998] will result in the right of privacy emerging in UK domestic law by the year 2000'.[202] He did, however, qualify this view with the

---

[199] The legislation was promoted, with cross-party support, and support from consumer groups, the CBI and the TUC, by the independent consultancy and legal advice centre Public Concern at Work, the concern of which was to encourage good governance and openness in organisations in the face of evidence that major incidences of corporate misconduct causing or contributing to major accidents or financial scandals might have been denounced by workers in good time if they had not been afraid to speak out. See G Dehn, 'Annotations to Public Interest Disclosure Act 1998' [1998] Current Law Statutes 23 at 23-2–23-3.

[200] This set of arguments, as applied in the particular context of protection of 'whistle blowing', is very usefully presented and analysed by L Vickers, *Freedom of Speech and Employment* (Oxford: OUP, 2002) at pp 29–36.

[201] Directive 95/46/EC of the European Parliament and of the Council of 24 October 1995 on the protection of individuals with regard to the processing of personal data and on the free movement of such data (OJ 1995 L281/31, 23 November 1995).

[202] J D R Craig, *Privacy in Employment Law* (Oxford and Portland Oregon: Hart Publishing, 1999) at p 238.

observation that 'it may be that ... the features of UK legal and political culture which have precluded the emergence to date [of a body of privacy law in relation to employment] ... will continue to make the UK a "divergent", as opposed to "convergent" jurisdiction [with other countries evolving such a body of law]'.[203]

Those hesitations were amplified in the subsequent writings of Gillian Morris and Hazel Oliver, each of whom demonstrated in different ways the extent to which the UK legislation had left the protection of workers' privacy vulnerable to waiver by the individual worker, or to reduction or constriction by the way in which personal work contracts are framed by employing enterprises.[204] One could go further and argue that the government's particular vision of managerial adaptability would induce a special concern to ensure that employing enterprises would retain a full capacity to take advantage of advances in information technology in maximising their capacity to monitor, and so more efficiently manage, the performance of their workers. This was manifested in the legislation which implemented the EC Directive of 1997 concerning the processing of personal data and the protection of privacy in the telecommunications sector.[205] This implementation was effected by the Regulation of Investigatory Powers Act 2000, under which were enacted the Lawful Business Practice Regulations 2000,[206] which were strongly and positively protective of managerial practices of electronic monitoring and surveillance, both in public and in private employment.[207]

The significant developments of this period in the field of equality rights consisted of the enactment, in the course of 2000, of the Part-time Workers (Prevention of Less Favourable Treatment) Regulations, and of the Race Relations (Amendment) Act, the first of which will be considered in the next sub-section and the second later in this chapter.[208]

2.3.3 Modifying legislation to non-standard employment

The foregoing discussion of the development during the first New Labour government of legislative policy, with regard to basic labour standards and human and equality rights, begins to build up a picture of a set of initially progressive intentions to increase the protections of workers, which are, as time goes on, qualified by a growing caution about re-regulation and a mounting concern to retain a robust version of managerial adaptability. The same tendency can be

---

[203] Ibid. Compare M Ford, 'Two Conceptions of Worker Privacy' (2002) 31 ILJ 135.

[204] G Morris, 'Fundamental Rights: Exclusion by Agreement?' (2001) 30 ILJ 49 especially at 61–65; H Oliver, 'E-mail and Internet Monitoring in the Workplace: Information Privacy and Contracting-Out' (2002) 31 ILJ 321, especially at 330–334.

[205] Council Directive 97/66/EC (OJ L24/1 30 January 1998).

[206] The Telecommunications (Lawful Business Practice) (Interception of Communications) Regulations 2000, SI 2000/2699.

[207] This argument is set out and developed more fully by M R Freedland, 'Privacy, Employment and the Human Rights Act 1998' in K Ziegler (ed), *Privacy and Human Rights in the European Union* (Oxford and Portland, Oregon: Hart Publishing, forthcoming).   [208] See 2.4.2 below.

observed in the context of measures and policies concerned with the modification of the law of personal work relations in favour of workers in non-standard patterns of employment—that is to say, essentially, temporary or casual and part-time workers. We can identify this tendency more precisely by distinguishing between two kinds of modification in favour of non-standard workers, the first consisting of enlargement of the personal scope of labour laws to include non-standard workers, and the second consisting of the creation of rights on the part of non-standard workers to equality or parity with 'standard workers' with respect to terms and conditions of employment.

The first Blair government seems to have begun with a real enthusiasm for the enlargement of the personal scope of its major worker-protective measures; the National Minimum Wage Act and the Working Time Regulations of 1998 were both applied[209] to 'workers' rather than to the 'employees' to whom the generality of the existing worker-protective legislation applied, with the significant exception of the employment provisions of the legislation relating to sex, race, and disability discrimination, where the very inclusive category of 'employed persons' was applicable.[210] The category of 'workers' was an intermediate one, apparently intended to bring in nominally self-employed workers who were in fact semi-dependent upon employing enterprises, while still excluding the 'genuinely self-employed'.[211] This represented what was clearly a free choice on the part of the legislators in the case of the National Minimum Wage Act, and was not, even in the case of the Working Time Regulations, a decision which was indubitably mandated by the Directives which they were intended to implement.[212]

In *Fairness at Work*, these extensions in personal scope were depicted as a first step to 'combine flexibility with fairness in the labour market' by 'reflecting in employment legislation greater flexibility in both working patterns and contracts';[213] and the intention was expressed to 'consult on the idea of legislation enabling [the Government] similarly to extend the coverage of some or all existing employment rights by regulation'.[214] Such powers of variation of the personal scope of existing employment legislation by governmental regulation were indeed

[209] NMWA 1998, ss 1(2)(a) and 54(3); Working Time Regulations use the term 'worker' throughout, defining it in Reg 2(1).

[210] Sex Discrimination Act 1975 (hereafter, SDA), s 82(1) defines employment as being 'under a contract of service or of apprenticeship or a contract personally to execute any work or labour'; similarly Race Relations Act 1976 (hereafter RRA), s 78(1), Equal Pay Act 1970 s 1(6)(a), and Disability Discrimination Act 1995 (DDA) s 68(1).

[211] See, for a fuller discussion, P L Davies and M R Freedland, 'Employees, Workers and the Autonomy of Labour Law' in H Collins, P Davies, and R Rideout (eds), *Legal Regulation of the Employment Relation* (London: Kluwer, 2000).

[212] The Working Time Directive used the term 'worker' throughout without defining or elaborating upon it; the Young Workers Directive, Art 2.1 stated that the Directive applied to 'any person under 18 years of age having an employment contract or an employment relationship defined by the law in force in a Member State and/or governed by the law in force in a Member State'.

[213] *Fairness at Work*, n 127 above, para 3.17.   [214] Ibid, para 3.18.

sought, and were conferred by the Employment Relations Act 1999;[215] but impetus seems to have been lost for this particular kind of extension of employment law, so that those powers had not been exercised even by the end of the second term in government of the Blair administration.[216]

If we turn to the evolution of policy with regard to the second kind of modification in favour of non-standard workers, we find that a similar loss of impetus, even a hardening of an anti-regulatory impulse, seems to have occurred in the course of the implementation in the UK of the Part-time Work Directive of 1997.[217] This Directive, a product of the Social Dialogue process of Community legislation,[218] was the first of what it was hoped might be a series of such Directives creating equality or parity rights with 'standard workers' for all the main types of 'non-standard workers'.[219] In the course of consultations by the DTI about the implementation of the Directive in the UK, a very significant attenuation seems to have taken place with regard to the right to not less favourable treatment which was conferred upon part-time workers. In the implementing Regulations, as finally enacted,[220] an apparent earlier intention to confine the Regulations to 'employees' was superseded by a decision to extend them to the whole larger category of 'workers'.[221] However, in a move which more than counter-balanced that extension, a provision was introduced[222] which severely fragmented this larger category[223] and limited the comparators who could be invoked by particular types of part-time

---

[215] Section 23. A very useful account of contemporary views about the extent and appropriate use of those powers is provided by S Deakin and G Morris, *Labour Law* (4th edn, Oxford: Hart Publishing, 2005) at 3.72.

[216] A Discussion Document on this question was published by the DTI in July 2002 (URN 02/1058); it resulted in nothing more than the publication by the DTI of a Summary of Responses to the Employment Status Review in March 2006 (URN 06/1050).

[217] Council Directive 97/81/EC of 15 December 1997 concerning the Framework Agreement on part-time work concluded by UNICE, CEEP, and the ETUC (OJ 1998 L014/9, 20 January 1998).

[218] See above, n 25. Because of the particular sequence of measures by which the Social Chapter and Directives made under its provisions became applicable to the UK, a special Directive was required to extend the Part-time Work Directive to the UK; this was Council Directive 98/23/EC of 7 April 1998 on the extension of Directive 97/81/EC on the Framework Agreement on part-time work concluded by UNICE, CEEP, and the ETUC to the United Kingdom of Great Britain and Northern Ireland (OJ 1998 L131/10, 5 May 1998).

[219] This Directive was in fact followed in 1999 by the Fixed-term Work Directive—see 2.4 below, but further proposals for a Temporary (Agency) Workers Directive continued to prove unsuccessful throughout the first and second Blair governments—see also 2.4 below.

[220] The Part-time Workers (Prevention of Less Favourable Treatment) Regulations 2000, SI 2000/1551.

[221] See DTI News Release P/2000/305 of 3 May 2000, 'More People to Reap Benefits of Working Part-time'—Mr Stephen Byers, Secretary of State for Trade and Industry.

[222] SI 2000/1551, Reg 2(3)–(4).

[223] Into the sub-categories of: '(a) employees employed under a contract that is neither for a fixed term nor a contract of apprenticeship; (b) employees employed under a contract for a fixed term that is not a contract of apprenticeship; (c) employees employed under a contract of apprenticeship; (d) workers who are neither employees nor employed under a contract for a fixed term; (e) workers who are not employees but are employed under a contract for a fixed term; (f) any other description

workers within the category.[224] The programme of modification of the law of personal work relations in favour of non-standard workers seems at this point to have hit the buffers which protected the government's particular vision of managerial adaptability.

2.3.4 The positive construction of managerial adaptability and public service reform

In the foregoing sub-sections we have surveyed the measures which were taken to implement the 'Third Way' strategy of *Fairness at Work* for the law of personal work relations. In the next section we discuss what followed on, for and around that strategy, during the second government of this administration. Before doing so, it is important to draw attention to the various ways in which, during its first period in government, this administration maintained and even began cautiously to build upon, the strategies, and many of the detailed tactics, for the positive construction of managerial adaptability and for the reform of public services in general and personal work relations in public services in particular, which had been developed during the previous administration (themselves, as we have seen, quite largely inherited from the Thatcher administration of 1979 to 1990). Behind a rhetoric of 'modernisation', there was more continuity of policy and practice in this area, albeit generally muted or slightly transmuted, than the government was keen to admit.

Following the sequence of discussion of the previous section, we first encounter this near-parallelism with earlier approaches in the way in which the first Blair government approached the ever-difficult issue of regulation of the practice of 'individualisation' of personal work relations, and the handling of the pressures to comply with ECHR and ILO standards of freedom of association.[225] This is considered in detail in the next chapter in the context of the development of collective labour law;[226] it suffices at this point to draw attention to the way in which, when seeking the powers to address these issues in secondary legislation which were conferred by Section 17 of the Employment Relations Act 1999, the government, by accepting the 'Miller amendment',[227] preserved the capacity for employing enterprises to introduce new practices of performance-related pay and performance

---

of worker that it is reasonable for the employer to treat differently from other workers on the ground that workers of that description have a different type of contract'. This Regulation originally included a distinction between fixed-term workers and other workers, but that distinction was removed by SI 2002/2035, Reg 2(a).

[224] This provision is analysed and criticised in detail by A McColgan, 'Missing the Point? The Part-time Workers (Prevention of Less Favourable Treatment) Regulations 2000 SI 2000 No 1551' (2000) 29 ILJ 260 at 263–264, and by M R Freedland and C Kilpatrick, op cit n 94 above, at 322–328.

[225] This was the set of problems which revolved around the *Wilson and Palmer* litigation; see above, text above n 97, and below, ch 3, text at n 49.

[226] Below, ch 3, text at n 50.   [227] Which was enacted as s 17(2) of the Act.

management in much the same way that the previous government had done by accepting the 'Ullswater amendment' in 1993 (which itself remained in force throughout the first New Labour government).

If, pursuing that same sequence of discussion, we turn our attention to reform of public services and personal work relations within those services, we similarly find that the approaches of the previous administration are being largely maintained behind a slightly changed rhetoric. The Citizen's Charter programme was 're-launched' by the Cabinet Office as 'Service First—The New Charter Programme'.[228] Under the aegis of the Treasury, the Private Finance Initiative was continued, and indeed further developed, for the provision of public services by this particular pattern of large-scale contracting out, both by central government and its agencies, by local government, and by the National Health Service; this continuation and extension of the earlier programme took place under the new umbrella heading of 'Public/Private Partnerships'.[229] Again under the aegis of the Treasury, the approach to public service provision by means of contract-like agreements between 'purchasers' and 'providers', which animated the 'Next Steps' initiative,[230] was greatly elaborated and extended by the introduction of a new system of 'Public Service Agreements', essentially a system of target-setting and target-enforcing running right through central government.[231]

Perhaps not to be outdone by the Treasury and the Chancellor, the Prime Minister and the Cabinet Office produced, in March 1999, a White Paper which sought to gather together and organise the multifarious discourse of public service reform under the general heading of '*Modernising Government*'.[232] Under this banner, an institutional focus was created for 'better regulation'[233] and the earlier discourse about 'deregulation and contracting out' was resumed under the heading of 'regulatory reform'.[234] More importantly in the present context, this White Paper signalled the concentration of a discourse about efficiency and performance management in public service personal work relations which was in substance very similar to the one which had been maintained by the previous administration.[235]

---

[228] Introduced by a document with that title published in June 1998 by the Cabinet Office as Pub J98 2861.

[229] This evolution is analysed by M R Freedland, op cit at n 111 above, at 88–90.

[230] See above, text above n 113 et seq.

[231] This was introduced by the Treasury, as part of its new annual Comprehensive Spending Review programme, in the White Paper, *Public Services for the Future: Modernisation, Reform Accountability—Comprehensive Spending Review: Public Service Agreements 1999–2002* Cm 4181 (London: TSO, December 1998).

[232] White Paper, *Modernising Government* Cm 4310 (London: TSO, March 1999).

[233] Though it is outside the scope of the present work to trace the transitions from the Better Regulation Taskforce which was set up in 1997 to the Better Regulation Executive, and then to the Better Regulation Commission which exists at the time of writing.

[234] Thus the Regulatory Reform Act 2001 represented a strengthening and extension of the powers of de-regulation and contracting out which had been created by the Deregulation and Contracting Out Act 1994—see above, text around n 101. At the time of writing, that line of policy is being further pursued by the Legislative and Regulatory Reform Bill currently before Parliament.

[235] See, in particular, chapter 6, 'Public Service'.

During the first New Labour government, this policy approach, and the evolutions which we have described in this sub-section, were not very prominent in the discussion of the law of personal work relations, although we suggest that they were of very considerable underlying significance to that discussion. In this first phase of the Blair administration, in appearance at least, the agenda for the regulation of personal work relations was essentially set by the White Paper *Fairness at Work*. In the next section, it will be argued that the priorities of this administration emerged as quite significantly different ones in the course of the second phase, to which we now turn our attention.

2.4 The second phase of the Blair administration, from 2001 onwards

We saw in the preceding section how, during the first Blair government, the focus of public policy in the sphere of individual employment law was primarily upon the realisation of the plan, laid out in the White Paper *Fairness at Work*, for the achievement of a socially progressive but not excessively re-regulatory closure upon what had hitherto been a deep conflict between extremes of legislative policy in this area. Although, as was indicated earlier, we do not suggest that the General Election of May 2001 marked any abrupt or conscious change of direction on the part of the New Labour administration, nevertheless that provides a point around which to organise an account of the way in which significant evolutions of policy and approach did take place over the eight-year period of the two governments, taken as a whole. We introduce that discussion by reflecting initially upon whether there were significant changes in the public policy discourse for the regulation of personal work relations, as between the two phases.

The results of that reflection are to suggest that there was in fact rather a significant difference in the way in which that public policy discourse was framed as between those two phases; and that the identification of this difference helps to understand the way in which the regulation of personal work relations developed during this second phase. During the first period in government of the Blair administration, as we have seen, the public policy discourse for the law of personal work relations, indeed for employment law at large, was essentially framed by the White Paper *Fairness at Work*, and, even if, as we have suggested,[236] there was a larger discourse standing behind it, about the competitiveness of the labour economy and of enterprise management, this policy framework still fairly closely conformed to the traditional one of seeking a durable legislative settlement of the conflict between management and labour.

However, as we have also noted at various points,[237] the government when presenting and invoking the *Fairness at Work* agenda was always at pains to emphasise

---

[236] Above, text around n 128.   [237] Above, text around nn 139, 176.

that, if their policy for labour law needed to be constructed in that form, that was only for a limited time, which would constitute the terminal or foreclosing phase of anything resembling an old-fashioned policy for industrial relations. In this second phase the administration did indeed move on from this kind of framework for the regulation of personal work relations into a state where the policy discourse was constructed in a different and more diffuse form. In a sense, it turned out that their new way or 'Third Way' of playing the traditional policy game in the traditional field of individual employment law was not to play that game at all, but instead to play a different game on a different pitch.

Hence it was that, whereas in its first phase, the government had, in the *Fairness at Work* White Paper, sought to bring together a number of different policy strands into a single discourse, in the second phase the approach to this policy discourse was much less unificatory. There was no single second-term manifesto for the regulation of personal work relations; instead, a number of different lines of policy were developed in a number of different areas or policy contexts. The nearest approach to a general overview policy document was a comprehensive policy paper published by Ms Patricia Hewitt as Secretary of State for Trade and Industry in July 2002, entitled *Full and Fulfilling Employment: Creating the Labour Market of the Future*;[238] it came from the discourse of employment policy, and was in the genre of the various European Employment Strategy policy pronouncements which stressed the importance of combining the promotion of full employment with the securing of good quality employment.[239] But, rather curiously, this paper never seems to have attained the character of an official policy document or the status of a departmental policy pronouncement.

Below that level of generality, there were several somewhat more specific policy documents, coming from different, but intersecting, particular areas or policy discourses. In 2000, Mr Stephen Byers as Secretary of State for Trade and Industry had published a Green Paper on family-friendly policies, *Work and Parents—Competitiveness and Choice*.[240] In July 2001, Mr Alan Johnson as Minister for Employment and the Regions presented a consultation document, *Routes to Resolution: Improving Dispute Resolution in Britain*[241] which developed a strategy for dispute resolution within the workplace rather than by litigation before employment tribunals. That strategy was loosely connected with an emerging policy genre of regulatory impact assessment, which was embodied in a policy document which emanated from the Better Regulation Taskforce in May 2002 under the interesting title of *Employment Regulation: Striking a Balance*.[242] In July 2002 the DTI published, in a somewhat different idiom, a Discussion Paper entitled

---

[238] DTI 11 July 2002 URN 02/1051.

[239] Compare D Ashiagbor, *The European Employment Strategy* (Oxford: OUP, 2005) at chapter 4 and especially pp 178–185 for a detailed critique of the main policy documents in which the strategy was presented.   [240] Cm 5005 (London: TSO, December 2000).

[241] DTI, July 2001.   [242] Better Regulation Taskforce, Cabinet Office, May 2002.

High Performance Workplaces: the role of employee involvement in a modern economy.[243] This had the specific purpose of initiating a discussion within the UK about the implementation of the Information and Consultation Directive,[244] but it also, in a wider sense, set forth a discourse about 'partnership' in the workplace which proclaimed a partly individualised approach to personal work relations in 'modern, high performance workplaces'.[245]

Finally among our set of relevant policy discourses and policy documents, we suggest that the agenda of reform of public services became even more central and important to the regulation of personal work relations in this second phase of the Blair administration than it had been in the first one. There is a real sense in which the White Paper *Modernising Government*, although, as we have seen, it was published during the first government, became one of the foundational policy documents for the second term in government. The policies which it articulated were reiterated and further specified in a document published in March 2002 by the then newly formed Prime Minister's Office of Public Service Reform, entitled *Reforming our public services: principles into practice.*[246] We shall suggest in the course of this section that the doctrinal and practical implications of this particular set of policy pronouncements, during this latter period, were very great indeed.

Although these different policy initiatives and policy documents relate to each other in complex ways, we can usefully group them in such a way as to identify two main policy constellations; first, a socially progressive one, increasingly strongly identified with notions of inclusion in employment and 'family-friendliness'; secondly, an approach seeking to maximise financial efficiency and cost-effectiveness, or competitiveness, both in the management of public and private sector personal work relations and in the methodology of its regulation by the state. If we had to say which of those two approaches was the prevalent one during this second phase of the Blair administration, it would be the latter; but this would risk misunderstanding the relationship between the two approaches, for these two policy constellations should not be regarded as polar opposites; it is rather that new and different versions of public policy for the regulation of personal work relations, and new ways of specifying the goal of managerial adaptability, resulted from the interplay between them.

This will emerge from a consideration of the measures which were taken, and discussed but not taken, during that period; we proceed with that consideration under the same set of headings, identifying different areas or aspects of the regulation of personal work relations, as was used in the two previous sections. In the course of that discussion, it will also be suggested that the reform of personal work relations in the public services played at least as important a role in the

243 DTI, 11 July 2002, URN 02/917.   244 See below 3.4.4.3.
245 See particularly chapter 2 under that title.
246 London: Office of Public Service Reform, 2002.

developments of this period as it had done in the previous two. It will be seen that the balance or relationship between the two underlying approaches differs from one area to another; on this occasion, we shall find that it was from the first and last of our four areas that the overall picture of public policy towards personal work relations at this period emerged most clearly.

2.4.1 Basic labour standards and general worker protection

During this second phase of the Blair administration, there was one key piece of legislation in the area of basic labour standards and general worker protection, namely the Employment Act 2002. There was further significant legislation in this area in 2004; both the Pensions Act and the Gangmasters (Licensing) Act of that year were important in very different ways. But it is the Employment Act of 2002 which best encapsulates the complex interplay of policy approaches which we have identified, and it is that Act which therefore deserves most of our attention in this sub-section.

In fact, the Employment Act 2002 represented an elaborate package of measures, almost entirely in the sphere of individual rather than collective employment law, and those measures include ones which fall within the subject areas of recognising equality rights[247] and modifying legislation to non-standard employment.[248] But it will be useful to concentrate on three sets of measures within the Act which in different senses concern basic labour standards and general worker protection; first, those in Part 1 concerning maternity, paternity, and adoption; secondly, those in Parts 2 and 3 concerning tribunal reform and dispute resolution; and finally those in Part 4 concerning 'flexible working'. Our argument will be that, while the first of these sets of measures represents the high-water mark of the government's family-friendly, worker-protective approach, and while the second of these, on the other hand, goes to the other extreme of business-protective de-regulation, the third set of measures is very interestingly poised between those two extremes.

2.4.1.1 'Family-friendly' measures

Thus, to begin with the measures in Part 1 of the Act, we find that they fit very squarely and straightforwardly into the 'family-friendly' part of the government's policy agenda for personal work relations. These measures, which incidentally went above and beyond what was required by the previously implemented Parental Leave Directive,[249] consisted essentially of, first, the introduction of paternity leave[250] and statutory paternity pay;[251] secondly, the introduction of

---

[247] Section 42—Equal pay questionnaires.
[248] Section 41—Amendment of the power to confer rights on individuals; section 45—fixed-term work; see below, 2.4.3.   [249] See above, nn 189 and 190.
[250] Section 1 and Regulations SI 2002/2788—the entitlement given was to two weeks' leave.
[251] Section 2 and Regulations SI 2002/2822—again, for two weeks.

adoption leave[252] and statutory adoption pay;[253] and, thirdly, the simplification and improvement of existing provision for maternity leave and statutory maternity pay.[254] In each case the length of the leave and payment entitlements attached were later extended by the Work and Families Act 2006.[255] These measures in various ways served the objectives identified in the Green Paper *Work and Parents—Competitiveness and Choice* of 'improving choice for parents and enhancing competitiveness for business by: keeping women's skills and knowledge in the economy and maintaining their attachment to the labour market...enabling business to benefit from a greater contribution from the workforce, maximising the contribution that working parents are able to make to their employers, safeguarding the health and welfare of the mother and child before and after birth, and improving the quality of family life'.[256]

That is, in fact, a mixture of objectives which may in certain respects be divergent ones—in particular, there may be a tension between labour-market inclusion for the benefit of the economy as a whole, and worker-protection for those workers who are parents or parents-to-be[257]—but it is not necessary to the present discussion to separate out the 'family-friendly' mixture in relation to these particular measures, because our main purpose is to contrast that bloc of measures with the other parts of the Act. There is, as we have begun to suggest, a radical contrast between the amelioration of the rights and protections of worker-parents intended and effected by that part of the Act, and the detraction from the rights of workers at large which resulted from Parts 2 and 3 of the Act—a set of de-regulatory aims and outcomes which were nonetheless potent by reason of being partly concealed in the language of 'tribunal reform' and 'dispute resolution'.

2.4.1.2 *Tribunal reform and dispute resolution*

The measures contained in Parts 2 and 3 emanate, as we have indicated, from the policy document *Routes to Resolution* issued in July 2001,[258] and from a discourse about the greater regulatory efficiency of either workplace dispute resolution or informal arbitration, as compared with litigation before employment tribunals,

---

[252] Section 3 and Regulations SI 2002/2788—the entitlement given was to 26 weeks' ordinary adoption leave, with the possibility of up to 26 weeks' additional leave; this corresponded to the entitlement to maternity leave.

[253] Section 4 and Regulations SI 2002/2822—for up to 26 weeks, again corresponding to maternity pay.

[254] Sections 17–18, extending both leave and pay from 18 weeks to 26 weeks.

[255] See Grace James, 'The Work and Families Act 2006: Legislation to Improve Choice and Flexibility?' (2006) 35 ILJ 272.   [256] Cm 5005 (London: TSO, December 2000) para 1.15.

[257] Compare, however, below 4.4.3; and see also a very useful discussion of this point by H Collins in J Conaghan and K Rittich (eds), *Labour Law, Work and Family: Critical and Comparative Perspectives* (Oxford: OUP, 2005) at 112–115.

[258] See n 241 above; a useful commentary is provided by S McKay in 'Shifting the Focus from Tribunals to the Workplace' (2001) 30 ILJ 331.

as methods of processing or adjudicating issues about the rights and protections of workers. A modest start down this particular road of reform had been made during the first New Labour government, when government support facilitated the passage of the Employment Rights (Dispute Resolution) Act 1998, derived from a Bill originally proposed by the previous Conservative government and re-presented by the Labour peer Lord Archer of Sandwell in order to permit and encourage alternative dispute resolution for employment law issues on a broader basis than had hitherto been possible under the system of mediation by ACAS in disputes over statutory employment rights such as the right not to be unfairly dismissed. However, that measure had not been a coercive one, and it achieved very little diversion of disputes from employment tribunal litigation towards alternative dispute resolution.

The Green Paper *Routes to Resolution* manifested much more robust intentions on the part of the second New Labour government and, despite the expressed concerns not to entrench upon existing workers' substantive rights,[259] or to restrict access to justice in respect of those rights,[260] it is hard to avoid the conclusion that its proposals quite extensively crossed the line which separates measures to facilitate the settlement of disputes from measures to stifle the assertion of the rights which might give rise to disputes.[261] In the event, one such proposal which was canvassed in the Green Paper, namely a proposal to introduce charging for applications to employment tribunals,[262] was not pursued into the Employment Bill.[263] But arguably no less discouraging of the pursuit of claims before employment tribunals or appeals before the Employment Appeal Tribunal were the proposals implemented in Part 2 of the Act to enable regulations to be made for tribunals to order not only a party to tribunal proceedings but also the representative of a party personally to pay costs incurred by any other party, including costs wasted in the preparation of cases, and also for tribunals to disallow costs of a representative 'by reason of that representative's conduct of the proceedings'.[264] To similar effect were provisions conferring

[259] Compare *Routes to Resolution* para 1.15, in which it was specified that the Review of Employment Tribunals which had been set up (under the chairmanship of Mrs Janet Gaymer) to consider how to achieve the goals of the Green Paper 'will not consider changes to underlying individual employment rights *unless these are concerned with procedural questions'* [emphasis added].

[260] Compare para 5.6: 'At the forefront of any consideration about change are the fundamental principles of access to justice, fair and efficient tribunals, a modern and user-friendly public service, and well-informed users.'

[261] An extended, powerful, and very fully documented presentation of a closely similar argument is offered by Anna Pollert in 'The Unorganised Worker: The Decline in Collectivism and New Hurdles to Individual Employment Rights' (2005) 34 ILJ 217.   [262] Paras 5.8–5.10.

[263] Such a proposal had similarly been made in 1986 as part of the de-regulation agenda of the Thatcher administration, but not pursued: see B Hepple and G S Morris, 'The Employment Act 2002 and the Crisis of Individual Employment Rights' (2002) 31 ILJ 245 at p 249, n 24; cf LLPP, 557–558.

[264] Section 22—employment tribunals; section 23—Employment Appeal Tribunal.

regulation-making powers to enable employment tribunals to impose conciliation periods before and as a pre-condition to the hearing of claims,[265] and to
determine proceedings without a hearing 'in such circumstances as the regulations may prescribe'.[266]

The indirect attack which was mounted by the Employment Act 2002 upon
employment tribunal litigation was a two-pronged one, the other thrust of which
came from Part 3 of the Act, under the heading of Dispute Resolution. The provisions of this Part of the 2002 Act made it clear how precise and narrow had been
the promise in *Routes to Resolution* not to encroach upon substantive employment
rights, and how fraught with meaning was the qualification which allowed for
changes 'concerned with procedural questions'.[267] Under that rhetorical guise of
improvement and effectuation of internal workplace dispute resolution mechanisms, a number of inroads were made into the capacity of employees successfully to articulate and pursue claims to have been unfairly dismissed. Whereas
the counter-balancing imposition of minimum procedural requirements upon
employers[268] was fairly rudimentary,[269] employees on the one hand suffered a
diminution of their rights to treat procedural defects as *per se* establishing the
unfairness of their dismissal,[270] while on the other hand being rendered open
either to finding their unfair dismissal claim barred from the outset by reason of
their having failed to pursue an internal grievance procedure,[271] or to a reduction
of compensation for the same reason.[272] The latter set of restrictions also applies
in relation to a wider set of claims to statutory employment rights,[273] including
the major discrimination and equality rights.

When the Employment Bill was presented to Parliament as a package designed
to promote 'high performance workplaces' where employers and workers could
work in 'effective partnership',[274] there was a dawning realisation that the

---

[265] Section 24.

[266] Section 26 (substituting new s 7(3)(A) of the Employment Tribunals Act 1996). At the time of
writing the DTI had begun to consult about reform in this area, and there were indications that
employers as well as employees were finding this set of provisions difficult to operate.

[267] Above, n 259.

[268] Section 29 of the Act gives effect to statutory disciplinary and dismissal procedures, (though
section 30, which would cause those procedures to operate as minimum procedural standards in contracts of employment, has not been brought into effect).

[269] The requirements, as formulated by Schedule 4 of the Act, are either for warning, hearing, and
appeal, or just for appeal; the Employment Act 2002 (Dispute Resolution) Regulations 2004 SI
2004/752, determining whether the greater or lesser set of requirements applies, give quite a wide
sphere of application to the latter lesser ones.

[270] Section 34(1) of the 2002 Act, inserting new s 98A into the Employment Rights Act 1996,
reversing the effect of the decision of the House of Lords in *Polkey* v *A E Dayton Services Ltd* [1987]
IRLR 503 and restoring the status quo ante in which the employee could not rely on a procedural
defect to establish the unfairness of dismissal except where the tribunal was content that the dismissal
would not have occurred 'but for' the procedural defect.   [271] Section 32(2).

[272] Section 31(2)–(5). This adjustment is mandatory as to 10% of compensation and discretionary up to 50% of compensation.   [273] Listed in Schedule 3 of the Act.

[274] *Hansard*, HL (series 6) vol 375, col 864 (27 November 2001; Ms Patricia Hewitt, Secretary of
State for Trade and Industry).

proposers of these particular measures, though they spoke in the honeyed tones of 'modernisation of employment tribunals' and 'promoting conciliation in the workplace',[275] were actually intent upon a subtle but effective[276] form of de-regulation of personal work relations. Lord McCarthy, in the House of Lords, famously denounced Parts 2 and 3 as the 'manky meat' of the Bill sandwiched between the more innocuous and 'family friendly' Parts 1 and 4.[277] Bob Hepple and Gillian Morris opined that:

Parts 2 and 3 of the Employment Act 2002 signify a moment of crisis as the UK, in common with several other European countries, tries to limit the cost of [individual employment] rights. The British response is essentially to attempt to privatise enforcement through management controlled procedures in preference to independent public tribunals.[278]

The New Labour administration was using procedural rather than substantive ways to limit the impact of unfair dismissal legislation upon managerial flexibility; this they had in common with their recent Conservative predecessors, although the precise means chosen were somewhat different.[279]

2.4.1.3 *Flexible working*

There is then a third set of measures in the Employment Act 2002 upon which it is useful to concentrate some attention, namely the provisions in Part 4 which concern 'Flexible Working'.[280] These are especially significant, we suggest, because they were pitched between the two extremes of worker protectiveness and business friendliness, but with an inclination in the latter direction, in a way which was to emerge as archetypal for this second phase of the Blair administration, and which we might identify as 'light regulation'. The typical features of this kind of 'light regulation' are, first, that the regulation in question takes place in response to some particular demand, such as one generated by a specific political event or need to comply with an EU obligation, rather than as the result of a general policy programme; and, secondly, that the response to such demands is, as far as possible, cast in terms of process regulation rather than in terms of hard

---

[275] The headings to chapters 4 and 5 of the Green Paper *Routes to Resolution*.

[276] B Hepple and G Morris record the government's expectation, in proposing these measures, of a reduction in the region of 25–30% in the caseload of employment tribunals: see (2002) 31 ILJ 245 (n 263 above) at 246, fn 3. There was in fact such a reduction in the period after these provisions came into effect, though how far propter hoc is necessarily controversial.

[277] *Hansard*, HL (series 6) vol 631, col 1369 (26 February 2002). ('Manky', according to the OED: *Brit. colloq.* Bad, inferior, defective; dirty, disgusting, unpleasant.)

[278] B Hepple and G Morris, 'The Employment Act 2002 and the Crisis of Individual Employment Rights' (2002) 31 ILJ 245, Abstract.

[279] Compare LLPP at 555–558, and B Hepple, 'The Fall and Rise of Unfair Dismissal', chapter 2 of W McCarthy (ed), *Legal Intervention in Industrial Relations: Gains and Losses* (Oxford: Blackwell Publishing, 1992).

[280] The provisions are those of section 47, which inserts a new Part 8A on Flexible Working into the Employment Rights Act 1996.

substantive rights—process regulation, moreover, the fine tuning of which is conducted by ministerial order rather than by primary legislation. By engaging in light regulation which conformed to this specification, the government could best realise and maintain its preferred version of management adaptability in personal work relations.

The need to devise some such form of light regulation was felt particularly acutely by the government in relation to the demand for provision for 'flexible working' to help working parents to combine work with the discharge of their parental responsibilities. There was a special demand for some regulation of this kind for two linked reasons; first, because some such measure was needed to give credibility to the government's political claim to be specially committed to 'family-friendly' legislation; and, secondly, because the logic of developing the notion of 'flexibility' in personal work relations required some demonstration of attachment to 'flexibility' for the worker as well as for the management of the employing enterprise. (There was also possibly perceived to be a lurking threat from the absence of any other measure which could claim to implement the provision of the Part-time Work Directive[281] about providing workers with opportunities to transfer between full-time and part-time work.[282]) Indeed, in the Work and Families Act 2006 the government extended its concept of 'family friendly' beyond parents by including 'carers' (to be defined in regulations) within the scheme.[283]

On the other hand, there were important reasons for keeping this regulation light; the government was in general increasingly keen to be seen to be listening to the business community in its development of 'family-friendly' policies, and the representatives of that community, generally adept at warning of the disastrous consequences of enhancement of worker-protective legislation, were especially eloquent with regard to anything which involved ceding control of the way in which working time was arranged and structured, such as might be involved in giving working parents rights to demand that they be accorded flexible working hours or 'flexi-time'.[284] In order to deal with this problem, Ms Patricia Hewitt as Secretary of State for Trade and Industry set up a Work and Parents Taskforce under the chairmanship of Sir George Bain, the Chair of the Low Pay Commission and highly skilled in tripartite negotiations; their report on this issue[285] delivered a legislative proposal in time for its inclusion as an amendment to the Employment Bill.

---

[281] See above, n 217.

[282] The provisions are contained in Clause 5 of the Part-time Work Agreement, to which the Directive gives effect. They fall short of specifically requiring Member States to provide for rights of transfer between full-time and part-time work.

[283] Section 12 of the 2006 Act, amending new s 80F of the ERA 1996.

[284] See, for a very useful discussion of why this particular demand is perceived as specially difficult, H Collins in J Conaghan and K Rittich (eds), *Labour Law, Work and Family: Critical and Comparative Perspectives* (Oxford: OUP, 2005) at 102–103.

[285] Published as *About Time: Flexible Working* in October 2001 (URN 01/1384, also the supporting document 01/1396), and followed by the *Government Response to the Recommendations from the Work and Parents Taskforce* issued by the DTI in November 2001.

The formula which emerged was indeed a carefully crafted compromise, perfectly embodying a notion of light regulation conferring relatively weak rights which are primarily procedural rather than substantive in character.[286] The central notion was that of conferring upon employees[287] with parental responsibilities a right to apply to their employer for a change in working time arrangements for the purpose of caring for a child,[288] and an obligation upon the employer to process the application by holding a meeting with the employee to discuss the application, by giving a written decision stating grounds for refusal, and by providing an appeal against refusal;[289] and the employer is allowed to refuse the request only where 'he considers that one or more of [a set of listed grounds] applies'.[290] The set of grounds for refusal was widely drawn, and capable of extension by ministerial regulation.[291] Crucially, it is provided in the supporting Procedural Requirements Regulations that 'where the decision is to refuse the application, [the notice of decision shall] state which of the [statutorily specified] grounds for refusal are considered by the employer to apply [and] contain a sufficient explanation as to why those grounds apply...'.[292]

There is scope for debate as to how strong or weak is the right which is thus conferred. It is not very meaningful simply to dismiss it as no more than a procedural 'right to request' as opposed to a substantive 'right to flexible working';[293] on the one hand because it would be very difficult on any view to frame an absolute substantive right of the latter kind, with any hope of its commanding political acceptance, and on the other hand because the liberty of the employer to refuse the request, although wide, is not unconstrained. The DTI claims in its guide to these provisions that the legislation has ensured that 'An employer may only refuse a request where there is a recognised business ground for doing so';[294] but the legislation in fact falls short of requiring objective justification for refusal, and defines the grounds for refusal in conspicuously permissive terms, including generalities such as 'the burden of additional costs' and 'detrimental impact on quality'.[295] Moreover, the legislation is so framed as to exclude any collective dimension to the process which leads to or follows from such a refusal.[296] So the

---

[286] So much so as to attract the characterisation of 'sound bite legislation' from L Anderson in a note at (2003) 32 ILJ 37.

[287] Though not other workers; and, rather strikingly, agency workers are expressly excluded vis-à-vis the end-user principal—new ERA, s 80F(8)(a)(ii).

[288] New ERA, s 80F. For the subsequent extension to include a wider set of family carers see n 283 above.   [289] S 80G.

[290] S 80G(1)(b).   [291] S 80G(1)(b)(i)–(ix).

[292] The Flexible Working (Procedural Requirements) Regulations 2002, SI 2002/3207, Reg 5(b)(ii).

[293] As some journalistic writing has been apt to do; compare an article on the website of 'Flexibility—the on-line journal of flexible working': <http://www.flexibility.co.uk/flexwork/general/flexible-right.htm>.

[294] DTI, *Flexible Working—The right to request and the duty to consider—a guide for employers and employees* (February 2003, URN 03/524) at 2.   [295] New ERA, s 80G(1)(b)(i),(v).

[296] H Collins in J Conaghan and K Rittich (eds), *Labour Law, Work and Family: Critical and Comparative Perspectives* (Oxford: OUP, 2005) at 117–123 usefully explores ways in which such a dimension could have been created.

right, when measured according to reasonably realistic political expectations, is more than a token one, but is less than fully robust.

We suggest that this last analysis captures quite well the flavour and aspiration of the light regulation approach of this second phase of the Blair administration in the sphere of personal work relations. We do not suggest that this 'light regulation' approach characterises each and every item of legislation in this second phase; we have already argued that within the compass of the Employment Act 2002 alone, there are sets of measures on either side of this centrist and somewhat employer-leaning path. But we think it is quite useful and accurate to depict in those terms many of the measures and policy decisions which followed after that Act in the course of this second phase, and even beyond it. We shall find that this analysis, if expanded and adjusted to take account of some situations where special policy considerations or special instrumentalities were at work, serves to carry us through the remainder of the history of the regulation of personal work relations during this period.

2.4.1.4 *Working time*

One very important manifestation of 'light regulation' consisted of minimal compliance with EU legislative obligations; during this second phase of the Blair administration that was to become a more prominent phenomenon, almost to the point of resemblance with the stance of the Major administration in its latter days—it became increasingly clear that, for New Labour almost as much as for the Conservatives, the European Social Model was one from which the British government wanted to distance itself. A good example is to be found in the field of regulation of working time; in this second phase, they duly though minimally implemented the Working Time Directive of 2000,[297] which extended the application of the original Working Time Directive of 1993 to certain sectors and activities which were previously excluded from its scope; various parts of the EU working time regime were now applied for the first time or more extensively than before to junior or trainee hospital doctors, road transport workers, crew members on board civil aircraft, and workers in the armed forces or emergency services.[298] However, the British government maintained throughout this period a determined insistence on the preservation of the individual opt-out from the 48-hour maximum working week, and was a major contributor to the resistance, successful throughout this period, to proposals from the European Commission to improve the effectiveness of EU working time regulation.[299]

---

[297] Council Directive 2000/34/EC (OJ 2000 L195/41, 1 August 2000).

[298] This is a summary statement of the effect of the Working Time (Amendment) Regulations 2003, SI 2003/1684.

[299] The Commission conducted a review of the operation of the Working Time Directive 1993 in 2003, as contemplated and required by the original Directive, and in 2004 presented legislative proposals as the result of the review; but agreement had not, by the time of writing, been forthcoming in the Council of Ministers.

2.4.1.5 Pensions

In quite a different way, but nevertheless equally significantly, we could even regard the Pensions Act 2004, and the other measures concerning occupational pension provision which were associated with it, as an important instance of light regulation. This observation might seem surprising, even ironical, to those concerned with the law and practice of occupational pensions schemes, who had to deal with a mountain of new legal and administrative requirements imposed by this legislation which dwarfed even those of the Pensions Act 1995,[300] but nevertheless there are real non-re-regulatory or even marginally de-regulatory aspects of the 2004 Act which make it more than slightly comparable with the Act of 1995. An amplification of this point may assist in the understanding, both of the particular conception of 'light regulation' which we are putting forward as typical of the personal work relations legislation and policy of this period, and of this particular set of measures; of which, however, we can offer no more than the merest summary of key points.

The conception of 'light regulation' which is deployed here is one which can be traced back to the Kahn-Freundian ideal for labour law; namely, that, it being admitted that the law is a secondary rather than a primary source of power in labour relations, it is nevertheless the mission of labour law to redress in favour of workers an inherent inequality of power between them and their employers. (This is not, however, to imply that Kahn-Freund would necessarily or even probably have regarded his ideal for labour law as having been realised in the New Labour brand of 'light regulation'.) In the field of personal work relations the terminology of 'de-regulation' generally refers to legislation and policy which resiles from earlier measures for the protection of workers; and we can think of 'light regulation' as consisting of measures and policies which are aimed at securing reasonably orderly and consensual governance of personal work relations, without, however, fundamentally restricting the freedom of action of enterprise management in favour of the protection of workers. That particular equilibrium, perhaps best conceived of as a balance between excessive regulation and insufficient regulation—using both those normative notions in a specifically contextual sense—is, of course, a notoriously elusive one for governments to achieve and maintain. In order to do so, they frequently find it necessary to engage in very intensive legislative activity, and they also need to require an immense amount of compliance activity on the part of the managers of enterprises to provide assurance that these delicate normative structures are being suitably operated. If the lightness of the Emperor's new clothes is not to be too painfully apparent, many tailors have to be seen to be doing a great deal of stitching.

If, therefore, a certain paradigm of 'light regulation' starts to emerge in the new millennium, consisting of the careful limitation of the coerciveness of worker-protection combined with deceptively intense regulatory activity in the face of

---

[300] See above, text at n 71.

major social and economic issues, that paradigm is perfectly instantiated by the programme or sequence of legislation constructed around the Pensions Act 2004. The major social and economic issues were, essentially, those of the increasing longevity of the population and the strains which it was starting to place, and were projected increasingly to place, upon the system or practice of provision for retirement; those issues had been the subject of a series of reports and policy documents throughout the life of the New Labour administration,[301] starting with the Green Paper of December 1998, *A New Contract for Welfare: Partnership in Pensions*.[302] The underlying question was whether and how far the government would cause that strain to be taken up either by reinforcement of state social security provision or by imposing more extensive obligations and expectations upon occupational pension provision by employing enterprises. The pensions legislation of 1994 neatly, if elaborately, sidestepped that question.

In order to understand how this somewhat paradoxical combination of substantive evasiveness with intensive regulatory activity could be effected, it is helpful to develop the distinction, which we began to introduce in relation to the Pensions Act 1995, between two divergent, even if not entirely mutually exclusive, kinds or levels of regulation of occupational pension provision. There is one kind or level of regulation in or at which the concern is with the protection of the accrued or specifically promised pension rights of workers; there is another kind or level of regulation in or at which there is a deeper and more general concern with ensuring the continuing efficacy of future provision by employing enterprises for the retirement of workers. The legislation of and around 2004 is reasonably robust at the former level, but rarely if ever intervenes with the same intensity at the latter level, and at that level is sometimes permissive to the point of being positively de-regulatory in character. We proceed to illustrate this contrast by recounting the story of this legislation in slightly more detail.

Throughout this second phase of the New Labour administration, there was a strong and widespread political perception of the existence of a 'pensions crisis';[303] this was generated mainly by an accelerating trend towards the closure of private sector final salary or 'defined benefit' pension schemes to new members (so that the pension provision offered to them would consist of the less favourable type of money purchase or 'defined contribution' savings scheme), but also by occasional specific incidents where concrete pension rights were effectively nullified by corporate and pension fund insolvencies.[304] The first New Labour government had in the view of many done little to prevent this crisis, and there was some feeling

---

[301] See Helen J Desmond, 'The Generation Game: Pensions and Retirement' (2003) 32 ILJ 218.

[302] Treasury and Department of Social Security, Cm 4179 (London: TSO, 1998).

[303] A useful body of reportage is to be found at <http://search.bbc.co.uk/cgi-bin/search/results.pl?scope=all&edition=d&q=pensions+crisis&go.x=45&go.y=9>.

[304] A telling incident was the insolvency in 2002 of the Allied Steel and Wire corporation, leaving 800 workers in Wales with greatly depleted pension provision; see <http://news.bbc.co.uk/1/hi/wales/3507624.stm>.

that it had actually been exacerbated by a fiscal measure taken by that government in 1997.[305] The responsive strategy of the second New Labour government was tentatively articulated in a Green Paper of December 2002 and confirmed in a White Paper of June 2003, both of which marched under the banner of 'simplicity, security and choice';[306] it was a strategy which claimed to address both the general and the specific problems, though in reality it was more apt to tackle the latter than the former.

In its aspect of developing robust protection of the accrued or specifically promised rights of pension scheme members, and building upon the notion of protection against fraud and misappropriation which was at the heart of the Goode Report and the Pensions Act 1995,[307] the 2004 Act created a new Pension Protection Fund to provide compensation to pension scheme members where their employing enterprise becomes insolvent and their pension scheme is underfunded.[308] This represented an anticipatory or proactive compliance with EU legislative obligations, in this case those imposed by the Pensions Directive of 2003;[309] so also, in a broad sense, did the decision to extend the TUPE system of protection of employees' acquired rights upon the transfer of undertakings, to include pension rights,[310] though there may in addition have been a domestic rationale for this measure, consisting of its facilitation of outsourcing of public services to the private sector.[311] A further political pressure was exerted by the realisation that a significant number of pension scheme members left severely deprived by the insolvency of their corporate employers would go uncompensated by the new Pension Protection Fund because the insolvencies had occurred before the beginning of its protective regime; a Financial Assistance Scheme was added to the legislation to address this particular need.[312]

These measures represent the main elements of 'heavy regulation' in the Pensions Act 2004; the rest of this programme of legislation consists quite largely of lightly regulatory, and even at times de-regulatory, interventions. This change

[305] This consisted in the abolition in 1997 of corporation tax credit in respect of share dividends, which effected a major transfer of resources from occupational pension funds to the Exchequer.

[306] The Green Paper was published as *Simplicity, security and choice: Working and saving for retirement* (Cm 5677), and the White Paper as *Simplicity, security and choice: Working and saving for retirement—Action on occupational pensions* (Cm 5835). In February 2004 the Secretary of State for Work and Pensions published a further associated White Paper on financial retirement planning, *Simplicity, security and choice: Informed choices for working and saving* (Cm 6111).

[307] See above, text above n 77.   [308] Pensions Act 2004, ss 173–181.

[309] The European Parliament and Council Directive 2003/41/EC on the Activities and Supervision of Institutions for Occupational Retirement Provision (OJ 2003 L235/10, 23 September 2003) was adopted in September 2003 for implementation by September 2005.

[310] Pensions Act 2004, s 258 and the Transfer of Employment (Pension Protection) Regulations 2005, SI 2005/649. This is not, however, to suggest that full rights to earn future pensions are transferred; compare D Pollard, 'Pensions and TUPE' (2005) 34 ILJ 127.

[311] Compare below, text and nn 473 to 475, for details of a probably similar rationale for some of the changes made to the TUPE Regulations themselves in 2006.

[312] Pensions Act 2004, s 286 and the Financial Assistance Scheme Regulations 2005, SI 2005/1986.

of character becomes the more apparent as the measures become less concerned with protection of accrued rights or concrete expectations, and more concerned with the general strategic regulation of occupational pension provision. In that larger hinterland there was created the new office of Pensions Regulator, an elaborately re-invented replacement for the Occupational Pensions Regulatory Authority (OPRA) which had been established by the Pensions Act 1995.[313] In this genre of re-working the regulatory systems of the 1995 Act, the Minimum Funding Requirement for occupational pension funds which that Act had instituted,[314] and which had operated under the supervision of OPRA, was replaced by a new Statutory Funding Objective, to be supervised by the Pensions Regulator.[315] The main *Simplicity and choice* White Paper, under the rubric of 'Making pension provision easier for employers',[316] makes it clear enough that this was intended to be a more 'flexible' set of requirements,[317] supervised by a correspondingly more 'flexible' regulator.[318]

This was not the only sense in which the Pensions Act 2004, often in the name of 'simplification' of existing legislation,[319] engaged in a degree of de-regulation and partial retrenchment upon existing controls, including some which had been introduced by the Pensions Act 1995. Thus, for example, the restrictions which the 1995 Act had placed upon the alteration of members' accrued rights were amended, essentially by replacement of requirements of consent with requirements of consultation.[320] Similarly, the 2004 Act removed the voluntary contribution requirement, which required occupational and personal pension schemes to allow additional voluntary contributions to be paid by members.[321] A third and concluding example is that of the relaxation by the 2004 Act of the requirement which had been introduced by the 1995 Act for indexation of pensions in payment under defined benefit pension schemes (known as Limited Price Indexation).[322] It could indeed be said of all these modifications that the measures which they superseded were modified in part because they had proved unsatisfactory ways of protecting scheme members' interests, and therefore not solely for the sake of alleviating regulatory burdens upon employing enterprises; and it could also be said that the new measures might themselves have imposed their own regulatory burdens; but nevertheless an underlying de-regulatory thrust is evident.

---

[313] Pensions Act 2004, Part I.   [314] See above, n 74.

[315] Pensions Act 2004, ss 221–233.   [316] Cm 5835, chapter 3.

[317] Para 3.4. 'Our proposals will allow schemes greater flexibility to match their investment strategy to the profile of their members.'

[318] Para 2.22 'Greater flexibility and proportionality will benefit both those the Pensions Regulator seeks to protect and those who provide and administer work-based pension schemes.'

[319] Compare Cm 5835, para 2.16: 'The Government has been consistently clear that simplification must lie at the heart of any strategy to encourage voluntary pension provision. The new regulatory framework...will enable us to simplify the legislation relating to scheme demonstration and governance'.   [320] Section 262 of the 2004 Act, replacing section 67 of the 1995 Act.

[321] Section 267 of the 2004 Act, providing for the repeal of Pension Schemes Act 1993, s 111.

[322] Section 278 of the 2004 Act, modifying section 51 of the 1995 Act. (Compare also section 279 of the 2004 Act, modifying section 162 of the 1995 Act as to certain personal pensions.)

There is, moreover, a further and more general sense in which the pensions legislation of 2004–5 amounted to 'light regulation'; we can identify it by reverting to the distinction which we drew earlier between regulation which concentrates upon the protection of the accrued or specifically promised rights or expectations of workers, and regulation which is more generally and strategically concerned with the protection of the security of workers. At the former level, the Pensions Act 2004 and the measures associated with it are quite heavily regulatory; but at the latter level they are much less so—in particular, because they tend to maintain and even to intensify a certain free-market approach to occupational pension provision which had been taken during the Thatcher and the Major administrations; in this sense, the Pensions Act 2004 really could be considered as the Pensions Act 1995 writ large. The 2004 Act essentially continued the occupational pensions system in its movement along a trajectory upon which it had been launched in the later 1980s and propelled in the earlier 1990s.

The key determinant of that trajectory was, as we have indicated, the shift away from defined benefit final salary pension provision towards defined contribution money purchase pension schemes. To shift the metaphor, we might say that the flow in that direction, which had been a trickle at the beginning of the first Major government, was becoming a flood by the end of the second Blair government. The channel for that flow had been opened up by a partial liberation of the regulatory and fiscal regime for 'personal' or 'portable' pensions in the 1980s,[323] this being one of the forms in which pension provision is wholly or partially detached and individualised in relation to the significantly mutualised paradigm of the final salary pensions scheme. A somewhat abortive attempt to aggrandise those personal pensions into a system of partly encouraged and partly mandated 'stakeholder pensions' was made during the first New Labour government by means of the provisions of Part I of the Welfare Reform and Pensions Act of 1999 and the Stakeholder Pensions Regulations of the year 2000.[324]

But it will, we think, with hindsight appear that it was the crucial role of the 2004 Act, as well as of the 1995 Act, to design the overall regulatory system for occupational pension provision, so as to protect and incentivise the dynamic towards money purchase pension provision, and, ultimately, money purchase from financial service providers rather than from pension funds run by or attached to employing enterprises. That set of incentives results in part at least from the way in which the 2004 legislation, while being substantively permissive in the ways discussed above, nevertheless extended, even more than the 1995 Act had done, the processual requirements placed upon the management of pension schemes—and most especially upon trust-fund-based defined benefit schemes.[325]

---

[323] In particular by Part I of the Social Security Act 1986; see LLPP, 572–573.

[324] SI 2000/1403 (as shortly afterwards amended by SI 2001/104 and SI 2001/1934). See, for an excellent survey, T Jarvis, *Stakeholder Pensions—House of Commons Research Paper 01/69* (House of Commons Library, 31 August 2001).

[325] Compare Alastair Meeks, 'The Pensions Act 2004—what does it mean for HR?' *Personnel Today*, 30 November 2004, at 12: 'To paraphrase the Prime Minister, companies can expect regulation,

It is debatable how far those particular consequences were intended ones, but there are many indications that the design of the legislative package of 2004–5 was shaped and informed by an ideological and political vision of the worker as the consumer of financial services in a free market of saving opportunities, rather than as the protected subject of labour law in retirement as well as in work.[326] In that larger sense, and behind an intricate façade of detailed and processual legislation, we discover an ironical reality of 'light regulation' in this important dimension of personal work relations.

The New Labour administration was conscious of the consequential strain which this light regulatory approach would place upon the social security system, and at the same period instituted a major review of the totality of pension arrangements by a Pensions Commission under the chairmanship of Adair Turner, formerly Director-General of the CBI. The Final Report of that body, published in April 2006,[327] indicated, even more forcefully than its two interim reports,[328] that these strains would before long become intolerable, and made recommendations for an essentially two-pronged medium- and long-term remedial strategy whereby government would on the one hand raise to 68 by 2050 the age of entitlement to the basic state retirement pension while enhancing the level of that entitlement and restoring its linkage to the rate of growth in earnings rather than to the (systemically lower) rate of general price inflation, and on the other hand institute a National Pension Saving Scheme which would be a state-provided low-cost vehicle for occupational pension provision, with strong pressure upon workers to participate in occupational pension saving by means of automatic enrolment, coupled with an element of mandatory contribution by employing enterprises.

Perhaps not having entirely foreseen the political pressure under which a Commission chaired by Lord Turner would place them, but feeling the need to be seen to yield to that pressure, the government published in May 2006 a White Paper *Security in retirement: towards a new pensions system*,[329] which essentially amounted to an acceptance of the proposals in a slightly moderated form,[330] and

regulation, regulation—if they have a final salary scheme. Companies with money purchase schemes escape largely unscathed.'

[326] This is a rhetoric which infused much of the *Simplicity* White Paper of 2003 (n 306 above), especially chapter 4: 'Choice for all—planning for retirement'. Compare the even more conspicuous display of this rhetoric by the then Pensions Minister Mr Malcolm Wicks, introducing on 14 March 2005 the new Stakeholder Pension Schemes (Amendment) Regulations 2005, SI 2005/577: 'These regulations will bring the stakeholder pension into the Government's new suite of stakeholder products. The key change is "lifestyling". "Lifestyling" will help provide people with a degree of certainty in the years leading up to their retirement. This will mean that people can have their pension moved into investments that will reduce the risk of an unexpected drop in value just before they retire.'

[327] *Implementing an Integrated Package of Pensions Reforms: The Final Report of the Pensions Commission* (April 2006).

[328] *Pensions: Challenges and Choices: The First Report of the Pensions Commission* (October 2004); *A New Pension Settlement for the Twenty-First Century: The Second Report of the Pensions Commission* (November 2005).

[329] Department of Work and Pensions, Cm 6841 (London: TSO, May 2006).

[330] For example, by avoiding a specific commitment to raise the state retirement pension age beyond 67.

with significant caveats about 'affordability'.[331] Although those proposals of the White Paper were too long-term in nature to justify detailed dissection at this juncture (beyond perhaps emphasising that the proposed National Pension Saving Scheme is limited in nature, so that neither the employer nor the state is obliged to take on board the obligation to provide a substantial pension), it is worth stressing the ways in which they support two central themes of our present work, namely the strength of the commitment on the part of the New Labour administration to 'light regulation', and to 'promoting work' in the sense of channelling state welfare provision through the maximising of employment. In our later chapter on 'promoting work' (chapter 4), we will be mainly concerned with measures and policies which concentrate on maximising entry into work; but another important element in the governmental strategy of 'promoting work' is that of creating the right conditions and incentives for the extension of the duration of working life in keeping with the increase in the longevity of the population. The proposals in this White Paper which couple the amelioration of state pension provision with its gradual postponement to a later age should therefore be seen as increasingly integral to that strategy.

An associated issue of more immediate concern was the question of whether and how to regulate the imposition by employing enterprises upon workers of requirements to retire at a fixed age;[332] we shortly turn to consider the way in which that was approached by means of policy and measures to control age discrimination, and we revert to that same issue in our subsequent chapter on 'promoting work'.[333] If the White Paper was of real future significance for the idea and politics of 'promoting work', it was also a vivid present illustration of the growing pre-occupation of the New Labour administration with 'light regulation'. Those drafting the White Paper clearly felt that, if they had spent most of their time on justifying the case for a strong future dose of relatively 'heavy regulation', they should also be seen to alleviate the regulatory mixture. The Executive Summary of the White Paper concludes its resumé of the government's intentions with such a classic exposition of the genre of 'light regulation' that it is worth quoting it almost in full:

Finally, we will streamline the regulatory environment. We will do this by:

[...]

- reducing burdens on schemes by bringing forward legislation to allow schemes to convert Guaranteed Minimum Pension rights into scheme benefits;
- introducing a rolling deregulatory review of pensions legislation, in light of the Pensions Act 2004;

---

[331] As, for example, in the Prime Minister's Foreword, and the Foreword of Mr John Hutton as Secretary of State for Work and Pensions. Contemporary political reportage strongly suggests that such caveats were insisted upon by the Chancellor of the Exchequer, Mr Gordon Brown.

[332] The relevance of this issue was identified in the *Simplicity* White Paper of 2003 (n 306 above) in chapter 4 under the heading of 'Greater choice about flexible retirement'.

[333] See below 2.4.2 and 4.4.2.

- piloting a Pensions Law Rewrite Project; and
- re-examining the existing regulatory landscape.

Any such simplification will be aimed at easing the regulatory burden on employers who provide good occupational pensions. They, and other measures in the proposed reform package, will be taken forward with regard to the Government's wider agenda to promote better regulation and reduce the administrative burdens on business.[334]

2.4.1.6 Gangmasters: and criminal liability for health and safety

We turn to consider two further and concluding examples of 'light regulation' in the general area of basic labour standards and worker protection. The first of those other episodes of 'light regulation' was of a very different kind from the one just described; it concerned the abuses and malpractices occurring in the course of the employment of labourers by gangmasters, especially though not solely in agricultural harvesting and in the gathering of shellfish. We could think of the regulatory response to those abuses and malpractices as a matter of adaptation to a particular kind of non-standard employment, namely that of employment by intermediaries or subcontractors, in this particular sector of the economy; but really it was, and is, not so much a problem of the failure of labour laws to apply to workers in such work relationships, as a shortcoming in enforcement of labour laws which were and are in theory applicable. This was a problem that had been exacerbated during the Major administration when the Deregulation and Contracting Out Act 1994[335] had abolished the previously existing system for the licensing of employment agencies,[336] which had been applicable at least to some forms of employment by gangmasters.[337]

The New Labour administration seemed not greatly more anxious than their Conservative predecessors to improve the quality of enforcement of basic labour standards against gangmasters,[338] until an urgent political pressure to do so was exerted by the incident in February 2004 of the drowning of a group of Chinese cockle-pickers working in gangmaster employment in Morecambe Bay, after which the government swung into a more vigorous support of the Gangmaster (Licensing) Bill proposed as a Private Member's Bill by Mr Jim Sheridan, MP, which was at that moment awaiting its Second Reading in the House of Commons.[339] However, the government's support was never fulsome or unstinting, as was indicated in the rather grudging re-joinder to Mr Jim Sheridan's presentation of his Bill by Mr Alun Michael as Minister for Rural Affairs and Local Environmental Quality: 'Does he agree that licensing is not a panacea—indeed,

---

[334] Para 41.   [335] See above, text around n 100.

[336] Section 35 and Schedule 10 of the 1994 Act, repealing Employment Agencies Act 1973, ss 1–3.

[337] See the very useful annotation to the Gangmasters (Licensing) Act 2004 by R Fortson, [2004] Current Law Statutes 2004/11 at 2004/11/1.

[338] A Private Member's Bill, the Licensing and Regulation of Gangmasters Bill, introduced in 2002–3, failed to attract government support; see R Fortson, loc cit (n 337, above).

[339] See R Fortson, loc cit (n 337, above).

he said that the Bill is not a panacea—but a necessary part of an effective system? . . . Indeed, our discussions about the Bill have concerned making it simple and effective.'[340]

In fact, as we have argued elsewhere,[341] the Bill, and indeed the Gangmasters (Licensing) Act 2004 as passed, did represent, potentially at least, quite a radical form of regulation of the gravely abusive employment practices with which it was concerned, insofar as the Act, by creating an offence of entering into arrangements with unlicensed gangmasters for the supply of 'workers or services' by the gangmaster,[342] did offer to impose criminal responsibility, for the observance of labour standards by the gangmasters as immediate employers or labour providers, upon enterprises such as major retailers further along the chain of commerce in the products which were harvested by means of this system of employment. We refer to a 'potential' rather than an actual effect of this legislation, because the price of government support was, not untypically, the inclusion of so much delegation of its implementation to ministerial regulations[343] as to give the Act the character of outline enabling legislation rather than that of an executive measure.

The government has certainly seemed minded to use those delegated powers to alleviate the impact of this legislation, so much so as to engender a suspicion that they might ideally prefer to limit its impact to cockle-picking in the particular part of Morecambe Bay in which the terrible incident of February 2004 occurred. The implementation, or non-implementation, of the legislation was entrusted not, as one might normally have expected of general employment legislation, to the Department of Trade and Industry,[344] but rather to the Department for Environment Food and Rural Affairs (DEFRA) so as to mark out its intended rigid confinement to the sphere of agricultural harvesting and shellfish gathering. Although the Gangmasters Licensing Authority was established by April 2005,[345] DEFRA engaged in a consultation about the terms of proposed Exclusions Regulations[346] which was so prolonged and so cautious as to ensure that the system of criminal sanctions against unlicensed operation by gangmasters did not come into effect until well after the end of the second term in government of the New Labour administration,[347] and even then was to do so on a severely restricted basis, excluding in particular the employment of workers in any subsequent part

---

[340] *Hansard*, HC (series 6) vol 418, col 521.

[341] P L Davies and M R Freedland, chapter 13, 'Identifying the Employer and its Complexities' in Davidov and Langille (eds), *Boundaries and Frontiers of Labour Law* (Oxford and Portland, Oregon: Hart Publishing, 2006) at 291–293.   [342] Section 13 of the 2004 Act.

[343] Section 25—Regulations, rules and orders.

[344] In the absence of a Department of Employment—for a critical analysis of this aspect of the institutional structure see M R Freedland and N Kountouris, 'The Institutional Structure at Departmental Level—Not the Department of Employment', chapter 2 in L Dickens and A Neal (eds), *The Changing Institutional Face of British Employment Relations* (Alphen aan den Rijn, The Netherlands: Kluwer Law International, 2006)

[345] The Gangmasters (Licensing Authority) Regulations 2005, SI 2005/448.

[346] *Consultation on the draft Gangmasters (Exclusions) Regulations 2005* (DEFRA, February 2005).

[347] This eventually took place in October 2006.

of the process of food production or provision other than its original harvest-ing.[348] To allay any remaining fears of heavy regulation, the DEFRA Minister, Mr Jim Knight, announcing this step in March 2006, offered the reassurance that 'We are also planning to review the system after one year to ensure it is working effectively. We are especially keen to ensure it doesn't become an excessive burden for small businesses.'[349]

A final example of the government's reluctance to introduce strong legal sanc-tions against management can be found in the area of the criminal law relating to health and safety at work. Reform of health and safety standards was not a major preoccupation of the government in general, but in one particular area they were the subject of a lively public debate in our period. In a number of cases—notably a ferry sinking in 1987 and, more recently, three railway crashes involving the deaths of both passengers and employees—prosecutions against the operating enterprises for manslaughter by gross negligence had either failed or not been instituted because it was thought they would fail. Certainly prosecutions for breaches of the Health and Safety at Work Act 1974 had been successful and had led in some cases to the imposition of substantial fines on the operators involved. However, prosecutions for the more serious and arguably more appropriate offence of manslaughter by gross negligence against the operating enterprises were normally not available, because the common law of crime, unlike the law of tort, did not apply the doctrine of vicarious liability, especially not to crimes involving a guilty mind. Only if very senior managers in the organisation had themselves been guilty of manslaughter by gross negligence would the operator itself be regarded as guilty of a criminal office (through the doctrine of 'identification').

In 1996 the Law Commission proposed a reform to deal with this problem in the shape of criminal liability on the organisation for substantial management failure leading to death.[350] The government consulted on the Law Commission's proposals in 2000 and put a commitment to legislate into its manifesto for the 2001 election, following one of the disasters referred to above. Yet it was not until 2005 that the government produced a formal response to the 2000 consultation and a draft Bill on corporate manslaughter.[351] This draft was put out for pre-legislative scrutiny, which was quickly provided by a Select Committee.[352] That in turn required a further government response, which, however, promised, in the time-honoured formula, only to 'legislate without delay as soon as Parliamentary time allows',[353] so that by the end of our period an enactment had not reached

---

[348] The Gangmasters Licensing (Exclusions) Regulations 2006, SI 2006/658; the exclusions are effected by reg 2 and set out in the Schedule.

[349] DEFRA News Release 107/06; see: <http://www.defra.gov.uk/news/2006/060313c.htm>.

[350] The Law Commission, *Involuntary Manslaughter*, Law Com No 237, March 1996.

[351] Home Office, *Corporate Manslaughter: the Government's Draft Bill for Reform*, Cm 6497 (London: TSO, March 2005).

[352] Home Affairs and Work and Pensions Committees, *Draft Corporate Manslaughter Bill*, First Joint Report Session 2005–06, HC 540–1, December 2005.

[353] *Draft Corporate Manslaughter Bill*, Cm 6755 (London: TSO, March 2006).

the statute book despite a manifesto commitment five years earlier to legislate on the topic.

Among the many difficulties which the government identified with the Law Commission's proposals, two areas are of particular interest to us. First, the government seems to have been concerned that too wide an offence might produce unduly cautious conduct on the part of managers as they sought to prevent the employing enterprise from committing a criminal offence. In order to prevent the introduction of a culture of excessive risk-avoidance throughout the enterprise, the offence was limited to gross negligence by senior managers (not any manager, as the Law Commission had proposed) and in situations where a duty of care at common law was owed to the person killed (not a restriction proposed by the Law Commission).[354] Secondly, this formulation of the corporate offence naturally raised the question of whether the individual senior managers should be criminally liable as well as the enterprise. The government steadfastly refused to create criminal liability for individual senior managers under the Bill,[355] sticking to the argument that the offence identified rested on a collective rather than an individual management failure. If any individual manager were individually at fault, that person could be prosecuted under the common law as it stood. That is perhaps a suitably characteristic note on which to conclude this discussion and turn to other aspects of regulation of personal work relations during this phase of the New Labour administration.

2.4.2 Recognition of human and equality rights in personal work relations

The foregoing discussion has indicated, in the sphere of basic labour standards, something of the ambivalence, even at times inconsistency, of the 'light regulation' approach of the second New Labour government, and of the notion of managerial adaptability which that government sought to foster or protect. In the context of the recognition of human and equality rights in personal work relations, we find a somewhat comparable degree of ambivalence or duality, but those qualities are differently manifested. As a broad generalisation, we suggest that the government at this period displayed itself as willing to engage in regulation of this kind where the aims or effects seemed to them to be predominantly the maximizing of social and economic inclusion in personal work relations, but markedly unwilling to do so where the aims or effects seemed to be those of constraining or rigidifying the structures or patterns of those personal work relations.

Many of the difficult choices which confronted a government with that essentially ambivalent approach were, as for its immediate predecessors, necessitated by

---

[354] Draft Bill, n 342 above, cll 1(1) and 4.

[355] This included ruling out secondary liability on individual managers in relation to the primary liability created on the organisation: cl 1(5).

EU initiatives and developments in EU law, and it is useful to analyse how the evolution of national policy and measures in this area relates to those initiatives and developments. From this analytical perspective, some interesting comparisons and contrasts present themselves. For instance, the government was in sympathy with the inclusionary impulses and the anxieties about racism and xenophobia, especially in an enlarging Community, which prompted the enactment in 2000 of the Race Directive,[356] in which, using the extended competence conferred by the Treaty of Amsterdam in 1997,[357] the Community engaged decisively in the combating of discrimination on grounds of racial or ethnic origin. In parallel with that Directive, though not specifically in reaction to it, but rather in response to the public exposure of the extent of the problem of institutional racism in the police service,[358] the government had brought forward the proposals for legislation which issued forth in the Race Relations Amendment Act 2000, which extended the Race Relations Act 1976 to cover policing and immigration functions and the employment of police officers,[359] and which imposed a set of legal duties on public authorities to work towards the elimination of unlawful discrimination and to promote equality of opportunity and good relations between persons of different racial groups.[360] In the latter respect, similar initiatives were later taken with regard to disability discrimination and to sex discrimination, eventually giving rise to parallel or similar provisions with respect to the former in the Disability Discrimination Act 2005,[361] and in the Equality Act 2006 with respect to the latter.[362]

So positive was this development that Sandra Fredman offered the speculation that the UK might be setting an example for the start of a new era of equality law in the EU.[363] However, if the New Labour administration had concluded its first term of government on that positive note, in fairly stark contrast to that approach was its stance towards an initiative which they found much more threatening to their vision of light regulation and managerial adaptability in personal work relations, namely the proposals for an EU Charter of Fundamental Rights; here, they evidently felt deep misgivings at the prospect of the inclusion of a set of economic and social rights in addition to the less controversial list of civil and political

[356] Council Directive 2000/43/EC (2000 OJ L180/22, 19 July 2000).
[357] By the addition of new ECT Article 13.
[358] *The Stephen Lawrence Inquiry*: Report Of An Inquiry By Sir William Macpherson, Cm 4262-I (London: TSO, February 1999).
[359] Race Relations Amendment Act 2000, s 1, inserting ss 19B–19F into the 1976 Act.
[360] Section 2 of the 2000 Act replaces section 71 of the 1976 Act, which imposed a general duty on local authorities to promote race equality, with sections 71–71E which provide for all specified public authorities to promote race equality.
[361] Disability Discrimination Act 2005, ss 1–3, implementing proposals canvassed in the consultation document *Towards Inclusion—Civil Rights for Disabled People—Government Response to the Disability Rights Taskforce* (DfES, March 2001).
[362] Equality Act 2006, s 84, inserting into the Sex Discrimination Act 1975 a new s 75A ('Public Authorities: General Statutory Duty').
[363] S Fredman, 'Equality: A New Generation' (2001) 30 ILJ 145.

rights, and at the possibility that this Charter might be enacted in a legally binding form.[364] The UK government did much during the discussion of the proposals to ensure that when the Charter was proclaimed by the Member States at the Nice European Council in December 2000,[365] it took a form in which it was not legally binding and created no new rights for workers in any concrete sense.[366]

Bob Hepple, characterising the contribution of the UK government to this outcome, concluded that 'Not for the first time in EU negotiations, the UK secured a number of important modifications in the interests of consensus, only at the end to resile from the legal consequences'.[367] Brian Bercusson has chronicled the way in which, in the subsequent phase in which the Convention on the Future of Europe formulated proposals for the embodiment of the Charter in the new Treaty which was intended to become the Constitution of the European Union,[368] the UK government played a comparably cautious and at times negative role.[369] The failure of the referenda held in France and the Netherlands in 2005 to secure majorities for the ratification of the Treaty, and the resultant abortion, at least for the short or medium term, of the initiative for an EU Constitution, avoided, perhaps not inconveniently for the government, the necessity for a full-scale public debate and decision about its acceptability in the UK; there can be little doubt that, had such a debate taken place, the government would have been at pains to assert that it had pursued a 'light regulation' approach to the role of the Charter in the Treaty, especially in the context of personal work relations, and that it fully intended to continue to do so.

A slightly comparable, though much more muted, contrast can be drawn between the responses of the second New Labour government to different aspects of the so-called Employment Framework Directive of 2000,[370] which complemented the inclusionary initiative taken, as we have seen above,[371] by the Race Directive of the same year by providing a framework for extending employment discrimination law to a set of grounds not previously addressed by EU law, that is to say, those of disability, religion or belief, sexual orientation, and age. The UK was in substantial compliance with this Directive so far as disability

---

[364] The proposals as they stood in 2000, and the arguments for and against them in their various formulations, were described by S Fredman, C McCrudden, and M R Freedland in 'An E.U. Charter of Fundamental Rights' [2000] Public Law 178.

[365] The Charter was promulgated as a 'Solemn Proclamation' (2000/C 364/01—OJ C364/1 18 December 2000).

[366] See, for a fuller analysis, B Hepple, 'The EU Charter of Fundamental Rights' (2001) 30 ILJ 225.   [367] Ibid, at 225.

[368] A slightly reformulated version of the Charter formed Part II of the Treaty establishing a Constitution for Europe, signed in Rome on 29 October 2004.

[369] B Bercusson, 'Episodes on the Path Towards the European Social Model', chapter 8 of C Barnard, S Deakin, and G S Morris (eds), *The Future of Labour Law—Liber Amicorum Sir Bob Hepple QC* (Oxford and Portland, Oregon: Hart Publishing, 2004).

[370] Council Directive 2000/78/EC of 27 November 2000 establishing a general framework for equal treatment in employment and occupation (OJ 2000 L303/16, 2 December 2000).

[371] Text around n 356.

discrimination was concerned, by virtue of the Disability Discrimination Act 1995,[372] but legislation was required with respect to the last three heads of discrimination. The contrast in approach to which we refer arises as between religion or belief and sexual orientation on the one hand, and age discrimination on the other. With regard to the former, the government seemed to have regarded the Directive as congruent with their own inclusionary policies, and were content to enact what is generally regarded as a reasonably whole-hearted set of implementing measures.[373] Indeed, in the matter of harassment of workers on the grounds of religion or belief and sexual orientation, it is arguable that those measures go further than was strictly speaking required, insofar as they seem to have come very close to creating a free-standing wrong of harassment on those grounds, rather than merely identifying harassment as a specific form of discrimination on those grounds.[374]

The attitude of the government was much less relaxed or positive with regard to the remaining obligation to legislate with regard to age discrimination in employment. The Directive itself was framed in terms which recognised that this was going to be a rather difficult matter for the Member States; they were allowed to request a deferment of the obligation to implement for up to three years, hence until October 2006;[375] and a broad substantive derogation enabled them to provide, if they wished, that 'differences of treatment on grounds of age shall not constitute discrimination if, within the context of national law, they are justified by a legitimate aim, including legitimate employment policy, labour market and vocational training objectives, and if the means of achieving that aim are appropriate and necessary'. It was further expressly provided that such differences might include the setting of age-related conditions for access to employment and vocational training for young people and older workers in order to promote their vocational integration, the fixing of minimum conditions of age, experience, or seniority, and the fixing of maximum ages of recruitment based on the training requirements of the post in question.[376]

Many Member States were content simply to replicate the terms of the Directive in their national legislation, albeit at the risk that important issues

---

[372] See above, 33 and n 86; any outstanding issues could be regarded as having been addressed by the Disability Discrimination Act 1995 (Amendment) Regulations 2003, SI 2003/1673—see 4.4.1 below, first para.

[373] The Employment Equality (Religion or Belief) Regulations 2003, SI 2003/1660 (EERBR); the Employment Equality (Sexual Orientation) Regulations 2003, SI 2003/1661 (EESOR); as to the former, see Lucy Vickers (2003) 32 ILJ 23, 188.

[374] EERBR, reg 6; EESOR, reg 6; the detailed argument is explored by S Deakin and G S Morris, *Labour Law* (4th edn, Oxford: Hart Publishing, 2005) at 6.44 (p 641). It should be noted, however, that the eventual introduction of a free-standing wrong of sexual harassment by the Employment Equality (Sex Discrimination) Regulations 2005, SI 2005/2467 took place by way of compliance with an EU requirement, that of Directive 2002/73/EC (subsequently re-cast into Directive 2006/54/EC: see n 92 above).   [375] Article 18; this was a facility which the UK invoked.

[376] Article 6.

would remain unresolved,[377] but the UK government was concerned to achieve a more fully worked-out set of formulae to avoid what they saw as a serious threat to managerial adaptability—in fact, one which was potentially much more serious than any which were posed by the requirements to legislate against discrimination on the other grounds which were addressed by the Directive. The most difficult issue was that of retirement age.[378] While, as we have noticed earlier,[379] the government had realised that, if it was to be able to deal with the rising costs of provision for the retirement of an ageing workforce, it had an important interest in persuading workers to prolong their working lives, on the other hand it was very reluctant to accord workers anything resembling a right to do so as against their employing enterprise. Rather as we saw earlier in relation to the claim that workers with parental responsibilities should have a right to demand flexible working,[380] the perception on the part of the government was that such a right would represent an especially significant encroachment upon the capacity of enterprise management to organise the structure of personal work relations.

The initial response to this dilemma was the imposition of a long period of stasis; a process of consultation about proposed age equality legislation initiated in 2001,[381] and originally expected to result in legislation in 2004, was still continuing by the time of the General Election of 2005; and it was not until April 2006 that the Employment Equality (Age) Regulations were finally made, to come into effect at the very last moment permissible under the Directive, in October 2006.[382] The central substantive product of this very long period of gestation was a very carefully crafted treatment of the retirement age issue, which in the midst of this prolonged period of ostensible consultation was announced to the House of Commons in a Written Ministerial Statement, rather as a fait accompli, in December 2004.[383]

This was a legislative strategy which as far as possible alleviated the regulation of the power of enterprise management to impose its chosen retirement age upon workers, while seeking to usher in a more than previously flexible approach to

---

[377] Details of national implementation are accessible via the website of the European Commission DG for Employment, Social Affairs, and Equal Opportunities at <http://ec.europa.eu/employment_social/fundamental_rights/public/pubst_en.htm>.

[378] A valuable survey of the complete set of issues is provided by S Fredman and S Spencer (eds), *Age as an Equality Issue: Legal and Policy Perspectives* (Oxford and Portland, Oregon: Hart Publishing, 2003).   [379] See above, text around n 332.

[380] See above, text around n 284

[381] By the publication by the DTI in December 2001 of the consultation document *Towards Equality and Diversity*; this was followed by three further consultation documents: *Equality and Diversity—The Way Ahead* in October 2002, *Equality and Diversity—Age Matters* in July 2003, and *Equality and Diversity—Coming of Age* in July 2005.

[382] The Employment Equality (Age) Regulations 2006, SI 2006/1031. (In September 2006 the Department of Work and Pensions announced a two-month deferment of the provisions of the Regulations relating to pensions.)

[383] *Hansard*, HC (series 6) vol 428, cols WS 126 et seq (Ms Patricia Hewitt, Secretary of State for Trade and Industry).

determining the time of retirement in individual cases. That strategy was implemented by means of a complete re-fashioning of the way in which the law of unfair dismissal was applied to the retirement of workers.[384] This new statutory regime for retirement was pivoted around two new conceptual and legislative devices, the first of which was the notion of a default retirement age of 65, and the second of which was the idea of a right to request working beyond retirement date. The significance of the default retirement age of 65 was that the imposition by an employer of a mandatory retirement age of less than 65 would require objective justification, whereas a requirement to retire at or over the age of 65 would not require such justification.[385]

Having by these means safeguarded the essential power of the employing enterprise to maintain a retirement age of 65, the legislation goes on to concede to employees a countervailing right to request a continuation of their employment beyond their retirement date.[386] This is modelled in part upon the newly introduced right of workers with parental responsibilities to request flexible working, which was considered in the previous section,[387] but it is even more cautiously conceived of and constructed. Like its counterpart in the flexible working legislation, this is primarily a right to a process of requesting and having that request considered, rather than a right to the substance of that which is requested; and, whereas in the case of the right to request flexible working it is stipulated that a refusal must demonstrably fall within a prescribed list of grounds,[388] albeit a very inclusive list, there seems to be no such substantive restriction upon a refusal to accept the request to continue working after the employee's retirement date. Equally, there seem to be no restrictions upon the grounds for rejection of the appeal—to itself—which the employing enterprise is obliged to provide.[389]

It is highly unusual for such a duty to be framed in such purely procedural terms; the regulatory touch upon the employer's discretion is at that point truly as light as a feather. This is a normative vacuum of the kind which Nature usually comes to abhor. It appears that the government was hoping that ACAS might fill this regulatory black hole with an informal code of practice, but the document which ACAS has produced[390] understandably confines itself to procedural guidance, since the legislation provides not even the most slender hook on which to hang a set of substantive principles. It is a telling illustration of the way in which the reality of light intervention may be concealed in the appearance of intense regulatory activity.

---

[384] A useful account of the legislative methodology is provided by the *Explanatory Memorandum to the Employment Equality (Age) Regulations 2006* which the DTI provided for the Joint Committee on Statutory Instruments.

[385] This is a summary of the effect of reg 30 and Sch 8, para 23 inserting new Employment Rights Act 1996, ss 98ZA–98ZF.   [386] Reg 47 and Sch 6.

[387] See above, text around n 280.   [388] See above, text at and n 291.

[389] 2006 Regulations, Sch 6, para 8.

[390] *Age and the Workplace: Putting the Employment Equality (Age) Regulations 2006 into practice— A guide for employers*, ACAS, May 2006.

2.4.3 Modifying legislation to non-standard employment

A similar story of light regulation in the midst of a flurry of regulatory activity is to be told, for the second phase of the New Labour administration, in the context of the modification of the law of personal work relations to non-standard employment. Even more obviously than in the sphere of human and equality rights which was under consideration in the previous sub-section, this is a story of reaction or resistance to EU legislation or proposals for legislation. There were two significant episodes of this kind during this period, the first concerned with the regulation of fixed-term work, and the second with the regulation of temporary agency work. Both of those episodes are sequels to the history of the regulation of part-time work during the first New Labour government which was recounted in the previous section.[391]

That exercise in the regulation of the relationship between part-time work and full-time work, initiated by the Framework Agreement and Directive on Part-time Work, was envisaged by the European Commission and the parties to the EU Social Dialogue as the first step in a sequence of measures which between them would comprehensively regulate the relationship between standard and non-standard forms of employment. The next step in that sequence was the conclusion in 1999 of the Agreement on Fixed-term Work and the making of the Fixed-term Work Directive[392] to give effect to that agreement. The Agreement and Directive had two main specific purposes, the first being to establish a measure of parity or equivalence between the terms and conditions of part-time work and those of full-time work,[393] and the second being to control the use by employers of successive fixed-term employment contracts or relationships as an abusive alternative to the making of open-ended or permanent work contracts or relationships.[394]

It appeared that by the time of its second term of government, the New Labour administration had outlived its first flush of enthusiasm, such as it had been, for EU Social Chapter measures.[395] The implementation in the UK of the Fixed-term Work Directive, after a not untypically extended period of consultation and elaborate regulatory impact assessment,[396] confirmed the tendency towards caution which had begun, as we have seen, to manifest itself in the earlier response to the Part-time Work Directive. Aileen McColgan regarded the Fixed-Term Employees (Prevention of Less Favourable Treatment) Regulations 2002[397] as representing the UK 'adopting its by now standard minimalist approach to transposition', in

---

[391] Above, text at and from n 217.

[392] Council Directive of 28 June 1999 concerning the framework agreement on fixed-term work concluded by ETUC, UNICE, and CEEP 99/70/EC (OJ 2000 L175/175, 10 July 1999).

[393] Agreement, cl 4.   [394] Agreement, cl 5.   [395] See above, text around n 159.

[396] Compare the *Government Response to the Public Consultation on the Fixed Term Work Directive* of January 2002 (DTI, URN 02/548), and the accompanying Regulatory Impact Assessment (URN 02/546).   [397] SI 2002/2034.

her view not only going no further than required by the Directive, but arguably even failing adequately to transpose it.[398]

We need not engage here in that latter debate; it is at least interesting that the government, clearly intent upon devising a 'light regulation' version of the fixed-term parity principle,[399] in much the same way as it had sought a restricted version of the part-time parity principle,[400] on this occasion chose to do so mainly by restricting its scope, indeed the scope of the Regulations as a whole, to 'employees'[401] rather than to the larger category of 'workers'—the category which it had been judged appropriate to adopt in order to give effect to the Part-time Work Directive,[402] cast in almost identical terms to those of the Fixed-term Work Directive with regard to its personal scope.[403] This seems to mark a turning point away from the enterprise of enlargement of the personal scope of employment legislation upon which the New Labour administration had embarked in its first term of government.[404] As to the second main principle of the legislation, that of the control of the abusive use of successive fixed-term contracts—which the Regulations chose to implement by converting a successive fixed-term contract into a permanent one[405] in the absence of objective justification for casting it in fixed-term form[406]—a relatively tight constraint upon its transposition from the Directive was achieved by confining this conversion effect to employment of a minimum of four years' continuous duration.[407]

In the second of these episodes, that concerning temporary agency workers, the government's predilection for 'light regulation' and the maintenance of managerial adaptability must be judged to have reached the heights of negativity in the face both of EU regulatory initiatives and domestic pressures for worker-protective legislation; this 'episode' of light regulation is thus very largely an 'incident of the dog in the night-time',[408] and can be recounted briefly. The situation and

---

[398] A McColgan, 'The Fixed-Term Employees (Prevention of Less Favourable Treatment) Regulations 2002: Fiddling While Rome Burns?' (2003) 32 ILJ 194 at 195.

[399] Embodied in reg 3 (less favourable treatment of fixed-term employees) as elaborated by reg 4 (objective justification).   [400] See above, text at and n 224.

[401] Regs 1 and 2, defining 'fixed-term employee', and deploying the notion of the 'comparable permanent employee'.   [402] See above, text at and n 221.

[403] Part-time Work Agreement, cl 2.1: 'This agreement applies to part-time workers who have an employment contract or employment relationship as defined by the law, collective agreement or practice in force in each Member State'. Fixed-term Work Agreement, cl 2: 'This agreement applies to fixed-term workers who have an employment contract or employment relationship as defined in law, collective agreements or practice in each Member State.'

[404] See above, text at and following n 209. Another symptom of this loss of interest was the failure to follow up on the review of employment status initiated by the DTI in 2002 to consider possible use of the extending powers conferred by the Employment Relations Act 1999, s 23 (see n 216 above).

[405] Reg 8 (Successive fixed-term contracts).   [406] Reg 8(2)(b).

[407] Reg 8(2)(a). A McColgan, 'The Fixed-Term Employees (Prevention of Less Favourable Treatment) Regulations 2002: Fiddling While Rome Burns?' (2003) 32 ILJ 194 at 198 rehearses the contemporary arguments for a shorter minimum period such as two years.

[408] The Sherlock Holmes mystery, *The Silver Blaze*, was about the theft of an expensive race horse from its stable. During the investigation, Inspector Gregory of Scotland Yard asked Holmes if there

regulatory needs of temporary agency workers had been a long-standing pre-occupation of the European Commission, from the perspectives both of Social Policy and of the European Employment Strategy, and it had been clear from the mid-1990s onwards that its aspirations for the regulation of non-standard employment, expressed in the initiatives leading to the Part-time Work and Fixed-term Work Directives, would not be fully realized until those Directives had been complemented by a further one on Temporary Agency Work. A central concern of the Commission was to establish a parity principle between temporary agency workers and their directly and more permanently employed counterparts, corre-sponding in some degree to the parity principles embodied in the Part-time Work and Fixed-term Work Directives for those non-standard work types and their 'standard' counterparts. In March 2002, the Commission sought to sidestep apparently irresoluble disagreement about this matter between the Social Partners to the European Social Dialogue by presenting its own proposal for a Temporary Agency Workers Directive.[409]

There was an additional local regulatory problem; from 2001 onwards,[410] if not before, it was evident that the British courts were experiencing real difficulty, or showing real unwillingness, in constructing or accepting the existence of contracts of employment within triangular personal work relationships between temporary agency workers, employment agencies, and end-user clients, with a resultant denial to those workers of most of the key statutory employment rights which were conditioned upon the existence of a continuous contractual employ-ment relationship.[411] From a worker-protective perspective, the government's policy response was not an encouraging one. Late in 2003, a set of Regulations was made for the reform of the legal regime governing the conduct of employment agencies,[412] which the government claimed would enhance the protection of agency workers.[413] However, these Regulations were mainly concerned with

---

was any particular aspect of the crime calling for additional study. Holmes pointed to 'the curious incident of the dog in the night-time'. Inspector Gregory replied, 'The dog did nothing in the night-time'. Holmes said, 'That was the curious incident'.

[409] COM (2002) 149, 20 March 2002. An admirably full history and useful analysis of this devel-opment is provided by L Zappala in 'The Temporary Agency Workers' Directive: An Impossible Political Agreement?' (2003) 32 ILJ 310.

[410] Following the decision of the Court of Appeal, in that year, in the case of *Montgomery* v *Johnson Underwood Ltd* [2001] ICR 819. An effort by a differently composed Court of Appeal to address this set of problems in *Dacas* v *Brook Street Bureau (UK) Ltd* [2004] IRLR 358 was only par-tially successful.

[411] See M R Freedland, *The Personal Employment Contract* (Oxford: OUP, 2003) at 43–45.

[412] The Conduct of Employment Agencies and Employment Businesses Regulations 2003, SI 2003/3319.

[413] For instance, in the presentation for approval of the draft Regulations to the House of Lords by Lord Sainsbury of Turville, *Hansard*, HL (series 5) vol 655, col 1331 (18 December 2003): 'The Government's main objective in putting forward these draft regulations is to safe-guard the rights of work-seekers, the interest of hirers and employers and the needs of the private recruitment industry.'

issues which were rather marginal or equivocal with regard to the protection of workers, such as restricting the imposition of 'temp-to-perm fees',[414] and were not at all concerned with the central worker protection issues of parity with directly employed and more permanent workers or contractual employment status.

This partial disjunction between the regulatory concerns of the legal regime for employment agencies and the mainstream preoccupations of employment law was not new—it had been a characteristic of the structure established by the Employment Agencies Act 1973.[415] It is, however, significant that the New Labour administration was not ready to recognise the extent to which the regulatory needs had been transformed in the succeeding thirty years by the enormously increased and increasing use which was being made of the temporary agency form of employment.

Moreover, it appears that the government devoted itself energetically over several years to opposition to the proposals for a Temporary Agency Workers Directive, forming shifting alliances with other Member States such as Germany for that purpose.[416] This opposition seems to have been unremitting, despite an apparent concession to the concerns of the TUC in the course of the talks leading to the notoriously obscure so-called 'Warwick Accord' of 2004.[417] It was perhaps a fitting, if somewhat ironical, culmination of this history that the proposals for the Temporary Agency Workers Directive ultimately received what seemed to be their quietus at the hands of a 'Better Regulation for growth and jobs' initiative of the European Commission; this conclusion was reached during and with the encouragement of the British Presidency of the EU in September 2005, when the proposals were in effect set aside for re-consideration at some unspecified future time.[418] It was an outcome which the British Prime Minister's two immediate predecessors might have welcomed, perhaps indeed did welcome, so closely did it echo their own de-regulatory initiatives of the later 1980s and early 1990s.

---

[414] Reg 10. The complexity of the debate about whether it is in the interests of temporary agency workers to restrict 'temp-to-perm fees' is indicated by the ambivalence of the treatment of this issue in the proposals for a Temporary Agency Workers Directive: see L Zappala, op cit (n 409 above), (2003) 32 ILJ 310 at 313–314.

[415] Compare LLPP at 344–345.

[416] It was reported in the *Times* for 19 May 2003 that 'Britain was supporting Germany in a campaign to strip meaning out of the Takeover Directive, in return for German support on sinking the Agency Workers Directive'.

[417] A news report in 'Online Recruitment' on 27 July 2004 recorded that 'Recruitment industry presses DTI for answers on agency workers directive—The Recruitment and Employment Confederation, the industry body for employment agencies was today seeking urgent clarification from the UK Government on its position with regard to the proposed Agency Workers Directive. At Labour's National Policy Forum in Warwick this weekend, it was suggested that the Government would now support the proposed Agency Workers Directive, currently being debated in Brussels.'

[418] European Commission Memo/05/340 on Better Regulation, 27 September 2005; DG Enterprise Communication, 'Outcome of the screening of legislative proposals pending before the Legislator', COM(2005) 462 final (27 September 2005) at p 4.

2.4.4 The positive construction of managerial adaptability and public service reform

If the foregoing discussion has served to show how the de-regulatory face of New Labour policies for the regulation of personal work relations revealed itself more clearly than before the second phase of the Blair administration, the ensuing one will seek to show how its other, re-regulatory, aspect also became more apparent in this second term in government. As we have indicated earlier,[419] this manifestation would occur, not so much in the arena of general employment legislation and policy which is the conventional focus of the discussion of the legal regulation of personal work relations, but rather in the realm of the reform of public services and of personal work relations with the institutions of public service. In this section, we shall explore the way in which a set of strongly normative intentions for such reforms, which had begun to be identified and articulated during the first phase of the New Labour administration, was implemented and realised on quite a grand scale during this second phase.

This was a set of intentions for imposing within the public service sector of the labour economy a certain mode or style of personal work relations which those in government regarded, rightly or wrongly, as the key to what they perceived as the success and efficiency of enterprise management in the private sector, especially in the private services sector. This mode or style of personal work relations was constructed around a certain notion or practice which we may identify as that of *individually contractualised performance management and pay*. It is strongly associated with a notion of the structural adaptability and reform of enterprise management. In this section, we shall examine some examples of the re-constituting, along these lines, of personal work relations in certain public services, during this second phase of the New Labour administration; the central case which will be so considered is that of the creation and implementation of the 'Agenda for Change' in the National Health Service.

2.4.4.1 *TUPE,* Wilson and Palmer, *and the Employment Relations Act 2004*

Before proceeding to that stage of our discussion, we should look at two areas of change in general labour law which relate to the facilitation of the changes mentioned above. The first was the adoption in 2006 of a new set of Transfer of Undertakings (Protection of Employment) Regulations,[420] wholly replacing the original regulations of 1981. Although these Regulations were a response to changes at Community level,[421] the relevant Directive, where it was not simply

---

[419] Above, text at and following n 228.   [420] SI 2006/246.
[421] Changes originally made by Directive 98/50/EC but later consolidated into Directive 2001/23/EC.

consolidating ECJ case-law, operated mainly so as to give Member States options to make the law on transfers more flexible where the transfer was by an insolvent transferor.[422] In the name of promoting the 'rescue culture' (ie, promoting the restructuring of failing businesses), the government took advantage of these options. In consequence, where an insolvent company is subject to a rescue rather than a liquidation procedure, the accrued entitlements of the employees will not go across to the transferee employer to the extent that they can be asserted against the Secretary of State under the guarantee provisions of the Employment Rights Act.[423] In addition, the transferee employer will have the freedom to agree with employee representatives (recognised trade union if there is one; elected or appointed employee representatives otherwise) adverse changes in the terms and conditions of the transferred workers.[424] Both changes were thought likely to promote the sale of businesses by insolvent companies to new owners.

Further, and more interesting, the government, although taking an unconscionable amount of time to do so (the DTI's original consultation document was issued in 2001), extended the British regulations so as to bring within the compulsory transfer principle types of transaction which were not required by the Directive to be covered. These are 'service provision changes'. It had long been a matter of controversy whether the contracting out of the supply of pure services (such as cleaning or security services) or indeed a change of service provider or a decision to bring service provision back 'in-house' were transactions which fell within the Directive. The ECJ had long grappled with the issue and had produced a somewhat circular and unsatisfactory rule that, in the case of service provision where no significant assets were transferred as well, the Directive applied only if the transferee took on a significant number of the transferor's employees.[425] The government could have stayed with this rule (although the British courts had shown themselves reluctant to so confine the application of the 1981 Regulations),[426] but in the name of clarity and protecting vulnerable groups of workers it chose to bring all service provision arrangements within the domestic Regulations. Along with the changes made in relation to the transfer of pensions in the previous year,[427] the effect was to put pressure on service providers to compete on the basis of factors other than driving down the terms and conditions of the employees concerned. Particularly interesting was the government's ultimate decision to reject an exception to the compulsory transfer

---

[422] See P L Davies, 'Amendments to the Acquired Rights Directive' (1998) 27 ILJ 365.

[423] Regulation 8: it has to be said that the Directive's terminology does not map easily onto existing British insolvency procedures.

[424] Regulation 9: a course of action firmly rejected by the ECJ under the original version of the Regulations, even if agreed by the employees concerned: Case C-362/89, *d'Urso* [1991] ECR I-4105.

[425] See P L Davies, 'Transfers—The UK Will Have to Make Up Its Own Mind' (2001) 30 ILJ 231.

[426] See, for example, *RCO Support Services Ltd* v *UNISON* [2002] ICR 751.

[427] See text at n 310 above.

provision for 'innovative' service providers, who would not necessarily have use for the existing workforce or all of them and whose bids would therefore have to absorb the costs of those workers' redundancy payments. To that extent competition in the service provider market would be reduced by being weighted in favour of the incumbent provider.[428] The government's overall strategy seems to have been to promote the acceptability of contracting out, in both the public and the private sectors, by reducing the potential for claims that the reconfiguration was being done at the expense of the employees.

There was a second location in which the government did regard it as necessary, as the immediately previous Conservative and New Labour governments had done, to engineer some general employment legislation in order to protect and safeguard their particular practical ideal for personal work relations. This was the area, primarily of collective labour law but with great secondary implications for individual employment law and for the regulation of personal work relations, in which the government advanced legislative measures to address the issues of freedom of association which, as we explain elsewhere in this work, were raised by successive episodes of the *Wilson and Palmer* litigation.[429] We have seen there how, in each of the two phases of legislative response to the pressure to bring the law of the UK into compliance with Article 11 of the European Convention on Human Rights (on Freedom of Association) in its treatment of incentives offered to workers to accept 'personal' or de-collectivised contracts of employment, the British government of the day had been concerned to make a saving provision to protect an underlying freedom of employing enterprises to re-structure their personal work relations.

In this third, and probably final, episode of that story, the screw of censure had been so far tightened by the adverse judgment of the European Court of Human Rights[430] that the government felt obliged to propose a durable legislative solution, which, as implemented by the Employment Relations Act 2004, consisted of the creation of new rights of workers not to have offers made to them by their employers with the sole or main purpose of inducing them not to belong to or take part in the activities of a trade union,[431] or, in the case of a member of a recognised union or of a union seeking recognition, with the sole or main purpose that the worker's terms and conditions of employment will not be or will no longer be determined by collective agreement.[432] However, as Alan Bogg has astutely observed, the government's response to the ECHR judgment was still a

---

[428] See J McMullen, 'An Analysis of the Transfer of Undertakings (Protection of Employment) Regulations 2006' (2006) 25 ILJ at 123–124. However, protection of competition does seem to be the reason for the exclusion of contracts wholly or mainly for the supply of goods from the extension: Reg 3(3)(b).   [429] Above, text at and following nn 97, 225 and 3.3.1.

[430] *Wilson and the National Union of Journalists, Palmer, Wyeth and the National Union of Rail, Maritime and Transport Workers, Doolan and Others v The United Kingdom* (2002) 35 EHRR 523.

[431] Employment Relations Act 2004, s 29 inserting new s 145A into the Trade Union and Labour Relations (Consolidation) Act 1992.   [432] Ibid, new s 145B.

'grudging and minimalist' one, and the restriction of these new rights to the case where the employer's 'sole or main purpose' was the statutorily proscribed one, was to allow scope for employers to pursue pay flexibility and performance-related pay.[433]

Indeed, in its *Review of the Employment Relations Act 1999* published in 2003,[434] the DTI had proclaimed that intention in notably robust terms, denoting a range of circumstances in which it was considered 'essential that employers and individuals should retain their freedom to agree individualised contracts'.[435] This was envisaged as a freedom 'to make arrangements giving necessary flexibility to employers to reward and retain key staff, and to shape working patterns to specific or particular circumstances'.[436] In its *Memorandum to the Joint Committee on Human Rights*,[437] the DTI was even more trenchant in the assertion of this position:

> The Department views it as extremely important that employers should be free to take the legitimate decisions they believe are needed to run their businesses effectively. Of course decisions are not legitimate if they infringe Article 11 or other ECHR rights but the Department is firmly of the view that nothing in the judgment in *Wilson and Palmer* was intended to or does prevent employers from taking decisions to reward particular employees more highly than others when the motivation for doing so is to reward such employees in the interests of the business.[438]

In the remainder of this section, we go on to detail the process of reform of personal work relations in the public service sector which was aimed at realising in that sector the particular vision of managerial freedom and adaptability which the DTI was there showing itself so concerned to protect.

2.4.4.2 Public service reform

This process evolved in the following way. We have observed in the previous section that the New Labour administration, and indeed the Prime Minister personally, clearly perceived themselves as having a mission of radical reform of public services—proceeding further along the lines laid down by the immediately preceding governments, that is to say towards devolved and marketised institutional and managerial structures, held together by a system of setting and enforcing targets for the delivery of public services which was to be administered from the centre of government downwards.[439] During the first New Labour government, while there were not yet many concrete outcomes of this process of further reform

---

[433] Alan Bogg, 'Employment Relations Act 2004: Another False Dawn for Collectivism?' (2005) 34 ILJ 72 at 73, and at 74 citing and drawing attention to the DTI Memorandum to the JCHR, to which we refer at n 437 below. [434] URN 03/606 of 27 February 2003.

[435] Para 3.13. [436] Op cit, para 3.12

[437] *Memorandum from the Department of Trade and Industry in response to concerns raised by the Committee in its Third and Fourth Progress Report of Session 2003–04*, published as Appendix 2 to the Thirteenth Report of the Joint Committee on Human Rights for the Session 2003–04.

[438] Para 31. [439] See above text at and nn 228 to 231.

of public services, there were nevertheless advances in policy formation which, it is clear in retrospect, were momentous ones.

These policy developments were, as we have indicated earlier, articulated in and focused by the 1999 White Paper *Modernising Government*.[440] The importance of that policy document, for the purposes at least of our present discussion, was that it placed special emphasis upon the reform and re-construction of personal work relations as a crucial element in the reform of public services, and that it set out a particular methodology for effecting that process of reform and re-construction. A set of ideas for the general reform of 'performance management' in the delivery of public services, which is set out in the White Paper,[441] is translated into a particular programme for the individualised management of the performance and pay for public service workers.[442] This programme seemed to be derived from the North American school of thought about 'strategic human resource management'; it is difficult to identify precisely its intellectual and practical foundations, but there are some striking similarities with the discourse and the practice of the United States Federal Government Office of Personnel Management.[443]

The articulation of such programmes of public service worker performance management tends to be wrapped up in obfuscatory clichés, and the White Paper *Modernising Government* provides no exception in this respect, for example stating that:

It is clear that performance management is not effective enough. The links between pay and objectives are not always clear. We must use our pay systems and performance pay in particular in creative ways to provide effective incentives to achieve sustained high quality performance and to encourage innovation and team-working.[444]

The essential idea which is concealed within this rhetoric is that of replacing standardised and collectivised job specifications and pay structures with arrangements for performance specification and performance-related pay which are individually contractualised. This is the approach which underlies the notion in the White Paper of 'reforming out-dated pay systems', formulated in the following terms:

Inflexible and inefficient practices in pay and conditions must be reformed so that pay can be tailored to the needs of the public service and provide suitable incentives for staff. This means challenging outdated assumptions about public sector pay, for example the idea that 'fair pay' means everybody should get the same increase, or that pay and conditions must all be set nationally.[445]

---

[440] See above, text at and around n 235.

[441] Particularly in chapter 4: 'Quality Public Services: We will deliver efficient, high quality public services and will not tolerate mediocrity.'

[442] That is the function of chapter 6: 'Public Service: We will value public service, not denigrate it.'

[443] Compare that Office's *Overview of Performance Management* at <http://www.opm.gov/Strategic_Management_of_Human_Capital/index.asp> and *Handbook for Measuring Employee Performance: Aligning Employee Performance with Organisational Goals* (Workforce Compensation and Performance Service, Performance Management and Incentive Award Division PMI—C13 September 2001).   [444] Para 6.21.

[445] Ch 6, para 20.

This particular programme of reform of public service personal work relations, launched during the government of the New Labour administration, became one of its central preoccupations during its second period in office. In 2001 an Office of Public Services Reform was established within the Cabinet Office, reporting directly to the Prime Minister, and in 2002 that Office produced a policy document, *Reforming our public services: principles into practice*;[446] the chapter on 'Flexibility and Incentives' in that document, when combined with the corresponding chapter in *Modernising Government*, demonstrates that the government was intent on introducing or imposing a method of management of public service personal work relations whereby the managers of de-centralised organisations of public service delivery, working within broad and open frameworks of job specification, grading, and pay, would engage in a continuous process of detailed specification and re-specification of jobs and rewards for the workers within each organisation.

This method of management, which has a distinctly individual and contractual character, would be implemented by means of appraisal systems through which the variables in detailed job specification would be adjusted, the measures of performance would be applied, and the units of currency of performance-related pay would be distributed. Those items of job-specification and measures of performance and pay would be integrally linked to the targets for the organisation itself; they would increasingly consist of normative notions such as leadership, initiative and acceptance of enhanced responsibility for the achievement of organisational goals; the capacities to display those qualities would increasingly be inculcated and measured by systems of specialised job training and the certification of individual workers' receptivity to such training. In these policy documents, these practical proposals are underpinned by an increasingly moralistic commitment to differentiation of pay as between individual workers according to the quality of their contribution to public service goals.[447]

The story of the implementation of these policies during the New Labour administration is indeed an interesting one, especially during its second term of government. There were several important initiatives to introduce schemes of performance management and performance-related payment systems; each of them was an attempt to introduce new working practices in an area of public services where personal work relations were perceived to have become problematical. There was of course nothing new about such attempts to restructure working and payment practices and systems in the public sector; for example, these initiatives had, in that sense, a significant precursor in the Fresh Start

---

[446] OPSR, Ref JO2-9201/0302/D2.4, March 2002.

[447] Thus *Principles into Practice* at 21: 'where front-line staff take on more responsibility for high quality service delivery, it is only right that their pay and conditions should reflect this fact. [...] And part of what makes people feel valued at work is the sense that they are being treated fairly—rewarded for their individual contribution and performance.'

Agreement for the Prison Service in 1987.[448] However, the particular design of the schemes for performance management and performance-related pay which were introduced under the New Labour administration, as it emerged in the *Modernising Government* White Paper, was a fairly novel one in the British public service context.

2.4.4.3 *Teachers and firefighters*

The Ministers in the New Labour government and their advisers had probably nursed an enthusiasm for this new mode of management of public service personal work relations even while still in opposition, for by December 1998 Mr David Blunkett, as Secretary of State for Education and Employment, was ready to launch in the Green Paper *Teachers: meeting the challenge of change,*[449] a set of proposals for a highly crafted and sophisticated scheme of performance management and performance-related pay for teachers and head-teachers. This was a plan to introduce a much elaborated performance appraisal system in order to establish and administer a complex set of career development steps for teachers and head-teachers, each with its own associated enhancement of payment.[450] Brought into effect by statutory regulations, for teachers and head-teachers in England, in September 2000,[451] the scheme was designed to help to address significant problems of recruitment and retention of head-teachers, and of teachers in some subject-areas, and also to pave the way for an increased use of unqualified support staff in classrooms. (It seems to have been less effective in the former respect than in the latter one.)

Tracing the further development of this approach to the reform of public service personal work relations during the subsequent New Labour governments yields some very interesting results. An initiative of this kind had, potentially at least, a significant role in the enterprise of 'modernisation' of the fire service in which the New Labour administration became increasingly involved during its second term of office, entrusting the responsibility for this initiative to the Office of the Deputy Prime Minister, Mr John Prescott. In an attempt to resolve a long-running and difficult set of negotiations between local authority employers and unions about pay and working practices in the fire service, arrangements were made in September 2002 for an 'Independent Review of the Fire Service' under

---

[448] See John Black 'Industrial relations in the UK prison service: The "Jurassic Park" of public sector industrial relations' (1995) 17 *Employee Relations* 64. Compare also *McLaren* v *Home Office* [1990] ICR 824 in which the legal effect of that agreement was considered.

[449] Apparently Cm 4164, though unusually (and perhaps because of a lingering sense that only White Papers or firm proposals should have the status of Command Papers) the document does not carry this citation.

[450] The details of the scheme as implemented were set out only in a guidance document issued by the DfEE in April 2000 (DfEE 0051/2000).

[451] The Education (School Teacher Appraisal) (England) Regulations 2000, SI 2000/1620, later revoked and replaced by SI 2001/2855. For Wales, SI 2002/1394 (W137).

the chairmanship of Sir George Bain. The report of that review, presented to the Deputy Prime Minister in December of that year,[452] coupled a recommendation for a national pay settlement with a set of proposals for the reform of the organisation and working practices of the fire services which provoked or further provoked a protracted and bitter industrial dispute. An important element in those proposals, for a 'modern, flexible, risk-based approach to allocating resources' to and within the fire services, consisted in plans for the development of a new performance management and reward management system.

In fact, the proposals in the report for the further development of the 'Integrated Personal Development System' in the Fire Services,[453] coupled with the adaptation of proposals for a new reward management system devised by the Hay Group of management consultants to the Independent Review,[454] amounted to a plan for performance management and performance-related pay of just the kind that seemed to be contemplated in the *Modernising Government* White Paper. However, these particular proposals, which admittedly did not seem to figure as the main bone of contention in the industrial dispute, did not seem to be of great interest to the Deputy Prime Minister: although they were referred to in passing in his statement to the House of Commons about the Bain Report[455] and in the subsequent White Paper, *Our Fire and Rescue Services*,[456] they seemed far from being central to the government's agenda for the future regulation of personal work relations in the fire service, perhaps because the Deputy Prime Minister belonged to a tradition of collective bargaining in which such plans had little part to play. The performance management programme of the Independent Review may well nevertheless have been influential upon the subsequent development of the Fire and Rescue Services, as they were re-named and re-organised by the legislation of 2004;[457] and in any event those plans remain as a significant instance of this particular form of 'new public management' of personal work relations.

2.4.4.4 The 'Agenda for Change' in the NHS

If plans for performance management and for a performance-related pay system were not, in the event, to assume a central role in the re-organisation of personal work relations within the fire and rescue services, it was quite otherwise in relation to the National Health Service. In that context, the most ambitious and extensive of all such schemes, the 'Agenda for Change' in the NHS, became the pivot

---

[452] *The Future of the Fire Services: reducing risk, saving lives*, Independent Review of the Fire Service presented to the Deputy Prime Minister on 16 December 2002.   [453] Ibid, paras 7.50–7.55.

[454] *Reward in support of strategic change in the Fire Service*, A paper for the Independent Review of the Fire Service by Hay Group, December 2002 (annexed to the Report of the Independent Review).

[455] *Hansard*, HC (series 6) vol 396, cols 554, 555 (16 December 2002).

[456] Cm 5808, presented by the Deputy Prime Minister, June 2003, paras 8.14–8.16

[457] Fire and Rescue Services Act 2004. At one stage during the industrial dispute of 2002–3 it had seemed likely that this legislation would further restrict the freedom of firefighters to take industrial action but in the event such suggestions were not pursued—see White Paper, paras 7.18–7.25.

around which an enormous process of organisational re-contracting was constructed—the process, in fact, of creating an 'internal market' for healthcare
within and around the National Health Service. That process had many complex
ramifications which it is beyond the scope of the present work to describe—
though certain episodes or aspects of that process, such as the re-contracting of
personal work relations between the NHS and its doctors, especially the general
practitioners, are of intense theoretical and practical interest to employment
lawyers; it is sufficient to consider the 'Agenda for Change' as a very large-scale and
paradigmatic example of the 'modernisation' of a public service pay system
according to the notions of performance management and performance-related
incentives which were at the heart of the whole New Labour initiative to 'modernise' public service personal work relations.

Although the crucial phase of development of the 'Agenda for Change' occurred during the second New Labour government, its foundations were laid down
during the first one. The plan emerged from protracted discussions and negotiations during the later 1990s about the payment and grading system for NHS
nurses and midwives, which from the point of view of the government had
become over-complex, over-costly, and inefficient (and also presented still unresolved problems of inequality of pay between women and men). The concern
to rationalise that pay and grading system became inter-linked with aims to
improve the general management of the performance of the NHS by means of
de-centralisation and the creation of internal 'purchaser and provider' organisational relationships. So this became a key location for the linking-up of institut
ional target-setting, and objectives-based organisational performance management,
with the re-organisation of performance and pay in personal work relations
according to parallel notions of objectives-based management. These plans were
announced by the Department of Health in the course of 1999 as the *Agenda for
Change in the NHS*;[458] the central feature of these plans was to create a pay system
which 'pays fairly and equitably for work done, with career progression based on
responsibility, competence and satisfactory performance', and 'simplifies and
modernises conditions of service, with national core conditions and considerable
local flexibility'.[459]

The announcement of these plans was only the beginning of a very long further sequence of negotiation with public sector unions and professional bodies
culminating in the publication of the *Agenda For Change Final Agreement* in

---

[458] The emergence of the nomenclature is interesting. A Department of Health press release of
27 January 1999 (ref 1999/0051) announced that Mr Frank Dobson (Secretary of State for Health)
'unveils new proposals for new pay and grading system for nurses'; the White Paper *Modernisation of
Government* in March 1999 refers at para 8.20 to 'the Department of Health's recent Agenda for
Change'; the Department of Health document, *Agenda for Change: modernising the NHS pay system*,
which is generally regarded as its main starting point, is variously cited as having been published on
1 January 1999 or 8 October 1999; the latter date is more probably the correct one.

[459] White Paper, *Modernising Government*, para 6.20, inset on 'Modernisation of the NHS pay
system'.

December 2004.[460] In that final agreement, pay modernisation is identified as 'an integral part of the human resource strategies of the NHS', to be 'implemented in a way which is consistent with the wider human resource policies set out in the relevant strategies'.[461] The previously existing NHS pay structure is replaced by a simplified system of three pay spines or series of pay bands, and staff are allocated to particular pay bands according to job weightings measured by the NHS Job Evaluation Scheme.[462] The crucial new element of performance management and performance-related pay is presented as a system of 'Career and Pay Progression'; it is instituted by means of an appraisal system called a 'Development Review Process' according to which 'All staff will have annual development reviews against the NHS Knowledge and Skills Framework (KSF) [. . .] which will result in the production of a personal development plan. Similar to current practice, development reviews will take place between staff and their manager, or, where appropriate, their supervisor, or professional adviser, or another appropriately trained senior team member.'[463]

Even if the staff conducting the development reviews are the same as under previously existing practice, the content of the reviews would seem to be very different from previous practice, in so far as the Knowledge and Skills Framework turns out to be a vehicle for a new style of performance management and allocation of performance-related pay, which those familiar with the current discourse of human resource management would be quick to recognise from the following clause in the agreement:

The output from the KSF for an individual job is a KSF post outline for that job and a subset of the full post outline known as the KSF foundation post outline. KSF post outlines identify the KSF dimensions, levels, indicators, and areas of application that are required for the holder of that post to undertake it effectively. KSF post outlines will provide prompts for action by individuals and their managers to update or develop their knowledge and skills, or address areas for development in the application of knowledge and skills.[464]

These provisions may present themselves to the uninitiated either as comical or as Kafkaesque in their obscurity. The indications are that the implementation of them consumes immense managerial resources and requires an extremely costly input of managerial consultancy. But these dispensations are detailed here, not for those reasons, but rather because, with their particular blend of managerialism and individualisation, they represent the very culmination and essence of the construct for the regulation of personal work relations which the New Labour

---

[460] Department of Health; see: <http://www.dh.gov.uk/PolicyAndGuidance/HumanResources AndTraining/ModernisingPay/AgendaForChange/fs/en>.
[461] *Final Agreement*, 3, point (iv).   [462] Ibid, 1.1–1.8.   [463] Ibid, 6.1.
[464] Ibid, 7.2. The next clause undertakes that 'The KSF will continue to be developed so that it is simple, easy to explain and understood.'

administration sought to put in place, even more fervently in its second term of government than in its first.

2.4.4.5 The 'two-tier workforce', the 'Warwick Accord', and the TUPE Regulations

That could be a suitable conclusion to this chapter, but some additional reflections are appropriate. They concern some incidental consequences, in and for the regulation of personal work relations, of the programme of public service reform which has been described in the preceding pages. In that programme, as we have observed, the reconstruction of personal work relations has been integrally linked to a larger restructuring of the institutional organisation of public services, typically involving the creation of units of public service provision in contract-like relations with governmental 'purchasers' of public services, and often involving the contracting out of the delivery of public services to private enterprises. It is of no small significance that, in order to secure consensus both among the workforce and the wider electorate, both for the general reforms of public services and for these particular reforms of public service personal work relations, the New Labour administration has found it necessary to take various measures to render those reforms acceptable, essentially by maintaining the security of employment and the level of terms of conditions previously enjoyed by the public service workers affected by the reforms in question.

This has meant, for the most part, taking measures to create protections equivalent to those afforded by the Transfer of Undertakings Protection of Employment (TUPE) Regulations in situations of re-organisation or outsourcing of public services to which those Regulations have not been applicable or where they have been of doubtful application.[465] There have been a number of such measures in the period under review, mostly taking the form of executive action or informal rather than formal legislation. Of just such a character was the Cabinet Office *Statement of Practice on Staff Transfers in the Public Sector* of January 2000,[466] to which was annexed the Treasury guidance document *Staff Transfers from Central Government: a Fair Deal for Staff Pensions* of June 1999; the composite effect of these was to state a governmental commitment to a practice, applicable both to organisational transfers within the public service and to the contracting out of public services by central or local government and the NHS, which was meant to ensure the equivalent of TUPE protection for transferred workers and to extend that protection to rights and expectations arising under public sector occupational pension provisions. Robert Davies has most usefully chronicled this and its associated developments, and has shown how, alongside that framework, there was created an alternative protective practice for some NHS

---

[465] See 2.4.4.1 above and nn 473–475 below for the subsequent changes to the TUPE legislation.
[466] Cabinet Office, January 2000.

workers affected by NHS Private Finance Initiative (PFI) projects, whereby those workers would remain in NHS employment and be treated as being on secondment to the PFI contractor, this being known as the Retention of Employment Model.[467]

These measures or exhortations to good practice lacked any statutory or clear legal force, and there was room for doubt as to their scope or effectiveness. At the same time, the concern about the exposure of public service workers to specific gaps in the TUPE regime[468] became part of a larger concern that the various forms of contracting out of public services were facilitating the evolution of a two-tier public service workforce, consisting of a more favoured group of directly employed or TUPE-protected public service workers and a less favoured group of indirectly employed and not TUPE-protected workers. In other words, the larger concern extended from the situation of transferees from public authority employment to the treatment of new joiners to an outsourced workforce. That larger concern was to some extent addressed with regard to public services for which local authorities were responsible,[469] by the issuing in March 2003, from the Office of the Deputy Prime Minister, of a *Code of Practice on Workforce Matters in Local Authority Contracts* which had some degree of statutory backing from the 'Best Value' system for the monitoring by central government of the activities and performance of local government authorities;[470] this Code represented a somewhat more specific set of commitments than had previously been made to ensure that both transferees in TUPE lacunae and new joiners to contracted-out workforces would be treated no less favourably than their counterparts directly employed by public authorities.

There still remained a corresponding set of concerns for workers involved in transfers and contracting out of public services by central government and the NHS. In an ever-deeper slide into informal executive regulation, those concerns were addressed, in advance of the General Election of 2005, by a commitment on the part of the Prime Minister to the extension of the *Code of Practice on Workforce Matters* from the sphere of local government to the public sector, which seems to have been embodied in the ever-mysterious 'Warwick Accord' of July 2004.[471] That was followed in March 2005 by a Prime Ministerial announcement of the 'roll-out' or publication of the now-extended *Code of Practice on Workforce Matters*

---

[467] R Davies, 'Contracting Out and the Retention of Employment Model in the NHS' (2004) 33 ICJ 95.   [468] See below, text and nn 473 to 475.

[469] In part at least to honour a Prime Ministerial pledge given at the Labour Party Conference of September 2002 in order to avert threatened strike action on the part of local government workers: see BBC News report, 'Blair pledge freezes strike ballots', 2 October 2002.

[470] The code was promulgated as Annex C of ODPM *Best Value and Performance Improvement Circular 03/2003* issued under Part I of the Local Government Act 1999.

[471] An agreement apparently reached, though not clearly recorded, between government Ministers and trade union leaders at a National Policy Forum at Warwick University on 25 July 2004. Compare above, n 417 and see also <http://www.eiro.eurofound.eu.int/2004/09/inbrief/uk0409102n.html> for another report regarded as being of significant authority.

in Public Sector Service Contracts.[472] It was even less than previously clear what the source of authority for such code-making was or what the normative impact of this pronouncement might be. Eventually, in 2006, the aspect of this set of problems which related to the application of the TUPE Regulations, was addressed by the long-delayed amendment (and indeed replacement) of those Regulations[473] in response to the Acquired Rights Directive of 1998;[474] the fact that this Directive created legislative options which bore upon this set of issues might have been one of the reasons both for delay in responding to that Directive and for the way in which the new Regulations were finally framed.[475]

We revert in the Conclusion to this work to evaluation of the developments which have been described in this chapter as a whole; but the regulatory events discussed in this sub-section themselves give rise to a brief concluding reflection as to their overall implications, so far as they can be judged at such a relatively short interval of time, for the whole New Labour construct of 'light regulation', and managerial adaptability in personal work relations which has been analysed in this and the previous section. We suggest that the developments considered in this sub-section, and in particular those which relate to the reform of public service personal work relations, serve to heighten a certain sense of irony and unintended regulatory consequences which has attended quite a lot of the discussion in the last two sections.

There is, of course, the continuing paradox of the intensity of regulatory activity which is needed to achieve the state of 'light regulation'; and that paradox is heightened when the regulatory activity becomes a mixture of formal legislation with informal executive lawmaking. But there is also another kind of irony, perhaps a recurring one in the history of labour legislation and public policy. It is the ironical effect whereby governments, when they engage in individualising and liberalising personal work relations, sometimes find that, in order to seek those outcomes, they find themselves impelled to engage not only in intense regulatory activity, but also in forms of 'social contracts' with collective labour of the kind which, as a general objective, they wish to avoid. There is some evidence of such unintended consequences in the history of New Labour public service reforms, especially during the second term in office; the government has seemed to be

---

[472] The only direct source of information about this announcement seems to be the Cabinet Office News Release CAB 18/05 of 18 March 2005. The text of the Code is accessible via the Cabinet Office website at <http://archive.cabinetoffice.gov.uk/opsr/workforce_reform/code_of_practice/index.asp>. The website of the TUC has an announcement of the same date which publishes the text of a letter from Mr David Milliband as Minister for the Cabinet Office to the TUC General Secretary Mr Brendan Barber in which he makes significant statements about how it is intended that the Code will operate.

[473] By the Transfer of Undertakings (Protection of Employment) Regulations 2006, SI 2006/246.

[474] Council Directive 98/50/EC amending Directive 77/187/EEC, later consolidated into Directive 2001/23/EC (2001 OJ L82/16, 22 March 2001).

[475] See John McMullen, 'An Analysis of the Transfer of Undertakings (Protection of Employment) Regulations 2006' (2006) 35 ILJ 113, especially at 117–125, concerning the new definition of a 'transfer' by Regulation 3. Compare also nn 420–426 and 465 above.

drawn further into high-level political collective bargaining and worker protective measures than it might initially have wished in order to effect and sustain those reforms. From a position which asserts the benefits of collectivised processes for the evolution of labour legislation and public policy, such as we asserted in the Conclusion of the first volume of this work, that might appear as an optimistic interpretation of the developments which we have considered in the last part of the present chapter. Such optimism might, however, be misplaced, because it would understate the negative effects of the inconsistency and ambivalence of intentions which sometimes seem to have attended upon these developments. Again, this is a reflection to which we revert in the Conclusion to this work as a whole.

3

Collective Labour Law

3.1 The policy context in 1997

The 'New' Labour government, elected in 1997 with a very large Parliamentary majority, came into office enjoying a much greater freedom in relation to the setting of the rules for collective labour law than any of its post-War predecessors. This position had arisen for a number of reasons. First, over the years since 1979, when the previous Labour government had been ejected from office, the industrial strength of the union movement had declined substantially. This is demonstrated graphically by the figures on union density (percentage of the workforce who are members of a trade union), union recognition (percentage of workplaces recognising a union in respect of any workers for the setting of terms and conditions of employment), and the coverage of collective bargaining (percentage of employees whose terms and conditions of employment are set by collective agreements, whether they are union members or not). On all three measures the influence of unionism had declined in this period.

In 1980 65% of workers were union members; by 1998 the figure had fallen to 36%. In 1980 64% of establishments recognised a union in respect of at least some of those working there; by 1998 the figure had fallen to 42%.[1] In 1980 about 70% of employees' wages were set by collective bargaining; by the mid-nineties this had fallen to 45%.[2] These overall figures obscured a sharp division between the private sector of the economy (both private manufacturing and private services), where unionisation was at a very low ebb, and the (now reduced) public sector where unionisation had declined much more slowly, with some of the privatised industries straddling the divide. Thus, not all trade unions felt that the ground was shifting beneath them, and some public sector unions later made significant membership gains on the back of greater public expenditure in the areas of health and education, especially after the re-election of the Labour government in 2001, but as a whole the trade union movement was on the defensive.

---

[1] N Millward, A Bryson, and J Forth, *All Change at Work?* (London: Routledge, 2000) 87 and 96. This work is based on the periodic Workplace Employment Relations Surveys which tend to produce more optimistic figures for unionisation than some other sources, probably because the surveys excluded (or did not report results for) establishments with fewer than 25 workers.

[2] S Machin, 'Union Decline in Britain' (2000) 38 BJIR 631.

Of course, a weak trade union movement does not necessarily increase the government's freedom of action, but in the context of the late 1990s in the UK that was the result. The unions in general and the TUC in particular were desperate to take action which would arrest the decline of unionisation. Many measures, no doubt, lay in their own hands, such as an increased emphasis on organising non-union workplaces, even if this meant fewer resources being devoted to the servicing of existing members.[3] However, a large part of the TUC's agenda consisted of securing, as far as possible, the repeal or amendment of the legislative reforms enacted by the Conservative government,[4] which were regarded as having contributed substantially to the current weakness of the unions. On a more positive note, the TUC also sought the enactment of new laws, for example on mandatory union recognition, which might help the unions to reverse the decline which they had suffered. Since a Labour government was the only credible source of such legislative reforms, the new government found itself in a strong position. To put the matter in terms of cold political exchange (which obviously does not capture the whole of the relationship between the unions and the Labour party), the new government, having a monopoly over the supply of the reforms the unions sought, needed to offer only a modest set of reform proposals to secure the unions' support.

The government's position might have been weaker, had its political programme required for its effective implementation some substantial input from the unions. Had that been so, something like the exchange which underlay the Social Contract of the mid-seventies might have eventuated.[5] However, by good fortune (from the government's point of view) the two industrial relations matters upon which governments had frequently sought the help of the TUC and the union movement in general in the post-War period, high levels of industrial action and high levels of inflation, were no longer pressing issues by the end of the 1990s. The contrast with the position in which earlier Labour governments found themselves is remarkable. Thus, whereas the Labour governments of 1964 to 1970 had to deal with a rising tide of concern, sometimes verging on panic, over levels of short, unofficial action, especially in manufacturing industry,[6] whilst the government of 1974 to 1979 both inherited and bequeathed a number of high-profile and intractable official disputes,[7] the Labour government of 1997 inherited and maintained a low level of industrial conflict. At least since 1992 the UK strike rate had been below the average for both the European Union and the developed countries which were members of OECD.[8] Thus, the government elected in 1997 was free

---

[3] On the stress placed by 'new' unionism on organising see F O'Grady and P Nowak, 'Beyond New Unionism' in J Kelly and P Willman (eds), *Union Organization and Activity* (London: Routledge, 2004).   [4] See *Labour Legislation and Public Policy* (LLPP) chapter 9.
[5] See LLPP, chapter 8.   [6] See LLPP, 6.1.   [7] See LLPP, chapter 8.
[8] J Monger, 'International comparisons of labour disputes in 2001' *Labour Market Trends*, April 2003, 181. The government claimed that the number of days lost through industrial action in 2005 was the lowest since records began in 1891 and the number of stoppages the lowest since 1930: DTI, *Success at Work*, March 2006, 5.

of significant political pressure from the electorate to 'do something' about strikes. In fact, industrial action remained politically unimportant for the government, despite predictions in some quarters that its election would trigger disputes in the public sector from workers seeking to recover ground lost under the previous governments, until well into its second term when there was a high-profile, but ultimately self-contained, conflict with the fire-fighters over the reform of working practices.[9]

In relation to inflation, a similar story can be told. The government inherited a situation of low inflation. More important, it inherited a new approach to macro-economic management of the economy, in which government's reliance on union co-operation was reduced.[10] The new government undertook to continue this policy of macro-economic stability, in particular a refusal to run substantial budget deficits in order to finance public expenditure. Furthermore, the government took an early decision to delegate the setting of interest rates to the independent Monetary Policy Committee (essentially the Bank of England reinforced by a number of prominent outsiders). By this (political) decision the setting of interest rates was substantially de-politicised. For those who remembered the levels of inflation reached in the 1960s and 1970s—and even the early 1980s—a startling reminder of how things had changed in this area was the level of the inflation target which was given to the MPC and which turned out to be eminently achievable—a mere 2.0% per annum. The government elected in 1997 thus had no need to delve again into the morass of prices and incomes boards, the setting of limits for wage increases or social contracts and compacts, which had so distracted its predecessors.[11]

Thus, union weakness coupled with the favourable economic environment inherited by the government (which included falling unemployment) meant that the union movement had greater need of the government than the government had of the union movement. This situation was reinforced by the electoral calculation made by the Labour Party in the pre-election period. Based on what had happened during the 'winter of discontent' in 1978[12] and the surprise defeat of the Labour Party in the 1992 election, the party's election strategists for the subsequent election took the view that the close link between the party and the union movement was a potential liability, not an advantage. This was a contrast with earlier elections, for example, that of 1974 when the party had campaigned on the basis that it could better handle the unions than the Conservatives because of its close connection with them. Coupled with this was the party's abandonment of certain socialist or social-democratic policies with which it had been associated

---

[9] At one stage it looked as though the government would be moved to enact special restrictions on industrial action by fire-fighters, but in the end it did not do so. For an account of the dispute see 2.2.2, above.   [10] See LLPP, 9.1.

[11] See LLPP, 4.3, 7.3 and 8.1, although, as ever, the government's attitude towards pay increases in the public sector was often influenced (in a downward direction) by the state of the public finances.

[12] LLPP, 366.

which were now perceived to be electorally unpopular, such as high levels of income tax to finance public expenditure. Since such policies were probably still thought to be appropriate by most unions, their abandonment gave rise to a further cooling of relations.

In the period before the election these two policy thrusts were symbolised by two changes in particular to the party's constitutional arrangements. First, the unions' share of the vote in a number of areas was reduced: from 40% to 33% in the election of the party leader (in 1992) and to 50% on conference resolutions (in 1995). Second, Clause 4 of the party's constitution, which had previously committed the party, at least theoretically, to common ownership of the means of production, was replaced in 1995 by wording which emphasised the value of the market and the promotion of competition. It is perhaps an indication of how weak the unions perceived their political position to be (both within the party and outside it) that they not only acquiesced in these changes but, in the case of some unions, actively promoted them.[13] Again, it was not until the government's second term that serious union/government disagreement surfaced in public.

It would be wrong, however, to present a picture of the unions and the party engaging in a divorce. The party was still substantially reliant on union donations to finance its election campaigns, despite successful attempts to increase the share of party income coming from individual donors—attempts which were to lead to adverse publicity in the government's third term.[14] Moreover, the party's policies were still more favourable to the interests (broadly conceived) of union members and those likely to join unions than were the policies of any of its competitors. What is suggested is the more limited proposition: that, in terms of formulating its policies on collective labour law, the incoming government had greater freedom of manoeuvre than any of its predecessors since the Second World War.

It is one thing to establish freedom of manoeuvre and another to decide how to exercise the freedom. We have already crossed that boundary by indicating that the new government did not wish to implement policies which could put it in danger of being portrayed as in the pockets of the unions, so that it was likely not to act on the whole or perhaps even substantial parts of the list of changes that the unions wished to see. More broadly, we have indicated that the new government inherited a mainly favourable economic situation and it was determined to do all in its power to maintain it and to shun policy initiatives which might again lay it open to the charge of economic mismanagement. The government committed itself to prudent economic management, notably to borrowing only to invest and not to fund current spending, and to keeping government debt at a stable level over the economic cycle. As a dramatic illustration of its prudence, it voluntarily committed itself to abide by the previous government's spending plans for the first

---

[13] For an illuminating account of these developments see J McIlroy, 'The Enduring Alliance? Trade Unions and the Making of New Labour, 1994–1997' (1998) 36 BJIR 537.

[14] Involving the non-disclosure of loans to both the main parties which, unlike donations, did not have to be disclosed.

two years of government.[15] Of course, these policies entailed continuing public sector pay restraint. Although these policies were focused on the area of macro-economic management, not collective labour law, they indicated a strong desire not to make changes that would endanger the achievement of the government's economic targets, which again suggested a bias against fundamental changes in collective labour law.

Whatever one may think of this policy towards collective labour law, it cannot be said that the party was not clear about it in the years before the election. The party's policy contained two main strands as far as collective labour law was concerned. On the law of industrial conflict there would be only minimal change and no repeal of the main elements of the changes put in place by the previous governments. The TUC may have voted in both 1994 and 1995 for the repeal of 'all anti-trade union legislation passed by the Tories',[16] but Mr Tony Blair told the same 1995 Congress that 'there is not going to be a repeal of all Tory trade union laws . . . Ballots before strikes are here to stay. No mass or flying pickets. All these are ghosts of time past . . . it is time to leave them where they lie.'[17] On the positive side, in terms of what the party would do, if elected, the commitments were limited. Only one specific collective labour law promise was made in the party's manifesto for the 1997 election. That concerned not the law of industrial conflict but the collective representation of workers as against their employer. This was the second strand of policy and involved the re-introduction of a statutory recognition machinery. As the party's manifesto for the election put it, 'where [workers] do decide to join [a union] and a majority of the relevant workforce vote in a ballot for the union to represent them, the union should be recognised'.[18]

Finally, there was no evidence that these proposals would constitute, as was the way with the Employment Act 1980,[19] the first in a series of reforms aimed at or in fact achieving a much more radical set of changes. On the contrary, the Prime Minister, in his Foreword to the White Paper[20] which preceded the Employment Relations Act 1999, stated that its proposals were for 'an industrial relations settlement for this Parliament'. Although there was a further Employment Relations Act in 2004 (ie, in the second term), it did not substantially add to the collective labour law changes made in 1999. However, legislation on collective representation at work did in fact proceed in dramatic new directions in the government's second term, not as a result of domestic legislative initiatives but as a result of legislation at Community level. Of the three main labour law pledges given in the

---

[15] A Glyn and S Wood, 'Economic Policy under New Labour: How Social Democratic is the Blair Government?' [2001] Political Quarterly, at 50–52.

[16] TUC, *Congress Report 1994*, 138 and *Congress Report 1995*, 34.

[17] Ibid, 112. This statement was repeated in Mr Tony Blair's Introduction to the *Labour Party Manifesto* for the 1997 Election (available on: <http://www.labour-party.org.uk/manifestos/1997/1997-labour-manifesto.shtml>). In 2006 the government reiterated its policy on collective action: 'we have no intention of changing industrial action laws or taking other measures that would damage employability or competitiveness in the UK.' (DTI, *Success at Work*, March 2006).

[18] Ibid.   [19] LLPP, 9.3.   [20] DTI, *Fairness at Work*, Cm 3968, 1998.

manifesto (in addition to the statutory recognition procedure there was an under-taking to introduce a minimum wage[21]) one was of a procedural rather than a substantive character. It was to 'opt into' the Social Agreement from which the UK had excluded itself at the negotiations at Maastricht on revisions to the EC Treaty.[22] Thus, the UK became fully bound by what is now the Social Chapter of the EC Treaty.[23] Since the Social Chapter provides a mechanism for making law (indeed, more than one route, since law can be made by a route involving the 'social partners' as well as through the standard Community method), it was not necessarily predictable what impact this step would have on domestic labour law. This unpredictability was enhanced by the Social Chapter provisions which permitted legislation to be made in some important areas by qualified majority vote, so that the consent of the UK to legislation which would bind it was not necessarily required. In the event, an important Directive was adopted requiring the introduction of continuous information and consultation mechanisms at establishment or enterprise level in all but the smallest workplaces as from March 2005.[24] Arguably, this Directive and the domestic rules transposing it introduced into the British structures relating to collective representation at work the most important changes since the reports of the Whitley Committee shortly after the First World War.[25] Certainly, it posed major challenges for government, unions, and employers about how the new provision should relate to the traditional mechanisms of collective bargaining.

We propose to proceed in this chapter to discuss the three main themes identified above: continuity in industrial conflict law, the introduction of the statutory recognition procedure, and the arrival of mandatory information and consultation mechanisms.

3.2 Industrial conflict law: continuity with some change

3.2.1 Continuity

In government the Labour Party stuck to its pre-election view that the structure of industrial conflict law—and the associated reforms of internal trade union law—put in place by its predecessor Conservative administrations would be retained. The point was reinforced in the Prime Minister's Foreword to *Fairness at Work*,[26] where it was said that 'the days of strikes without ballots, mass picketing, closed shops and secondary action are over'. When the 1999 Act was reviewed in 2003 the government stated its view to be that the structure of industrial conflict law

---

[21] Discussed below at 4.3.1.   [22] See 2.2, above.
[23] Part Three, Title XI of the EC Treaty.
[24] Directive 2002/14/EC. The UK, as a country with no established system of mandatory works councils, was permitted a transition period: the requirement was applied to enterprises with 150 or more workers initially, reducing to 50 by March 2008.
[25] See LLPP, 1.2.   [26] See n 20, above.

was 'well established and ensures that the inevitable disruption inherent in industrial action is confined as far as possible to those directly involved in an industrial dispute. The Government therefore re-affirms its commitment to retain the essential features of the pre-1997 law on industrial action.'[27]

Although this was the reaffirmation of a policy of not legislating, it is worth spending a moment considering its profound significance. The legal centrepiece of the doctrine of collective laissez-faire was the enactment of legislation which excluded the common law economic torts (and certain associated crimes) from the area of peaceful industrial disputes, so that the outcome of those disputes could be settled by the free play of the economic resources available to workers and employers.[28] For a century after the Trade Union Act 1871 it was the peace-time policy of nearly all governments to exclude the relevant liabilities from the area of trade disputes by providing immunities for those 'acting in contemplation or furtherance of a trade dispute' (even if judicial policy-making often frustrated the governments' intentions). The beginnings of a different policy can be detected in 1971 when the Conservative government of Edward Heath adopted a strategy of using common-law based notions of unfair industrial practices to regulate even peaceful industrial action, in the event in a more rigorous way than it had intended because of the unions' policy of non-registration.[29] However, the Industrial Relations Act 1971 was promptly repealed by the succeeding Labour government.[30] From 1980 onwards came the second wave of reform as the administrations of Mrs Margaret Thatcher allowed the common law liabilities an even more far-reaching scope for operation.[31] This set of reforms was substantially complete by the end of the 1980s, though the administration of Mr John Major made a significant addition as part of its 'Citizens' Charter' initiative.[32] On this occasion, however, the succeeding Labour government did not engage in root and branch reform so as to restore the policy of collective laissez-faire.

The failure of the Labour government elected in 1997 to take similar action in relation to the reforms of the 1980s marked a shift in the political consensus of the most significant kind. No major political party was now seeking to convince the electorate that peaceful industrial action should be unregulated or even that the particular controls put in place by the previous Conservative administrations should be substantially amended. One can see the decline over recent decades of the other elements of the policy of collective laissez-faire, notably the increasingly direct legislative regulation of the employment relationship from the middle of

---

[27] DTI, *Review of the Employment Relations Act 1999*, February 2003, para 3.22 (URN03/606).

[28] See LLPP, 1.1(a), where we make clear the distinction between a policy of collective laissez-faire and the legal rules necessary to bring such a policy into existence.

[29] LLPP, 7.2.   [30] LLPP, 8.2.   [31] LLPP, chapter 9.

[32] See 2.2.4, above. The insertion was of what is still s 235A of TULRECA 1992, allowing an individual to sue organisers whose unlawful industrial action interferes with the supply of good or services to that individual. However, the special publicly funded enforcement mechanism through the somewhat Gilbertian 'Commissioner for Protection Against Unlawful Industrial Action' was repealed by the 1999 Act.

the 1960s onwards. However, cross-party acceptance from the middle of the 1990s onwards that economic torts had a continuing role to play in the control of peaceful industrial action constituted the posting of a formal obituary of collective laissez-faire and underscored the need for new guideposts in the analysis of labour law. In effect, legislating to control the externalities generated by industrial action was given priority over the untrammelled operation of the principle of self-regulation or private ordering by employers and trade unions. More speculatively, acceptance of the Conservative governments' reforms can be seen as evidence of a general shift in political power from producers (both employers, employees and, indeed, the liberal professions) to consumers of goods and services (whether produced by the public or the private sectors) which affected many areas of life in this period.

This change of policy was naturally subject to continuing criticism from the TUC and individual trade unions. Legal writers tended to focus their criticism on the incompatibility of the industrial conflict rules with the Conventions of the ILO, notably the basic Conventions 87 and 98 on freedom of association.[33] Although some of this criticism was overdone, it is clear that the ILO supervisory bodies continued to identify two aspects of British industrial conflict law as incompatible with international labour law. These were the almost complete prohibition of secondary and sympathy action[34] and the prohibition on unions taking disciplinary action against members for refusing to take part in even lawful (and thus properly balloted) industrial action.[35] In the diplomatic language in which the reports of these bodies are couched, the Committee of Experts in 2005 said that it 'requests the Government to continue to keep it informed in its future reports of developments' and 'is raising a number of points in a request addressed directly to the Government'.[36] However, the impact of these comments on the government was not such as to cause it to change its policy.

3.2.2 Change: the position of individual workers

The strand of continuity identified above relates to the legal position of the organisers of industrial action. With regard to the legal position of participants in industrial action, however, a significant change did take place. Its significance is

---

[33] For an excellent early analysis along these lines see T Novitz, 'International Promises and Domestic Pragmatism' (2000) 63 MLR 379. See also, on the similar relationship between British collective action law and the European Social Charter, E Kovács, 'The Right to Strike in the European Social Charter' (2005) Comparative Labour Law and Policy Journal 445.

[34] Secondary action is still lawful if carried out in the course of lawful picketing (which is itself tightly defined). See LLPP, 9.3(e), for the first attempt to legislate against secondary action under the previous administrations in the Employment Act 1980, and LLPP, 9.8 for the current rule, introduced by the Employment Act 1990.

[35] See LLPP, 9.7(a)—a rule introduced by the Employment Act 1988.

[36] ILO Conference, 93rd Session, 2005, Report of the Committee of Experts on the Application of Conventions and Recommendations, Report III(A), Part II, p 123.

underlined by the fact that it involved a change in the basic stance taken from the very beginning by the law of unfair dismissal towards those dismissed for taking part in industrial action. Not only had the common law of the contract of employment failed to conceptualise the standard forms of industrial action as anything other than a breach of contract, but governments, both Conservative and Labour, when introducing the unfair dismissal law in the 1970s, sought to replicate the common law position by excluding those dismissed whilst taking industrial action from the protection of the new laws, provided the employer did not discriminate among those engaged in the action.[37] The aim, it was said, was to prevent the tribunals from having to take a view on the merits of the underlying industrial action. In the Employment Relations Act 1999[38] the government moved, however, to permit those dismissed whilst engaging in lawful, official industrial action to bring claims of unfair dismissal, even though there was no element of discrimination. The objection about tribunal evaluation of the merits of the industrial action was met by making dismissal for taking part in such industrial action automatically unfair. As initially enacted, this protection was confined, normally, to the first eight weeks of the industrial action,[39] but in the 2004 Act that period was extended to twelve weeks, with the possibility of further extension in the case of a lock-out.[40] In the current industrial relations climate, only a very small number of strikes will exceed the protected period.

However, whilst one can point to change in one fundamental aspect of the law of unfair dismissal in relation to industrial action, one finds continuity in relation to an equally fundamental aspect of that relationship and one, this time, introduced by the previous Conservative administrations. In 1990 the government considerably worsened the unfair dismissal protection of those engaging in unofficial industrial action by depriving them of access to the tribunals even if they were treated in a discriminatory way by the employer (who might, for example, simply dismiss those regarded as the ring-leaders of the industrial action).[41] Coupled with the new provisions on union liability for the actions of its officials, including lay officials, the unfair dismissal rules put the union in a demanding legal situation if its members engaged in action without explicit union sanction. In order to protect its funds, because no ballot had been held, the union would have to repudiate the action but, having thus made the action unofficial, it had then to urge its members, especially the activists, to return to work in order to protect them against discriminatory dismissal—at least until such time as a ballot could be organised. The new government explicitly refused to alter this position.[42]

---

[37] See LLPP, 7.2(c) and 8.2.   [38] Introducing a new s 238A into TULRECA 1992.

[39] More accurately, to the first eight weeks of the dismissed employee's participation in the industrial action, which might not always be the same thing.

[40] S 26 of the 2004 Act, amending s 238A. The government had not intended initially to extend the eight-week period: DTI, *Review of the Employment Relations Act 1999*, February 2003, para. 3.37 (URN03/606).

[41] LLPP, 9.8(b).   [42] DTI, *Fairness at Work*, Cm 3968, 1998, para. 4.22.

3.2.3 Change: industrial action ballots

This was an area where there was considerable tinkering with the law, but no commitment to change its policy thrust. As we have noted, the pre-strike ballot was an element of the existing law which the Labour Party in opposition had indicated it would retain. The critique developed in *Fairness at Work* was that the existing provisions were 'unnecessarily complex and rigid'.[43] A number of detailed changes were made,[44] probably the most important of which concerned attempts to relieve the union from any obligation to give the employer a pre-strike notice containing lists of the names of its members who were proposing to take industrial action.[45] In some instances, including the pre-strike notice, the reform efforts were almost counter-productive, and the issue had to be revisited in the 2004 Act.[46] Overall in this area, however, continuity was a much stronger part of the picture than change, despite the amount of legislative time spent on the change.

3.3 Freedom of association and the recognition of trade unions

3.3.1 Freedom of association

The most important single change made by the 1999 Act was the re-introduction of a statutory recognition procedure. Before dealing with that, however, we should say a little bit about the changes made in the law dealing with workers' rights to join and be members of unions. The issue which occupied the greatest attention was how best to respond legislatively to a decision of the House of Lords in 1995 in two joined cases,[47] where their lordships had articulated a very narrow interpretation of the statutory provisions giving employees the right not to have action short of dismissal taken against them for the purpose of preventing or deterring them from being members of or taking part in the activities of an independent trade union.[48] Both cases involved the de-recognition of trade unions by an employer and came to symbolise the hostility of the law to unionism and the decline of trade unions under the Conservative administrations, even though statistical analysis showed that the fall in trade union membership was due mainly to the unions' failure to secure recognition in new workplaces rather than to their loss of recognition in existing workplaces.[49]

---

[43] Ibid, para 4.26. [44] Keith Ewing identified ten: (1999) 28 ILJ at 294.

[45] The pre-strike notice requirement was another innovation of the Major administration, which had introduced s 234A into TULRECA 1992 (in TURERA 1993, s 21)

[46] DTI, *Review of the Employment Relations Act 1999*, February 2003, paras 3.21 ff (URN03/606). The defects of the original drafting on pre-strike notices were exposed in *London Underground Ltd* v *National Union of Rail, Maritime and Transport Workers* [2001] ICR 647, CA. And only judicial benevolence prevented other amendments made in the 1999 Act from leaving the law in a worse state than before: *P* v *National Association of School Masters/Union of Women Teachers* [2003] ICR 386, HL.

[47] *Associated Newspapers Ltd* v *Wilson; Associated British Ports* v *Palmer* [1995] ICR 406, HL.

[48] Then s 23 of the EPCA 1978, later s 146 of TULRECA 1992. [49] See Machin, n 2 above.

In these two cases the employers had de-recognised the union, were willing for workers to remain members of the union, but wanted to move them onto 'individual' contracts and away from the terms previously agreed with the unions. To that end the employer offered certain inducements (namely, pay rises) to workers who moved onto the new contracts and abandoned collective representation, inducements which were not available to those workers who insisted on the status quo. From a broad freedom of association perspective the appropriate answer to the question of the legality of such action seems rather clear: the law ought not to permit employers to offer financial benefits for the purpose of persuading employees to abandon collective bargaining. It was a mark of the tentativeness of the freedom of association rules introduced in the 1970s[50] that the domestic law did not yield this clear answer. Equally striking was the slow and timid approach on the part of the new government to reforming the law in this area: the changes made in the 1999 Act were ineffective and the area had to be revisited in the 2004 Act, under pressure from an adverse judgment of the European Court of Human Rights. The impediment to reform, in the government's mind, seems to have been the difficulty of drafting new rules whilst preserving the traditional freedom of British employers, even when collective bargaining was in place, to agree different terms with particular workers. In short, the government did not want any reform to imperil the traditional principle of British labour law that the terms of a collective agreement do not automatically and compulsorily become part of the contracts of the workers covered by the agreement.

In deciding in 1995 that the employers' action was lawful the House of Lords adopted an uncharacteristically literal interpretation of the section: since the matter complained of was a failure to offer a benefit rather than the deprivation of a benefit already held, this was not 'action' within the meaning of the section but an omission. The government did not have much difficulty in coming to the conclusion that this position should be reversed and the 1999 Act amended the 1992 Act so as to introduce, where appropriate, the additional words 'or any deliberate failure to act'.[51] Much more complex was their lordships' second reason for finding the employers' actions to fall outside the statutory protection; and the legislative response to this second argument, both when the case was being decided and after the election of a different government in 1997, was equally complex, not to say labyrinthine. Their lordships' second reason was that the employers' actions were not taken with a view to deterring the employees from being members of the union because, even if the right to membership involved the right to use the essential services of the union (upon which differing views were expressed), the service of collective bargaining was not an essential service of the union.[52]

---

[50] See LLPP, 8.3(c).   [51] See Schedule 2 to the 1999 Act.
[52] See Lord Bridge (with whom Lord Keith concurred) at p 418E, Lord Slynn at p 422F, and Lord Lloyd at p 425A. As stated, the employers were happy for their employees to remain members of the union and held out no inducements conditional upon forgoing membership.

This second argument was one which had not attracted the Court of Appeal in their judgment, given in April 1993,[53] and since the 'action/omission' point had not been run in the Court of Appeal, the employers had lost in that court. This outcome in turn did not appeal to the then government which, at a late stage in the passage of the Trade Union Reform and Employment Rights Act 1993, introduced an amendment, the famous 'Ullswater' amendment named after its proposer in the (legislative) House of Lords, to reverse the Court of Appeal. In the light of the subsequent House of Lords' judgment this legislative action turned out to have been unnecessary, but it formed part of the legal framework which the new government had to consider in the late 1990s. The amendment provided that where an employer's purpose was to 'further a change in his relationship with all or any class of his employees' a complaint of infringement of the statutory right could not be made unless the action was such as no reasonable employer would take.

Thus, there were two questions, beyond the act/omission distinction, facing the new government: what would it do about the second strand in the House of Lords' interpretation of the statutory provision as it stood before the 1993 change and what would it do about the Ullswater amendment? The answer in 1999 was: 'nothing directly'. The 1999 Act did not remove the Ullswater amendment, but, on the other hand, the government took power in section 17 of the 1999 Act to make regulations for cases where an employee is dismissed or suffers a detriment on the grounds that he or she refused to enter into a contract which contains terms different from those in an applicable collective agreement. However, this government, too, accepted an amendment in the House of Lords, this time from the opposition peer Baroness Miller, which constrained the definition of detriment in section 17 by excluding more favourable pay and other associated terms where the worker receiving the more favourable pay was not inhibited from being a member of a union and the higher pay was reasonably related to the services provided by the worker under his contract.

The purpose of the Miller amendment, and the government's acceptance of it, seems to have been to safeguard the freedom of employers to pay above the collectively bargained rate to particularly meritorious workers, without being in danger of facing a claim of infringement of the statutory provisions on freedom of association. A government committed to labour market flexibility would naturally want to secure this objective. However, the legislative tension produced by section 17, as originally drafted, on the one hand, and the Ullswater and Miller amendments, on the other, was sufficiently intense to make the drafting of effective regulations difficult. Indeed, perhaps for this reason, none was ever produced. Whether domestic pressures would eventually have led to a resolution of the issue is difficult to say. It is possible that they would not have done so. The industrial relations and legal situation had changed in the UK so as no longer to encourage employers to

---

[53] But reported in [1994] ICR 97.

de-recognise where the union still enjoyed a good level of support. After the introduction of the statutory recognition procedure (discussed below) a union facing the loss of its voluntary recognition in such circumstances would simply put in a claim for recognition under the statute. A number of employers which had de-recognised unions in the 1990s quietly re-recognised them either shortly before or shortly after the new procedure was introduced.[54] Thus, it may be that the underlying social problem had largely gone away in any event.

However, the matter did not rest in a purely domestic forum. Although the condemnation by the ILO's supervisory bodies of the *Wilson and Palmer* decisions had had little impact on governmental policy,[55] the success of the employees before the European Court of Human Rights in 2002 produced a much more visible result which the government could not easily ignore. In *Wilson and National Union of Journalists* v *United Kingdom*[56] and associated cases the European Court of Human Rights articulated the basic objection to the employers' conduct from a freedom of association perspective: that conduct 'constituted a disincentive or restraint on the use by employees of union membership to protect their interests'[57] and the UK was thus in breach of Article 11 of the European Convention on Human Rights by permitting such conduct within its legal system. Although this decision was notable for its reliance on the views of the supervisory bodies of the ILO and under the European Social Charter, it is not clear that the case marked a major extension of the Court's definition of freedom of association.[58] However that may be, the Court's decision clearly required radical revision of the British law discussed above. In the 2004 Act the government proceeded to repeal the Ullswater amendment and also the never-used regulation-making power in section 17 of the 1999 Act (and thus also the Miller amendment). On the positive side, it extended the existing protections against dismissal or action short of dismissal in respect of union membership and activities so as to embrace explicitly the use of union services.[59] It also introduced two new rights[60] for individuals: not to have inducements offered where the purpose is to induce the worker not to be or become a member of a union or take part in its activities or use its services or, where the worker is a member of a recognised union or one seeking recognition, to induce the worker not to have terms and conditions determined by collective agreement. The flexibility for employers which the government had been keen to protect seems to have expressed itself in the restriction that liability should arise in the above cases only if the forbidden objective was the employer's 'sole or main' purpose, so that the employer who can convince a tribunal that the main purpose

---

54 See generally S Oxenbridge et al, 'Initial Responses to the Statutory Recognition Provisions of the Employment Relations Act 1999' (2003) 41 BJIR 315.

55 See ILO Committee on Freedom of Association, *Case No 1730 (UK)*, 294th Report (1994).

56 [2002] IRLR 568, ECtHR.   57 At para 47.

58 For a contrary view see K Ewing, 'The Implications of *Wilson and Palmer*' (2003) 32 ILJ 1.

59 S 146 of TULRECA, as amended by s 31 of the 2004 Act.

60 New ss 145A and B, inserted by s 29 of the 2004 Act.

of an action was to reward employees for flexible working would not be caught under the new provisions.

In *Fairness at Work*[61] dealing with the act/omission point was coupled with the introduction of a prohibition on blacklisting of trade union members. This was a rather mysterious proposal. Blacklisting (ie, co-operation among employers to refuse to hire known union activists)[62] has a long, if submerged, history in some industries in the UK, notably construction. However, there was little hard evidence that it was a pressing current problem. Nevertheless, in the 1999 Act the government took powers to make regulations prohibiting the operation by employers of blacklists (thus aiming to deal with the problem before it affected the hiring of a particular worker). Somewhat in the manner of the inducement regulations, however, this power was not exercised, and in its review[63] of the 1999 Act the government came around to the view that the problem was not pressing and all it offered to do was to draft regulations to be kept in reserve if the problem re-emerged.[64] All in all, this was a curious episode of legislative shadow-boxing.

3.3.2 Trade union recognition

The promise to re-introduce a statutory recognition procedure was the single most important undertaking which the union movement secured from the Labour Party in the area of collective labour law in the period running up to the election of 1997. In contrast to the industrial action area, the field of collective representation at work was one where the new government was prepared to take significant action which would be helpful to the unions. Moreover, given the centrality of collective bargaining to the unions' role in society, legal machinery which aimed to promote that activity was bound to be regarded as a major gain in union circles. However, it is one thing to give a commitment in principle to introduce a statutory recognition machinery and another thing to produce an effective design for it. There could be no question of simply re-introducing either of the previous two sets of provisions, those contained in the IRA 1971 and EPA 1975 respectively, for both were regarded in different ways as having been failures.[65] In fact, the new provisions, inserted by the 1999 Act as Schedule A1 to TULRECA 1992, were designed in many ways as a reaction to the perceived weaknesses of the previous

---

[61] DTI, *Fairness at Work*, Cm 3968, 1998, para 4.25.

[62] An actual refusal to hire a particular person might constitute a breach of the existing legislation relating to discrimination on grounds of membership at the point of hiring, though that provision does not extend to discrimination on grounds of union activities: see TULRECA 1992, s 137. However, a rule against blacklisting would operate whether the blacklist could be shown to have been implemented in any specific case or not.

[63] DTI, *Review of the Employment Relations Act 1999*, February 2003, para 3.18 ff (URN03/606).

[64] See DTI, *Draft Regulations to Prohibit the Blacklisting of Trade Unionists—A Consultation Document*, February 2003 (URN 03/648). The government, surprisingly, seems not to have considered the alternative of repairing the lacuna in TULRECA 1992, s 137 (see n 62, above).

[65] See LLPP, 7.2(a)(vi) and 8.3(c).

provisions, especially those of 1975.[66] Those reactions can be divided into those concerning underlying principle and those concerned with the machinery in operation.

3.3.2.1 *Underlying principle*

In terms of underlying principle, the most important difference lay in the government's reasons for promoting collective bargaining. In 1975, despite the problems of industrial action and inflation, public policy still regarded collective bargaining as the best way of settling terms and conditions of employment and the government was, for that reason, committed to promoting it. To this extent the government's policy on collective bargaining still reflected the enthusiasm for joint regulation which had built up during the Second World War.[67] In 1999, by contrast, the government presented itself when introducing the recognition machinery as implementing the majority view of a particular group of workers—a democratic rather than a broader social rationale for collective bargaining. *Fairness at Work* failed to endorse collective bargaining as the most desirable form of collective employee representation. On the contrary, the government stated its belief to be 'that mutually-agreed arrangements for representation, whether involving trade unions or not, are the best ways for employers and employees to move forward'.[68] Only where a majority of workers were in favour of collective bargaining would the law come off the fence and mandate this particular form of representation. Of course, the two rationales overlap to some degree. However, the two approaches led to important differences of emphasis in the design of the statutory provisions.

This can be seen most clearly in the contrasting mechanisms for the choice of the union to represent the workers. Stripped to essentials, the recognition machineries which have operated in the UK are designed to settle two core substantive questions: what is the appropriate bargaining unit, and which is the appropriate bargaining agent? The first question asks: which workers are to be put together for the purposes of representation in collective bargaining; and the second: which body is to represent those workers? The democratic principle cannot logically be applied to answer the first question (since the question in effect requires the constituency to be defined),[69] but it can, though need not, be used to answer the second question. Under the 1975 procedure the democratic principle was given

---

[66] S Wood and J Goddard, 'The Statutory Union Recognition Procedure in the Employment Relations Bill: A Comparative Analysis' (1999) 37 BJIR 203; Lord McCarthy, *Fairness at Work and Trade Union Recognition: Past Comparisons and Future Problems* (London: Institute of Employment Rights, 1999). (The IRA machinery was regarded as having been part of legislation with such very different objectives that it provided few guide-lines for the drafters of the 1999 Act.)

[67] See LLPP, 1.3.   [68] DTI, *Fairness at Work*, Cm 3968, 1998, para 4.10.

[69] A thorough-going human rights rationale for recognition might regard the first question as redundant: an individual worker should have the right to be represented by the union of his or her choice, but the 1999 Act adopted a collective rather than an individual approach to representation at

much less weight in answering the second question than under the 1999 procedure, where it is central.

Thus, under the 1975 Act, ACAS, the body charged with operating the recognition procedure along with its many other functions and which, significantly, was under a duty 'of promoting the improvement of industrial relations and in particular of encouraging the extension of collective bargaining',[70] determined both core questions. True, ACAS was under a duty to ascertain the opinions of the workers to whom the recognition claim related and could even conduct a formal ballot,[71] though it rarely did so, preferring opinion surveys. Nevertheless, in the interests of encouraging the extension of collective bargaining, ACAS could and would recommend recognition where there was not majority support among the employees for this step, provided it thought there was sufficient support to make collective bargaining viable. ACAS thus could, and sometimes did, take the view that support for collective bargaining would grow once the institution was in place. Contrariwise, it would sometimes, though much less often, not recommend recognition even though there was majority support among the employees for the applicant union, because it thought recognition of that particular union would not be conducive to good industrial relations.[72] Overall, the approach was that of an expert and specialised body doing its sensitive best to promote collective bargaining and good industrial relations.

By contrast, although the Central Arbitration Committee (CAC) decides the first core question under the 1999 procedure (in the absence of agreement between the parties), the second core question is a matter solely for the employees falling within the bargaining unit. If the applicant union has majority support within the unit, then the union must be declared by the CAC to be entitled to be recognised by the employer, even if the CAC thinks the union a wholly inappropriate representative of the workers; and equally, and more important, the CAC may not order recognition of a union which does not currently have the majority support[73] of the workers, even if the CAC is confident such support would grow if the union were recognised. This emphasis on majority support represents, we suggest, a certain retreat by the government from a full commitment to collective bargaining: it was because the workers wanted collective bargaining in a particular case, not because the government wanted it as the general or paradigm case,

work. For the alternative approach see J Hendy and M Walton, 'An Individual Right to Union Representation in International Law' (1997) 26 ILJ 205.

[70] EPA, s 1(2).   [71] S 14(1).

[72] Stephen Wood, 'Recognition', in B Towers and W Brown (eds), *Employment Relations in Britain: 25 Years of the Advisory Conciliation and Arbitration Service* (Oxford: Blackwell Publishing, 2000); *United Kingdom Association of Professional Engineers* v *Advisory, Conciliation and Arbitration Service* [1980] ICR 201, HL.

[73] Majority support can be tested in two ways: either a majority of the workers in membership of the union, or a majority of those voting in a secret ballot representing at least 40% of the bargaining unit. The addition of the 40% requirement where there is a ballot, and the CAC's discretion to insist on a ballot in some cases even where there is majority membership, are both controversial features of the procedure, but neither affects the principle being argued for in the text.

that it should be imposed on employers. As *Fairness at Work* put it: 'While many employers and employees will continue to choose direct relationships without the involvement of third parties, these procedures will provide a new settlement which will enable trade unions to be recognised for collective bargaining where the relevant workforce chooses such representation.'[74] The tone is one of governmental neutrality, which is abandoned only where the democratic principle can be invoked.

It would be wrong to leave the impression that the democratic principle suffuses the whole of the new procedure: as we have pointed out, it operates only for the determination of the second core issue and therefore its boundaries are set by the prior determination of the bargaining unit, which is, in the absence of agreement, a decision for the CAC. However, in a different way the more distanced attitude of the government towards collective bargaining shows itself in relation to the first issue also. Under the 1975 procedure ACAS was given a broad discretion to define the bargaining unit, but subject to its overriding duties to promote good industrial relations and collective bargaining. Under the 1999 procedure the CAC's discretion is constrained by the overriding requirement that the CAC take account 'of the need for the unit to be compatible with effective management'; and other relevant factors are to be taken into account only insofar as compatible with this overriding 'need'.[75] In other words, the government's approach requires the CAC to be accommodating of the difficulties which employers' existing employee relations structures may have in adapting to bargaining units proposed by trade unions. Thus, even if a union puts forward a proposed bargaining unit which has the support of all the workers in it, the CAC is still required to scrutinise the 'appropriateness' of the union's proposal (unless the employer accepts it) and to give priority in its scrutiny to the compatibility of the proposal with the company's managerial arrangements (for example, where the union's proposed bargaining unit contains only manual workers but the employer has developed common terms and conditions for its manual and white-collar workers). As the DTI's review of the 1999 Act put it, the recognition procedure 'was designed to balance the desire of a workforce to have a union bargain collectively on their behalf with the need for effective management'[76]—but the balance is one which the legislation seeks to shift in favour of the employer.

3.3.2.2 Detailed design

The detailed design of the 1999 procedure is very different from that of the 1975 one and in many ways can be seen as a response to the history of that procedure. The 1975 procedure was operated by ACAS, which found the task incompatible

---

[74] DTI, *Fairness at Work*, Cm 3968, 1998, para 1.9.

[75] TULRECA 1992, Sch A1, para 19B(2).

[76] DTI, *Review of the Employment Relations Act 1999*, February 2003, para 2.2 (URN03/606). The rigour of the 'effective management' criterion was diluted somewhat by the decision of the Court of Appeal in *R (Kwik-Fit (GB) Ltd)* v *Central Arbitration Committee* [2002] ICR 1212, to the effect

with its voluntary functions.[77] Under the 1999 procedure the task is given to the CAC, leaving ACAS to act in a voluntary role in support of the CAC and the statutory procedure more generally. More important, but linked to this, the task of producing a 'recommendation' in favour of or against recognition seems to have been viewed by the drafters of the 1975 Act as an essentially administrative task, which ACAS was left to get on with on the basis of relatively little statutory guidance. Under the 1999 procedure the CAC is given a series of well-defined decisions which it has to take at various points in a procedure which is spelled out in considerable detail in the statute, before it can order recognition. In the words of Abel-Smith and Stevens,[78] the CAC is clearly a 'court-substitute', not an administrative or policy-making body, a fact which was underlined by the government's decision to appoint a High Court judge[79] to be the first chairman of the CAC in its new role. If an aim of these steps was to protect the new procedure from the intrusive judicial review which the 1975 Act suffered,[80] then it has been successful so far, the decisions of the appellate courts on review being supportive of the CAC's view of its role.[81]

Partly for this reason, there is also an immense contrast in legislative styles in the drafting of the 1975 and 1999 procedures and something of a paradox at the heart of the 1999 procedure. On the one hand, the government aimed to produce a procedure which was 'simple, clear and quick'.[82] On the other hand, the 1999 procedure was set out in some 172 paragraphs of a schedule (to which the 2004 Act added further paragraphs), whilst the 1975 procedure was set out in six sections of a statute. The steps in the 1999 recognition procedure are set out in enormous detail, from acceptance of an application, determination of a bargaining unit, establishing whether there is majority support, conducting a ballot (if necessary) and determining the method of bargaining, with further, virtually distinct, procedures dealing with the various ways in which an application may be made for a union to be de-recognised. Why should the drafters of the 1999 procedure have adopted this approach?

A number of factors may have contributed to this approach. Spelling out in as much detail as possible what is to happen leaves the parties in a reduced state of uncertainty about the consequences of invoking or continuing with the procedure.[83] Another feature of the 1999 procedure which contributes to this result is the

---

that the union's proposal must be compatible with effective management, but not the most compatible proposal which could be devised. See further A Bogg, 'Politics, Community, Democracy: Appraising CAC Decision-Making in the First Five Years of Schedule A1' (2006) 35 ILJ at 257–261.

[77] See LLPP, 9.3(f).

[78] B Abel-Smith and R Stevens, *In Search of Justice* (London: Alan Lane, 1968) 218–224.

[79] Sir Michael Burton.　　　　[80] See LLPP, 8.5(c).

[81] See in particular *R (Kwik-Fit (GB) Ltd)* v *Central Arbitration Committee* [2002] ICR 1212, CA and *R (Ultraframe (UK) Ltd)* v *Central Arbitration Committee* [2005] ICR 1194, CA.

[82] DTI, *Fairness at Work*, Cm 3968, 1998, para 4.19.

[83] It has to be said that the parties are unlikely to derive this knowledge from reading the Schedule itself, for its detailed drafting style is off-putting in the extreme, but rather from secondary guidance

precise and limited specification of what recognition means for the purposes of the procedure, ie, recognition over pay, hours, and holidays. The CAC cannot order recognition over a broader range of subject-matters but, if it orders recognition at all, must include all three matters.[84] In this respect its powers differ from those of ACAS under the 1975 procedure which could 'recommend' recognition generally (ie, in relation to all terms and conditions of employment) or in relation to one or more specified matters.[85] Thus, the parties know in advance what will result from a successful application under the Schedule. Equally, and again in contrast to the 1975 procedure, the exclusion of the CAC's jurisdiction in virtually all cases where there is an element of inter-union competition makes for simplicity in the CAC's work. For example, the machinery cannot be used to run a referendum on whether an existing voluntary bargaining arrangement with union A should be replaced by recognition under the statute with union B.[86] Making it clear to the parties ex ante how the recognition procedure will (or will continue) to work might be thought to encourage the parties to settle the dispute, either without invoking the statutory procedure at all or without going all the way through it.

A second impact of the detailed drafting style is that it reduces the discretion of the CAC. This may in turn reduce the scope for argument over the CAC's decisions. Some evidence for this proposition can be deduced from the fact that, by the end of its sixth year of operation, the CAC had handled 502 applications for recognition but had faced only six applications for judicial review.[87] A third impact of the detailed drafting style is that it reduces the chances of the CAC developing the procedure in ways not intended by those who drafted it. Some evidence that this has occurred is derivable from the limited changes made to the procedure by the 2004 Act, which reversed a CAC decision in only one minor area,[88] but endorsed a central element of its operation, ie, the approach it had developed to test whether a majority of the proposed bargaining unit would be likely to support the application.[89]

However, providing procedural transparency for the parties and a narrow role for the CAC assumes that the legislature can set out ex ante rules which will

---

produced by advisers or the CAC itself. In fact, the drafters of the Schedule managed even to deceive themselves in one respect in 1999 and the nonsense produced had to be amended in the 2004 Act: see its s 12.

[84] Para 171A was added to the Schedule by the 2004 Act so as to effect a further simplification, by taking pensions out of the definition of pay for the purposes of the Schedule, unless the Secretary of State by regulation brings them back in.   [85] EPA, s 12(5).

[86] These are, no doubt, the factors the government would point to as supporting its view that the procedure is 'simple'.

[87] CAC, *Annual Report 2005–2006*, 19. The judicial review decisions can be found at: <http://www.cac.gov.uk/recent_decisions/judreview.htm>. As we have noted above, those reviews have also been favourable to the CAC, by and large, and that too may in part result from the courts' perception of the CAC as dealing with rather limited and detailed issues of industrial relations within a rather firm statutory framework.

[88] S 20 (taking pensions out of the statutory definition of pay—see above).

[89] S 19 (power to require parties to supply information to case manager).

govern what is to happen and does not need to resort to ex post standards which necessarily confer much more discretion on the adjudicatory body (ie, the CAC). The recognition procedure is predominantly a rule-based system, but some of the decisions which the procedure requires the CAC to take defy ex ante specification and thus the statute has to resort to alternative ways of constraining the CAC's discretion. Thus, the decision on the appropriate bargaining unit is peculiarly dependent on the facts of particular industrial relations situations and so the most that can be done and is done (see above) in the 1999 procedure is to specify the relevant factors which the CAC must take into account and to give those factors some rough type of prioritisation, notably the prioritisation accorded to the factor of 'compatibility with effective management'. Despite this legislative help, it is difficult for the parties to predict in advance how the CAC will define the bargaining unit, if it is called upon to do so.

Two further examples areas where ex ante rules have not been easy to formulate can be given. First, if the CAC decides to hold a ballot to determine majority support, the employer comes under a duty to give the applicant union reasonable access to the workplace to seek the workers' support. 'Reasonable access' is a classic example of an ex post standard and, in this case, one dealing with a very sensitive subject, ie, from the union's point of view, its ability to put its case to the workers and, from the employer's point of view, the need to admit the union onto its premises for that purpose. Guidance to the parties is provided nevertheless, although not primarily through the legislation but rather through a somewhat lengthy Code of Practice, issued by the Secretary of State.[90] This seems to have been largely successful in guiding the parties towards agreements on access arrangements and to reducing the need for the CAC to specify the access arrangements. Secondly, if the CAC orders recognition and the parties cannot agree a method of bargaining through which to carry out that order, then the CAC must specify to the parties a method of bargaining. Here, as well, the CAC's discretion is reduced by the specification of a detailed model method of bargaining set out in a statutory instrument[91] of which the CAC must 'take account'[92] if it is required to specify a method of bargaining in a particular case. In practice, the detailed specification in the subordinate legislation is usually enough guidance for the parties to agree on their own adaptations of the statutory model, without the need for CAC decision.[93]

---

[90] Employment Code of Practice (Access to Workers during Recognition and Derecognition Ballots) Order 2000, SI 2000/1443. As a result of the introduction of 'unfair practices' into the ballot rules (see s 9 of the 2004 Act, and 3.3.2.3 below), the Code of Practice was re-issued in 2005.

[91] Trade Union Recognition (Method of Collective Bargaining) Order 2000, SI 2000/1300.

[92] TULRECA 1992, Sch A1, para 168.

[93] As at the end of the year 2005/6 the CAC had ordered recognition in 142 cases but had had to specify a method of bargaining in only 13: CAC, *Annual Report 2005–2006*. The method of bargaining has been criticised as being both unsophisticated and incomplete, but its drafters, again, seem to have preferred simplicity and precision over other virtues.

The desire for precision carries through under the 1999 procedure to the crucial question of how the duty to recognise the union is to be formulated and enforced. The most well-known approach, because it was the centrepiece of the Wagner Act in the United States, is to impose upon the employer a duty to bargain in good faith, an obligation compliance with which, however, it is very difficult to test. This is due to the problem of disentangling an obligation to agree or even to make reasonable concessions (which is not what is required) from a mere obligation to bargain, whilst avoiding the pitfall of simply requiring the employer to go through the motions of sitting down and talking to the union without any subjective intent of taking the union's arguments seriously.[94] Nevertheless, under the 1975 procedure a British circumlocution of the bargaining in good faith test was imposed: the union could complain that the employer was 'not then taking such action by way of or with a view to carrying on negotiations as might reasonably be expected to be taken by an employer ready and willing to carry on such negotiations as are envisaged by [ACAS'] recommendation'.[95] Under the 1999 procedure, the legislature has come much closer to a requirement that the employer simply go through the motions of talking to the union. There is no explicit obligation to bargain in good faith. Rather the obligation, on both parties, is to abide by the method of bargaining specified by the CAC, which is to have effect as if it were a legally-binding contract made by the parties.[96] The extent of the employer's obligation is thus determined by the statutory model of bargaining, as amended by the CAC in any particular case. That model method has at its centre a six-stage procedure, with tight time limits, which envisages proposals and counter-proposals being made by union and employer. It is true that the method requires the reasons for the proposals and counter-proposals to be set out in writing, together with any accompanying 'evidence', on which a bold court might perhaps build a duty to bargain in good faith, but no such obligation, either in its pithy American form or as a British circumlocution, is actually set out.[97]

What is clear is that the issue of non-compliance with an imposed method of bargaining is not for the CAC but for the ordinary courts. Having used the CAC to determine whether an obligation to recognise should be imposed, the legislature did not want to use the CAC to adjudicate upon breaches, as it had done under the 1975 procedure (where the decision on recognition was given to ACAS). The legislation is, however, unusually unforthcoming on the procedure

---

[94] H H Wellington, *Labor and the Legal Process* (New Haven, Conn: Yale University Press, 1968), chapter 2.   [95] EPA 1975, s 15(2).

[96] TULRECA 1992, Sch A1, para 31(5). The parties may, and normally do (see n 93, above), agree a method of bargaining themselves, but, if the voluntary agreement is broken, the only recourse is to the CAC, which may impose a binding statutory method. This set of provisions provides some incentive to the union not to agree a voluntary method with an employer whose good faith it does not trust but to try to go directly to the CAC for an imposed and legally binding method.

[97] The government seemed to think that it had not created a duty to bargain in good faith. See letter from the Minister of State at the DTI, the *Guardian*, 12 February 1999, stating that such a formula would lead to 'complicated legal wrangles over a highly subjective concept'.

for handling complaints of non-compliance with an imposed method, other than to state that the only remedy available shall be specific performance.[98] However, this area has so far proved to be one of the untested parts of the legislation. As indicated above,[99] very few bargaining methods have been imposed by the CAC and none seems to have given rise to litigation for breach of contract. The current and rather traditional remedy of an action for breach of contract before a non-specialised court again perhaps indicates why the drafters of the legislation adopted such a highly specified model for the method of bargaining to be imposed by the CAC: it was important that it should be easy to establish whether the method had been followed or not.

3.3.2.3 *The impact of the procedure and further reform*

It seems clear that the statutory procedure introduced in 1999 did help to generate a climate more favourable to collective bargaining, by stimulating unions to put more resources into organisation and employers to look more favourably on recognition claims. A major part of this stimulus showed up, not in applications to the CAC, but in recognition agreements achieved wholly outside the statutory process.[100] A number of large employers, which had de-recognised unions in the 1980s or early 1990s, quietly re-recognised them and often did so in the period after it was clear that legislation to create a statutory recognition procedure would be put on the statute book but before it was enacted or came into force. However, the overall impact of the more favourable climate on the state of unionisation and collective bargaining in the UK, although significant, was not such as to bring about a reversal of the trends of the previous period. At best, the preliminary findings from the 2004 WERS survey[101] suggested that the previous decline had been halted; at worst, only that it had been significantly slowed down. Thus, union

---

[98] TULRECA 1992, Sch A1, para 31(6). Under the 1975 procedure the CAC's remedy was to adjudicate upon a claim by the union for improved terms and conditions of employment. Thus, an employer who would not bargain in good faith became subject to a form of compulsory unilateral arbitration—arguably a rather appropriate remedy. In Canada there is extensive use of compulsory arbitration if there is a failure to agree in the first negotiations post recognition, whether that failure involves bad faith or not.   [99] See n 93, above.

[100] See S Wood, S Moore, and K Ewing, 'The impact of the trade union recognition procedure' in H Gospel and S Wood (eds), *Representing Workers* (London: Routledge, 2003) at 136–140 and, further, S Moore, S McKay, and H Bewley, *The content of new voluntary recognition agreements 1998–2002* (DTI, Employment Relations Research Series, No 26, 2004). Controversially, however, employers who together with associated employers employ fewer than 21 workers are excluded from the procedure. However, provided this threshold is met, there is no need for the bargaining unit to contain more than 20 workers. For arguments in favour of reform see K D Ewing and Anne Hock, *The Next Step: Trade Union Recognition in Small Enterprises* (Kingston upon Thames: Popularis, 2003).

[101] B Kersley et al, *Inside the Workplace: First Findings from the 2004 Workplace Employment Relations Survey* (London: DTI, URN 05/1057). One difficulty about comparing the 1998 and 2004 surveys, which are otherwise well placed to measure the impact of the Labour governments' legislation, is that the 2004 preliminary results are reported in relation to workplaces with 10 or more workers, whereas the main dissemination of the 1998 findings was based on workplaces with 25 or more workers (see M Cully et al, *Britain at Work* (London: Routledge, 1999). The point is important in this area since small workplaces are less prone to unionisation.

membership was reported at 34% of the workforce (as against 36% in 1998), whilst recognition of unions in workplaces with 25 employees or more was reported at 39% of workplaces in 2004 as against 41% in 1998.[102] Thus, from the unions' point of view, recognition was far from being a problem which had been solved. In particular, the divide between the public and the private sectors of the economy, already evident in 1998, seemed to have become even deeper. Thus, whereas collective bargaining had maintained its position as a determinant of pay in over three-quarters of workplaces in the public sector as between 1998 and 2004, in the private sector it was a determinant in only 11% of workplaces as opposed to 17% in 1998.[103]

One impact of this situation, which was known to those involved in industrial relations, at least in outline, before the WERS survey charted it in detail, was to generate pressure from the unions for reform of the statutory procedure, when the DTI came to review the workings of the 1999 Act in 2003—pressure to which the government was prepared to succumb only to a limited extent.[104] However, in terms of the overall level of collective representation of employees at work, there are inherent limitations on the results likely to be achieved by a union recognition procedure of the type which has been enacted, now on three occasions, in Britain, no matter how much reformed. Recognition is understood in these procedures as essentially a function of union membership, or at least of employee support. Broader notions of union 'representativity', which are not purely membership-driven, as used in some continental labour law systems, have never been part of the British recognition procedures, and would certainly not be consonant with the notion of employee choice which is one of the mainstays of the 1999 procedure.[105] As we have noted above, employee support may be required in a strong form, as under the current procedure, or in a softer form, as under the 1975 procedure, but this should not obscure the fact that both ACAS could not and the CAC cannot accept recognition claims without adequate levels of worker support. From a union organiser's point of view, this creates something of a methodological problem: the best way of showing employee support for recognition is to demonstrate high and growing levels of union membership, but workers are likely to be more willing to join a union once it has been recognised and they are able to obtain relevant services in exchange for their subscriptions. Thus, the thing which is needed to obtain a recognition order is most easily available only once that order has been made (when it is no longer needed for that purpose).

---

[102] Kersley, op cit (n 101, above), 12–13. If workplaces with 10 to 24 workers are taken into account, a significant decline in the rate of recognition can be observed: from 28% of such workplaces in 2004 to 18% in 2004.   [103] Ibid, Table 6.

[104] See DTI, *Review of the Employment Relations Act 1999*, URN 03/606, February 2003.

[105] Linked to this is the limitation that the procedures can be used to obtain recognition only against a single employer (not against multiple employers). In the case of the 1999 procedure, unlike the 1975 one, even associated employers cannot be subject to a single recognition application. For the early post-War decline of multi-employer bargaining in the UK, see LLPP, 3.3.

A union organiser thus has to secure membership, or at least support, in a non-unionised workplace on the promise, explicit or implicit, that recognition will be obtained on behalf of the group in the near future. For this reason, the 1999 procedure contains tight time-limits, often impracticably tight ones, which the CAC must observe[106] in relation to the various stages of the application, for fear that the employer will be able to dissipate support for the recognition claim simply through delay. For the same reason, a neuralgic point about the procedure has been the issue of union access to the workforce in order to solicit support. As we have noted, once the CAC has determined to hold a ballot, the union has a right of access to the employer's premises in order to meet the workers, but no such right is given prior to that, so that the union has to secure the level of support necessary for the CAC to accept its application[107] without a statutory right of access. The 2004 Act added a right for the union, once its application has been accepted but before a ballot is decided on, to have information distributed to the workforce through an independent person, but this new right involves no entitlement of access to the employer's premises.[108] The 2004 Act also strengthened the legal position of the union in the pre-ballot period by introducing[109] the concept of 'unfair practices' which would be committed if either employer or union took certain proscribed actions 'with a view to influencing the result of a ballot' in that period.[110] Initially, the DTI did not propose to make this amendment in the 2004 Act and seems to have been persuaded to do so as a pre-emptive measure rather than because there was extensive evidence of this sort of employer behaviour.[111]

Despite these changes, the fact remains that an application for recognition is likely to be the end rather than the beginning of a union organising process in a

[106] Most of these time limits can be extended by the CAC for good reason, but the Committee attracts criticism if time-limits are extended routinely. Furthermore, the policy underlying the imposition of tight time limits on the CAC is somewhat undermined by the often generous periods afforded to the parties to reach agreement (for example, on the bargaining unit: see para 18 of the Schedule). The policies of encouraging expedition and voluntary agreement are thus in conflict to some degree.

[107] Essentially, that 10% of the proposed bargaining unit are in membership of the union and a majority of the unit 'would be likely' to support the application.

[108] ERA 2004, s 5, adding new paras 19C–F to the Schedule. The distribution, which is at the union's cost, is made via a qualified independent person and the employer is required to make the relevant names and addresses available.

[109] Or, perhaps better, re-introducing. See LLPP, 7.2(a)(ii).

[110] ERA 2004, s 10, introducing new paras 27A–F into the Schedule and supplementing the existing provisions in Part VIII of the Schedule protecting individual employees against detrimental action (which are justiciable before employment tribunals). The action prohibited consists essentially of bribes, coercion, and undue influence. However, it seems not to have been the intention to restrain the employer from putting its case forcefully. As the (draft) Code of Practice on Access and Unfair Practices (2005) puts it: 'It is a fine line, therefore, to distinguish between fair comment about job prospects and intimidatory behaviour designed primarily to scare the workers to vote against recognition'. For an analysis of the operation of such prohibitions in North America see J Godard, *Trade union recognition: statutory unfair labour practice regimes in the USA and Canada* (DTI, Employment Relations Research Series No 29, 2004).

[111] See K Ewing, S Moore, and S Wood, *Unfair Labour Practices: Trade Union Recognition and Employer Resistance* (London: Institute of Employment Rights, 2003).

particular workplace, and the statutory procedure assumes, but does not provide for, success in the earlier stages of union activity. Of course, other parts of labour law do protect the earlier stages of organising, for example, the rules governing a worker's right to be a member of and take part in the activities of a trade union at an appropriate time, which, as we have seen in 3.3.1 above, were also reformed in the 1999 and 2004 Acts. Nevertheless, the union does face a very real difficulty in persuading a sceptical worker that it is worthwhile joining, and remaining for any length of time a member of, a union which does not have collective bargaining rights as against the employer. The union will find it difficult to provide full value to the member in the absence of such rights.[112] This is not an issue which British labour law has traditionally addressed in a direct manner, although indirectly the law has an impact, for example, where a union offers a member in a non-unionised workplace free representation over an employment tribunal claim or in connection with an accident at work.

For this reason a certain amount of excitement was generated by the creation in the 1999 Act of a right in the individual worker to be accompanied at a disciplinary or grievance hearing, normally of course held on the employer's premises, the category of eligible accompanists including a trade union official (whether full-time or lay).[113] The thought was that these provisions, although creating a right only in relation to individual disputes,[114] would give a non-recognised union a basis in the workplace from which it could demonstrate the benefits of membership to the workforce,[115] and some even thought these provisions might be more effective than the recognition procedure itself in expanding union membership.[116] In fact, their impact seems to have been at a rather low level, perhaps because disciplinary and grievance hearings are rather episodic events and so do not afford the union a continuous mechanism for involving itself in the workplace. Nevertheless, the issue of a legal requirement for a form of representation in the workplace, falling short of recognition for collective bargaining, did emerge as a major issue in the second term of the new government as a result of developments in Community labour law, to which we now turn.

---

[112] For this reason some unions offer discounted membership until such time as the union is recognised. The argument in the text does not aim to suggest that an instrumental analysis of what the union can deliver for a prospective member is the only determinant of whether workers are prepared to join trade unions, simply that it is an important factor. See generally A Charlwood, 'Why Do Non-Union Employees Want to Unionize? Evidence from Britain' (2002) 40 BJIR 263.

[113] ERA 1999, ss 10–14. The accompanist has no right to answer questions put to the worker but does have rights to address the meeting on the worker's behalf, which rights were clarified and to some degree extended by the ERA 2004, s 37.

[114] And until the enactment of Part II of the Employment Act 2002 (see above p 66) a right to be represented only if the employer made a disciplinary or grievance procedure available.

[115] Lord McCarthy described the new right as 'a direct inducement to membership': 'Representative consultations with specified employees—or the future of rung two' in H Collins, P Davies, and R Rideout (eds), *Legal Regulation of the Employment Relation* (London: Kluwer Law International, 2000) 530.

[116] William Brown, 'Putting Partnership into Practice in Britain' (2000) 38 BJIR 299 at 303: 'a surer base'.

3.4 Mandatory consultation of employee representatives

3.4.1 Background

The British tradition in workplace representation is the creation of voluntary bargaining arrangements between employers and unions where unions seek to use social sanctions (or the threat of them) to secure both initial recognition and, subsequently, effective bargaining with the employer over terms and conditions of employment. The union acts principally in the interests of its members, though employers for obvious reasons normally seek to apply the outcomes of bargaining to non-member employees, thus creating for unions a considerable free-rider problem, since non-members can usually obtain at least the financial benefits of union membership without joining the union. There is another model[117] of workplace representation varieties of which can be found in some continental European countries and which can be referred to as the 'works council' model of representation. Here, as with a recognition procedure, the representation is required[118] by law, rather than being dependent upon employer and trade union agreement. However, the representatives act in the interests of the workforce as a whole and, most important, are chosen by the workforce as a whole, both union and non-union. The law requires the employer to deal with the employee representatives, not normally through a bargaining mechanism but rather by requiring the employer to supply information about the enterprise to those representatives and to consult with them about certain actions which the employer proposes to take. In some systems the law may even provide that certain decisions may not be taken without the consent of the employee representatives, in which case it must supply some mechanism for dealing with disagreements between employer and representatives, for example, compulsory arbitration. Finally, in a few cases, it may vest the decision wholly in the employee representatives, where it thinks the matter of high importance to the employees and a matter of relative indifference to the employer. The system is normally financed, as far as its direct costs are concerned, by the employer. The law provides sanctions if the employer fails to engage in the necessary interactions and it may, in addition, prohibit the employee representatives from organising industrial action, ie, it may make the legal sanctions the exclusive remedy within the works council system.

Traditionally, British unions have been hostile to such forms of representation. They have preferred the 'single channel' system of representation, where the union is the sole interlocutor between the employer and the employees collectively. This is hardly surprising. Employees may display a lesser propensity to join trade

---

[117] What follows is not an attempt to describe the works council system in any particular country, such structures in fact varying fairly widely across countries.

[118] Generally, the employer's obligation to establish a works council is dependent upon its being asked to do so, by a group of employees or a trade union (the so-called 'trigger mechanism'). On the other hand, there is usually no formal mechanism for abolishing a council, once it has been created.

unions if they think they can obtain the benefits of a collective voice as against the employer through a representation system which they themselves do not have to finance. They may persist in this view, even if in fact the effectiveness of the employee representatives in the statutory system depends heavily upon the training, information, and other resources provided by the union to those representatives, because the union may find it less easy to claim the credit for the beneficial outcomes of a representation system which it does not fully control and where its role is backstage. Even worse, the employer may positively take advantage of the mandatory consultation system to persuade its employees that they do not need the benefits of unionisation and collective bargaining: their desire for 'voice', the employer may argue to the workers, is adequately met by the mandatory consultation system. Of course, there are ways of tying the system of mandatory consultation into that of voluntary collective bargaining, of which some countries have made extensive use and which reduce the threat of the former to the latter. However, there is no guarantee that the system of mandatory consultation will be designed by the legislature so as to minimise the threats to collective bargaining and so pressing for the introduction of a mandatory consultation system has seemed historically to British unions to be a highly risky policy—and certainly not a risk worth taking so long as voluntary collective bargaining flourished. One particular feature of the structure of collective bargaining in Britain has promoted union fears about works councils: its post-war focus on the establishment or enterprise. In those countries where collective bargaining is focused at industry-level, there is potentially space for the development of complementary systems of representation in the establishment or enterprise (through mandatory consultation) and outside the enterprise through multi-employer collective bargaining.[119] Where both systems operate at single-employer level, the chances of destructive competition can be seen to outweigh those of mutual reinforcement.

Thus, for most of the twentieth century British unions did not press for the introduction of mandatory bodies, representative of all the employees, into the enterprise, and seem to have been powerful enough to resist pressures in this direction from other quarters (which pressures were in any event not strong, outside war-time). The exceptions to this statement were periods of national emergency, as with the creation of joint production committees during the Second World War under governmental pressure.[120] After the Second World War the growth of the shop-stewards' movement and workplace collective bargaining pushed mandatory general consultation mechanisms even further down the public policy

[119] The paradigm example is Germany, where the legislature took steps to give the unions some influence over the operation of the works council system. Even where collective bargaining has not occupied the regulatory space within the workplace, the functioning of the works council may still be contested: does it operate, for example, to prevent the spread of union influence within the workplace or does it, rather, reinforce at establishment level the rules agreed in external collective bargaining?

[120] See LLPP, 2.2. Even these were not universal but were strongly encouraged by government in the munitions industries.

agenda. However, it should be noticed that unions were not opposed to legally required consultation mechanisms where they could be sure that these presented no threats to collective bargaining and would serve to extend union influence, as in the nationalised industries.[121] Moreover, although neither government nor unions normally pressed for the creation of consultation machineries, employers remained free to create them and they were always part of the landscape of representation in Britain. In particular, under the influence of human resource management theories in the 1980s and 1990s mechanisms for collective and individual consultation became popular in some quarters. Thus the WERS 2004 survey found that 20% of workplaces with 10 or more employees had joint consultative committees, whilst a further 27% had committees at a higher level within the organisation. And nearly all workplaces used some form of direct communication.[122]

Despite this lack of pressure for a statutory basis for a consultation mechanism, the government, with the enthusiastic support of the TUC, introduced the Information and Consultation of Employees Regulations,[123] which ushered in, as from April 2005, precisely such a system of mandatory, all-employee consultation at enterprise level, initially only for enterprises with 150 or more workers but, by 2008, for all enterprises with more than 50 workers. What produced such a dramatic change in the laws concerning the structures of collective representation at enterprise level in Great Britain? The answer to this question requires an analysis not only of the change of policy which the TUC underwent in this area in the 1990s, but also of the development of the social policy of the European Community in that period and the British government's reactions to these developments.

3.4.2 Union policy: mandatory consultation as a route to collective bargaining

The development of the TUC's policy on mandatory consultation was very much a response to the steep decline in union membership and collective bargaining coverage which was experienced in the 1980s and 1990s, to the point where, as we have seen, the private sector of the economy became a predominantly non-union area. It did not take much insight to realise that the re-introduction of a statutory recognition procedure, based on some notion of majority support, would not by itself be enough to reverse this decline. From the early 1990s the TUC began to produce policy documents which sought to give unions a statutory role in the workplace even where their levels of membership fell short of that needed to secure recognition for the purposes of collective bargaining over terms and conditions of employment. In so doing the TUC aimed to generalise from the limited

---

[121] Ibid.
[122] B Kersley et al, *Inside the Workplace: First Findings from the 2004 Workplace Employment Relations Survey* (London: DTI, URN 05/1057) 14 and 17–19.   [123] SI 2004/3426.

examples of mandatory consultation already present in British law, often as the result of European Directives.[124]

In the first substantial document reflecting a new openness to consultation mechanisms, *Trade Union Recognition* (1991),[125] a phased approach to recognition was put forward, in which a union lacking sufficient support for recognition would obtain lesser rights. In fact, recognition appeared as the 'third rung'[126] on a ladder of which the first rung was the right to facilities provided by the employer and the second was the right to be consulted by the employer over certain issues. However, the crucial feature of this set of proposals, indicating how controversial was the works council model described above, was that the rights so proposed were rights for the union alone, ie, 'single channel' still prevailed. Employee-based, as opposed to union-based, consultation rights were thus rejected at this point. The move beyond union rights was signalled only in 1974 (after a further Labour Party defeat in a general election) when in an interim report to the 1994 Congress, *Representation at Work*,[127] a task force described (though fell short of recommending) a three-rung model in which the second rung of mandatory consultation would consist of a right vested in the employees as a whole to be consulted by the employer over a range of matters through elected representatives

The Report devoted considerable attention to the need to avoid the new structure undermining collective bargaining; indeed, the aim was to use it to promote collective bargaining. Thus, where there was a recognised trade union, the consultation rights were to be vested in the union and there would be no role for the body elected by the employees as a whole; and the consultation rights were not to extend to terms and conditions of employment, which were regarded as the sole province of collective bargaining through a trade union. This latter point would obtain even if there was no recognised trade union in the particular workplace; if the workers wanted collective bargaining over terms and conditions of employment, that would be available only through the union. The policy was to create a situation in which the union could 'demonstrate the benefits of unionisation' (by being active in the consultation system) but also hold out the carrot of the full benefits of unionisation being obtained only by workers who joined the union in sufficient numbers to enable it to claim recognition (thus 'moving to a situation where recognition becomes a natural development for at least some groups of employees').[128]

However, this suggested system proved too much for the union movement as a whole. The final report to the 1995 Congress, *Your Voice at Work*, moved back very substantially to the idea of attaching consultation rights to the union alone

---

[124] See 3.4.4.1, below.
[125] Report to the 1991 Congress. See also K D Ewing, 'Trade Union Recognition—A Framework for Discussion' (1990) 19 ILJ 209.   [126] Lord McCarthy: see n 115, above.
[127] See also Mark Hall, 'Beyond Recognition? Employee Representation and EU Law' (1996) 25 ILJ 15 (this author's work had considerable influence on the formation of TUC policy).
[128] TUC, *Representation at Work*, Interim Report, 1994, para 9.72.

(a threshold of 10% membership was proposed), thus putting on the unions the burden of reaching this membership threshold before any legal rights could be asserted, rather than giving them the opportunity of using a universal system of consultation to build up union membership, if necessary from scratch.[129] There was a rather unclear additional proposal that non-union representatives elected for the purposes of redundancy and transfer consultation (as required by EU law) might in some cases become the bearers of wider consultation rights, but even this proved unacceptable to Congress, and thus by the middle of the 1990s TUC policy was that wider consultation rights were to be via the trade union alone.

It might be thought that the TUC's rejection of a more radical approach to consultation rights did not much matter, since the Labour Party, in its discussions with the TUC in the run-up to the 1997 election, had committed itself only to the implementation of 'rung three' (ie, the statutory recognition procedure) and some minor items at the level of 'rung one', notably the right to be accompanied at disciplinary and grievance hearings.[130] However, as a result of developments in EU law, to which we now turn, the TUC was presented with the opportunity to see mandatory consultation rights become part of British law, albeit in the form akin to that described in the 1994 document and rejected by Congress in 1995.

3.4.3 EU policy on employee involvement

3.4.3.1 Background

For more than a decade after the signing of the Treaty of Rome in 1957 the Community had no significant social policy beyond guaranteeing the free movement of workers. Only in 1972 did the Member States, at a summit in Paris, commit themselves to substantial initiatives in this direction and, even then, without embarking on any amendments to the Treaty which would facilitate social action at Community level. Nevertheless, the Council's Social Action Programme of 1974,[131] which followed up the political agreement reached at the 1972 meeting, was a remarkably wide-ranging document, and it identified as a priority area for Community action, along with eight other topics, 'the progressive involvement of workers or their representatives in the life of undertakings in the Community'. At this period the policy of involvement of workers in employing enterprises was high on the political agenda throughout Europe. In the wake of the waves of

---

[129] The WERS 2004 preliminary results reported that in 64% of workplaces there were no union members (77% in the private sector but only 7% in the public sector), which might be thought to be an argument in favour of the 1994 proposals. The contrary argument (Lord McCarthy, n 115 above, at 458) was that 'it is not easy to see how unions can be expected to do much to promote rung two rights in this vast and unpromising wasteland'.

[130] Above. It should be noted that the government interpreted 'rung one' as an individual, not a union, right in two senses: the right to be accompanied was vested in all employees and the accompanist did not have to be a union official but might be any fellow worker.

[131] OJ C13/1, 21 January 1974.

industrial and political protest which occurred in Europe in the late 1960s, governments were looking anxiously for ways to diffuse workplace discontent. This tended to strengthen the position of trade unions, as the organisations in civil society likely to be able to perform a major role in this process, and of social democratic governments, as more likely than conservative governments to be able to mobilise unions to undertake this task. Part of this process reflected itself in the 'neo-corporatist' involvement of unions in 'social contracts' and such like at the level of the economy as a whole,[132] but an equally important strategy was employee involvement at enterprise level. As a token of the strength of these pressures, it should be remembered that it was at this time that the UK came close to taking the radical step of requiring employee representation on the boards of large, private-sector companies.[133]

At the level of the Community, however, initiatives for employee involvement actually achieved only a very limited success in the 1970s—in essence, Directives dealing with employee consultation over two specific areas of business decision-making, which are discussed further below. Not until the 1990s or even the new millennium did the 1974 initiative achieve significant results, after the Treaty had been amended to facilitate legislation to promote a social policy[134] and, paradoxically, after the initial political impetus for radical involvement mechanisms had dissipated itself.[135] Besides being a tribute to the elephantine nature of policy-making at Community level, the lapse of time between proposal and enactment meant that the ultimate legislation was rather different from what had been envisaged initially. In order to assess this example of late (even retarded) development, however, it is necessary to distinguish firmly between the two types of involvement into which EU policy in this area is conventionally split: participation (meaning employee influence at board level within companies), and information and consultation mechanisms existing outside the corporate structure.

3.4.3.2 Participation and the European Company

The first can be dealt with quite briefly. Although the Community had ambitions in the 1970s to require all Member States to introduce mandatory systems of employee representation at board level, these ambitions have faded over the years. Only in the area of cross-border mergers of companies has Community legislation

---

[132] See LLPP, 7.3(a) and 8.1 for the British experience at this level.   [133] See LLPP, 8.4.

[134] See Title XI of Part Three of the EC Treaty, as established by the Treaty of Amsterdam (1997) and as amended by the Treaty of Nice (2001), which provides an explicit legal base for some types of social legislation. For the history of the changes from 1957 onwards see P L Davies, 'The Emergence of European Labour Law' in William McCarthy (ed), *Legal Intervention in Industrial Relations: Gains and Losses* (Oxford: Blackwell Publishing, 1992) and J Kenner, *EU Employment Law: From Rome to Amsterdam and beyond* (Oxford: Hart Publishing, 2003).

[135] As S Simitis and A Lyon-Caen have remarked, 'it is difficult to identify what social forces influence the legal activity of the Community; to a large extent, its authorities and institutions are free from social pressure': 'Community Labour Law: A Critical Introduction to its History' in P Davies et al (eds), *European Community Labour Law: Principles and Perspectives (Liber Amicorum Lord Wedderburn)* (Oxford: OUP, 1996) 3.

emerged containing a (limited) mandatory participation requirement. Failure here is probably due to the fact that, no matter what the make-up of the Community has been over the years, only about half its members have had national systems requiring participation in private sector companies;[136] and those Member States which did not know such a system were reluctant to accept it via Community law. The most direct assault on the susceptibilities of Member States was the never-adopted draft Fifth Directive in the company law series, which, in its initial form, would have required all Member States to amend their national laws so as to adopt the German or Dutch systems of mandatory employee representation on the upper tier of a two-tier board system in large companies. Although later made more flexible by widening the range of involvement mechanisms available, this proposal has not come close to adoption, even though it was first put forward in 1972.[137]

The Commission's second participation initiative from this period, which has reached the Community statute book (but not until 2001 and coming into effect in October 2004) was the proposal for a European Company (or SE). The SE is an optional form provided by Community law for the incorporation of a company. It is an alternative to the forms of incorporation made available by the national laws of the Member States. It is designed, in particular, to foster cross-border mergers, whether among independent companies or within corporate groups. Again, the original version of the SE proposal would have required participation on the upper tier of a two-tier board.[138] Since the SE is an optional form of incorporation, this requirement might have been thought to be less threatening than the proposed Fifth Directive to the interests of Member States without mandatory participation in their national laws. However, conflict between the two groups of states was as acute here as well. Those without mandatory participation at national level were not willing to forgo the advantages[139] of the SE in order to avoid mandatory participation, whilst those with mandatory participation at national level feared that an SE without mandatory participation would provide an escape route from participation for their national companies. The SE legislation[140] was adopted only on the basis of a compromise by which the Community gave up any ambitions to have a common rule on participation for the SE and dealt with the matter

---

[136] For the position at the time of the adoption of the European Company Statute see the Davignon Report: Group of Experts, *European Systems of Worker Involvement*, Final Report, Brussels, May 1997; for the current situation, see N Kluge and M Stollt, *Board-level Representation in the EU 25*, ETUI, 2004. The figure for mandatory participation looks more impressive if state- or former state-controlled enterprises are included, but the heart of the controversy has always been in the private sector.

[137] For the history of this Directive in more detail see C Barnard, *EC Employment Law* (2nd edn, Oxford: OUP, 2000) chapter 8. [138] For details, see Barnard, ibid.

[139] The extent of which has been subject to debate: cross-border combinations can be achieved, after all, also by means of a take-over or a merger using purely national law mechanisms (see n 141 below). It seems unlikely that many SEs will be formed.

[140] Council Directive 2001/86/EC (OJ L294/22, 10 November 2001) (hereafter 'SE Directive') contains the involvement rules for the SE, transposed into domestic law by Part 3 of the European Public Limited-Liability Company Regulations 2004, SI 2004/2326 (hereafter 'SE Regulations').

simply on the basis that the aim was to prevent opportunistic use of the SE mechanism to avoid national requirements. The compromise, known as the 'before and after' principle, means that an SE is required to have participation arrangements only where one or more of the companies forming the SE is subject to participation arrangements under its national law (and, where there is more than one system operating in the founding companies, the 'most advanced' system will be used in the SE).[141] Companies from national systems which have no mandatory participation requirements can thus form an SE which will not be subject to them either, even if the SE is registered in a state which requires participation in companies formed under its national law.

3.4.3.3 Works councils and similar bodies in continental Europe

By contrast, the Commission's initiatives in the areas of mandatory information and consultation have been much more successful, albeit time lagged. Probably, this can be put down in large part to the different configuration of Member State laws in this area, as contrasted with participation requirements. To be sure, there are again two groups, one with effectively mandatory information and consultation mechanisms in the workplace and one without, but in this case the groups are of unequal size, the 'withouts' consisting principally of the UK and Ireland and the 'withs' of virtually every other Member State. As hinted above, what is revealed is a profound difference in the systems of workplace representation in the UK and Ireland, on the one hand, and in continental Europe, on the other, even taking into account the differences among the continental systems themselves. As we have noted, in Britain the unions, in the shape of active shop stewards, moved into the area of workplace representation after the Second World War, displacing the war-time Joint Production Committees, and carried on collective bargaining at that level in such a way that in the end it undermined multi-employer bargaining at industry level.[142] In continental Europe, by contrast, the period of economic re-building immediately after the Second World War saw the widespread creation of works council-like structures within the workplace, whose purpose was 'to enable employers to consult with their workforces on how to improve economic performance ... and in the process build consensus for managerial decisions in the pursuit of economic progress'.[143] Distributional

---

[141] Actual implementation of this principle is more complicated than it might seem at first sight. See P Davies, 'Workers on the Board of the European Company?' (2003) 32 ILJ 75. The same solution is used in the 10th Directive in the company law series, which also promotes cross-border mergers but where the resulting company is not an SE but a company formed under national law (Directive 2005/56/EC, OJ L310, 25 November 2005).

[142] See LLPP, 6.1.

[143] W Streek, 'Works Councils in Western Europe: From Consultation to Participation' in J Rogers and W Streek (eds), *Works Councils* (Chicago: University of Chicago Press, 1995) 317. This book contains a wealth of insights into the post-War history of works councils in Europe. Some works councils systems pre-date the Second World War, of which the most well-known is the German. See Ruth Dukes, 'The Origins of the German System of Worker Representation' (2005) 19 Historical Studies in Industrial Relations 31.

conflict, by contrast, expressed itself through collective bargaining, which took place largely outside the workplace through multi-employer bargaining.

Although works councils on the Continent went into a period of decline thereafter, the events of the late 1960s led to their revitalisation (or the creation of new structures in the workplace) in the 1970s but now with as much emphasis on the representation of workers' interests as on providing employers with a mechanism through which to consult their employees. The importance placed on representation meant closer ties between the works councils and the unions,[144] but the works councils were still kept separate from collective bargaining which continued to occur either wholly outside the workplace or, if also within the workplace, within a tight framework set by the parties to multi-employer bargaining. It is easy to understand why the continental works councils developments of the 1970s passed the British system by, even though the UK was by no means immune to the industrial and political pressures of that period. Rather, in the UK these pressures expressed themselves in a consolidation of the system of workplace collective bargaining through shop stewards. As we have noted, it was only in proposals for participation at board level that the UK seemed to be part of the Europe-wide institutional changes of the 1970s, because at that level there was indeed a domestic representation gap—albeit one which was not filled in the event because of opposition from a combination of employers and some trade unions to such a radical innovation.[145]

Although the political situation changed again in the economic downturn of the 1980s, on this occasion the works councils structures continued to be important, because their functioning was sufficiently flexible to accommodate without major legislative change a renewed emphasis on the advantages to employers of the consultation mechanism. With the decline of mass-production industries in Europe under the impact of increased global competition in the manufacturing sector and the corresponding growth of flexible and decentralised production strategies, the works councils could be presented as a way of securing the employee commitment (going beyond mere passive obedience to lawful orders) which the new production methods needed for their fully effective implementation. The Community's documentation in the 1990s tended to emphasise as much the value to employers of consultation in producing a flexible workforce as its value to employees in protecting their interests in the continual process of organisational change.[146] What needs to be noticed, however, is that none of the three main rationales for mandatory consultation which have been influential in continental Europe in the post-War period—promoting co-operation on the part of the workforce with the business strategies of the employer, representing the interests of

---

[144] In Streek's words unions were 'given a range of privileges inside the council system to ensure its representativeness' (loc cit, note 143 above, 337). In some cases, as in Italy, the work place structures were in fact union-based, albeit representative of all employees.   [145] See LLPP, 8.4.

[146] See, for example, European Commission, *Green Paper—Partnership for a New Organisation of Work*, COM (1997) 128 final, 16 April 1997.

those at work, and facilitating the 'flexible firm'—neatly align themselves with the narrow rationale developed by the TUC for the 'second rung' in the 1990s, ie, as smoothing the path to recognition for the purposes of collective bargaining at workplace level. Although frequently operating, especially in the second and third phases of their development, as mechanisms for spreading union influence in the workplace, the goal of achieving workplace collective bargaining would have appeared strange to both continental works councils and trade unions, embedded as they were in systems of multi-employer bargaining external to the workplace. Such a development might well also seem threatening to both—facing the works council with the potential loss of its autonomy to the union and the union with possible loss of control over collective bargaining. Consequently, when in the early years of this decade the UK had to implement Community legislation derived from the continental tradition, it was faced with a number of fundamental uncertainties about how the new rules would fit in with established patterns of workplace representation, only some of which uncertainties were resolved in the process of transposition.

3.4.3.4 *From subject-specific consultation to European Works Councils*

However, this is to get somewhat ahead of ourselves. The initial Community commitment to mandatory consultation produced little in the way of legislation, namely subject-specific consultation over redundancies (1975),[147] and transfers of business (1977).[148] The limited nature of these initiatives probably reflected the need to secure unanimous consent of the Member States to mandatory consultation rules under the then available legal bases for Community legislation, thus enabling the 'withouts' to veto any more general proposals and discouraging the Commission from putting them forward. The Single European Act of 1987 made majority voting available in the area of health and safety and the 'framework' health and safety Directive (1989)[149] introduced mandatory consultation obligations in that specific area as well. However, this had little impact in the UK, where mandatory consultation over health and safety matters had been part of domestic law since 1974[150]—an interesting domestic example of a submerged strain in British legislation in favour of consultation in areas not seen as containing topics likely to generate significant distributional conflict.[151]

[147] Directive 75/129/EEC (OJ L39/40, 14 February 1976), now the Council Directive 'on the approximation of the laws of the Member States relating to collective redundancies', 98/59/EC (OJ L255/16, 12 August 1998); see LLPP, 8.3(c).

[148] Directive 77/187/EEC (OJ L61/26, 5 March 1977), now the Council Directive 'on the approximation of the laws of the Member States relating to the safeguarding of employees' rights in the event to transfers of undertakings, businesses or parts of undertakings or businesses', 2001/23/EC (OJ L82/16, 22 March 2001); see LLPP, 10.4(a).

[149] Council Directive 89/391/EEC (OJ L183/1, 29 June 1989), art 11.

[150] See LLPP, 7.3(b).

[151] Also purely domestically driven was the obligation upon employers to disclose information for the purposes of collective bargaining: see LLPP, 8.3(c), provisions currently in TULRECA 1992, ss 181–185.

Any substantial impact of Community consultation legislation on the UK would require the Community to generalise its rules beyond the specific topics mentioned above. That process of generalisation occurred after the amendments made to the EC Treaty as a result of the agreement reached in Maastricht in 1992. This provided for legislation on 'the information and consultation of workers' to be adopted by qualified majority vote.[152] Thus, the states probably most opposed to such legislation at Community level (the UK and Ireland) could no longer block on their own Commission initiatives in this area. Indeed, by opting out of the 'social agreement,' as the arrangements agreed at Maastricht were known, the UK probably facilitated the adoption of such legislation by excluding itself from the debates on it, since, at that time, the results would not be applicable in the UK. It was in this period that the first general consultation instrument was adopted, the Directive on the European Works Council (EWC),[153] which was later extended[154] to the UK without debate when the UK 'opted back' into the social policy arrangements immediately after the election of the Labour government in 1997. This Directive requires multinational undertakings (normally companies, though they need not be)[155] to consult with employee representatives over:

[...] the structure, economic and financial situation, the probable development of the business and of production and sales, the situation and probable trend of employment, investments, and substantial changes concerning organisation, introduction of new working methods or production processes, transfers of production, mergers, cut-backs or closures of undertakings, establishments or important parts thereof, and collective redundancies.[156]

It thus covers a wide range of fairly high-level business decisions likely to have an effect on employment, but steers clear of terms and conditions of employment, which would be regarded as the stuff of collective bargaining.

In fact, the Commission's first successful attempt at general consultation legislation was carefully designed so as to secure Member State agreement.[157] First, by concentrating on top-level decisions in multi-national companies (the Directive

---

[152] Now article 137(1) and (2) EC. By contrast, legislation on the 'representation and collective defence of the interests of workers and employees, including codetermination' requires unanimous consent of the Member States (Art 137(3)).

[153] Council Directive 94/45/EC (OJ L254/64, 30 September 1994)—hereafter 'EWC Directive'.

[154] By Council Directive 97/74/EC (OJ L10/22, 16 January 1998). In fact, many British-based multinationals, being obliged to establish EWCs for their continental European workers, had voluntarily included their British workers in the arrangements in advance of this Directive.

[155] For example, a partnership and many public sector bodies would be covered. However, those parts of the public sector solely concerned with the exercise of public authority are excluded: see Cases C-298/94, *Henke* [1997] ICR 746; C-343/98, *Collino* [2002] ICR 38; C-175/99, *Mayeur* [2002] ICR 1316. The point is important for the scope of all the Community consultation Directives which refer to 'undertakings' rather than 'employers'—for reasons related to the scope of the Community's lawmaking powers.   [156] Annex, para 2.

[157] See M Hall, 'Behind the European Works Councils Directive: the European Commission's Legislative Strategy' (1992) 30 BJIR 547.

applies only to undertakings or groups of undertakings employing workers in at least two Member States of the EEA),[158] the Commission effectively addressed the 'subsidiarity' requirement, that in areas of joint competence the Community should act 'only if and so far as the objectives of the proposed action cannot be sufficiently achieved by the Member States'.[159] By aiming the proposal at the creation of consultative structures operating at the top of the multi-national structure, the Commission sought to legislate on a matter which was necessarily outside the competence of any national legislature, at least on normal principles of comity. The British legislature might legislate, for example, on how a British-based multinational company consulted its workers employed in Britain, but would not normally seek to legislate for the consultation of employees based in other countries, even if decisions taken in Britain were likely to affect the workers employed elsewhere.[160] Secondly, for the same reason, the consultation structure created by the Directive sits on top of and does not seek to replace the existing representative structures created by national law, for the EWC is designed to deal only with decisions having cross-border implications.[161] The Directive thus largely avoided the problem of competition with existing national structures but did at the same time create a major issue about how the Community-level consultation body should be linked to the existing national structures, a problem in effect passed on to the Member States by use of the formula '"employees' representatives" means the employees' representatives provided for by national law and/or practice'.[162]

However, generalisation of the consultation obligation was only one of two significant features of the EWC Directive. The other was the transformation of the consultation rule from a mandatory rule (as it had been in the earlier Directives) into a default rule, ie, a rule capable of being displaced by alternative arrangements agreed between the management of the company and the employee representatives or, in some cases, adopted by the employee representatives unilaterally, which arrangements might even include a decision by the employee representatives to have no special consultation arrangements at multinational level at all.[163] Of course, the default rules (called 'subsidiary requirements' and set out in an Annex to the Directive) substantially constrain the negotiations for alternative arrangements, since each side has an incentive to come to an agreement only if,

[158] That is, the EC, plus Norway, Iceland, and Lichtenstein.
[159] Art 5 EC. An earlier version of the proposal from the Commission, the so-called 'Vredeling' Directive, which applied to all corporate groups, whether national or multinational, had failed over a number of years to obtain sufficient support among the Member States.
[160] Even the Community legislature has this problem, but at a higher level of coverage, so that the Directive applies only to those working within the Community. A further problem arises if, besides having workers outside the Community, the company's headquarters are outside the Community, as they may well be. This problem is solved, or at least addressed, by a rule identifying one of the group's subsidiaries in the Community as the headquarters for the purposes of the Directive. See Art 4(2).
[161] Under the 'subsidiary requirements' (see below) the competence of the EWC is limited to matters concerning the multinational as a whole, or at least two undertakings situated in different Member States: Annex, para 1(a).   [162] Art 2(1)(d).   [163] See Arts 5(5) and 6.

overall, the agreement is viewed as more favourable to it than the default rules. In short, this is an example of bargaining 'in the shadow of the law'. In the EWC Directive displacement of the default rules was provided at two stages. In the period after the Directive was adopted at Community level, but before it was transposed into national law (in principle some two years later), management was given a very wide freedom by Article 13 of the Directive to reach an agreement 'covering the entire workforce, providing for transnational information and consultation of employees'. Article 13 was widely criticised for it seemed to permit the employer to reach this agreement with any interlocutor, no matter that it was not an effective representative of the employees, and the agreement to contain any form of information and consultation arrangement. Nevertheless, it was highly effective in producing action and some three-quarters of the EWC agreements in force today are 'Article 13' agreements.[164]

Article 13 is now a dead letter, even for companies brought into the scope of the Directive by its extension to the UK. However, a group of 100 employees or their representatives may at any time trigger the process for the creation of an EWC, the first stage of which is the establishment of a Special Negotiation Body (SNB), of representatives from each Member State in which the company has employees, whose role is to explore the possibility of agreeing with the employer an alternative to the default rules. Here, the transposing national law is required to specify how the members of the SNB are to be chosen (so that the employer no longer has a free choice of interlocutor), different selection methods thus being quite likely to operate in different Member States. Assuming the SNB does not decide to reject the whole notion of mandatory consultation under the Directive, it and the management have a wide discretion as to the arrangements they negotiate, including a consultation procedure rather than an EWC, but the minimum structural and procedural matters that must be covered in an EWC agreement are specified. These are the so-called 'Article 6' agreements.

If there is failure to agree (though the parties are given the extraordinarily long period of three years to do so),[165] the subsidiary provisions for the establishment of an EWC come into force. These mandate one regular annual meeting of the EWC, the management of the multinational to consider the matters specified above, and extraordinary meetings 'where there are exceptional circumstances affecting the employees' interests to a considerable extent, particularly in the event of relocations, the closure of establishments or undertakings or collective redundancies'.[166] Of course, the subsidiary requirements can operate only if there is some mechanism to select national representatives to the fall-back EWC, which is

---

[164] EC Commission, *Report on the application of the EWC Directive*, COM(2000) 188 final, 4 April 2000, 6. Trade unions in particular had an incentive to reach such agreements since they could operate in their own right under Article 13 and did not have to proceed through the SNB (see below).

[165] Art 7: the parties can truncate this period by simply agreeing to apply the subsidiary requirements.   [166] Annex, para 3.

again a matter for the transposing national laws. There appears to be no obligation on the Member States to choose the same method for selecting representatives to the SNB and fall-back EWC.

Since its introduction in the EWC Directive, the principle of making the Community involvement rules default rules, capable of being displaced by unilateral decision of the employee representatives or by agreement between them and the management of the company, has become an established feature of Community legislation. It is to be found in the Directive dealing with involvement in the SE (discussed above), which, besides provisions on participation, contains consultation rules heavily influenced by the EWC Directive. Both the participation rules and the consultation rules for the SE are default rules, though the freedom of the SNB, either unilaterally or jointly with management, to displace the participation rules is sometimes restricted.[167] The principle is also to be found in the framework Directive on consultation at national level, to which we turn below. The principle represents a recognition on the part of the legislature that those closest to the workplace may be in a better position than the lawmaker to determine how the principle of involvement is to be implemented in a particular enterprise, and even to determine whether that principle should apply at all.

The overall impact of the EWC Directive is difficult to assess. Some quantitative data are available.[168] As of 2004 (ie, before the latest round of enlargement of the Community) it was estimated that 1,800 multinational companies fell within the scope of the legislation (ie, employed at least 1,000 workers in the Community and at least 150 in each of two Member States).[169] Some 640 only (thus slightly over one-third) had established EWCs, despite the ease with which the trigger to establish an EWC can be pulled, ie, by 100 employees or their representatives. In fact, some 400 of the existing EWCs were established under the Article 13 procedure (above) and so without the need to pull the trigger and establish an SNB. Of the rest, probably all were 'Article 6' agreements, though the evidence suggests that the content of such agreements has been heavily influenced by the subsidiary requirements which apply in the absence of agreement. The number of EWC arrangements continues to grow slowly. As is often the case with such structures, an EWC is more likely to exist the larger (in terms of employment) the multinational company is. Thus, three-fifths of companies employing more than 10,000 workers have EWCs, whilst only slightly above one-fifth of companies employing fewer than 5,000 workers have established one. The impact of the EWC on the quality of industrial relations in multinational companies and groups has not been established clearly by empirical research.

---

[167] See P Davies, n 141 above (notably where the SE is formed by transformation of an existing single national company).

[168] See n 164 above; M Carley and M Hall, 'The Implementation of the European Works Council Directive' (2000) 29 ILJ at 107–109; ETUC, 'European Works Councils' <http://www.etuc.org/a/125?var_recherche=works+council+>.   [169] Art 2(1)(a).

3.4.3.5 *National consultation arrangements*

The second general consultation Directive from the EC extended the principle of consultation from multinational companies to purely national employers. This was the Directive establishing a general framework for informing and consulting employees in the European Community (2002).[170] As soon as the EWC Directive was on the Community statute-book, the Commission indicated its intention to initiate the legislative process in relation to national undertakings.[171] Its success in this respect was a singular achievement, not because the arguments for (or against) mandatory consultation at national level are any weaker than those at cross-border level, but because the subsidiarity argument against Community action to bring about such consultation was much stronger in relation to national level consultation. Clearly, the Member States can legislate, and most have legislated, for mandatory consultation within the workplace. The recitals in the 2002 Directive and the arguments in the Commission's earlier consultation documents address subsidiarity mainly through arguments which posit the inadequacy of the existing national laws. However, it is far from clear that the Community satisfies the requirements of Art 5 EC simply by taking a different view of the policy balance from that adopted at Member State level.

For more pragmatic reasons Member States might also oppose Community legislation in this field, those without mandatory legislation at national level wishing to maintain that position and those with it seeing no need for Community legislation and perhaps not wishing to have to change particular aspects of the national rules. The concerns of the latter and bigger group of states the Directive seeks to address by remaining at the level of high principle and explicitly making the Directive's provisions minimum standards. Article 4(2) of the Directive obliges Member States to introduce information provision in respect of 'the recent and probable development of the undertaking's activities and economic situation'; consultation over 'the situation structure and probable development of employment' within the undertaking; and consultation 'with a view to reaching agreement' over decisions 'likely to lead to substantial changes in work organisation or in contractual relations'. However, the Directive does not seek to lay down the mechanisms through which these interactions should take place, even to the limited extent that the EWC Directive does. The Member States in their transposing legislation are to 'determine the practical arrangements' for exercising the rights created by the Directive (Art 4(1)). Thus, it is inaccurate to speak of this Directive as the 'national works council Directive' since it does not require the Member State to establish a system of works councils.

The Commission was also keen to introduce the default-status principle, as successfully deployed in the EWC Directive, but again this was not welcome in all

---

[170] European Parliament and Council Directive 2002/14/EC (OJ L80/29, 23 March 2002)— hereafter 'national framework Directive'.

[171] Medium Term Social Action Programme 1995–1997, Communication from the Commission, 12 April 1995, p 16.

Member States, most of whose national consultation laws were entirely mandatory in character. On the other hand, the Commission could see that the principle might help to make its proposals more palatable to the 'without' states. These conflicting considerations were resolved by making the choice between mandatory and default status for the consultation principle of the Directive itself a matter for Member State choice.[172] The Directive also refrained from laying down any mechanism, equivalent to the SNB, through which negotiations over an alternative to the Directive's provisions could be facilitated, in Member States which chose the default approach. Again, such matters were left to the Member States.

As to the 'without' states, mainly the UK and Ireland, they could not block the proposal by themselves and so meeting the concerns of the 'with' states helped the Commission ultimately to isolate the 'withouts'. The only substantial concession obtained by the UK and Ireland, simply on grounds of being 'withouts', was to be found in the transitional provisions of Article 10, whereby states where 'there is no general, permanent and statutory system of information and consultation of employees' had until March 2008 to apply the Directive to all undertakings with more than 50 employees (150 being the threshold from 2005 until March 2007 and 100 in the following year).[173]

However, the Commission suffered a significant defeat by being forced to drop a part of its initial proposal to which it attached considerable importance. In the Commission's eyes one of the weaknesses of national consultation laws lay in the inadequacy of the sanctions which could be applied to employers for breach of the consultation obligations, and it proposed to remedy this by making a managerial decision so taken ineffective, at least in relation to the contracts of employment of the workers concerned. This was a novel proposal for a number of Member States and it was not universally welcomed. The provision does not appear in the adopted version of the Directive even though it was still there as late as the Commission's amended proposal of May 2001.[174]

3.4.3.6 Assessment

The Community, and especially the Commission, has had considerable, though not unqualified, success in pushing forward Community initiatives requiring consultation of employees across the Community, at least on a default basis. This was reflected in the Charter of Fundamental Rights of the European Union of 2000,[175] article 27 of which lists consultation as a fundamental right: 'workers or their representatives must, at the appropriate levels, be guaranteed information and consultation in good time in the cases and under the conditions provided for by Community law and national laws and practices'. Participation requirements at Community level, by contrast, have emerged only in relation to cross-border

---

[172] Art 5.
[173] There is an alternative set of thresholds based on establishment size, but the UK has chosen to apply the Directive to undertakings, not establishments.
[174] COM (2001) 196 final, 23 May 2001.   [175] OJ C364/1, 18 December 2000.

mergers, and then in a highly relativistic form. They were not mentioned in the Charter, probably wisely in view of their absence from the private sector of half the Member States of the Community, but nevertheless the absence of a reference to participation constitutes a contrast with the earlier Community Charter of the Fundamental Social Rights of Workers (1989)—which the UK did not sign— where participation was dealt with alongside consultation. Collective bargaining, by contrast, does appear as a fundamental right in the 2000 Charter. Article 28 provides:

Workers and employers, or their respective organisations, have, in accordance with Community law and national laws and practices, the right to negotiate and conclude collective agreements at the appropriate levels . . .

This is a surprising provision, since the Community has done little to promote collective bargaining, other than the political version of it known as the 'social dialogue', which constitutes an alternative to traditional lawmaking at Community level.[176] However, more closely considered, Article 28 perhaps is dealing not so much with any entitlement[177] of the union to be recognised by the employer but with entitlements (as against the state) of employers and unions jointly to engage in collective bargaining if they so wish.[178] Whatever the true import of Article 28, the current position seems clear: of the three main methods of representation within the undertaking which can be identified in Europe, Community law contains significant provisions on consultation through non-union bodies and little on either participation within the company or collective bargaining. The absence of significant participation requirements posed no particular policy challenges for the British government, but the question of how to relate the consultation rules to the existing system of collective bargaining certainly did and it is to that issue that we now turn.

3.4.4 Mandatory consultation and British labour law

3.4.4.1 *Subject-specific consultation*

The issue identified at the end of the previous paragraph presented itself even when Community law contained only subject-specific consultation requirements. In the 1970s, British governments (both Labour and Conservative) adopted what then seemed the obvious approach of linking the consultation obligation firmly to

---

[176] See Arts 138 and 139 EC. The absence of collective bargaining, as normally understood, from the Community's agenda was roundly criticised by Professor Wedderburn, 'European Community Law and Workers' Rights after 1992: Fact or Fake?' in *Labour Law and Freedom* (London: Lawrence & Wishart, 1995).

[177] The extent to which the Charter creates rights is in any event debatable. See B Hepple, Note (2001) 30 ILJ 225.

[178] Article 6 of the European Social Charter 1961 (of the Council of Europe) is much clearer on this point, treating the right to bargaining collectively as encompassing a duty on states party to the Charter to promote voluntary collective bargaining.

the institutions of collective bargaining. Relying on the standard provision in the consultation Directives that the employee representatives were those 'provided for by national laws and/or practice', the legislation transposing both the redundancy and transfers Directives required the employer to consult only with the representatives of any recognised trade union, which had the consequence that, in the absence of a recognised trade union, no consultation obligation arose. This rule eliminated any competitive threat to collective bargaining from the consultation requirement; on the other hand, it also removed any potential for the consultation function to be used by non-recognised unions to obtain a foothold in the undertaking. Some twenty years later, in 1994, the ECJ, in what was surely a misreading of the Directive, held that this tight linkage to collective bargaining was an inadequate transposition of the Directive on the part of the UK and that where there was no recognised union some other mechanism had to be put in place for the selection of employee representatives who could engage in the required consultation.[179] The British governments responded to the judgment by providing for a system of elected representatives for consultation in these two areas. In the case of the then Conservative government this was done by permitting the employer to consult through the alternative mechanism, even if there was a recognised trade union in place—a provision more ideological than practical.[180] However, the Labour government elected in 1997 changed the law to the present configuration, in which consultation must be through the recognised trade union, if there is one ('union priority'), as well as making some further changes designed to enhance the independence and effectiveness of the elected representatives.[181]

In this way the debate over 'single channel' (union only) or 'dual channel' (union and elected representatives of the whole workforce) forms of workplace representation was launched in the UK. There is little doubt that, had the ECJ taken its decision in the 1970s, it would have been met with the strongest condemnation from the trade unions (and, indeed, many employers). However, given the decline of collective bargaining since then and the development within the union movement itself of a debate on the role of mandatory consultation (see 3.4.2 above), the ECJ decision served to stimulate that debate, though in an often confused way, and to strengthen the position of those who were arguing

---

[179] Cases C-382 and 383/92, *Commission v UK* [1994] ECR I-2479; see P Davies, Note (1994) 23 ILJ 272: the Directives were adopted on the basis that the consultation obligations would be attached to whatever national representative institutions existed, not on the basis that new institutions would have to be created for this purpose.

[180] Collective Redundancies and Transfer of Undertakings (Protection of Employment) (Amendment) Regulations 1995, SI 1995/2587.

[181] DTI, *Employees' Information and Consultation Rights on Transfers of Undertakings and Collective Redundancies: Public Consultation*, February 1998, URN 97/988. The changes were made by the Collective Redundancies and Transfers of Undertakings (Protection of Employment) (Amendment) Regulations 1999, SI 1999/1925. For the current provisions see TULRECA 1992, ss 188 and 188A and the Transfer of Undertakings (Protection of Employment) Regulations 2006, SI 2006/246, regs 13–14.

that mandatory consultation should not be viewed in single channel terms. The principle raised by the ECJ decisions was a fundamental one for the British system of workplace representation, but subject-specific consultation constituted only a minor part of the landscape of employee representation. Much more challenging for the British government was the question of how it should transpose the EWC and national framework Directives into domestic law.

3.4.4.2 Transposition of the EWC and SE Directives

The central issue in relation to the general Directives was how the British government would exercise the powers given it to determine the rules for the selection of the employee representatives of the British workers. As far as the EWC Directive and its close companion, the SE Directive, were concerned, the Directives themselves made it clear that the 'recognised union only' solution was not permissible. Thus, the EWC Directive, whilst leaving it to the Member States to establish the machinery for choosing the members of the SNB, stated that in undertakings 'where there are no employees' representatives through no fault of their own, [employees] have the right to elect or appoint' its members.[182] Equally, the members of the fall-back EWC were to consist of employees of the multinational 'elected or appointed from their number by the employees' representatives or, in the absence thereof, by the entire body of employees'.[183] The national framework Directive, as befits its more general level, contained no such provisions, but it is clear that the approach of the ECJ in the case of the specific Directives had to be applied to it, if only because of its close linkage with those specific Directives.[184] However, this still left to be decided at national level the crucial question of how closely the traditional union-based collective bargaining system was to be linked to the consultation arrangements and, in particular, whether the potential of the consultation system to promote union membership and collective bargaining was going to be maximised in the design of the transposing domestic legislation. For example, would the rule of 'union priority', so recently adopted in relation to redundancies and transfers, be applied here as well?

It quickly became clear from the DTI's consultative document of July 1999 on the EWC Directive[185] that it did not intend to apply any principle of union priority in the domestic regulations, ultimately adopted as the Transnational Information and Consultation of Employees Regulations 1999.[186] Its argument was that the 'democratic legitimacy' of the representatives would be enhanced if they had been elected in a secret ballot or ballots of the whole workforce. This principle was to be applied to the selection of the British representatives on both

---

[182] Art 5(2)(a). Ditto the SE Directive: Art 3(2).

[183] Annex, para 1(b). Ditto the SE Directive, Annex, Part I(a).

[184] Framework Directive, Art 9.

[185] DTI, *Implementation in the UK of the European Works Council Directive*, July 1999, URN 99/926, pp 22–23.   [186] SI 1999/3323—hereafter the 'TICE Regulations'.

the SNB and the fall-back EWC—the selection method for representatives in voluntary agreements being left to the parties to those agreements. With one limited exception, a recognised union was to have no formal role in the selection of the representatives. This approach was in sharp contrast with the transposition rules adopted in the continental European states, where the works council or the trade union was given either an exclusive or a priority role in the selection of representatives.[187]

In the case of the SNB representatives the TICE Regulations provided for selection in a ballot of the employees (organised by the employer but under the gaze of an independent scrutineer), except in the rare case where there already was an elected general consultation body in the undertaking which represented all its employees—in which case that body would make the selection.[188] Union activists, including non-employee officials of a recognised union who represented the employees in negotiations with the employer,[189] might stand in the elections, but their selection would depend upon their obtaining the requisite support in the ballot. As to the members of the fall-back EWC, the wording of the Directive (above) might appear to give the employee representatives (ie, the recognised union if there was one) the task of selecting the representatives. However, the government interpreted that wording as requiring the recognised union to represent all the workers in the undertaking (again, a rare situation), in the absence of which (or a general elected consultative body meeting the same criterion) a ballot of the workforce was again imposed.[190] It is perhaps unnecessary to add that the union, in contrast to the position in some continental countries, was given no preference in the ballot arrangements, for example, an exclusive right to nominate candidates. Thus, the approach favoured by the TUC as a consequence of its debates in the middle of the 1990s (either union-only consultation rights or elected representatives only as a fall-back where no union mechanism existed) failed to carry the day.

It is not at all easy to understand why the government sought to keep collective bargaining structurally separate from the system of consultation through the EWC, having only the previous year adopted a rather different policy in the area of subject-specific consultation. In part, the timing of the need to transpose the EWC Directive was unfortunate, coinciding as it did with the discussions on the Employment Relations Bill, which contained the proposed statutory recognition procedure. Given its general policy of seeking to keep business support for its policies, the government may have thought it should give priority to the recognition

---

[187] Carley and Hall, n 168 above, at 110–111.

[188] TICE Regulations, 13–15. However, such general consultative bodies may become a more general feature of British industrial relations under the impact of the ICE Regulations, discussed below.

[189] Reg 13(3)(c) and 2(1)—definition of 'employees' representative'.

[190] Schedule, para 3 and reg 2(1)—definition of 'employees' representative'. The Regulations did not seek to depart from the provision of the Directive that the members of the default EWC should be employees of the undertaking, so that full-time union officials were excluded.

procedure, where it had given a clear political commitment to the unions and which it may have though likely to be more important than a measure applying only within multinational undertakings. Business itself was strongly opposed to the EWC Directive. The CBI played an important part within the European employers' federation, UNICE, in securing the latter's refusal to negotiate with ETUC over this proposed Directive, thus forcing the Commission to proceed with legislation of the standard type rather than being able to delegate the matter to a social partners' agreement.

However this may be, the principle set out in the TICE Regulations was maintained in the transposition of the later Directives. The European Public Limited Liability Company Regulations 2004,[191] transposing the SE Directive, adopted the same approach to the selection of the British members of the SNB required under that Directive, with the unfavourable twist from the unions' point of view that union full-time officials could stand as candidates only if the management agreed.[192] With regard to the selection of the members of the fall-back representative body, however, under the 2004 Regulation the method of selection was left to the SNB,[193] perhaps so as not further to delay the formation of the SE, whose registration is conditional upon employee involvement matters having been settled. Nevertheless, even then, it is still elected representatives, rather than union appointees, who choose the method.

3.4.4.3 *The framework Directive and the ICE Regulations*

The transposition of the EWC Directive presented the government with major issues to resolve, especially in the area of choice of representatives, but even more significant policy challenges faced it as a result of the adoption of the framework Directive on consultation, transposed into British law by the Information and Consultation of Employees Regulations 2004.[194] The framework Directive was politically a much more sensitive instrument because it would apply eventually to a much larger number of undertakings than the EWC Directive. Moreover, as we have seen, the Directive, whilst laying down the principle of consultation, contained very few provisions about the machinery by which the principle was to be implemented, whether by way of voluntary agreement or fall-back provisions. The government's strategy for effecting the transposition of the Directive was to generate a high level of consensus between employee and employer representatives on the new legislation. It consulted on the proposed legislation on three occasions (2002, 2003, and 2004) and achieved the considerable political coup of inducing the CBI and TUC to produce an agreed set of principles for the transposition of the Directive.

---

[191] SI 2004/2326.
[192] Regs 23–25. Moreover, under the 2004 Regs the consultative committee, which displaces the ballot process, does not have to consist of elected members.
[193] Sch 3, para 1(c).   [194] SI 2004/3426—hereafter 'ICE Regulations'.

The DTI's first consultation document[195] set the broad outlines of the government's approach. It put forward the view that consultation of employees in advance of important decisions was a way of both securing fairness for workers and promoting productive efficiency, by generating high levels of trust and cooperativeness between employers and employees. It was equally concerned to stress that its support for consultation did not translate into support for a particular mechanism for delivering the consultation. In particular, whilst continental works council mechanisms might be useful sources of ideas for appropriate machinery, the framework Directive did not mandate their use, and the document indicated some scepticism about their general value in a British context. Moreover, despite the absence in the past of a legal requirement for general consultation mechanisms, a wide variety of such mechanisms could be found in practice in Britain and the government wished to permit as many as possible to qualify under the transposing legislation. Thus the WERS 1998 survey had found that 50% of workplaces with 25 or more employees had some form of joint consultative committee, though employers and employees differed markedly on how well they thought these bodies functioned.[196] Further, nearly all workplaces had some form of system for direct communication with the employees (ie, not through representatives) but the implications of this fact for the design of the transposing legislation were to turn out to be controversial. Overall, in the document's hackneyed phrase, it would be wrong to adopt a 'one size fits all' approach to the transposition of the Directive. The approach of the 2002 document was consistent with the stance which had been adopted by the UK in the negotiations at Community level on the framework Directive: scepticism about mandatory consultation through Community law (but not opposition to the practice of consultation) coupled with a strong desire, if there was to be Community-level legislation, for as much flexibility as possible for Member States and the social partners in the implementation of the principle.[197]

Between this first consultation document, which remained at a high level of debate and contained no draft regulations, and the second,[198] which did contain such a draft, the government achieved its goal of engaging the CBI and TUC in the transposition process. Whilst these two organisations had made some headway in reaching an agreement on the recognition procedure in advance of the 1999 Act, most of the difficult issues relating to that machinery could not be agreed and had to be settled by the government. By contrast, the two organisations, with governmental assistance, managed to reach agreement on the way to

[195] DTI, *High Performance Workplaces: the role of employee involvement in a modern economy*, July 2002 (hereafter '2002 consultation document').

[196] 70% of employers thought they functioned well but only 30% of employees did so.

[197] Mark Hall, 'Assessing the Information and Consultation of Employees Regulations' (2005) 34 ILJ 103 at 108.

[198] DTI, *High Performance Workplaces: Informing and Consulting Employees*, July 2003 (hereafter '2003 consultation document').

transpose the framework Directive within the structure of principles set out in the 2002 consultation document. The 2003 consultation document reproduced that agreement but sought no consultation on it;[199] consultation (which included 'ten regional roadshow events')[200] was confined to the draft Regulations, which the government had produced on its own responsibility in order to put the tripartite agreement into legislative form. After considering the responses to the 2003 document,[201] the government held one further brief round of consultation in the draft Regulations, which were then enacted in a form which embodied, substantially unaltered, the original tripartite agreement. For the government this way of proceeding enabled them to tie the top representative organs of both employers and employees into the resulting rules, whilst those organisations presumably obtained more influence over the rules than would have been the case had they been simply lobbying from outside. However, both organisations had to work within a basic framework laid down by the government in the 2002 consultation document.

The main features of the final Regulations, based on the CBI/TUC agreement, were the following. First, the regulations did not operate automatically in relation to the employers covered by them but began to bite only if a 'trigger' was pulled. Secondly, the option to make the Directive's provisions default rules was taken up and two main ways of opting out of the default rules provided. Thirdly, maximum flexibility was given to the parties in the negotiation of arrangements to replace the default rules. Fourthly, broadly the same policy in relation to the choice of employee representatives was adopted as under the ICE Regulations, except that greater legislative effort was devoted to ensuring the democratic legitimacy of the agreements arrived at by those representatives. Each point will now be briefly elaborated.

On the employee side the trigger was set at a request from at least 10% of the workforce, subject to a minimum of 15 employees and a maximum of 2,500, but without, in contrast to the TICE Regulations, any provision for a representative of the requisite number of employees (for example, a trade union) to pull the trigger on their behalf.[202] The employer, by contrast, was free to pull the trigger at any time.

Two opportunities for negotiating alternatives to the default rules were provided, one before the trigger was pulled and the other after it, the so-called 'pre-existing' and 'negotiated' agreements respectively. It is to be noted, however, that,

---

[199] See its chapter 1.

[200] DTI, *Responses to the Consultation Document High Performing Workplaces – Informing and Consulting Employees*, July 2004, para 1. This wording perhaps indicates that the government was as much concerned with selling as with consulting about the draft Regulations.

[201] The most significant changes made were probably those which enabled pre-existing or negotiated arrangements concluded at higher or lower levels than that of the undertaking to count under the Regulations, provided they met the Regulations' other requirements.

[202] ICE Regulations, reg 7. Because of the need for individual requests, elaborate arrangements had to be made to enable the employees, if they wished, to keep their identities from the employer by making the request via the CAC.

in contrast to the EWC provisions, an agreement counts as 'pre-existing' under the ICE Regulations even if it is negotiated after the transposition of the framework Directive into national law, provided it is agreed before the trigger is pulled in relation to a particular undertaking.[203] There are interesting variations between the TICE and ICE Regulations in respect of the regulation of the agreements reached to displace the default machinery. Along one dimension, such agreements are more stringently regulated than their equivalents under the TICE Regulations, because of the requirements in the ICE Regulations for employee approval of such agreements. The TUC had lost the battle for union exclusiveness or even priority, but one can perhaps detect its hand in these approval provisions. Especially in relation to pre-existing agreements, the TUC may well have feared that, without these controls, the employer would be well placed to do a 'sweet heart' deal with inadequately prepared and non-union employee representatives, thus both failing to give the employees any real protection and blocking later access to the legislation on the part of the employees, perhaps now encouraged and supported by a union.

Employee approval has two main aspects.[204] First, pre-existing agreements do not count at all for the purposes of the Regulations unless they have been approved by the employees. Merely reaching agreement with representatives is not enough, although the Regulations do not specify what employee approval means.[205] Secondly, a pre-existing agreement, even one meeting the legislative criteria, does not of itself protect the employer against the need to negotiate if the employees pull the trigger. Instead, in such a case the employer may, if it so wishes, hold a ballot on whether the pre-existing agreement shall continue in force or whether negotiations shall begin for a new arrangement. If the majority of those voting in a ballot, representing at least 40% of the employees as a whole, vote in favour of the request for fresh negotiations, the employer must enter into them, despite the existence of the pre-existing agreement.[206] In other words, the pre-existing agreement does not prevent the employees from pulling the trigger, but it does make the trigger a heavy one to pull, by in effect raising the level of employee approval required to initiate the negotiations (unless the employer is willing to forgo the pre-existing agreement).

---

[203] Reg 2.   [204] Reg 8.

[205] This is left for the CAC to decide, with such help from the DTI's Guidance (DTI, *The Information and Consultation of Employees Regulations 2004: DTI Guidance* (2005)) as it may derive. It has been held that approval can be given by a recognised trade union where that union has majority membership among the workers concerned: see *Stewart* v *Moray Council* [2006] IRLR 592 (EAT). The CAC is the main dispute resolution body under the Regulations, though disputes arising out of the operation of a pre-existing agreement (as opposed to a dispute about the impact of such an agreement on the operation of the trigger) do not fall within the jurisdiction of the CAC; rather the parties are left to specify the relevant machinery as part of their agreement.

[206] Again this tracks the recognition legislation, where these criteria (related to a bargaining unit) are applied to ballot approval of a union's claim to recognition. If the proposal to initiate negotiations fails to attract the stipulated level of support, another challenge to the pre-existing agreement may not be mounted for three years: reg 12(1)(c).

In addition to using pre-existing agreements the employer may displace the standard rules[207] by negotiating an agreement with the employee representatives after the trigger has been pulled, either by the employees or itself. If an agreement is reached,[208] it will be effective to displace the standard rules, which apply in default of agreement, but again subject to approval conditions. If all the representatives sign the agreement, that will meet the approval requirement. If they do not, a ballot of the workforce must be held and 50% approval of those voting obtained.[209] In other words, the Regulations seem to envisage the risk of the employer 'buying off' some of the representatives, perhaps those closest to management, so as to secure majority approval for a weak agreement.[210] Where the negotiating representatives are split, the Regulations thus put the matter into the hands of the employees as a whole, rather than letting the representatives decide on a majority basis, as the EWC Directive does.

Along a second dimension, however, agreements displacing the fall-back machinery are unregulated. Continuing the approach adopted in the EWC provisions, very little is said about the substantive content of negotiated or pre-existing agreements. They must cover the whole workforce (though this may be done in more than one agreement) and must set out the circumstances in which information is to be provided and consultation is to take place, but are not required to track the consultation requirements of the standard provisions.[211] Thus it appears that a voluntary agreement might fail to cover any of the topics required to be consulted on under the default rules, and might instead provide for consultation over terms and conditions of employment, and yet still qualify under the Regulations. This approach again underlines the crucial importance of the approval requirements as the main protection for the employees against inadequate agreements.

Even more important, both pre-existing and negotiated agreements may provide for the information to be given to, and the consultation to take place with, the employees directly rather than through their representatives.[212] Given the prevalence of direct communication in existing practice, the CBI and the government were keen to preserve its legitimacy under the Regulations. However, the legality of this method of transposing the Directive is open to question. The purpose of the Directive was to establish information and consultation mechanisms and both these terms were defined exclusively by way of an interaction between the employer and the employees' representatives.[213] For this reason,

[207] Set out in Part IV of, and Schedule 2 to, the Regulations.

[208] In this case the period for agreement is the much more reasonable one of, in effect, nine months from the date of the employee request to begin negotiations, unless extended by agreement of the employer and majority of the representatives: reg 14(3) and (5).

[209] Reg 16. Alternatively 50% approval in writing from individual employees is enough—a potentially useful provision in small workplaces, especially as reg 16(5) does this time require the ballot to be fair and secret, though still not independently supervised.

[210] The scope for such opportunistic behaviour is enhanced by the employer's power to pull the trigger itself (reg 11), so that it can choose the moment for the negotiations.

[211] Regs 8 and 16.   [212] Regs 8(1)(d) and 16(1)(f).

[213] Arts 1(1) and 2(f) and (g) of the framework Directive.

among others, the Regulations were made, not under the European Communities Act 1972, which permits the use of delegated legislation to transpose Community *obligations* of the UK, but under the specially enacted section 42 of the Employment Relations Act 2004, conferring wider powers. However, the crucial question is not whether the provisions on direct consultation are required by the Directive—they clearly are not—but whether their inclusion has prevented proper transposition by the UK of the obligations which have been created by that Directive, ie, to provide for information and consultation of employee representatives, as there defined. The consequences of an agreement on direct consultation are that, in the case of a pre-existing agreement based on this form of consultation, the trigger is made substantially more difficult to pull; and, in the case of a negotiated agreement, access to the standard information and consultation provisions, which envisage consultation only through representatives, is blocked for at least three years,[214] potentially contrary to the wishes of at least a minority of the workforce. It is difficult indeed to see the three-year bar as falling within the Directive's permission for the Member States to allow management and labour to define through negotiated agreement 'the practical arrangements for informing and consulting employees',[215] given the definition of those terms in the Directive. Recital 16, whilst stating that the Directive is 'without prejudice' to systems of direct consultation, adds the crucial rider that the employees 'are always free to exercise the right to be informed and consulted through their representatives'. As to the 40% trigger, the issue would seem to be whether such a high level of 'trigger' is contemplated by Recital 15, as interpreted together with Recital 16.

Finally, in relation to choice of employee representatives, the ICE Regulations largely tracked the policy choices made in the TICE Regulations, ie, no union priority and a strong preference for representatives elected by the whole workforce. In relation to pre-existing agreements, as under the TICE Regulations, nothing is said about the persons with whom the agreement must be negotiated.[216] As far as negotiated agreements are concerned the Regulations do here specify how representatives are to be chosen. Once the Regulations have been triggered, the employer's first duty in such a case is to make arrangements for the employees to elect or appoint 'negotiating representatives'.[217] Beyond giving each employee an entitlement to participate in the selection process, the Regulations are sparse on the details of that process, not even providing that, in the case of a ballot, the ballot must be secret or supervised in any way and leaving it unclear whether non-employee union officials may be candidates. Finally, under the standard rules applying in default of agreement, the employer must make arrangements for a ballot of the workforce to elect representatives (normally on the basis of one representative for every twenty-five employees), who must themselves be employees of the undertaking. The ballot must be a secret one and compliance with this and the other requirements of the ballot is to be ensured by the

---

[214] Reg 12(1)(a).   [215] Art 5.   [216] See reg 8(1).   [217] Reg 14.

appointment of a ballot supervisor.[218] This tracks pretty closely the procedure for the appointment of representatives under the subsidiary requirements of the TICE Regulations, except that, apparently, a ballot has to be held under the ICE Regulations even if a recognised trade union does represent all the employees in the undertaking. Moreover, the fallback arrangements under the ICE Regulations are even more exiguous than those under the TICE Regulations in providing a framework for the representatives, once chosen, to interact with the employer: the ICE Regulations simply deal with the substance of the interaction (by copying out the Directive's requirements) but leave it to the parties to generate the machinery through which that interaction shall happen.[219]

3.4.4.4 Assessment

The ICE Regulations produced in the event an almost complete formal divorce between the rules on consultation and the rules and practices of collective bargaining. On the one hand, the existence of an agreement establishing collective bargaining over terms and conditions of employment and applying to the whole workforce of an undertaking would not prevent 10% of the workforce from triggering negotiations over a consultation mechanism, leading to either a negotiated consultation agreement or the application of the standard provisions, operating alongside the collective agreement and through a set of elected non-union representatives. This would be the case even if the collective agreement had been imposed by the CAC as a result, initially, of a recognition application. On the other hand, the existence of a consultation mechanism covering the whole of the workforce, even one imposed under the Regulations, would not prevent a union from applying to the CAC for collective bargaining over pay, hours, and holidays or the CAC from imposing a recognition order, provided the application had the requisite degree of support from the employees. Thus, the statutory recognition machinery and the ICE Regulations seem to run on parallel tracks. At a formal level, the only awareness of the potentiality for overlap between union- and non-union-based forms of representation is to be found in relation to consultation over redundancies and transfers. The framework Directive states that it operates without prejudice to those provisions,[220] so that an employer must consult over those matters as prescribed by the subject-specific Directives, ie, under the UK rules with the recognised union if there is one.[221] Consultation over these matters also falls within the framework Directive,[222] in the UK thus normally with elected representatives, even if there is a recognised union. The conflict was resolved, but for the standard provisions only, by releasing the employer from its consultation duty under the ICE Regulations, once its specific obligations to consult have come into force and upon notification to the 'standard' employee representatives.[223]

---

[218] Reg 19 and Sch 2.   [219] See reg 20.   [220] Art 9.
[221] See 3.4.4.1, above.   [222] Art 4(2)(c).
[223] Reg 20(1)(c) and (5). For negotiated and pre-existing agreements the parties are left to sort out the issue for themselves, though clearly they cannot contract out of the specific statutory obligations.

In practice, of course, in well-organised workplaces such parallelism is not likely to be found, for there are many ways in which, as a matter of fact, the collective bargaining and consultation systems may link up with one another. For example, in a well-organised workplace the union may well be able to dissuade the employer[224] or the employees from pulling the trigger. To this end, the union and the employer may agree to extend their collective agreement to cover consultation over the issues dealt with in the Regulations. Such an extended collective agreement, either on its own or together with other arrangements, may qualify as a pre-existing agreement, thus raising the level of employee support needed effectively to pull the trigger.[225] Even if the trigger is pulled, the union activists may succeed in getting themselves elected as negotiating representatives and then secure a close alignment between the collective agreement and the negotiated consultation agreement. It may not be too optimistic to predict that in such workplaces the Regulations will operate so as to deepen the interaction between employer and union, rather than lead to the setting up of a competing structure.

However, we have seen that the domestic debate has not focused on such workplaces but rather on the impact of the consultation requirements on the majority of workplaces, at least in the private sector, where there are some union members, but no recognition, or no union members at all. What impact could the Regulations have there? One possible outcome is that very little will happen because neither employees nor employers have an interest in setting in motion the machinery for establishing consultation arrangements. The initial reaction to the ICE Regulations coming into force in April 2005 was certainly muted, in contrast to the flurry of activity which preceded the adoption of both the new recognition machinery[226] and the EWC Directive.[227] This was perhaps due to the unfamiliarity of local union officials with employee-based structures and the fact that the pre-existing agreement provisions of the ICE Regulations provided less of an incentive to employers to take immediate action than did Article 13 of the EWC Directive, because the former did not expire on the transposition of the framework Directive into national law.[228] Given the novelty of the new consultation requirements, however, it would be unwise to extrapolate from the initial lack of reaction to a lack of impact in the future.

In the absence of the union exclusivity argued for by the TUC in the mid-1990s, union officials will need to learn the skills of making use of machinery which is not fully under their control, if they are to capitalise on the new consultation rules to establish a union presence in the workplace and build up membership to a level

---

[224] In one collective agreement seen by the authors it is provided that 'the intention is that [the Union] representatives will be the sole employee representatives . . . for the purpose of . . . information and consultation with the employer' and consequently 'the Employer will not commence any procedure provided for in [the] Regulations which would have the effect of initiating a procedure for the election of alternative representatives for any purpose who may include individuals who are not existing accredited or elected [union] representatives'.

[225] But it must provide at least a minimally detailed consultation procedure: see *Stewart* v *Moray Council* [2006] IRLR 592 (EAT).

[226] See 3.3.2.3, above.   [227] See 3.4.3.4, above.   [228] Hall, n 197 above, at 118–126.

from which a claim for recognition can plausibly be made. Whereas the recognition machinery is fully under union control (because only unions can make a claim for recognition), the consultation machinery can be triggered only by the employer or the employees, who may not wish to act when the union thinks it is opportune to do so or may act at a time when the union thinks it is not. On the other hand, if union organisers can acquire the necessary skills, there are, as we have seen, plenty of possibilities for the union de facto to dominate the operation of the consultation machinery. Moreover, since the topics for consultation set out in the Directive fall short of the core items for collective bargaining (ie, pay, hours, and holidays), there is also scope for unions which have established themselves as interlocutors for consultation to persuade both employers and employees of the value of supplementing the consultation with collective bargaining. Thus, although difficult, supplementing consultation with bargaining appears to be an available strategy for unions, just as is the opposite one of supplementing bargaining in unionised undertakings with consultation.

However, the spread of consultation will depend not only on the propensity of employees to support the new arrangements and of unions to encourage them to do so, but also on the propensity of employers to make use of them. The traditional fear of the unions, supported by some historical experience, is that employers will establish consultation arrangements in order to reduce the propensity of employees to support trade unions and collective bargaining. This may be less of a threat in current circumstances where unions have shown themselves unable to make significant headway in reversing their declining presence in the private sector, even with the benefit of a statutory recognition machinery. To put the matter more dynamically, employers' use of the consultation machinery in this defensive way on any scale may not occur until the unions have demonstrated an ability to make positive use of it, as discussed in the previous paragraph. However, it would be wrong to see employers' likely evaluation of the utility of the consultation machinery solely in defensive terms (ie, to keep the union out). Giving the employees a voice in the taking of corporate decisions which affect their working lives can be of advantage to employers. Indeed, as we have seen, the standard arguments for mandatory consultation depend as much on its benefits for employers as for employees. Research suggests that the percentage of workplaces where there is some system for giving employees 'voice' in management decisions has not altered in recent years nor has the level of demand on the part of employees to have 'voice', but that what has occurred is a marked reduction in the propensity of employers to enter into voice arrangements with trade unions and a corresponding increase in voice arrangements provided unilaterally by employers, whether through consultative committees or direct communication methods.[229] Equally important, that shift in voice arrangements seems not to be the result of a growth

---

[229] A Bryson, R Gomez, and P Willman, 'The end of the affair? The decline of employers' propensity to unionize' in J Kelly and P Willman (eds), *Union Organisation and Activity* (London: Routledge, 2004).

in hostility on the part of employers towards trade unions but of 'indifference, or neutrality, that is born of limited experience with unions and the potential costs of switching from one voice regime to another . . .'.[230] In other words, finding a way to make use of the new machinery may be a method for unions to alter both the propensity of employees to join trade unions and of employers to deal with them—and that the greatest potential for union gains lie where it can use the new machinery to both these ends.

3.5 Conclusions: partnership?

In its descriptions of its policy on collective representation at work the word used most often by the government in its early years was 'partnership'. In its manifesto for the 1997 election[231] the Labour party stated that industrial relations were an area 'where our aim is partnership not conflict between employers and employees'. In his foreword to *Fairness at Work*[232] the Prime Minister reiterated the point: 'This White Paper is part of the Government's programme to replace the notion of conflict between employers and employees with the promotion of partnership.' What did 'partnership' mean for the government? It is clear that the main focus of the government's policy was at the level of the workplace. Partnership in terms of tripartite institutions at the level of the economy as a whole, often involving government as well as employers and trade unions, received only a modest boost in this period, in the form of the creation of a tripartite Minimum Wage Commission and the Skills Alliance, both of which we discuss in chapter 4. None of the tripartite institutions terminated by the previous Conservative administrations was resuscitated.[233] In fact, as we have noted, the most prevalent form of tripartite institution in the post-war period, the various, short-lived machineries set up to promote prices and incomes policies, were not needed under the form of macroeconomic management established in the 1980s and carried on by the new government. In some continental countries such national tripartite institutions were used in this period for 'solidarity' bargaining (wage restraint in exchange for job creation), but, with continuing high levels of employment in the UK, there was little pressure to try to replicate such ideas in this country. Probably few practitioners of British industrial relations regretted the absence of prices and incomes machinery, for the institutional structures of both trade unions and employers were ill-adapted to support it and it had never looked like taking root in Britain on the previous occasions upon which it had been tried. At a more analytical level some scholars might regret that this was so and see it as yet another facet of the highly decentralised organisation of collective bargaining in the UK, but re-structuring collective bargaining was not part of the government's partnership agenda.

[230] Ibid, 144.
[231] Available on: <http://www.labour-party.org.uk/manifestos/1997/1997-labour-manifesto.shtml>.
[232] DTI, *Fairness at Work*, Cm 3968, 1998.
[233] See LLPP, 9.2, where the decline and fall of the NEDC is chronicled.

Even at the level of the workplace, partnership is, of course, a word that does not carry an unambiguous meaning. Nor is it made much clearer by the contrast with conflict and adversarialism. The term might be taken to express a unitary theory of industrial relations, ie, one which considers the interests of employers and employees to be entirely congruent. If so, it is a theory hardly worth debating, so clearly is it wrong. In 1999 the TUC produced a more defensible gloss on the word in *Partners for Progress: New Unionism at the Workplace*.[234] For the TUC partnership involved, among other things, a commitment, shared by employers, workers, and trade unions, to the business goals of the organisation, but also a recognition that there might well be from time to time differences of interest and priorities among the partners (as, indeed, in a partnership among business people). Since the TUC document was warmly welcomed by the Prime Minister, speaking at the conference at which it was launched, and was even endorsed by the CBI, it presumably contained no ideas contradictory to government policy.

Even on this more realistic definition of partnership, there is a curious lack of fit between the government's proclaimed goal and the policies actually adopted. One might say, somewhat tongue-in-cheek, that, by altering little of the inherited industrial conflict laws, the government encouraged, in a negative way, a partnership approach on the part of trade unions, because this policy deprived trade unions of the instruments necessary to promote a more adversarial culture. However, this argument can easily be over-stated. Even after the Thatcherite reforms industrial sanctions could be deployed relatively freely by workers against their own employer, provided their use had been sanctioned in a secret ballot. Employees with market power, such as the London Underground workers, continued to make credible threats of, and engage in, occasional lawful industrial action throughout our period. The continuing low levels of industrial conflict[235] were due only in part to the restrictive legal framework. As for the centrepiece of the government's policy on workplace relations, the statutory recognition procedure, it is difficult to detect any particular elements in it designed to promote a partnership, as opposed to a more traditional type of relationship, between employer and trade union. As we have seen, compulsory recognition under the procedure was confined to the limited and traditional agenda of pay, hours, and holidays. The statutory procedure studiously ignored matters likely to be found in a genuine partnership agreement, such as the organisation of work, job security, or training.[236] Nor did the method of bargaining,[237] which the CAC could impose if the parties failed to agree one

---

[234] TUC, May 1999.　　　[235] WERS 2004, 23.

[236] Though a union which was recognised under the statutory procedure and subject to a method of bargaining specified by the CAC did obtain the right to be consulted over training: TULRECA 1992, s 70B. See 4.5, below. For an empirical analysis of partnership principles and practices adopted by some companies, which demonstrates how far short of such matters the statutory agenda for bargaining fell, see D Guest and R Peccei, 'Partnership at Work: Mutuality and the Balance of Advantage' (2001) 39 BJIR 207.

[237] Trade Union Recognition (Method of Collective Bargaining) Order 2000, SI 2000/1300; see para 17 on out-of-round meetings.

after recognition was agreed or imposed under the statutory procedure, provide machinery through which partnership was likely to develop, since it was based on the model of an annual pay round, with virtually no interaction between the parties being required between rounds—only for the purpose of dealing with employer proposals to alter contractual terms relating to pay, hours, and holidays outside the annual round where the employer had failed to bring the proposals forward at the annual meeting. The method was based on a model of episodic, not continuous, interaction between employer and trade union, ie, a rather distanced relationship which might be thought to be the opposite of a partnership. Of course, the parties might voluntarily agree something more demanding, but there was no particular statutory incentive for them to do so.[238]

By contrast, the framework Directive was explicitly based, as we have seen, on a partnership analysis of relations between employers and employees and their representatives: consultation over planned or anticipated organisational change was seen as promoting both employee security and flexible forms of production. Indeed, perhaps in recognition of the above arguments, by the beginning of its third term the government seemed to have moved to identifying partnership largely with the consultation machinery.[239] Moreover, the consultation machinery fitted in well with the government's reforms in the area of company law. The proposed Companies Act 2006 makes it clear that the duty of directors is to promote the success of the company for the benefit of its shareholders, but nevertheless formulates that duty in an inclusive way so as to require directors to take account of, inter alia, the interests of the employees, so far as the basic duty to shareholders requires it.[240] Mandatory consultation provisions could be seen as putting some backbone into an otherwise imprecise obligation. Yet the Directive was implemented in the UK in such a cautious way that it cannot be predicted whether the ICE Regulations will lead to a genuine and substantial involvement of employees in strategic decisions affecting employment. It is really left to employers (and to some extent employees and trade unions) to determine whether or not to use the ICE Regulations as a springboard towards partnership. So, the legislation does no more than provide an opportunity; whether it will be taken up depends upon factors outside the government's policy reach. Indeed, it seems overwhelmingly likely that, in the absence of the Community initiative in this direction, there would have been no expansion of the domestic laws on consultation. Nevertheless, it might be thought that the framework Directive contains greater potential than the statutory recognition machinery to promote partnership. It at least aims at an employee input into decisions which bear directly upon

---

[238] S Moore et al, *The content of new voluntary trade union recognition agreements 1998–2002* (DTI, Employment Relations Research Series No 43, 2005, URN 05/1020), in a study of voluntary agreements reached both within and without the statutory procedure, found that there was some extension of the subjects of bargaining outside the core area.

[239] DTI, *Success at Work*, March 2006 (URN 06/1024), 50–51. Interestingly, by now 'partnership' was almost the last item discussed in this statement of achievements to date and proposals for the third term. [240] HC Bill 218, cl 173 (20 July 2006).

business efficiency and long-term security of employment, whereas the recognition machinery deals with the core and often zero-sum matters of pay and hours. Yet the government was more committed to the recognition machinery than to the consultation system. Why, in the name of promoting partnership, did it not give more, perhaps all, of its support to an effective mandatory consultation system and ignore proposals to re-introduce a statutory recognition machinery?

No conclusive answer can be given but some suggestions can be offered. It may be that the government was not convinced by the arguments in favour of mandatory consultation or thought its benefits were exaggerated. However, the DTI's first consultation document on the framework Directive suggests the opposite, consultation being analysed in very positive terms.[241] Alternatively, it might be thought that the timing was bad from the government's point of view. It had already committed itself, before the election, to mandatory recognition and was unwilling to impose on employers a further round of legislation concerning collective representation in the workplace. However, this argument raises the question of why the government committed itself at that time to recognition (the TUC's 'rung three') rather than to mandatory consultation ('rung two'), leaving recognition to grow voluntarily out of the rung two arrangements, if rung two legislation would have been more consistent with its policy of encouraging partnership. Again, no firm answer can be given. Nevertheless, we have noted[242] the government's cautious attitude to making the promotion of union rights part of its election campaign and thus its unwillingness simply to adopt the whole of the TUC's representation agenda (rungs one, two, and three), whilst it also needed to make some promises to the unions to secure their support in the forthcoming election. In this context, a commitment to compulsory union recognition machinery may have seemed a better choice than mandatory consultation, despite the latter's arguably stronger partnership credentials, since the unions themselves were united in their support for mandatory recognition but somewhat divided over the form of any mandatory consultation machinery. Moreover, both unions and employers would have greater familiarity with the concept of mandatory recognition procedures, such machinery having previously been introduced by a Conservative government (in 1971) and a Labour government (in 1975), so that such a proposal was less risky politically. General consultation obligations, by contrast, were a step into the unknown for British industrial relations. Wherever the truth lies about the process of policy-making, the outcome was paradoxical. The mandatory recognition procedure, promoted by the government, appeared in a form which could be characterised (or perhaps caricatured) as the last and enfeebled gasp of an old and rather narrow approach to workplace relations, whilst 'modern' partnership came in as a result of legislative pressures largely from outside the 'New' Labour government.

---

[241] DTI, *High Performance Workplaces: Informing and Consulting Employees*, July 2003.
[242] At 3.1, above.

4

Promoting Work

4.1 'Welfare to Work'

When the New Labour government came to power in 1997 it quickly moved to make proposals for reform in an area which was to remain at the centre of its concerns for the remainder of its time in office and which was to constitute a central plank in its appeal to the electorate in subsequent general elections. The proposals were aimed at revitalising the welfare state. In 1998, in a document pointedly entitled *A New Contract for Welfare*,[1] the government presented itself as engaging in the first comprehensive review of provision since the report of Sir William Beveridge in 1942. Like Beveridge, the government took a broad view of what the welfare state encompassed—not just the payment of cash benefits to claimants, but also the provision of public services, such as education and health, to citizens, and mechanisms for securing full employment. Education, indeed, was probably the area which the government regarded as the most important for securing both the life chances of citizens and the future health of the economy.

It would be out of place to discuss the whole of this programme in a book on the law relating to employment. However, some elements of it do deserve attention from labour lawyers. This is because promoting work was presented as a key element in the process of reform outlined in 1998 and carried out over the succeeding years. Under the banner of moving the welfare state from a goal confined to 'preventing poverty' to that of 'promoting opportunity and developing potential', the government laid down eight key principles to guide the reform programme. The first of these was that 'the new age of welfare should help and encourage people of working age to work where they are capable of doing so'.[2] Under the slogan 'From Welfare to Work' this policy was to be applied not only to young unemployed persons and to the long-term unemployed—for many years the focus of governmental concern[3]—but also and more controversially to lone parents, the disabled and long-term sick, and older workers.

It is easy to reach glib conclusions about the reasons for the government's insistence on the central role of work in its new vision of the welfare state. Obviously,

---

[1] *A New Contract for Welfare*, Cm 3805, 1998, iii. The Beveridge Report appeared as *Social Insurance and Allied Services*, Cmd 6404, 1942. See *Labour Legislation and Public Policy* (LLPP) 2.1(b).
[2] Ibid, chapter 2.   [3] See LLPP, 10.5(c).

those in work have fewer claims to cash payments from the state than those out of work. So, increasing the employment rate (the percentage of the working age population actually in work) is likely to reduce the demands of the welfare state on the government's budget. Moreover, those in work will in due course contribute to the government's revenues and the growth of the economy. The government was concerned that over the fifty years since 1949 governmental spending on social security had risen eight-fold in real terms and from one sixth to one third of all governmental spending; and that in the two previous decades the real growth of social security spending had been higher than that in any other major area of governmental responsibility, including education and health.[4] Moreover, the government clearly had some items of social security expenditure in its sights for reduction, notably the amount spent on Incapacity Benefit, and had a general target of reducing the levels of fraud within the system.[5]

However, there is no reason to doubt the government's sincerity in its statements about the non-budgetary value to be attached to improving access to work. Apart from the potential value of work to an individual's self-esteem and security,[6] the government saw its programme as part of a broader attack on social exclusion. It was struck by the changing pattern of 'worklessness', whereby, within a stable employment rate, 'more people live in households with no one in work' than had been the case twenty years previously. Moreover, such households had 'become more geographically concentrated in urban areas' so that 'unemployed or poor households are increasingly likely to live in communities with high levels of unemployment and benefit dependency'.[7] Breaking out of this pattern was regarded as a crucial step in both reducing poverty and increasing social cohesion.

The centrality of promoting the move 'from welfare to work' in the government's reform proposals gives us the key to understanding which elements of its overall programme need to be brought into an analysis of employment or labour law. At a very general level, it may be said that the government's policy restored some sense of the linkages between employment law and social security law which had been gradually lost over the previous fifty years. Social security law after the Beveridge reforms became increasingly the study of the policies underlying, and the functioning of, a large state bureaucracy for making cash payments to those out of work, whilst labour law focused on the individual or collective relationships between those in work. The points of contact between the two were limited[8] and

---

[4] *A New Contract for Welfare*, n 1 above, 11.

[5] Ibid, 54, for an argument addressing the general cost issue, where Incapacity Benefit was described as 'a simple but costly escape route for government to keep the unemployment numbers down'; and chapter 9 entitled 'Rooting out fraud', dealing with the second point. The concern about fraud led to the passing of the Social Security Fraud Act 2001, partly based on a report from Lord Grabiner (see G McKeever, 'Tackling Benefit Fraud' (2003) 32 ILJ 326).

[6] Ibid, 3.   [7] Ibid, 10.

[8] There was a period when the issue of the payment of benefits to strikers constituted a cross-boundary issue, but with the decline of strikes and the reform of the benefit system the issue ceased to be a live one. See LLPP, 327–328 and 467–469.

in academic life the two topics tended to go their separate ways.[9] The policies of the new government, by focusing on the movement from welfare into work, brought employment law and social welfare law into a greater degree of proximity than had been the case for many decades.

Emphasis on the relationship between social security and the labour market represented a highly significant policy choice on the part of the new government. As Raymond Plant has pointed out, there were two competing visions of the welfare state operating in Britain in the last quarter of the twentieth century, based on competing versions of citizenship.[10] One vision was based on the notion of citizenship as status, so that social security was viewed as an entitlement. On this view increased conditionality of benefits and means testing were regarded as steps down the wrong path. Competing with this was a more active notion of citizenship, where social security was viewed as a reciprocal arrangement provided in exchange for contributions (no doubt widely conceived) to society. On this alternative view stressing the linkage between work and benefits was not in principle improper but on the contrary gave operational meaning in many cases to the reciprocal nature of social security (though of course there was room for debate about how stringently the idea of reciprocity should be translated into the law). The alternative view was supported to some degree by the re-definition of 'poverty' which had occurred in the period since the Second World War.[11] For Beveridge, following tradition and perhaps giving it its most sophisticated expression, poverty had been conceived in absolutist terms, ie, relief against poverty involved bringing citizens up to a bare subsistence level, meaning a level sufficient to preserve physical well being. That citizens should have an unconditional entitlement to be relieved of poverty, as so defined, was a relatively easy argument to make. The relative definition of poverty, by contrast, involved measuring it by reference to the material standards of society as a whole. A variety of measures could be argued for, but a commonly adopted official measure was an income of less than 50% of average earnings. Since poverty was now measured by reference to the earnings of those engaged in productive activity in the economy, it could be argued to be indefensible for those capable of work, and for whom work was available, to claim access to a standard of living determined by reference to the working economy whilst not being prepared to participate in the activities which supported that standard.

The entitlement view was the dominant view in academic circles from the 1960s onwards, though it had never been clearly adopted in the British social security system, which reflected an uneasy compromise between the two approaches. Nevertheless, when the Conservative governments of the 1980s began to move the

---

[9] A notable exception to this statement was the work of Professor Paul O'Higgins. For a recent work which insists on the relevance of social security law to modern labour lawyers see S Deakin and F Wilkinson, *The Law of the Labour Market* (Oxford: OUP, 2005).

[10] R Plant, 'Supply Side Citizenship?' (1999) 6 Journal of Social Security Law 124.

[11] See N Harris, *Social Security in Context* (Oxford: OUP, 1999) 41–47.

social security system more firmly in the direction of reciprocity, notably in the shape of the 'Fowler reforms' of the middle 1980s,[12] the opposition of the Labour party was expressly based on the entitlement view.[13] Thus, for the Labour party in government from 1997 onwards to make central to its policies the notion of 'welfare to work' was a highly significant choice. It meant that the new government substantially adopted, but also took forward in more positive ways, the reforms of its predecessors in this area. It rejected the entitlement view as demoralising for those dependent upon welfare benefits, as unattractive to taxpayers who had to fund the social security scheme, and as limiting the productive potential of the national economy. The new approach was captured in its slogans: 'work for those who can; security for those who cannot' and 'a new contract between the citizen and the state, where we keep a welfare state from which we all benefit; but on terms that are fair and clear'[14] and 'rights balanced with responsibilities'.

One significant consequence of the 'welfare to work' approach in our area is that the government was no longer concerned solely with the *unemployment* rate (important though that was), ie, the percentage of people seeking work (in other words, those in the labour market) who were not employed. In fact, the unemployment rate fell and remained around 5% for much of the period after 2000, a low figure compared with what had often been the position over the two previous decades and a reduction of one third on the situation which the government had inherited on coming into office.[15] It was equally concerned with the *employment* rate, ie, the proportion of people of working age who were in employment, whether or not they were seeking work and thus could be said to be in the labour market. A central component of the 'welfare to work' strategy was to move those who had dropped out of the labour market back into it and then into work, of which the employment rate was a better measure than the unemployment rate. This measure improved by almost three percentage points to nearly 75% between 1997 and 2005,[16] but in 2006 the government set itself an ambitious new target of an employment rate of 80%, although no specific date was attached to the target.[17]

The stress on the rate of employment made social security law and the associated parts of employment law much more important elements in 'active labour market' policies than had been the case for Beveridge. For him, the main determinant

[12] Leading to the Social Security Act 1986. See N Wikeley, A Ogus and E Barendt, *The Law of Social Security* (5th edn, London: Butterworths, 2002) 6–7.
[13] Desmond King and Mark Wickham-Jones, 'From Clinton to Blair: the Democratic (Party) Origins of Welfare to Work' (1999) Political Quarterly 62. They identify the shadow Chancellor's (Mr Gordon Brown) proposals of 1995 to tackle youth unemployment through what was later called the 'New Deal' (see below) as the significant turning point. (The authors perhaps exaggerate the extent to which, even pre-Fowler, the benefit system lacked conditionality rules.)
[14] *A New Contract for Welfare*, n 1 above, Foreword and Introduction (by the Prime Minister).
[15] HM Treasury, *Britain Meeting the Global Challenge: Pre-Budget Report*, December 2005, Cm 6701, chart 4.1.   [16] Ibid.
[17] Department for Work and Pensions, *A New Deal for Welfare: Empowering People to Work*, Cm 6730, January 2006, 18 (composed, of course, of different target rates for different groups of people).

of whether those seeking work obtained a job was the number of offers employers were making at any one time, whilst those who had dropped out of the labour market were either incapable of work or were not entitled to benefits. On this view, macro-economic policy, by affecting the demand-side of the labour market, was a crucial part of the context of social security law, for without the adoption of macro-economic policies aimed at running the economy at a high level of activity, there was unlikely to be adequate demand for workers. However, at an operational level there was no linkage between the social security rules and demand management. The approach of the new Labour government challenged this analysis on two fronts. First, and less radically, it was pointed out that job vacancies and unemployment could coincide if those seeking the jobs were not appropriately qualified to take them up. This rider to the basic Beveridge analysis had been recognised in the 1946 National Insurance Act, but the government now placed much more emphasis on this argument. In an early analysis of the nature of the labour market the new government argued that globalisation, by reducing the demand in the domestic economy for unskilled jobs as those jobs were increasingly performed outside the UK, had produced a situation in which running the British economy at a high and constant level (an objective which was in fact substantially achieved over the coming years) could no longer be relied upon to absorb all the unskilled workers available to work.[18] It pointed to the fact that the unemployment rate had fluctuated between 1% and 3% of the workforce until the middle 1970s, but had averaged about 8% since 1980, no matter what the state of the economy. Since the government saw the trend towards globalisation as irreversible, it was forced to the conclusion that it needed to supplement effective macro-economic demand management with supply side measures. This did not mean that macro-economic measures were regarded as unimportant. On the contrary, the government presented macro-economic stability in 2006 as one of 'five pillars' on which its labour market policies were founded.[19] Rather, the government no longer believed it could rely on a high level of economic activity to provide jobs for all those of working age who were capable of work without adopting additional supply-side policies.

The above argument generates a natural focus, initially, on the skills of those seeking but not finding work. As we shall see below, this is where the government directed its efforts in the period immediately after 1997. Its first New Deals were aimed at those in receipt of unemployment benefit (now called Jobseeker's Allowance) and made continued receipt of benefit conditional upon participation

---

[18] HM Treasury and the Department of Education and Employment, *Employment Opportunity in a Changing Labour Market*, 1997, 3.01–3.11. Of course, the point should not be exaggerated. Some unskilled jobs cannot be exported, notably those in the service industries where a physical presence of the worker in the UK is required, but the point remained that the demand for unskilled jobs had declined significantly and, in the government's view, that tendency was irreversible.

[19] *A New Deal for Welfare*, n 17 above, 15. The other four were: minimum standards of employment (mainly labour law rules), ensuring that work pays, skills and training policies, and an active labour market policy.

in employment or training programmes. However, secondly, and more radically, the government challenged the perception that those not in the labour market (whether for social or for medical reasons) were necessarily incapable of work. Thus, the government extended its New Deal programmes in due course to, and took other measures[20] to encourage work by, those who were not seeking employment and so were not in the labour market. In particular, it applied its philosophy to the disabled and long-term sick, and lone mothers. Both these policy initiatives involved a rejection of the proposition that the pool of jobs available was influenced only by demand-side measures. Whilst it was true to say that the number of jobs on offer at any one time set a limit to the chances of those without work obtaining it, on a dynamic basis supply-side measures, coupled with appropriate demand-side measures, could increase the number of jobs available over time. This was on the theory that an increase in the supply of appropriately qualified labour would enable the economy to be run at a higher level than otherwise before the point was reached at which supply constraints led to the development of inflation and the government (or the Bank of England) taking measures to reduce economic activity to control inflation. Thus a greater supply of appropriately qualified workers would support a higher but non-inflationary level of demand in the economy, and the higher level of demand would call for more jobs.[21] In fact, in 2006, after a long period of macro-economic stability, the government could go so far as to declare that 'the problem is not lack of jobs' but rather the 'problem is connecting people with the work that they want and need and also with the jobs that employers need done'.[22]

Thus, our main concern in this chapter is to identify how active labour market policy made use of social security and labour law to effect the policy of 'welfare to work'; and to examine the linkages created between those two bodies of law. It is suggested that policy can be analysed under three main headings: an increased 'conditionality' for cash benefits, 'making work pay', and 'lowering the barriers to work'—to use in the last two cases the labels employed by the government itself.[23] The first mechanism operated almost entirely within social security law. The availability of an increasing range of benefits was made dependent upon the claimant satisfying an increasingly demanding set of conditions relating to job search or

[20] For example, tax credits and anti-discrimination laws.

[21] 'As we have said, at all times the number of jobs will depend on aggregate demand. But, because of the inflation constraint, aggregate demand will be restricted by the amount of available labour. So, over a run of years, the number of jobs will ultimately depend on the available supply of labour—that is, on the number of those who are ready and willing to take up jobs.' (J De Koning, R Layard, S Nickell, and N Westergaard-Nielsen, *Policies for Full Employment*, Department for Work and Pensions, March 2004.)   [22] *A New Deal for Welfare*, n 17 above, 18.

[23] *A New Contract for Welfare*, n 1 above, 23. Curiously, the traditional mechanism within the social security system for reflecting reciprocity, ie, the insurance principle (that benefits were conditional on a satisfactory contributions record) was not strengthened by the government, and national insurance contributions continued their general drift away from insurance-like premia towards general tax payments. This was perhaps a reflection of the government's desire to target welfare payments on the worst-off.

preparation for job search. If these conditions were not satisfied, entitlement to benefit could be suspended for a period or withdrawn altogether. The second mechanism operated in both social security/tax law and in employment law, and its aim was to maximise the chances of the claimant being better off in work than out of work. The government's enthusiastic adoption of tax credits was a major example of this second mechanism. Through tax credits the government was prepared to countenance the payment of cash benefits to those in work, thus removing or at least reducing the disincentive to move from benefit to work if the consequence of that move would be the loss of social security payments and a possible reduction in living standards. However, making work pay could also be seen from the viewpoint, not of loss of benefit, but of pay from work. Here, the government aimed to make work more attractive by introducing a National Minimum Wage. This was a policy located within employment law and can be analysed as the government shifting part of the cost of its policies onto employers, including, of course, itself in its capacity of employer in the public sector. Thus, within the second mechanism, social security and labour law work in tandem.

Finally, 'lowering barriers to work' might also have both social security and employment law dimensions. For example, social security measures designed to improve the skills of jobseekers could be regarded as improving the supply of labour, whilst laws dealing with disability or age discrimination could be regarded as increasing the demand for labour on the part of employers for these categories of worker. Equally, the presence of anti-discrimination laws might operate so as to improve the supply of labour, as those previously discouraged from entering the labour market for fear of discrimination against them changed their minds about their chances of obtaining work. Indeed, a more general consequence of the Labour government's focus on the supply side of the economy was that it abandoned its predecessors' attachment to the view that reductions in employment protection would necessarily improve the chances of people obtaining work. In the 1980s reduction of employment rights to boost demand for labour had been a governmental policy which had led to substantial reductions in the scope of employment protection laws.[24] Under the post-1997 policy, conferring rights on individual workers could be seen as a way of improving the supply of labour. Although cautious in its reforms and anxious to keep business on side (and so less radical than some of its supporters wished), the new government engaged in a fairly extensive programme of extending workers' individual rights, much of which could be seen as part of its active labour market strategy. It also reversed some of its predecessors' more dramatic reductions of entitlement.[25]

[24] LLPP, 10.3(b)—a policy still attractive to governments, as the (failed) attempts of the French government in 2006 to remove unfair dismissal rights from young workers and the (successful) efforts of the Australian government to remove unfair dismissal rights more generally showed. On Australia, see J Murray, '*Work Choices* and the radical revision of the public realm of Australian statutory labour law' (2006) 35 ILJ, 343.

[25] Thus, the qualifying period for unfair dismissal protection was reduced from two years to one in 1999 (SI 1999/1436), but not to six months as it had been before the reforms of the 1980s.

We shall look at each of these strategies in a little more detail in this chapter. However, the productivity of the economy, even in labour terms, does not depend solely on the employment rate but also on the skill levels of those who easily find employment in the labour market and move from job to job without significant state intervention. The level of skill in the workforce as a whole, whether at a basic or more advanced level, constitutes an area where the British labour market has traditionally shown up badly in international comparisons. In recent years, British governments have not been significantly interventionist in relation to the training of those in work. As we shall see, the post-1997 government continued this policy in only a slightly modified form, putting most of its efforts into medium- and long-term policies to improve education in schools. Nevertheless, it did take some steps to improve in-work training. It also sought to meet short-term pressures through a more welcoming policy towards skilled migrant workers.

4.2 Labour market conditionality

4.2.1 Availability for work

The extent to which those seeking benefit on grounds of being out of work should be subject to conditions based on their relationship with the labour market has long been debated. What is clear is that there has always been an element of labour market conditionality attached to the benefit system; what is equally clear is that from the late 1980s onwards the then Conservative government increased the stringency of those conditions and the succeeding Labour government, far from repealing those changes, adopted them and used them as a basis for implementing its welfare to work policies. When unemployment benefit was introduced in the National Insurance Act 1911 it was made conditional upon the claimant being 'capable of work but unable to obtain suitable employment'.[26] When re-enacted post-Beveridge in the National Insurance Act 1946, the requirement was that the claimant be 'available' for employment.[27] So, availability for work has always been the minimum requirement in this area. In the terms of the then main rationale for unemployment benefit (ie, that it was a form of national (compulsory) insurance against involuntary unemployment), this restriction was fully understandable. Contributions have been paid in exchange for benefits in respect of the risk of involuntary unemployment. Those who became or remained unemployed voluntarily fell outside the risk insured against: choosing to leave employment or choosing to leave the labour market represented acts outside the scope of the insured risk. Considerable discussion, in both case law and legislation, developed over the question of when a person could be said to have left work voluntarily, including

---

[26] S 86(3).
[27] S 11(2)(a)(i). The current requirement is set out in the Jobseekers Act 1995, s 1(2)(a).

on the question whether loss of employment through a trade dispute disqualified one from benefit.[28] There was rather less debate over the meaning of being available for work. Though generally thought to be an undemanding test, it can put the claimant at risk of loss of benefit if he or she seeks to confine availability to the type of work or work producing the level of remuneration enjoyed in the previous employment. Thus, the present Regulations do not permit any restriction on the level of remuneration to be imposed after a period of six months and restrictions on the type of work, although not time-limited, must nevertheless not put the claimant in a position where he or she does not have 'reasonable prospects of securing employment'.[29]

4.2.2 Actively seeking work

Thus the principle of being available for work as a condition of receipt of unemployment benefit is long-established. For many years, it translated itself in practical terms into the weekly obligation to 'sign on' at the labour exchange or equivalent office, ie, availability was demonstrated largely through physical presence on a weekly basis in a government office.[30] However, there has always been a body of thought to the effect that the relevant condition should require a more active commitment to job search on the part of the claimant. Indeed, the 1911 formulation hinted at something more demanding through its reference to 'unable to obtain suitable employment'. In 1921, in the face of an unexpectedly rapid rise in unemployment, the Unemployment Insurance Act of that year changed the condition to 'genuinely seeking whole time employment',[31] but it was repealed in 1930 on the basis that it was having no significant impact on the behaviour of the unemployed. As we have seen, Beveridge endorsed the 'availability' condition and thus the law remained until the Social Security Act 1989[32] re-introduced the 'actively seeking employment' test which was carried forward into the current law in the shape of the Jobseekers Act 1995.[33] Under the modern legislation, the active condition is applied both to contributory

---

[28] LLPP, 7.2(c) and 9.3(g).

[29] The Jobseeker's Allowance Regulations 1996, SI 1996/297, regs 9 and 10—hereafter Jobseekers Regulations. In addition, the rules on the jobseeker's agreement (see below) state that under such an agreement insistence on the previous type of work or previous level of remuneration should be limited to a maximum of a thirteen week period under the agreement (reg 16), which may give a better idea of the practice of employment officers.

[30] For Beveridge it was the obligation to report weekly to a labour exchange, where all local job vacancies would be registered, which helped him to support a simple 'availability' test. The worker did not need to 'hawk himself' around because the public labour exchange would bring the jobs to him: W H Beveridge, *Unemployment: A Problem of Industry* (London: Longmans, Green and Co, 1931) 280. The role of the public labour exchange was thus crucial for him, although the state was never given a monopoly of job-broking in the UK. From this point of view, splitting the benefit offices from the employment exchange offices, as happened for a period in the UK in the mid-1970s, was a major error.

[31] S 3(3)(b).   [32] S 10.   [33] S 1(2)(c).

benefit (formerly unemployment benefit) and to non-contributory benefit (formerly supplementary benefit or, later, income support), which are dealt with together in the 1995 Act. In any week where the active condition is not satisfied, the claimant will not be entitled to contributory benefit and may claim only a discretionary 'hardship' payment on a non-contributory basis (where the stringent conditions for such a payment are satisfied).

It is difficult to assess the impact of the change made in the late 1980s. On the one hand, the government produced survey evidence of unemployed claimants failing to engage in job search and pointed to the coincidence in particular areas of high levels of unemployment and job vacancies. On the other hand, there was evidence that the adjudicatory bodies did not regard the previous 'availability' test in a purely passive light and so already required some job search. Further, the evidence from the 1920s was that benefit officers found it difficult to give operational effect to the active test.[34] Although regulations made under the 1995 Act attempted to put some flesh on the bare bones of 'actively seeking employment'— including the remarkable provision that a claimant should be deemed not to meet the active test if 'by his behaviour or appearance' he undermined his prospects of obtaining employment[35]—any significant impact of the active test would depend on the efforts of individual employment officers, upon whom an extensive discretion was conferred.

4.2.3 Jobseeker's agreements

Probably more significant in giving effect to the active condition was a further condition for eligibility for the Jobseeker's Allowance introduced by the 1995 Act. Besides being available for and actively seeking employment, the claimant must enter into a 'jobseeker's agreement' with the employment officer.[36] This is 'agreed' between the employment officer and the claimant, put into writing, signed by each, and a copy is given to the claimant. It is clear that a main purpose of the jobseeker's agreement is to spell out in the individual case what is required of the claimant to meet the availability and activity tests. Thus, an employment officer may not enter into an agreement unless its terms would bring the claimant into compliance with the availability and activity tests.[37] Furthermore, the regulations require the agreement to specify the steps the claimant will take 'to seek employment' and 'to improve his prospects of finding employment'.[38] These provisions thus attempt to put some legislative pressure on both claimant and, perhaps as important, employment officer to direct their minds to what the general tests require in each particular case. However, the employment officer is not confined

---

[34] The arguments at the time of the passing of the 1989 Act are discussed by Buck (1989) 18 ILJ 258.
[35] Jobseekers Regulations, reg 16—discussed by Wikeley (1996) 25 ILJ 71. It is perhaps significant in this context that the 1995 Act replaced the term 'unemployment benefit' with that of 'jobseeker's allowance', thus shifting the emphasis from the claimant's current state (unemployed) to that which he or she hoped to attain (having a job).   [36] Jobseekers Act 1995, ss 1(2)(b) and 9.
[37] S 9(5).   [38] Jobseekers Regulations, reg 31(e).

to the jobseeker's agreement as the method for securing specific behaviour from the claimant. Even outside the agreement, and even though the claimant is available for and actively seeking work, the 1995 Act empowered the officer to give 'jobseeker directions' (a written direction given with a view to assisting the claimant to find employment or improving his chances of being employed), noncompliance with which would disqualify the claimant from benefit for at least two weeks.[39]

The contractual terminology deployed in support of the jobseeker's agreement has proved to be controversial.[40] Although it may capture the reciprocal view of citizenship, identified above, when applied at an individual level it suffers from the lack of persuasiveness which attends any contract proffered by a monopoly provider, arising out of the fact that the counterparty has no option to get better terms by going elsewhere, so that his or her consent to the terms of the agreement is highly constrained. Monopoly providers of services in the private sector of the economy increasingly have their terms and conditions of trade subject to a review by a regulator. In the public sector, such review is provided partly by a right of appeal (in this case, against employment officers' decisions) and partly by political scrutiny, the former requiring more resources for effective use than many claimants have at their disposal and the latter operating only episodically and unpredictably. Clearly, the choice between the two versions of citizenship identified above is ultimately a political matter, each containing risks (of coercion of the individual on the one hand, of exploitation of the system on the other) which the other aims to contain. It should be noted, however, that the illiberal tendencies of the Jobseeker's Allowance are not associated wholly with the contractual aspects of the jobseeker's rules. The regulation, noted above, relating to appearance stems from the non-contractual duty actively to seek work, and the power to issue directions exists independently of the jobseeker's agreement. The choice between rule-making which takes an apparently contractual form[41] and rule-making of a more traditional administrative character is mainly a matter of choice on the part of the government, with little significant importance beyond the rhetorical or psychological.

4.2.4 New Deals

4.2.4.1 Jobseekers

Thus by the middle 1990s the labour market conditions for eligibility for unemployment benefit had been tightened considerably beyond the simple

---

[39] Jobseekers Act 1995, s 19; Jobseekers Regulations, reg 69.

[40] Mark Freedland and Desmond King, 'Client Contractualism between the Employment Service and Jobseekers in the United Kingdom' in E Sol and M Westerveld (eds), *Contractualism in Employment Services* (The Hague: Kluwer Law International, 2005); P Vincent-Jones, 'Contractual governance: Institutional and organisational analysis' (2000) 20 OJLS 317.

[41] S 9(2) of the 1995 Act provides that the agreement shall have effect 'only for the purpose of section 1', ie, of determining eligibility to benefit, and so is not enforceable as a standard contract.

availability test used in the 1946 National Insurance Act. 'Welfare to work' analysis made the Labour government elected in 1997 now supportive of the supply-side measures which its predecessor had adopted. However, its was an analysis which led to the conclusion that its predecessor's reforms were insufficiently far-reaching. If a central problem was that the unemployed lacked the skills which the available jobs required, then something more was going to be required of claimants than that they energetically look for jobs. Before reaching the stage where such activity was likely to be successful, claimants might need a period of training or skill-acquisition or even just 'confidence building'. However, as we have noted, the ambition of the government was to apply its vision of the value of work not only to those who were seeking work (albeit without much success) but also to those who perceived themselves to be outside the labour market but who, in the government's view, could ultimately be encouraged or cajoled into work. It was both problems which the government's 'New Deals' were aimed at addressing. Indeed, by the beginning of its third term the second problem began to loom larger in the government's thinking than the first.[42]

The initial funding of these arrangements, from a one-off 'windfall' tax on the profits of privatised industries, was one of the few large expenditure decisions which the government made in its early years—an indication of the importance it attached to the initiative. The importance of the New Deals has been somewhat obscured by the fact that they needed little in the way of new legislation. The necessary powers of compulsion as against claimants were already available in the Jobseekers Act 1995—in particular, section 19(5)[43] provided that a claimant could be disqualified from benefit for failing to take up or continue with a place on a training scheme or employment programme—or in other social security legislation applying to other groups of claimants; and authority to set up the New Deal schemes themselves could normally be found in the Employment and Training Act 1973.[44] However, although legislative power to create New Deal schemes existed, the exercise of that power in the most effective way required a certain degree of trial and error (or 'reflexive regulation' as it is often more grandly termed) on the part of the Department for Work and Pensions. Consequently, the Department engaged in trials in particular areas of novel schemes before introducing them nationally. Further, the effective implementation of the New Deal schemes required a significant reform of the bureaucracy of the Department: Job Centres became Jobcentre Plus and some employment officers 'personal advisers', whilst some of these more sophisticated services began to be provided through private sector organisations

---

[42] *A New Deal for Welfare*, n 17 above, 18.

[43] An equivalent power was contained in the National Insurance Act 1946, so that it was not the principle which was new so much as the extensive commitment of resources to compulsory training programmes. See also Jobseekers Regulations, reg 75, introduced by the Social Security Amendment (New Deal) Regulations 1997, specifying various New Deal arrangements and reg 140(4A) imposing particularly strict requirements on the availability of hardship payments to those who refused New Deal places.   [44] See LLPP, 7.3(b).

rather than directly by the state.[45] The Jobcentre Plus changes began in 2002 and represented in many ways the second stage of the new government's welfare reforms, which began with the first of the New Deals in 1998. We do not propose to go through the detail of all these changes but to focus instead on the broad outlines of the main New Deals.

The New Deals were aimed at different groups of claimants, were developed over time, and came with differing levels of compulsion. The first target was the young unemployed (those aged 18 to 24), for whom entering into a New Deal programme was the only form of state support on offer after a period of six months in receipt of Jobseeker's Allowance, so that there was a high level of compulsion for this group. There was an initial period of assessment and preparation (referred to as the 'gateway'), which could last up to four months, after which the young person had to accept an offer of a place on one of four types of programme for a period of six months: subsidised employment, full-time education or training, work with a voluntary sector organisation, or work on the environmental taskforce. The government undertook to make one or more (but not necessarily all) of these options available to each person falling within the scheme. With regard to its subsidised employment option, this New Deal could be viewed as an expanded version of the Youth Training Scheme, which operated in the 1980s.[46] However, it contained greater protections against New Deal young workers simply replacing existing employees (so that the overall volume of employment remained unchanged), and put some pressure on employers to retain competent trainees after the six month period of subsidised employment came to an end. If, however, the programme (of whatever type) did not lead to employment, at its end the trainee could re-claim benefit.

Also introduced at the same time (in 1998) was a New Deal for the long-term unemployed, ie, those over 25 who had been unemployed for more than eighteen months (initially two years), so that only a longer period out of employment triggered governmental intervention of a New Deal type for the over-25s. This New Deal was also mandatory (for workers under the age of 50), and followed a similar pattern to that for Young Persons. After an initial 'gateway period' of up to four months, during which an 'action plan' would be drawn up with a personal adviser, there would be an 'intensive activity period' (but of three months' duration only) consisting of a similar range of options as that made available for those under 25.

4.2.4.2 The disabled and long-term sick

By 2006 the government felt confident enough of the success of its policies for the general unemployed aged 50 or under to drop them from its list of priority

---

[45] 'Employment Zones' constitute a good example of both local focus and the use of non-governmental providers. See Mark Freedland and Nicola Countouris, 'Diritti e doveri nel rapporto tra disoccupati e servizi per l'impiego in Europa' (2005) Giornale di Diritto del Lavoro e di Relazioni Industriali 557. [46] LLPP, 10.5(c).

groups.[47] Those in receipt of Jobseeker's Allowance had fallen by 700,000 since 1997 and the number of claimants had remained below one million since the beginning of 2001. Although this result was attributed to the success of the government's policies in combination, rather than just to its social security changes, nevertheless this outcome reduced the pressure on the government to further reform the jobseeker's rules. However, the government did focus on the administration of the rules, stressing increased local discretion and flexibility in the operation of the rules (the title of 'Jobcentre Plus' being used to denote the importance attached to adapting the rules to the needs of local labour markets and individual claimants).[48]

However, as *A New Deal For Welfare* 2006 acknowledged,[49] progress in relation to other groups of claimants had been more limited, notably the disabled, lone parents, and those over 50. This was hardly surprising. The potential for active labour market measures to take these groups from welfare into work was obviously more limited than in relation to the general unemployed, whilst there was greater political resistance in these cases to the forms of compulsion which had been applied to jobseekers under 50. Perhaps the area of greatest government concern was with the disabled and long-term sick, where, on a cross-OECD comparison, the UK displayed high rates of inactivity due to disability.[50] The number of workers on incapacity benefit had expanded very rapidly in the 1980s and 1990s, from about 750,000 to 2.5 million. The previous Conservative government had begun the process of reform, through the Social Security (Incapacity for Work) Act 1994, notably by making the test for access to the benefit more stringent by introducing the 'all work test'. This replaced the previous test of whether there was work which a disabled person could 'reasonably be expected to do' (requiring a consideration of the claimant's overall social situation) with one which focused exclusively on the claimant's mental and physical capacities.[51] Those who failed the test would not be entitled to this benefit; they would be permitted to claim the Jobseeker's Allowance, but only subject to the compulsory labour market conditionality noted above. As was now the pattern, the new Labour government, which had opposed the 1994 reforms, adopted and extended the earlier changes through the Welfare Reform and Pensions Act 1999.[52] The 'all work test' was re-named the 'Personal Capability Assessment' (PCA) and, in line with the new government's greater commitment to active labour market policies, acquired a

---

[47] *A New Deal for Welfare*, n 17 above, 18. Also, 'Youth unemployment has virtually been eradicated', ibid, 'Ministerial foreword'.

[48] Department for Work and Pensions, *Building on New Deal: Local solutions meeting individual needs*, June 2004. [49] n 17 above.

[50] *Financial Times* (UK Edition), 25 January 2006, p 3.

[51] Wikely, Ogus and Barendt, n 12 above, 541.

[52] Introducing a new s 171C into the Social Security Contributions and Benefits Act 1992. See generally G McKeever, 'Welfare to Work for the (In)Capacitated—the Reform of Incapacity Benefit' (2000) 29 ILJ 145. The 1999 Act also tightened the contribution conditions for this benefit and introduced an element of means-testing.

positive as well as a negative aspect.[53] A claimant might now be required to provide evidence to a medical practitioner (or otherwise be disqualified from benefit) not only to determine whether he or she was capable of work but, even if the claimant was entitled to the benefit, for the purpose of 'assisting or encouraging a person to obtain work or of enhancing his prospects of obtaining it'.[54] Information of the second type was not permitted to be sent to the officer who had to determine whether the claimant was entitled to the benefit,[55] but rather went to the claimant's personal adviser whose task was to help the claimant, in an appropriate case, to take steps towards a job.

However, at this stage the element of labour market conditionality was limited to undergoing a PCA at stated intervals[56] and attending work-focused interviews at a Jobcentre.[57] Thus, the government's steps of a compulsory nature towards implementing its policy of 'work for those who can; security for those who cannot' were tentative. The view that taking steps towards obtaining a job should be an entirely voluntary matter for the disabled received a high level of political support,[58] and so the government felt the need to tread extremely carefully. It was not until 2006 that the government produced a consultation document proposing significant additions to its compulsory powers.[59] By that stage it felt confident that it had developed effective methods of helping the disabled who might eventually be capable of work to prepare for work and find jobs (notably through its 'Pathways to Work' pilots),[60] so that it could protect itself against the charge that further compulsion was simply a way of reducing expenditure rather than helping the disabled to achieve their own goals. Even so, it proceeded cautiously. Its proposals for a new benefit to replace Incapacity Benefit[61] were located deep in a chapter which dealt with other matters as well (such as 'developing healthy workplaces', 'reducing sickness absence', extending the Disability Discrimination legislation, and so on), and it was proposed that the new benefit be obligatory only for

---

[53] The 'all work test' was described at a 'key problem' with Incapacity Benefit: 'It writes off as unfit for work people who might, with some assistance, be able to return to work . . . It is an all or nothing test, in the sense that it assesses people as either fit for work or unfit for any work.' *A New Contract for Welfare*, n 1 above, 54.

[54] Social Security (Incapacity for Work)(General) Regulations 1995, reg 6(1), as amended.

[55] Reg 6(4).   [56] Social Security Contributions and Benefits Act 1992, s 171C(5).

[57] Social Security Administration Act 1992, ss 2A–2B, inserted by the Welfare Reform and Pensions Act 1999.

[58] McKeever, n 52 above, 154–158. Part of the problem consists in the wide range of disabilities covered by incapacity benefit. For some the typical disabled person is someone with a permanent and serious disabling condition; for others a male worker who formerly worked in manufacturing and is now seen as a victim of deindustrialisation; for yet others a person suffering from a real but nevertheless temporary or manageable physical or mental condition. These differing stereotypes make policy agreement difficult.   [59] *A New Deal for Welfare*, n 17 above, ch 2.

[60] At the same time as the introduction of the Welfare Reform Bill 2006 (see below) the government announced the national roll-out of the Pathways to Work scheme by April 2008 (Department for Work and Pensions, Press Release, 4 July 2006). It was also reported that private and voluntary sector organisations were to have a substantial role (perhaps as much as 60%) in the delivery of the advice and training measures to those claiming incapacity: *Financial Times* (UK Edition) 5 July 2006, p 2.

[61] And, indeed, income support on the grounds of incapacity.

future claimants. The new benefit, Employment and Support Allowance (ESA), would be available only after a re-vamped and again re-named PCA has been carried out (during which time the claimant would receive only the lower Jobseeker's Allowance), which would sort the claimants into two groups. Those (the minority) of whom 'it would be unreasonable to expect that they engage in work-related activity'[62] would receive the 'Support' element of the allowance, whilst those ('most people') for whom 'a return to work (full-time or part-time) is feasible in the short or medium term'[63] would receive the 'Employment Support' component of the allowance.[64] As with the Jobseeker's Allowance, the ESA involved a renaming of the benefit designed to focus attention not on the conditions which gave the claimant access to the benefit but on the conditions which would see him or her move off it. Crucially, however, the ESA would come with a higher level of labour market conditionality. Those in receipt of it would be required to draw up a 'personal action plan' with their personal adviser, which would focus on 'rehabilitation and eventually on work-related activity'.[65] 'Work-related activity' would include work 'tasters', action to improve employability, job search assistance, and action to stabilise elements of the claimant's personal life (eg, health, accommodation). Failure to agree and implement a plan would lead to reductions of benefit in tranches, until it rested at the JSA level.

These proposals were put forward in the Welfare Reform Bill 2006. Overall, one can say that, even though the numbers claiming Incapacity Benefit had continued to rise under the new government, albeit much more slowly than previously,[66] the element of labour market conditionality proposed for those claiming incapacity was less stringent and carried less draconian financial consequences than that which had actually been applied for some years to the general unemployed. This was a testament to both the practical and political difficulties raised by more stringent levels of compulsion in respect of this group of claimants.

4.2.4.3 Lone parents

The second group of claimants identified by the 2006 document as requiring further governmental attention were the approximately 750,000 lone parents on income support.[67] The government's concern was that the employment rate among lone parents was only 56.6% compared with 75% for the population as a

---

[62] *A New Deal for Welfare*, n 17 above, 39.   [63] Ibid, 42.

[64] After consultation, the government decided to stick to its proposed two-tier system of benefits even though that proposal was heavily criticised by consultees, but it did agree to make the PCA more robust—and in the usual modern form to re-name the two proposed benefits (perhaps using 'Work-Related Activity Component' rather than 'Employment Support Component'). See Department for Work and Pensions, *A New Deal for Welfare: Empowering people to work, Consultation Report*, Cm 6859, June 2006, 20. See also Work and Pensions Select Committee, Third Report, Session 2005–6, *Incapacity Benefits and Pathways to Work*, HC 616 and the government's *Response*, Cm 6861, June 2006.

[65] *A New Deal for Welfare*, n 17 above, 20.

[66] It had reached some 2.75 million by the end of 2005 and some 35% of claimants had been in receipt of benefit for eight years or more: ibid, 25–26.   [67] Ibid, 52.

whole. More significantly, this was another area of worklessness where the international figures did not show the UK to advantage, since it had in 2003 a lower employment rate for this group than any other EU Member State except the Netherlands.[68] The government's position was that it was helping to make provision to enable lone parents to work 'but in return we believe that lone parents have a responsibility to make serious efforts to return to work, especially once their youngest child reaches 11'.[69] However, the government's use of compulsion against lone parents was confined to the work-focused interview. From 2000 onwards regulations[70] were progressively strengthened so as to impose interview requirements upon a wider range of lone parents, and at ever-shorter intervals. By 2005 any lone parent, entitled to income support and responsible for and living in the same household as a child, was subject to a requirement to attend such a work-focused interview (provided the parent had attained the age of eighteen).[71] The interview process must be repeated every six months in the normal case, and every three months in the case of a parent with a (youngest) child over the age of fourteen who had been claiming income support for at least twelve months.[72] The increased frequency of interview as the child approached 16 (and thus ceased to be of compulsory school age) was designed to avert what the government saw as a particular problem, namely, lone parents moving straight onto incapacity benefit at that point. The purpose of such an interview was to help the interviewee into work, either directly (by identifying job opportunities) or indirectly by identifying ways of increasing the prospects of the interviewee's obtaining a job. Failure to attend the interviews as scheduled without good cause would lead to a reduction or cancellation of benefit.

The 2006 consultation document proposed to lower the (youngest) child's age at which three-monthly interviews become mandatory to eleven but notably did not propose, as it did in the case of the disabled, to make work-related activity compulsory.[73] In other words, although the interviews were mandatory, taking up any of the suggestions emerging from the interview or taking advantage of the facilities of Jobcentre Plus was to remain voluntary in the case of lone parents. Instead, a reward rather than a sanction was to be deployed to encourage work-related activity: a premium of £20 per week was proposed for lone parents who had been on benefit for at least six months and whose youngest child was aged 11 or over who committed themselves to a programme of work-related activity agreed with the personal adviser.[74] Why did the voluntary principle continue to play a greater part in the arrangements for lone parents as compared with the disabled, especially as moving lone parents into work was seen as the main mechanism for relieving child poverty? The document gives no direct answer to the question. However, it can be said that, whereas the numbers on Incapacity Benefit

[68] Ibid, Figure 3.1.   [69] Ibid, 52.

[70] Social Security (Work-focused Interviews for Lone Parents) and Miscellaneous Amendments Regulations 2000, SI 2000/1926, as amended.   [71] Reg 1(3)(g).

[72] Regs 2 and 2A.   [73] *A New Deal for Welfare*, n 17 above, 56.   [74] Ibid, 57–58.

had remained stubbornly high, the employment rate of lone parents, although low on an international comparison, had improved by eleven percentage points since 1997 under the regime where compulsion was confined to interviews. Moreover, in the case of lone parents with a youngest child aged at least 11 the employment rate was 68%, not far short of the government's target of 70% for lone parents as a whole.[75] There was thus reason for thinking that there was a close alignment between the government's goals and those of lone parents themselves, at least in relation to older children. In relation to lone parents with younger children, the government seemed to take the view that the main obstacle to work was the non-availability of flexible, affordable child-care, rather than an unwillingness of lone mothers to work, so that it proposed to put resources into a programme to provide by 2010 to all parents 'school-based care for 5 to 11-year-olds . . . from 8 am to 6 pm all year round'.[76] A further consequence of this approach was that the government could preserve its political capital to fight for compulsion in the areas where it thought it most needed.

4.2.4.4 Older workers

For the government the position of workers over the age of 50 presented a serious policy challenge. On the one hand, life expectancy had increased substantially over the post-War period, whilst, beginning in the 1980s, economic activity among the over-50s had fallen, partly because of the use of early retirement to deal with the growing level of redundancies in that period, thus helping to create 'a culture of early retirement'.[77] Taken together, these trends meant that people were spending a lower proportion of their lives in work than had been the case for previous generations.[78] Although in many ways welcome, these developments created policy challenges along two dimensions. On the one hand, the economy would find it increasingly difficult to support the retired at an appropriate material level through transfer payments from those in work; on the other hand, workers who retired early would be in a less good position to contribute financially to their own (extended) retirement. *A New Deal for Welfare* (2006) did not locate its solutions to this problem mainly in the area of social security reform. Rather, it emphasised the introduction of age discrimination laws and the reform of pensions—both of which might have as much, if not more, impact on keeping the over-50s in their existing jobs and thus combating the 'early retirement culture'.[79] However, it did propose to introduce an element of compulsion which had previously been lacking into the social security rules.

---

[75] Ibid, 57. The National Statistical Office reported that between 1992 and 2006 the proportion of one-parent households without a job had fallen by more than a quarter, so that the overall proportion of households consisting of a lone parent with at least one dependent child where the parent was in work was 60% in 2006: *First Release*, July 26, 2006, Table 1(ii).

[76] *A New Deal for Welfare*, n 17 above.   [77] Ibid, 62.

[78] Retirement as a percentage of adult life rose from 18% in 1950 to 31% in 2005: ibid, 63.

[79] The Age Discrimination rules are discussed at 4.4.2 below; pensions reforms at 2.4.1.5 above.

The government had introduced a New Deal 50 Plus in 2000 (for those on benefit for at least six months), but this was a voluntary programme and consisted of access to a personal adviser to draw up an action plan to re-enter the job market. It also followed from the voluntary nature of New Deal 50 Plus that there was no obligation on the claimant to implement the action plan, though a worker who qualified could choose to take up the options available under New Deal 25 Plus (see above). However, one innovative feature of New Deal 50 Plus was that, once work was obtained, an In-Work Training Grant of up to £1,500 was available to help the worker improve his or her skills. *A New Deal for Welfare* proposed to pilot schemes based on the principle that New Deal 50 Plus would become mandatory and to make New Deal 25 Plus mandatory for the over-50s (ie, for those claiming benefit for 18 months).[80] This was a significant change of policy in relation to the over-50s.[81] It occurred despite the fact that the employment rate for the over-50s had increased by six percentage points between 1997 and 2005 (to 71%) and that, in comparative EU terms, this was an area where the UK did well—only Sweden and Denmark having higher employment rates in this age group in 2004.[82] That compulsion was introduced despite these countervailing factors perhaps indicated the government's concern with the whole area of retirement provision.

4.2.4.5 Conclusion

We have dealt with the traditional social security aspects of the government's policies in this section under the heading of 'labour market conditionality'. This has correctly reflected the main legal change which the policy has entailed, ie, making entitlement to benefit conditional upon participation in an increasing range of schemes designed to promote employability or employment. However, the political acceptability of the compulsion can be said to depend upon the effectiveness of the schemes which claimants are encouraged and increasingly required to join. As we have noted, the schemes themselves, and the bureaucratic changes needed to deliver them, have not required much legislative change. However, there is scope for wondering about the overall quality of the substance behind the creation of 'personal advisers' for claimants and the operation of Jobcentre Plus,[83] though the government was assiduous in piloting proposed changes and commissioning research on the outcomes of its initiatives.[84] There is also a question of judgment as to whether the government had got the best balance between compulsion, on the one hand, and facilitation or encouragement on the other. However, in 2006 the government seemed protected from fundamental criticism by its success in raising the employment rate overall and in reducing to insignificance the problem

---

[80] *A New Deal for Welfare*, n 17 above, 70.

[81] Though it should be noted that only 140,000 over-50s were claiming Jobseeker's Allowance, whilst 1.4 million were claiming sickness and disability benefits and so would be subject to the rules attached to those benefits, as discussed above.   [82] *A New Deal for Welfare*, n 17 above, 67.

[83] SSAC, *Sixteenth Report April 2002–July 2003*, 2003, paras 1.8ff.

[84] The research is to be found at <http://www.dwp.gov.uk/asd/asd5/>.

of youth unemployment which had plagued its predecessors and still plagued other European governments. By 2003 the UK was the only EU Member State with an unemployment rate at 5% or below, an employment rate amongst the working age population generally at nearly 75% and an employment rate among older workers at 50% or above.[85] However, the legitimacy of the increased emphasis on labour market conditionality was also dependent upon the jobs into which claimants were encouraged or compelled actually improving their economic situation, and it is to the government's policies directed at this objective that we now turn.

4.3 Making work pay

4.3.1 The National Minimum Wage (NMW)

4.3.1.1 *The NMW and Wages Councils*

The Labour government made only two promises for reforms of substantive labour law in the period prior to its election in 1997: one was the promise to introduce a statutory recognition procedure, discussed in chapter 3, the other to introduce a statutory national minimum wage. Although a statutory minimum wage is a feature of many, though by no means all, countries in the developed world, in fact in the British context its introduction was in many ways a more radical initiative than that of a statutory recognition machinery, which had already been tried twice before in the UK in recent decades. For Britain the national minimum wage was a new departure. It is a measure of the government's commitment to 'make work pay' that it gave this new measure such high prominence and, in fact, translated it into law in the National Minimum Wage Act 1998 and accompanying Regulations a year before the statutory recognition procedure achieved the same status. If government was to place such a high premium on increasing the rate of employment, including, as we have seen, putting some not inconsiderable pressure on individuals to move from welfare benefits into jobs, it was inevitably required to protect itself from the counter-argument that the jobs into which it was forcing its citizens were exploitative and thus unacceptable. More positively, its policy of combating social exclusion was likely to be more successful if the jobs on offer met some minimum standards of reward for those who took them. As the government spokesperson put it in the Second Reading debate on the NMW Bill: 'Such a wage is a key part of our strategy to enhance employability and to help those at

---

[85] De Koning, Layard, Nickell, and Westergaard-Nielsen, n 21 above, Table 1. The Netherlands had a lower unemployment rate, but had an employment rate among older workers of only 42%; Sweden had a higher unemployment rate (5.6%) but better employment rates, especially among older workers. According to the OECD, in 2005, of the EU Member States only Luxembourg and Ireland had lower unemployment rates than the UK and only Sweden and Denmark had higher employment rates: OECD (2006), n 273 below, Figures 1 and 2.

present without jobs to move into work'.[86] The argument amounted thus to a rejection of the contention that lower rates of pay would necessarily lead to higher levels of employment because low pay would increase the number of jobs on offer. Although sensitive to the argument that, at some level, a national minimum wage would have an impact of the availability of jobs, as we shall see below, the government was persuaded by the counter-argument that a minimum wage would improve the supply of workers available to be employed. A satisfactory labour market had to provide both offers of jobs and workers prepared to take the jobs on offer.

However, although the NMW was a new venture for the UK, the use of law to protect the low paid was not. Such legislation could be found in Britain since shortly before the First World War, in the shape of what eventually came to be known as the Wages Councils Acts.[87] In their heyday in the 1950s over 60 wages councils had been in operation, though their powers were later much reduced by the Wages Act 1986 and they were abolished by the Trade Union Reform and Employment Rights Act 1993 (with only the Agricultural Wages Councils, established under separate legislation, surviving the 1993 Act and continuing to do so). A first question to address is thus why the wages councils were not revived. However, a quick glance at their structure and operation shows how they were not well adapted to solving the problem which the 1997 government perceived itself as facing. The government's view was that those out of work over a period of time (and thus most at risk of social exclusion) were likely to be able to obtain work, initially, only at the bottom end of the earnings league and it was the jobs at this level which needed to be made more attractive financially. Legislation thus needed to be targeted at the lowest paid and to have no other, complicating objectives. From this perspective a number of defects with the wages councils can be identified. First, wages councils were established on an industry-by-industry basis where pay overall was low, and so would not catch pockets of low paid work in industries which were not as a whole low-paying, whereas a NMW would not suffer from this defect in scope. Secondly, the wages councils machinery was carefully designed so as not to cut across collective bargaining (as one would expect of legislation of that period) but in consequence the scope of the legislation was constrained. Thus, as reformulated in 1945, the conditions for the establishment by government of a wages council were not simply that low wages prevailed in an industry but also that no adequate collective bargaining machinery existed or, if it existed, it was not likely to continue to operate effectively for the regulation of terms and conditions of employment.[88] Thus, if collective bargaining machinery existed, there could be no wages council, even if the industry had a significant low pay problem.

---

[86] Ms Margaret Beckett, *Hansard*, HC (series 6) vol 303, col 165 (16 December 1997).

[87] For a brief history of the wages councils see P Davies and M Freedland, *Labour Law: Text and Materials* (2nd edn, London: Weidenfeld and Nicolson, 1984) 144–154.

[88] Wages Councils Act 1945, s 1.

Thirdly, as embryonic collective bargaining bodies, the wages councils were organised on a tripartite basis, with employers' and union representatives and a small number of neutral members, to which the setting of rates was in effect delegated for the industry for which the works council was responsible.[89] The government in 1997, by contrast, wished to keep the level of the NMW in its own hands in line with its view about the likely macro-economic consequences of getting a national rate wrong. Consequently, it is the Secretary of State who from time to time prescribes the national minimum wage.[90] Tripartism survives, however, in the shape of the Low Pay Commission, a national body with employer and union representatives and independent members, which the Secretary of State was required to consult before setting the initial rates under the Act and which could be, and in fact always has been, consulted in advance of further amendments of the rates.[91] The Commission is required to consult widely on the references made to it by the Secretary of State and in making its recommendations to have regard in particular to 'the effect of this Act on the economy of the United Kingdom as a whole and on competitiveness',[92] a clear indication that the potential adverse economic effects of a NMW were to be fully assessed before rates were set. If the Secretary of State does not accept the Commission's recommendations, the reasons for so doing have to be explained to Parliament,[93] thus giving the Commission's views a status somewhat above mere recommendations.

Fourthly, whereas the wages council, again as an embryonic bargaining body, determined, not just a single minimum rate, but a minimum wage structure (ie, it set minimum wages not just for the lowest paid in the industry), as well as holidays,[94] the Secretary of State under the 1998 Act sets only a single minimum wage (albeit a different minimum wage for workers of different ages, as we shall see below). Fifthly, the complexities resulting from each wage council setting different wage structures, often for relatively small groups of workers, meant that the legal minima were often not well known, despite attempts to publicise them. It could be hoped that a small number of hourly rates[95] applying across the economy would increase the visibility of the new legislation. Finally, the wages councils' record of effectiveness was not impressive. In the middle of the 1960s the Royal Commission on Trade Unions and Employers' Associations reported that the wages

[89] With the consequence that in periods of incomes policy there might be clashes between the wages council and the government about the setting of the appropriate rate: see LLPP, 3(2)(b).

[90] National Minimum Wage Act 1998, s 1(3).   [91] Ibid, ss 5–6.

[92] S 7(5)(a).   [93] Ss 5(4) and 6(3).

[94] At least until the powers of the wages councils were reduced by the Wages Act 1986: see LLPP, 10.2(b).

[95] The NMW is required to be expressed as an hourly rate: NMW Act 1998, s 1(3). Working out whether this requirement has been met in the cases of workers not paid on a time but an output basis is necessarily complicated. See National Minimum Wage Regulations 1999 (SI 1999/584), regs 24–26A, as amended in 2004 (by SI 2004/1161). S 50 requires the Secretary of State to give publicity to the NMW rates and s 12 contains a power to make regulations to require employers to give workers a NMW statement. The latter would seem likely to be more effective than the former in disseminating knowledge of current rates, but it proved surprisingly controversial with employers and has never been invoked.

councils had achieved neither of their main objectives—to improve the position of the lowest paid and to encourage the spread of collective bargaining—and some unions, in the event probably mistakenly, thought that the wages councils were actually a barrier to the development of collective bargaining in these industries.[96] A clearer focus on the objective of raising the pay of the worst-off might lead to better results.

To sum the matter up, for the Labour government of 1997 support for collective bargaining was to be provided via the statutory recognition machinery, leaving the wages legislation to concentrate wholly on the substantive level of pay. Thus, the government was probably correct to conclude that, given the focus of its policies on combating social exclusion, the introduction of a NMW was the correct tool to choose, rather than a revival of the wages councils. For similar reasons it hardly needs to be said that the new government showed no interest in reviving the 'fair wages' legislation which the previous Conservative governments had repealed. This legislation in one way or another enabled workers not covered by collective bargaining to seek pay parity with those who were. For the new government such legislation did not focus sufficiently, or even primarily, on those at the bottom of the wages distribution.[97] However, setting a national minimum rate was a step in the dark and both the government and the Low Pay Commission were aware of the pitfalls. On the one hand, unless the new legislation did significantly improve the position of those on the lowest wages, its contribution to the fight against social exclusion would be minimal. On the other hand, setting the NMW too high might lead to a loss of jobs which would cut right across social inclusion policies.

4.3.1.2 Setting the NMW

The government and the Low Pay Commission began their task cautiously, with the former being rather more cautious than the latter.[98] This caution showed itself in three ways in particular: the level at which the NMW for adult workers[99] was set; the introduction of a 'development' rate for those below the adult age and certain other groups; and the exclusion of 16- and 17-year olds from the

---

[96] Davies and Freedland, n 87 above, 149–152.

[97] For a discussion of this legislation see Davies and Freedland, n 87 above, at 154–163 and LLPP, 10.2(a). For an argument that the NMW should be supplemented by the reintroduction of the 'fair wage' principle see Unison and the Low Pay Unit, *Justice, Not Charity: Why Workers Need a Living Wage*, 2002.

[98] An illuminating account of the early deliberations in the Low Pay Commission can be found in D Metcalf, 'The British National Minimum Wage' (1999) 37 BJIR 171 (Prof Metcalf was and is a member of the Commission).

[99] In line with its aim of encouraging work the NMW Act adopts the term 'worker' (s 1(2)), rather than the narrow 'employee', as the definition of its personal scope, and it also explicitly applies to agency workers (s 34—the agency or user being treated as the employer according to which is responsible for paying or actually pays the worker in question) and home workers (s 35—where the home worker is included even though she or he has not personally contracted to perform the work in question). Home work is a particularly intractable area of low pay and of pay below the NMW.

NMW.[100] After the NMW had bedded down, some relaxation was shown on each of these dimensions. The initial NMW for those aged 22 and over was set at £3.60 per hour as from April 1999, the rate recommended to the government by the Commission. This was much less than some unions were pressing for (about a £1 per hour less), but put the UK rate (as a proportion of median full-time adult pay) about in the middle of the NMW rates set by comparable countries.[101] Until 2003 the rate was increased only roughly in line with the increase in average earnings, but the 2003 and 2004 increases together amounted to a 15.5% increase in the NMW at a time when average earnings increased by only 8%, and the 2005 and 2006 increases continued at above average earnings to reach £5.35 in 2006.[102] A reading of the Commission's Reports gives the impression of a strong commitment to proceeding on the basis of only reliable economic evidence and, in particular, of ensuring that the NMW was not having an adverse impact on the availability of jobs and on the ability of firms to survive. Although the NMW applies across the economy and areas of low pay are to be found in many industries, it is well-known that its impact is felt heavily in certain sectors, such as the retail, hospitality, residential social care, and cleaning sectors, because it is there that low paid jobs are clustered. It is on these sectors that the Commission's attentions centred and, having established that the effects of the NMW were not on the whole adverse, it and the government were prepared to be somewhat bolder in setting the adult rate.

A particular concern of the Commission in terms of the potential job-reduction effect of the NMW was the position of young workers. Both the Commission and the government were convinced that job opportunities for non-adults were particularly sensitive to increases in wage levels (because of young persons' lack of job-related skills) and since, as we have seen above, youth employment was a particular target of the government elected in 1997, it was not likely to take risks with this sector. Consequently, the Commission recommended initially the exclusion of 16- and 17-year olds from the NMW and the setting of a lower 'development' rate for those aged 18 to 20 inclusive (at about 85% of the adult rate).[103] The government in fact chose a somewhat lower development rate for the first year than that recommended by the Commission and made the full adult rate available only for those who had reached the age of 22,[104] a position to which it has adhered ever since, despite the Commission's continuing recommendations to lower the adult age to 21. In 2004, however, the Commission recommended the

---

[100] However, the Act rules out setting different NMWs for different geographical areas, which some had recommended: NMW Act, ss 2(8) and 3(3).   [101] Metcalf, n 98 above, 179.

[102] *National Minimum Wage: Low Pay Commission Report 2005*, Cm 6475, 2005, chapters 2 and 7. It is far from clear that above-trend increases will continue after 2006. It should be noted that there is no provision for automatic up-rating of the NMW: the rate is such as the Secretary of State prescribes 'from time to time': s 1(3).

[103] *The National Minimum Wage: First Report of the Low Pay Commission*, Cm 3976, 1998, chapter 5.

[104] Statement by the President of the Board of Trade on the Low Pay Commission's Report, *Hansard*, HC (series 6) vol 314, col 508, 18 June 1998.

introduction of a NMW for 16–17 year-olds at more than £1 below the development rate and the government accepted the recommendation.[105] This was because of evidence of substitution in some sectors of workers in this age band at very low rates of pay for those covered by the development rate.

4.3.1.3 Impact and enforcement

Although the introduction of a NMW without any significant adverse impact on inflation, job growth, and firm productivity was an important achievement, because it laid the foundation for the acceptance of the NMW as a permanent feature of the regulation of industrial relations by employers and the general public, it was in itself not a major contribution to governmental policy of combating exclusion unless significant numbers of workers benefited from the NMW, so that the jobs held by them could realistically be regarded as having been made more attractive. The numbers of jobs benefiting from the NMW do seem to be substantial. The government estimated that 2 million jobs benefited from the initial introduction of a minimum wage.[106] The Commission estimated that between 1.1 and 1.6 million jobs were affected by the 2004 up-rating (admittedly a very significant one), with the true figure being probably at the upper end of the range.[107] Within the overall number of beneficiaries of the 2004 up-rating, a significant proportion were women (68% of all beneficiaries), especially women part-time workers (49% of all beneficiaries). Young workers were also significant beneficiaries (7–8% of 16–25 year-olds, as against 4% in the range 25 to 54), as were members of the Pakistani/Bangladeshi ethnic group (but otherwise whites and non-whites benefited relatively equally). These disaggregated figures for the beneficiaries indicated by the same token the groups at the bottom end of the wages dispersion.

Whether the holders of the jobs which benefited from the introduction and subsequent up-rating of the NMW actually received those benefits is, of course, a different question and raises issues about the effective enforcement of the minimum wage. The minimum rate displaces any less favourable term in the worker's contract of employment and the rights thus created can be enforced in an ordinary court or before an employment tribunal under Part II of the Employment Rights Act 1996.[108] However, it is unlikely that many low-paid workers would take such action on their own behalf—and even less likely that they would do so whilst their employment was on foot, despite the existence of statutory protections against victimisation for enforcing NMW rights.[109] Consequently, the NMW legislation relies heavily on public resources being devoted to its enforcement, as did the wages council legislation before it. The Act gives powers to 'enforcement officers'—in

---

[105] Low Pay Commission, *Protecting Young Workers: Low Pay Commission Report 2004*, Cm 6152, March 2004, chapter 3. A perverse potential result of the NMW for those in the youngest age bracket, which the Commission wished to avoid, is providing them with an incentive to abandon full-time education. [106] n 104 above.

[107] Ch 2, n 102 above.   [108] NMW Act 1998, ss 17–18.   [109] Ss 23–24.

practice, a specialist team within HM Revenue and Customs—to issue enforcement notices requiring employers to pay workers (including former workers)[110] at the NMW where the officer is of the opinion that the required rates are not being met and the notice may require specific sums of money to be paid to particular workers within a set time-period. The employer may appeal against the notice within four weeks of its issue, but the burden is on it to do so. If the notice is not complied with (and survives any appeal against it), the officer may bring proceedings in an employment tribunal for the recovery of the money on behalf of the workers as an unlawful deduction from wages and the employer is also liable to a financial penalty, of twice the wages withheld for each day of non-compliance with the enforcement notice, payable to the Secretary of State.[111] The latest report shows that the Revenue's activities have identified some £2.5 million per year in wage arrears due under the Act in a normal year, with the occasional large case increasing that figure considerably in particular years. The average deficiency in the most recent year is about £300 per worker.[112] The Revenue has a good record of success when challenged in tribunal on its enforcement notices. As Simpson has commented, 'the statistics clearly provide broad endorsement of the profile of the Revenue as an effective and efficient enforcer'.[113]

4.3.1.4 Conclusion

Overall, the NMW can be counted as a success for government policy, in three senses. First, the new principle of the state determining minimum rates of pay across the board (and not just in specific industries, as under the wages councils legislation) seems to have been accepted by employers and trade unions, though, naturally, there is continuing dispute about the level at which the minima should be set. Employers clearly had to be won around to this new mechanism, but until the early 1990s majority sentiment in the trade union movement was also against the NMW, because it provided by law, to a large group of low-paid workers, a benefit which they might otherwise seek to obtain through collective bargaining, and so the NMW could be seen as a threat to collective bargaining.[114] Secondly,

---

[110] The unhelpful decision of the Court of Appeal in *IRC* v *Bebb Travel plc* [2003] ICR 1271 in relation to former employees had to be reversed by the National Minimum Wage (Enforcement Notices) Act 2003 and there was further amendment of the provisions on enforcement notices in the Employment Relations Act 2004, s 45.

[111] Ss 19ff. The Commission has recommended that interest should be payable on amounts withheld from the workers, which currently it is not. The interest would run, apparently, from the date of non-payment rather from the date of the enforcement notice and would give employers some incentive to comply with the NMW before their non-payment is discovered by the Revenue: 2005 Report, Chapter 6. The NMW Act, Sch 2 extends its enforcement powers to the Agricultural Wages Councils' orders. Those councils may not fix wage rates below the NMW.

[112] DTI/Inland Revenue, *National Minimum Wage Annual Report 2004/5*, January 2006. (The document is dated in fact January 2005, but this seems to be an error, since its Ministerial Foreword is dated, accurately, October 2005.)

[113] Bob Simpson, 'The National Minimum Wage Five Years On' (2004) 33 ILJ at 38.

[114] Hence the decision to tailor the earlier wages councils legislation in such a way as to exclude if collective bargaining machinery existed: see above.

unlike with the wages councils legislation, there is evidence that the NMW has improved the position of the low-paid relative to the general movement of earnings in the economy and so has not operated merely to keep the low-paid in the same relative position (ie, to prevent their position from deteriorating further).[115] Thirdly, the gains for the low-paid have been achieved without significantly deleterious impacts on the overall availability of jobs at this level of wages, on inflation, or on the viability of firms employing the low paid.

At a more strategic level, the NMW represented the transfer to employers (including the government as employer) and away from the state (ie, the general taxpayer) of part of the cost of the welfare to work programme. This was not the first time the government had engaged in such a transfer. In the 1980s statutory sick pay, paid by employers, replaced short-term sickness benefit paid by the state. Initially, this was simply aimed at saving state administrative costs, because many employers had their own, more generous, occupational sick-pay schemes—and thus the machinery to administer them—and employers could recoup from the state the amount of SSP paid to employees.[116] As was perhaps predictable, employers' recoupment rights were later reduced (in fact effectively abolished) so that today, normally, only SSP expenditure in excess of 13% of the employer's gross National Insurance liability is recoverable from the state.[117] The threshold was aimed ostensibly at giving employers an incentive to control sickness absence, but it also, clearly, transferred a financial obligation from the state to employers. By contrast, the introduction of statutory maternity pay in 1975 led later only to the transfer of administrative responsibility to the employer, when the previously available maternity allowance payable by the state was rolled up into SMP in the standard case.[118] Maternity and (now) paternity and adoption pay remain largely recoverable from the state by employers, thus making the cost of this support a charge on society as a whole, not on the person who happens to be the employer at the time of the event.[119] The NMW may thus appear to be closer to the SSP than to the SMP model, since the employer cannot recoup from government any part of the NMW. However, in fact it lies in between them. The government was

---

[115] The Treasury has claimed that 'the introduction and up-rating of the NMW has brought to an end the long-term trend of average wages rising faster than those of the lowest paid workers': *Tax Credits: reforming financial support for families (The Modernisation of Britain's Tax and Benefit System Number Eleven)*, March 2005, Box 4.1)—hereafter *Tax Credits*.

[116] Social Security and Housing Benefit Act 1982, Pt I. See LLPP, 558–560.

[117] Statutory Sick Pay Act 1994 (introducing a new s 159A into the Social Security Contributions and Benefits Act 1992) and the Statutory Sick Pay Percentage Threshold Order 1995, SI 1995/512. As Wikeley, Ogus, and Barendt remark, 'this Percentage Threshold Scheme effectively requires a positive epidemic of sickness in the workforce before reimbursement becomes available' (n 12 above, 528).

[118] By the Social Security Act 1986, now the Social Security Contributions and Benefits Act 1992, s 35. It was perhaps thought both contrary to public policy and likely to be ineffective to give the employer an incentive to reduce the incidence of pregnancy among the workforce.

[119] Social Security Contributions and Benefits Act 1992, s 167, as amended, for maternity pay; Employment Act 2002, s 7 for paternity and adoption pay (recovery is set at 92% of the amount paid, except for small employers).

unwilling, for the reasons explored below, to transfer on to employers the whole of the burden of providing the financial incentive to move from welfare to work. Instead, part—indeed a considerable part in the case of families with children—of the burden remained with the state, through the payment of in-work benefit, now reorganised as 'tax credits'.

4.3.2 Tax credits

4.3.2.1 Incentives to work and the relief of poverty

We have discussed the NMW above as providing a financial incentive to move from welfare into work. The force of the incentive is easy enough to grasp in the case of a single worker, without dependants, whose benefit entitlements are limited. When, however, one turns to a workless household with, for example, two dependent children, the power of the incentive provided by the NMW may be attenuated or eliminated altogether. This is likely to be the case if the benefit payments made in respect of the dependants cease upon entry into work. This is an example of the 'unemployment trap', ie, the situation in which some people are better off on benefit than at work—or, at least, secure very little financial benefit from being in work. There are several conceivable strategies for dealing with the unemployment trap. One would be to make the minimum wage vary according to the number of the worker's dependants. However, society has never accepted the principle that a person's wages for work should vary significantly according to that person's family responsibilities, so that it is very difficult to address household poverty in this way. Another would be to set the NMW at a level which would enable the worker to meet the needs of a 'standard' family unit—if such a thing can any longer be defined. Some unions and anti-poverty campaigners advocated this approach to the NMW, but the government, as we saw above, rejected it. It would have required a very much higher NMW—some estimates put the required level at twice the level actually set[120]—thus generating a significant risk that the NMW would reduce the demand for workers, an effect likely to affect adversely the very group the high NMW was intended to protect. It would certainly go against the government's 'welfare to work' policy. The third strategy, and the one actually adopted by the government, was to continue some level of benefit payment (in the form of a tax credit) even after the worker took up employment. Thus a worker with dependent children and in a low-paying job would receive an income consisting partly of a wage, underpinned by the NMW, and partly of a tax credit. It is to the development of the tax credit system that we now turn.

However, before doing that it is important to understand that the government's commitment to tax credits was not aimed solely at bolstering its 'welfare to work' strategy. Independently of that objective, it had committed itself to reducing child

---

[120] HM Treasury, *Government's Evidence to the Low Pay Commission*, 2002, Annex A, para 30.

poverty, ie, the number of children living in households whose income fell below the poverty line.[121] This could not be achieved solely through a NMW. First, and rather obviously, a NMW can do nothing for the relief of poverty of those who are unable to work, but a policy of relieving child poverty cannot leave such households out of account. Secondly, the NMW turns out to be a rather unfocused way of relieving child poverty. This is because a surprisingly high proportion of recipients of the NMW turn out not to be members of poor households. An OECD study found that only 10% of low paid workers were in poor households.[122] So, for the relief of child poverty the government preferred a more 'targeted' mechanism than the NMW and this was provided by the benefit or tax credit system, because it made receipt of benefit dependent upon low levels of household income. The two aspects of the tax credit regime (incentives to work and relief of child poverty) were made explicit after 2002 (see below) with the introduction of a Working Tax Credit (paid to the worker) and a Child Tax Credit (paid to the main carer). Thus, although our main focus is the relationship between tax credits and the 'welfare to work' strategy, we should be aware of their broader purpose.

Indeed, the government's argument for in-work benefits could be taken further, as it was by the opposition in the debates on the NMW Bill,[123] to the extent of saying that both the incentive to work and the relief of poverty objectives could be met entirely through social welfare law and that there was no need to set a NMW. The focus should be on setting minimum income levels for households, whether they contained members in work or not, through social welfare law rather than setting minimum wage levels through labour law. The government's rejection of this policy and its adoption of a NMW sheds light on its perception of the problem facing it. First, it can be said that the approach of relying entirely on social welfare law makes the incentive to work less effective, since the minimum wage provides a positive incentive to work whereas the minimum income approach has to rely on probably less effective negative sanctions (for example, deprivation of benefit) against those not genuinely seeking work. Secondly, the minimum income approach gives employers at the bottom end of the wages distribution a perverse incentive to reduce wages, knowing that the difference will be taken up by the state. In this way, the minimum income approach can be said to involve a state subsidy to low-paying employers, an approach the government strongly rejected.[124] Thus, the government's position was that there was a further argument

---

[121] Usually defined as some percentage (not less than 50%) of median household income.

[122] OECD, *Employment Outlook*, 1998. On this basis the government concluded that 'low pay is only weakly (although positively) correlated with poverty': HM Treasury, *Evidence*, n 120 above, para 27. On the other hand, one quarter of people in low income households are employees (HM Treasury, *Tackling Poverty and Making Work Pay—Tax Credits for the 21st Century (The Modernisation of Britain's Tax and Benefit System Number Six)*, March 2000, para 3.9)—hereafter *Tackling Poverty*. Metcalf, n 98 above at 188–191, argued that the NMW's effects would be felt, within households with at least one working adult, by those households at the bottom end of the distribution.

[123] Mr John Redwood, *Hansard*, HC (series 6) vol 303, col 176 (16 December 1997).

[124] Statement by the President of the Board of Trade, n 104 above.

for the NMW in the context of its anti-poverty strategy, even though its direct contribution to the reduction of household poverty might be limited: it under-pinned its tax credit strategy.

4.3.2.2 Development of policy to 2002

What is a tax credit? In the case of a person in work, then the ideal of a tax credit (from the government's point of view) is that it is a balance standing to the credit of the employee, which the employer utilises in calculating the sum of money due to the employee on a weekly or monthly basis—or whatever other interval wages are paid at. The credit is used first to reduce any payments due from the employee to the state (by way of income tax or national insurance contributions), so that the absurdity of the state giving with one hand but taking away with the other is ended. If, after this exercise is completed, the credit has not been exhausted, then the remainder of the credit is paid over to the worker as an addition to wages, the employer reimbursing itself from the amounts of tax or national insurance contri-butions deducted from other employees' wages. From the state's point of view an administrative burden is thus passed to the employer. However, a tax credit falls short of a 'negative income tax' in that different factors are taken into account to calculate, on the one hand, the employee's income tax liability and, on the other, the size of the credit, whereas under a negative income tax these two bases of cal-culation would be unified. In particular, tax liability is calculated on an individual basis whilst tax credits depend on the calculation of household income.[125] From the worker's point of view the credit system may be simpler than separate systems of payment of benefit from the state and wages from the employer, though the model of separate systems does leave open the possibility of paying the benefit to some other member of the household than the member in work, which might be advantageous, for example, if the person in practice responsible for the children were not the person in work.

In its first term the government's main response to the issue of tax credits was contained in the Working Families Tax Credit (WFTC),[126] introduced by the Tax Credits Act 1999.[127] The credit was available only where the adult or adults in the household were responsible for at least one child. It was thus not something

[125] For this reason raising the personal tax threshold is not as effective a way of targeting poor households as the tax credit, because the former benefits those on low incomes who are nevertheless not members of poor households, so that some of the resources put into the higher tax threshold 'leak' away from those intended to be benefited. Nevertheless, the tax credit system did involve the whole-sale transfer of the benefits payment apparatus from the Department for Work and Pensions to the Inland Revenue (ie, ultimately to the Treasury).

[126] We wish to acknowledge the research assistance provided by Nicola Countouris which helped to guide us through the thickets of legislation generated by the tax credit system. The Disabled Person's Tax Credit, also introduced at this time, is discussed below.

[127] The policy behind the Act was much influenced, especially on the integration of the tax and benefit systems, by a report commissioned by the Treasury from Martin Taylor, then chief executive of Barclays Bank: HM Treasury, *Work Incentives: A Report by Martin Taylor (The Modernisation of Britain's Tax and Benefit System Number Two)* 1998.

available to single persons or childless couples, but it did seek to address the argument that a minimum wage might not be, by itself, sufficient to support a household where there were dependent children.[128] The principle of payment of benefit to a household where one of its members was in fact in work was not, however, new. This principle underlay the Family Credit introduced in 1988 (by a Conservative government) and it can be traced back to the introduction of Family Income Supplement as long ago as 1971. However, although not new, the payment of benefit to persons in work is controversial, partly because it evokes memories of the 'Speenhamland' system which operated spasmodically in England for some forty years after 1795 and which involved providing what today would be called a 'minimum income guarantee' to those in work, whatever the level of their wages. The Speenhamland system, however, was not buttressed by a minimum wage and was abandoned in the 1830s by which time there was overwhelming evidence that it operated, at least in times of economic depression, so as to give employers an incentive to reduce wages and thus to throw an increasing burden of support on the public authorities.[129]

Although the tax credit dealt with the unemployment trap, at the same time it created a 'poverty trap'. Since the benefit paid to (the families of) those in work was designed to address the position of the low-paid, it necessarily followed that, as earnings increased, the benefit would be reduced or withdrawn. Depending on the rate of reduction, the low-paid would thus suffer high marginal rates of 'tax' on their additional earnings, especially if besides loss of benefit from central government, the worker lost benefits paid by local authorities, such as housing and council tax benefit, and began paying income tax or making national insurance contributions.[130] The new government took a number of steps to reduce the impact of the 'poverty trap'. It introduced a new lower rate of income tax of 10%, so that the income tax take from the initial extra earnings of the low paid was reduced by half from its previous level.[131] Further, it lowered the rate of reduction of benefit as earnings increased from 70p in the pound (as under Family Credit) to 55p in the pound. However, it could be said that, on the one hand, a 'tax' rate of 55% was still very high and, on the other, the effect of making the reduction was, ironically, to increase the number of people subject to the disincentive to increase

---

[128] The amount of the credit increased according to the number of children. It also included an element directed at child-care costs.   [129] See Deakin and Wilkinson, n 9 above, 126–134.

[130] The marginal rates could easily exceed 100% in this situation. The disincentive effect of the withdrawal of benefit paid by local government is still a live issue. Even as late as 2005 the Treasury admitted that 'the improvements [in financial incentives to move into work] have been modest for those households in receipt of Housing Benefit': *Tax Credits*, n 115 above, para 7.11.

[131] The government preferred this solution to that of an equally costly raising of the threshold at which any income tax was paid because of its greater incentive effect: 'A lower starting rate of tax, combined with changes to the benefit system, is likely to have a more positive effect on work incentives, because a greater number of low paid workers would see a reduction in their marginal rates . . . ' (HM Treasury, *Employment Opportunity in a Changing Labour Market (The Modernisation of Britain's Tax and Benefit System Number One)*, November 1997, para 4.26). There were similar reforms to the National Insurance Contributions rules to remove the 'entry fee' whereby, once the minimum earnings threshold was reached, an employee had to pay a 2% contribution on the whole of his or her earnings.

their earnings.[132] It should also be said that it is far from clear how, or how power-fully, these disincentives to work, or to work more, operate in practice. That they are disincentives to work or work more seems plausible on a common sense approach, but their strength is another matter.[133] However, as indicated above, a government committed to applying pressure to the workless to move into the world of work would find it hard to justify this policy if it could be shown that the unemployment and poverty traps existed, even if their effect was to some degree speculative. Indeed, the government was concerned to show that it funded WFTC more generously than Family Credit had been supported so that the gains from work to families with children were correspondingly increased.[134]

4.3.2.3 Development of policy, 2002 and after

The scheme described above was taken further in the government's second term in the Tax Credits Act 2002. This reorganised the existing system around two main tax credit systems: a Child Tax Credit (CTC) and a Working Tax Credit (WTC). The former, available both to those in work and those not, brought together all (or nearly all) the benefits payable to parents in respect of their children, whilst the latter provided in-work support for those with or without children (though sup-port for the costs of child care continued to be part of the WTC, because it was seen as a work-related cost).[135] From our point of view the main focus is on the WTC for, as the Inland Revenue's consultation document preceding the legisla-tion put it, one main aim of the reforms was 'to separate the support for adults in a family from support for the children, so as to provide a clearer focus on making work pay for those in low-income households, including those without children, through the employment [working] tax credit . . . '.[136]

Thus, the rationalisation and extension of the tax credit system in 2002, which had been envisaged as early as the 1999 budget,[137] made clear its twin objectives: relief of child poverty through the CTC and providing incentives to work through the WTC.[138] Aligning the tax credit system with those groups identified (see

---

[132] This is because on, for example, a pound-for-pound reduction basis, the number of people subject to the disincentive is minimised: once the benefit has been withdrawn entirely, the disincen-tive ceases to operate and a pound-for-pound reduction system achieves that result most quickly. Under the Tax Credits Act 2002, discussed below, the reduction rate was lowered to 37%. The disin-centive effect of the poverty trap on those in work to seek additional earnings has been emphasised by the Institute of Fiscal Studies: S Adam, M Brewer and A Shephard, *The Poverty Trade-Off* (Bristol, The Policy Press, 2006) ch 3.

[133] See House of Commons Library, *Working Families Tax Credit and Family Credit*, Research Paper 98/46, April 1998, section IV.A.3.   [134] HM Treasury, *Tax Credits*, n 115 above, Box 4.2.

[135] See generally on the reforms, Inland Revenue, *New Tax Credits: Supporting families, making work pay and tackling poverty*, Consultation Document, July 2001.

[136] Ibid, para 9. The Employment Tax Credit was later termed the Working Tax Credit. However, since money paid to adults in respect of children will inevitably go to meet general household needs, there is a potential conflict between relief of child poverty and strengthening incentives to work: *The Poverty Trade-Off*, n 132 above, ch 4.   [137] *Tackling Poverty*, n 122 above, para 1.5.

[138] Though, of course, the government would maintain that work was also the best means of end-ing child poverty.

above) as the main focus of the government's efforts to raise the employment rate had already been a part of the pre-2002 system. Thus, although single people and childless households were excluded from the WFTC, some such people were brought back into tax credits through additional schemes. Thus, at the same time as it introduced the WFTC, the government brought in a 'New Deal 50+ Employment Credit' which gave a credit of up to £60 per week for the first year of employment to all those aged over 50 going into a full-time job after a spell of unemployment of six months, provided their annual income was less than £15,000 per year. This was a recognition of the difficulty those losing jobs in this age group faced in obtaining fresh employment at a wage equivalent to that which they had previously enjoyed. Also introduced at this time was the Disabled Person's Tax Credit, which did not require dependent children as part of its eligibility requirements. However, the adult elements of both these tax credits were now rolled up into the WTC, which was extended generally to single people and to households without children. This was an important extension of the tax credits and was a step taken expressly because the gains from work for those without children and not entitled to either the 50+ or Disabled Person's Tax Credit were thought to be too modest.[139]

However, the extension of the tax credit system to households without children was subject to certain restrictive conditions. First, the person in work was required to be aged 25 or over. Those below this age would benefit only from the NMW (at its full or development rate) because, in the government's opinion, 'for younger people, low pay is more likely to be transitory and active, intensive labour market policies ... and training and education are key to helping them with employment and to improving their earnings'.[140] Further, those newly brought within the credit would benefit only if they took on full-time work (30-plus hours per week; childless couples could aggregate their working hours) whereas those with children benefited (albeit at a lower rate) if they worked part-time (more than 16 hours per week). The 30-hour requirement, although at first sight restrictive, did mean that the tax credit system did not operate as a major incentive for childless workers to take on part-time or casual jobs, knowing that their income would be made up by the tax credit. As far as single persons were concerned, it might be wondered why they could not be catered for simply by raising the level of the NMW. One answer, which was likely to appeal to the government, was that the WTC was available only to those on low incomes: a person with a significant income, say from investments, should not be entitled to state aid just because he or she chose to take on a low-paying job. In other words, the WTC fitted in with the government's commitment to 'targeted' benefits.

---

[139] HM Treasury, *Tackling Poverty*, n 122 above, para 3.12. The gain needed was thought be about £40 per week and childless couples in particular, where one member went into work, were likely not to make that gain as compared with their benefit position.
[140] Inland Revenue, *New Tax Credits*, n 135 above, para 44.

4.3.2.4 *Operation in practice*

One important element of the government's reforms was not successfully maintained. As we have noted, the government had attached considerable significance to the wages and the state benefit being paid through a single payment made by the employer (though the Revenue, as with the income tax system, has to make the calculations and tell the employer how much to deduct from, or pay to, the worker). This was the way in which the WTC was introduced. However, there was considerable opposition by employers to this system, despite the recoupment provisions. Eventually, the government abandoned this system and decided that amounts would be paid directly by the Revenue to the workers in question.[141]

Secondly, the system generated high levels of inaccurate payments, especially over-payments. A Report of the Parliamentary and Health Service Ombudsman[142] indicated that, by the end of the 2003/4 tax year, one third of tax credit awards had been over-assessments (involving the overpayment of £1,931 million); that 630,000 awards had involved over-payments of £1,000 or more; and that two thirds of the over-payments were to households on modest incomes. The overpayments continued at a not much lower level in 2004/5 and were expected to be the same in 2005/6.[143] The Revenue then, subject to certain relaxations, sought to recover the overpayments, often within the same financial year in which they had been made, with the result that people on very low incomes, who had received the money in good faith, had spent it and had no reserves on which to draw as their benefit disappeared, often found themselves in severe financial difficulty. The overpayment problem revealed a potential disadvantage for claimants arising out of the move to a 'tax' model from the 'social security' model of assessing payments. Under the latter, assessments are made on the basis on the claimant's current circumstances at the time the award is made (not the previous year's income) and, equally important, the award is then fixed for a period of six months. Thus, no question of claw-back arises in respect of payments during that sixth-month period, but equally no entitlement to greater payments can arise in that period. The adoption of the tax model was designed to produce a system more responsive to changes in the claimant's situation, but its tendency to produce overpayments of a substantial character which were then clawed back tended to show the system up as oppressive rather than responsive.

In addition, the tax credit system was subject to large-scale and organised attempts at fraudulent claims, which caused HMRC to close down its tax credits

---

[141] Tax Credit (Payment by Employers etc) (Amendment) Regulations 2005, SI 2005/2200, revoking the Working Tax Credit (Payment by Employers) Regulations 2002, SI 2002/2172.

[142] *Tax Credits: Putting Things Right*, 3rd Report, Session 2005/6, HC 124, June 2005.

[143] National Audit Office, *HM Revenue and Customs 2005–06: The Comptroller and Auditor General's Standard Report*, HC 1159, July 2006, para 2.14. The overpayments in 2004/5 were £1.8bn, which the Treasury welcomed as a drop of 20% on the previous year, a calculation achieved only by revising upwards the overpayments in 2003/4 from £1.9bn to £2.2bn!

e-portal in December 2005;[144] and the new IT system procured by the Revenue did not function properly, its providers eventually paying the Revenue some £71 million worth of compensation.[145] In an attempt to fix the overpayment problem, the Chancellor announced in the Pre-Budget Report 2005 that the amount of increased income a family could acquire before the repayment of tax credits would be required would rise from £2,500 in the relevant year to a huge £25,000, thus catering for most of the system's mis-projections of current income.[146] It also proposed to strengthen the reporting obligations on claimants in respect of changes of circumstances.

Apart from these (severe) delivery problems, what impact did the tax credit system, and the resources put into it, have on the incentives to move into work? Obviously, a lot depends on the assumptions one makes about the type of household in question and their remuneration from work. However, at least in some cases the increase in incentive seems to have been substantial. Thus, for a one-earner couple with two children the point at which the tax credits exactly cancelled out the worker's tax and national insurance liabilities rose from £13,600 in 1997/8 to £18,700 in 2005/6,[147] a very substantial rise in the threshold at which deductions began to bite. At lower levels of income, the tax credits could effect a substantial addition to wages produced by the NMW for some groups of worker. So, in October 2005 a single-earner family with one child working 35 hours per week at the then-prevailing minimum wage would receive nearly £177 weekly from the employer, but the tax credits would not only eliminate any tax or national insurance charge on this amount but also increase the household income to £260. By contrast, a single worker aged over 25 and working the same amount would receive £169 (ie, the credit would operate so as to reduce but not eliminate tax and national insurance deductions), whilst a childless couple would receive a modest addition to wages so as to bring their income up to £200.[148]

4.3.2.5 Conclusion

Leaving aside the delivery problem, which in principle ought to be reparable, what can we conclude about the government's policy to 'make work pay', as expressed in the NMW and the tax credit system? Three things can be said. First, the government did not see the burden of implementing this policy as one that should fall on

[144] Ibid, paras 2.30ff. To add insult to injury, the fraud sometimes involved identities stolen from staff working at the Department for Work and Pensions.

[145] *Financial Times* (UK Edition 23 November 2005), p 2. The Treasury Select Committee was subsequently highly critical of the opacity of this settlement: *The administration of tax credits*, Sixth Report, Session 2005/6, HC 811–1.

[146] HM Treasury, *Pre-Budget Report 2005*, Cm 6701, December 2005, paras 5.18ff. However, overpayments resulting from other causes, such as official error or fraud, would not be affected by these changes. [147] *Tax Credits*, n 115 above, Table 3.1.

[148] Figures calculated from ibid, Table 4.1. Thus, despite the extension of WTC to childless households, the biggest gainers from the tax credits remained households with dependent children.

state resources alone. The NMW clearly indicates the government's view that the state should not subsidise wages; and the NMW and the tax credit system taken together have the result that the lion's share of the financial incentives to move into work are to be provided for single persons and even childless couples, under the age of 50, through wages rather than benefits. Secondly, the government does accept as a charge on its resources an obligation to relieve poverty. A major source of household poverty it has identified as being the costs associated with bringing up children. Indeed, it has stated its objective to be to abolish child poverty 'within a generation'.[149] However, a policy aimed at achieving the elimination of child poverty must necessarily involve making payments to parents, whether they are in work or not, as the separate identification of a CTC in 2002 indicates. This puts a natural limitation on the policy of 'making work pay'. The government's response to this was to design WFTC and CTC in such a way as to allow parents to secure significant gains from work, for example, by a gentle rate of reduction of the tax credit as wages increased[150] and including in the credit system an element for child-care costs. Thirdly, the integration of the tax and benefit systems has been achieved only partially. At the level of the state apparatus, the Benefits Agency has been increasingly merged into the Revenue, but the government has not achieved its objective of making benefit payments to those in work solely through the employer—partly because of employer resistance and partly because it may not be appropriate to channel both wages and benefit solely through the parent who is in work.

4.4 Reducing barriers to work

Reducing barriers to work can be viewed from both the demand side (ie, from the side of employers) or from the supply side (ie, from the perspective of employees). From the demand side the government viewed the matter as one of reducing what it viewed as the irrational reluctance of employers to employ (or retain) certain types of worker, notably the sick or disabled and old workers. Its main legal strategy was to give to workers or potential workers individual rights as against the employer not to be discriminated against on the relevant ground, thus using discrimination law as a way of furthering its labour market aims. In rather similar fashion its commitment to 'family friendly' policies, which extended beyond the law of discrimination, promoted its policies of increasing the employment rate, by maximising the chances that parents (especially women) with children would remain in or return to work. Such laws, however, are likely to have an effect on the supply side as well: those in whom the new rights are vested may now perceive

---

[149] See, for example, HM Treasury, *Tax Credits*, n 115 above, para 5.
[150] HM Treasury, *Modernisation*, n 131 above.

themselves as part of the labour market when previously they did not; or they may make greater efforts to obtain work, bolstered by their perceived entitlement to be considered fairly for jobs. Supply side measures aimed at overcoming barriers to work may take, of course, a number of different forms. In particular, policies aimed at equipping workers with the skills sought by employers operate in this way. As we have noted, at 4.2 above, the New Deals contained a considerable element of helping or requiring claimants to prepare themselves for work, in other words the conditionality of the benefits was not a mechanism simply for throwing burdens onto unaided individuals. There is no need to go over that ground again here, except to note its relevance to 'reducing barriers to work'. In this section, therefore, we will concentrate on the strategy of conferring rights on individuals as against the employer.

4.4.1 Disability discrimination

The Disability Discrimination Act 1995 was passed by a Conservative government. Implementing a manifesto commitment, the Labour government appointed a ministerial Task Force in December 1997 to review the 1995 Act and its final report, *From Exclusion to Inclusion*,[151] foreshadowed the three significant changes or additions to the 1995 Act which the Labour government later effected. These were the Disability Rights Commission Act 1999;[152] the Disability Discrimination Act 1995 (Amendment) Regulations 2003;[153] and the Disability Discrimination Act 2005. The first established a Disability Rights Commission along the lines of the Equal Opportunities Commission and replaced the ineffective National Disability Council established under the original Act. (The DRC was later to be amalgamated into the Commission for Equality and Human Rights by the Equality Act 2006, along with the EOC and the Commission for Racial Equality.) The second, and most important from our point of view, made substantial changes to the basic duties laid upon employers by the 1995 Act. The third established a duty upon public bodies (but only them) to promote equality of opportunity for disabled people, along the lines of a similar duty imposed by the Race Relations (Amendment) Act 2000 within its scope of operation. The process of reform was also aided to some degree by the adoption by the Community of the Directive establishing a general framework for equal treatment in employment and occupation, which embraced among other things disability discrimination.[154] The government's view, however, was that the Directive required it to do nothing that it had not already planned to do on the basis of the Task Force report, so that

---

[151] A Report of the Disability Rights Task Force on Civil Rights for Disabled Persons, December 1999.

[152] This Act was passed in fact on the basis of an interim report from the Task Force and before it even delivered its Final Report.   [153] SI 2003/1673.

[154] Council Directive 2000/78/EC (OJ L303/16, 2 December 2000) (hereafter the 'general framework Directive').

its main impact was to permit the second set of reforms to be effected by means of Regulations under the European Communities Act 1972 rather than through primary legislation.[155]

The discourse in which the original Act was debated in Parliament, and that of the Task Force, was almost entirely that of civil rights.[156] That discourse has continued, rightly, to be the dominant one through which discussion of disability law is conducted. However, it would be inaccurate not to notice the labour market implications of the legislation. From within its civil rights approach, the task force stated: 'It is a myth that most disabled people are unable or reluctant to work.'[157] Moreover, it put forward as a criticism of the operation of the then current law 'the fact that disabled people are only half as likely as non-disabled people to be in employment'—although it is unclear whether they were arguing that in a non-discriminatory environment the employment rates of the disabled and the non-disabled would be the same. The government's response to the taskforce was couched predominantly in civil rights language as well, but it quoted with approval its own earlier observation that eliminating unjustified discrimination 'is not only inherently right, it is also essential for Britain's future economic and social success . . . '.[158] More revealing of governmental policy were its publications dealing with its approach to the welfare state generally. Thus, in *A New Contract for Welfare*,[159] issued at the beginning of its period of office, the government placed the disability discrimination legislation alongside the New Deal for disabled people, the disabled person's tax credit, and the reform of incapacity benefit as part of a coherent overall package. Some years later the government was more explicit in identifying the connections between the disability discrimination legislation and its various policies of promoting work. Thus, in *Improving the Life Chances of Disable People* (2005), the Prime Minister's Strategy Unit remarked:

A number of changes have been made since 1997, including the strengthening of the Disability Discrimination Act, the New Deal for Disabled People, and the National Minimum Wage . . . These changes have improved incentives and assistance for people to move off benefits and into work, and have placed additional requirements on employers to employ disabled people.[160]

---

[155] On the relationship between the Directive and national law, see Katie Wells, 'The Impact of the Framework Employment Directive on UK Disability Discrimination Law' (2003) 32 ILJ 253, taking a somewhat more positive view of the potential impact of the Directive.

[156] The terms of reference of the Task Force were: 'To consider how best to secure comprehensive, enforceable civil rights for disabled people within the context of our wider society, and to make recommendations on the role and functions of a Disability Rights Commission.'

[157] n 151 above, 37.

[158] DfEE, *Towards Inclusion—Civil Rights for Disabled People*, March 2001, 8.

[159] n 1 above, chapter 6.

[160] Prime Minister's Strategy Unit, *Improving the Life Chances of Disabled People* (January 2005) 156. However, the Report also noted subsequently the view that discrimination legislation has made employers cautious about employing disabled persons and that the legislation's main impact has been in relation to those who become disabled in employment (p 186). It recommended only exhortatory work by government to address this problem.

Again, in *A New Deal for Welfare* (2006),[161] the Department for Work and Pensions remarked, somewhat menacingly, as a prelude to its discussion of the disability discrimination legislation: 'We need to change the current culture and raise the expectations of employers, health professionals and disabled persons themselves that these barriers [to work] can be overcome.'

Can the disability discrimination legislation be viewed in the same way as we have presented the NMW, ie, is the government shifting part of the costs of its labour market policies onto employers? Had the DDA stopped at prohibiting discrimination on grounds of disability, it might have been possible to answer this question clearly in the negative. It might then have been said that the government's aim was simply to combat 'irrational' discrimination, and that by preventing employers from taking such action, it was in fact promoting their best interests (by expanding the supply of suitable workers). However, the DDA makes the employer liable, not only for direct discrimination ('on grounds of' the disability), but also for discrimination which 'relates to' a person's disability, which the Court of Appeal[162] held to involve comparison with the employer's actual or likely treatment of a person who does not have the disability in question. This appears at first sight to mean that an employer must assess the applicant's suitability for a job on the artificial basis that the applicant is not disabled, and, in consequence, might have to employ a person who was incapable of performing the tasks demanded by the job. However, such considerations can in fact be relied on by the employer because disability-related discrimination can be justified, provided the reason put forward is 'both material to the circumstances of the particular case and substantial'.[163]

Further, the DDA does go beyond these two categories of discrimination. From the beginning it identified a form of discrimination consisting, as now defined, of a failure to make 'reasonable adjustments' to the physical features of the employer's premises or to any 'provision, criterion or practice' applied by the employer, which places the disabled person at a substantial disadvantage in comparison with non-disabled persons. By requiring reasonable adjustments the disability discrimination legislation, uniquely among current discrimination laws, imposes a form of mandatory positive discrimination upon employers. In other areas, the starting point is one of a prohibition on positive discrimination, with some mild forms of such policies being permitted, but not required.[164] By contrast, the duty to make reasonable adjustments, as the Act recognises,[165] may require an employer to treat a disabled person more favourably than non-disabled employees. Until the changes made by the 2003 Regulations such a failure to make reasonable adjustments

---

[161] n 17 above, 49.   [162] *Clark* v *Novacold Ltd* [1998] ICR 951.

[163] DDA 1995, s 3A(1). In fact, the main purpose of the amendments made in 2003, by which s 3A was introduced, was to remove the defence of justification from direct discrimination (not previously separately identified as a form of discrimination under the DDA) rather than to threaten its availability in respect of disability-related discrimination.

[164] Council Directive 2000/78/EC, art 7.   [165] S 18D(1).

could be justified by the employer, but at that point, following the Task Force's recommendation,[166] the defence was removed, on the grounds that the employer did not need it to protect its legitimate interests, because only 'reasonable' adjustment was required in any event.[167] At the same time the scope of the disability discrimination legislation in the employment area was expanded by the removal of the small employer exemption and the inclusion within it of various types of 'employee-like' relationships, most notably contract workers.[168]

Thus, the extent to which the costs of securing or maintaining employment of disabled persons falls on employers depends to a large extent on how the courts interpret 'justification' in relation to disability-related discrimination and, especially, 'reasonableness' in relation to the duty to make adjustments. The policy, as articulated by the Task Force, was that 'the DDA's approach to allowing employers to appoint the best person for a job, *once they have made any reasonable adjustment, should continue in civil rights legislation'.*[169] This suggests that the main cost-shifting element for employers was the reasonable adjustment duty. However, the Act does not make it clear what level of resources the employer may have to commit to discharging the duty, merely setting out a lengthy list of factors for the courts and tribunals to take into consideration.[170] The courts, to whom the matter is passed, have adopted a relatively robust approach by taking a wide view of the matters to which the adjustment duty applies[171] and conceptualising the duty in objective terms, so that little deference is given to the employer's view of what is reasonable in the circumstances.[172] Whatever private sector employers may have thought of the disability discrimination legislation,[173] they will have known that these duties applied equally to the public sector as employers as well. Indeed, the Disability Discrimination Act 2005, by imposing on public employers a duty to promote equality of opportunity, subjected them to a duty not required of private sector employers. As the Strategy Unit remarked, an important aim of the 2005 Act was that 'Government departments, government agencies and local authorities ... should take the lead in demonstrating, promoting and reporting on best practice in the recruitment and retention of disabled people.'[174] Thus we find in the area of discrimination law an interesting revival of the idea that the public sector should be a 'model employer', an idea in earlier times formulated mainly by reference to collectively bargained terms and conditions of employment but one

---

[166] n 151 above, 40.

[167] DDA 1995, s 4A, as introduced by the 2003 Regulations. Failure to comply with the duty has the further consequence that disability-related discrimination cannot be justified unless it would have been justified had the employer complied with the adjustment duty: s 3A(6)   [168] S 4B.

[169] n 151 above, 40 (emphasis added).   [170] S18B.

[171] *Archibald* v *Fife Council* [2004] ICR 954, HL.

[172] *Smith* v *Churchill's Stairlifts plc* [2006] IRLR 41, CA, as contrasted with the greater deference afforded to the employer's view on the matter of justification of disability-related discrimination: *Jones* v *Post Office* [2001] IRLR 384, CA,

[173] Some are openly supportive, such as the members of the Employers' Forum on Disability (see <http://www.employers-forum.co.uk>).   [174] n 160 above, 191.

explicitly rejected by the Conservative governments of the 1980s.[175] In this way, the Disability Discrimination Act 2005, together with its counterparts, the Race Relations (Amendment) Act 2000 and Part IV of the Equality Act 2006 (for sex discrimination), resuscitated the 'model employer' role for the state but in a significantly different area of employment law.

4.4.2 Age discrimination

Thus, in relation to disability discrimination, the Labour government coming into office in 1997 found the anti-discrimination principle already enshrined in legislation, was elected on a manifesto commitment to extend the reach of the legislation, and proceeded to implement most of the recommendations of the Disability Rights Task Force. Its response to age discrimination was rather different. There was no existing legislation on the topic in 1997; its original response was to address the issue without the use of legislation; but it changed its mind, partly in response to evidence that the voluntary process was having little impact and partly as a result of the adoption of the general framework Directive (2000), which included age within its scope. It would be wrong to suppose that this aspect of the Directive was included over the bitter opposition of the British government; on the contrary, the government welcomed the Directive, which, being put forward under Article 13 EC, required the unanimous consent of all the Member States, though the legislative initiative at Community level perhaps increased the speed of the government's conversion to the use of legislation in the area of age discrimination. However, since the Directive allowed Member States a particularly long period to transpose its age discrimination provisions,[176] the domestic rules did not come into force until October 2006.[177] Thus, it was nearly a decade after its first election that the government implemented legislation prohibiting discrimination on grounds of age.

Despite the length of time it took for legislation to arrive, the government put the issue of age discrimination on its agenda from an early stage. In May 1997 it announced its intention to consult on the best way of tackling age discrimination. The results of that consultation showed, in the government's view, a lack of a consensus on the use of legislation and a failure on the part of those supporting legislation to make out a strong case for it.[178] It therefore proceeded to adopt in 1999 a voluntary Code of Practice on Age Diversity in Employment.[179] However, that there were elements in government who took the view that legislation was going

---

[175] LLPP, 10.2.

[176] General framework Directive, art 18. A similar relaxation applied to its provisions on disability discrimination, but the government did not seek to make use of it in that sphere.

[177] The Employment Equality (Age) Regulations 2006 (SI 2006/1031)—hereafter Age Regulations. The pension provisions of the Regulations were delayed for a further two months.

[178] DfEE, *Action on Age: Report of the Consultation on Age Discrimination on Employment* (1998).

[179] The current version of which can be found on <http://www.agepositive.gov.uk/>.

to be necessary to produce a significant change in attitudes towards, especially, the recruitment of older workers was demonstrated as early as the following year, when a Cabinet Office Report concluded that 'age discrimination legislation would have a positive effect on British culture and would build—as other discrimination Acts have—on a growing sense of public interest'. It therefore recommended that 'the Government should make clear that it will introduce age discrimination legislation if evaluation of the Code of Practice on Age Diversity shows that it has not been effective. That is, Government should decide to legislate unless a clear shift in attitudes and behaviour has occurred.'[180] That evidence was duly forthcoming in a 2001 study which concluded:

Overall, the research programme indicates that awareness of the Code is far from universal among employers although awareness is increasing. In particular, those in smaller companies tend to show patchy awareness and many have no recall that a copy of the Code was ever sent to them ... There is some slight evidence of change as a result of the Code's publication ... However, the level of change experienced and expected is still very low and many employers confidently assert that age discrimination is not an issue for them.[181]

The adoption of the Framework Directive in December 2000, requiring anti-age discrimination legislation, was thus in tune with the development of policy at domestic level.

The potential relevance of age discrimination legislation to the government's labour market policies is clear enough: as we have seen, at the beginning of its period of office it was much exercised about improving the employment prospects of young workers and later the same issue in relation to older workers was seen to be pressing. Age discrimination legislation could help remove the barriers to work for both these groups. In its first post-Directive consultation devoted specifically to the issue of age discrimination legislation, the government stated:

Legislation on age discrimination is likely to result in increased participation rates for older and younger workers. This will lead to a wider pool of workers whose abilities and talents better match the requirements of employers when recruiting and developing their staff ... The Cabinet Office report, *Winning the Generation Game*, published in 2000, discussed the cost of low participation rates amongst older workers. It gives us an idea of the possible scale of impact in this policy area. It said: 'The total economic cost is high. The drop in work rates among the over-50s since 1979 costs the economy about £16 billion a year in lost GDP and costs the public purse £3–5 billion in extra benefits and lost taxes'.[182]

However, it is one thing to adopt the principle of age discrimination legislation and another to translate that principle into legislation. As far as the labour market impact of the legislation is concerned, the two most important legislative issues were the rigour with which the anti-discrimination principle was to be applied to

---

[180] Cabinet Office, *Winning the Generation Game*, April 2000, 60.
[181] Department for Work and Pensions, *Evaluation of the Code of Practice on Age Diversity in Employment*, September 2001, para 8.7. [182] DTI, *Age Matters*, URN 03/920, July 2003, 7.

employment practices in general and the specific issue of how mandatory retirement ages were to be handled in the legislation. As to the first, the government's perception and that of most of those it consulted was that the use of age as a criterion for awarding employment and the benefits associated with it, although normally inappropriate, was legitimate in a wider range of cases than in the area of sex or race discrimination.[183] Thus, the Directive envisages,[184] and the domestic Regulations provide,[185] that even direct discrimination on grounds of age may be justified. In all other areas of current discrimination law,[186] justification of direct discrimination is not allowed. Of course, there are situations in these other areas where direct discrimination is permitted, but these are identified ex ante by the legislature (usually under the heading of 'genuine occupational requirements') and are very narrowly drawn. The use of ex post justification in the Age Regulations (in addition to the category of ex ante genuine occupational requirements) indicates a greater willingness on the part of the government to contemplate the continuing use of age as a criterion for the award of benefits in the employment area. This is so despite the test for justification being fairly narrowly drawn, ie, 'a proportionate means of achieving a legitimate aim'.[187] It also means that the answer to the first question of the rigour of the anti-discrimination principle in this area will depend in part on the case law developed by the courts, up to and including the European Court of Justice, which may take a tighter view of justification than the British government might think desirable.[188] The Directive gives examples, which the government initially intended to turn in the Age Regulations into an exhaustive list, of potentially justifiable age restrictions, but it later decided to make the category of justifiable aims open-ended.[189] The Directive's list is: fixing minimum conditions of age, professional experience, or seniority; fixing a maximum age for recruitment to jobs where there is a significant training requirement; and setting favourable conditions for access to employment for young people, old

---

[183] The Secretary of State, Ms Patricia Hewitt, captured the point well in her Foreword to *Age Matters*, where she said: 'In the work we have been doing on implementing the European Employment Directive I have been struck by how ageism is widely held to be a milder form of discrimination. It is not viewed as seriously as sex discrimination, say, nor as being as socially divisive as race. It's true that, unlike other areas of discrimination, differences of treatment based on age are not often based on hostility or ill feeling. That might simply reflect the fact that age is a condition we all have in common, and that we're resigned to having been younger and to getting older. But the inevitability of age is no excuse for discrimination; nor should we ignore people's abilities just because they are the "wrong" age. Such attitudes damage individuals, employers, and the country.'

[184] General Framework Directive, art 6, permitting Member States to introduce a justification provision but not applying this permission to the other grounds of discrimination covered by the Directive. [185] Age Regulations, reg 3.

[186] As we have seen above (n 163), justification of direct discrimination on grounds of disability was available until the reforms of 2003. [187] Age Regulations, reg 3(1).

[188] Case C-144/04, *Mangold* v *Helm* [2006] IRLR 143, ECJ, cf J Swift, 'Justifying Age Discrimination' (2006) 35 ILJ 228.

[189] DTI, *Coming of Age*, URN 05/1171, July 2005, p 30. It was also decided at a late stage not to included the Directive's list of examples, apparently out of concern that such a list would lead the courts to read down the range of non-listed situations which would be justifiable.

people, or carers in order to promote their employment opportunities. As far as the latter example is concerned, we have seen above that the government's different New Deal programmes are explicitly age-based. However, the government will be relieved of the necessity to justify its choice of age criteria, since neither the Directive nor the Regulations apply to social security or social protection schemes.[190]

The issue of mandatory retirement ages is one which the government found very difficult and on which its proposals varied considerably in the policy-formation process. On the one hand, facilitating work beyond normal retirement age would help with the problems of financing retirement, which, we have noted above, the government had identified as a major policy concern. By extending working life and reducing the period of retirement the financing problem would be alleviated. The government was proposing a number of initiatives in related fields to encourage such an extension of working life, most notably in the area of pensions. Thus in 2002 the government proposed to remove the rule preventing pensions schemes from making payments to members, once they had reached pensionable age, if the member still worked for the employer, thus encouraging part-time work after the normal retirement age. In the long term, much more important was likely to be the raising of the state pension age to 68.[191] At the other end of the scale, the minimum age for putting pensions into payment (whilst retaining tax relief for the scheme) was to be raised from 50 to 55.[192] On the other hand, some employers were resistant to the removal of mandatory retirement ages on the grounds that they provided a trouble-free way of ending the employment of often long-serving employees, without the need for proving that their performance had fallen below acceptable standards of competence. Employer attitudes to the Age Regulations as a whole were likely to be significantly affected by the government's stance on mandatory retirement ages.

The government's initial view in 2000 was that the abolition of mandatory retirement ages should not be a short-term objective and that US experience with the policy should continue to be monitored.[193] By 2003 the government's main policy had become that mandatory retirement ages would need to be justified by reference to the (in the government's view, restrictive) criteria discussed in the previous paragraph. In principle, therefore, mandatory retirement ages would be a breach of the age discrimination regulations and so no longer maintainable by employers, but employers in certain exceptional cases might be able to justify their continuance. However, the government consulted on the notion of introducing a

---

[190] Directive Art 3(3). The Age Regulations apply only to employers, unless their provisions are explicitly extended beyond that group. Reg 22 applies to governmental activities under the Employment and Training Act 1973, but only to the extent of outlawing harassment and subjection to a detriment. However, the age provisions of the minimum wage legislation do appear to be challengeable, the most likely challenge being to the decision to implement the adult rate at age 22 rather than 21. See 4.3.1.2.   [191] See 2.4.1 above.

[192] HM Treasury and Inland Revenue, *Simplifying the Taxation of Pensions: Choice and Flexibility for All*, December 2002, 4.   [193] Cabinet Office, *Winning the Generation Game*, April 2000, 59.

'default' retirement age of 70. A 'default' age of 70 would mean a mandatory retirement age at this age or later would not need to be justified and that employers would be free to end employment at that retirement age without being subject to a challenge under the age discrimination laws or under the unfair dismissal legislation. At this stage, therefore, the government appeared to be giving more weight to the policy of facilitating continuance in work by older workers rather than their smooth exit from the workforce.

By the time the government issued its final consultation document on the Age Regulations in 2005 it had decided not only to introduce a 'default' retirement age but also to set it at age 65.[194] In other words, mandatory retirement ages were to be permitted to continue, provided the age of retirement was not set below 65. Below that age, they would be lawful only if justified. Thus, the policy of facilitating smooth exit was given greater priority than two years earlier, and that of facilitating work in old age given less. This seems likely to have occurred because of pressure from business. As the 2005 consultation document stated: '[it is] clear that significant numbers of employers use a set retirement age as a necessary part of their workforce planning ... This is our primary reason for setting the default retirement age.'[195] However, this policy was accompanied by two qualifications. First, there would be a review after five years of the decision to set a default retirement age,[196] thus perhaps salvaging the 2000 policy that abolishing mandatory retirement ages should not be a short-term objective of the government but a longer-term aim. Secondly, employers of those subject to a mandatory retirement age, whether one implemented under the default rule or justified under the direct discrimination provisions, would have a duty to consider requests from employees to continue working beyond the mandatory age. The duty to consider a request for continued working was framed in essentially procedural terms which leave the employer a considerable measure of freedom over the policy to be adopted in the case of post-retirement work.[197] The ostensible sanction for non-compliance with the procedure is an award of up to eight weeks' pay, but the bigger sanction is the risk of an unfair dismissal claim.[198]

In fact, the relationship between the Age Regulations and the law of unfair dismissal is crucial in the area of mandatory retirement and has arguably produced a legal framework which makes it less likely that employers will allow workers to work beyond normal retirement age. In the case of a normal retirement age under the age of 65 the employer may well feel that the chances of justifying the lower age are likely to be decreased if the employer too freely allows workers to continue

[194] DTI, *Coming of Age*, URN 05/1171, July 2005, 55.   [195] Ibid, 59.   [196] Ibid, 71ff.

[197] Age Regulations, sch 6. The procedure consists essentially of a duty on the employer to notify the employee in good time of an intended retirement, to hold a meeting with the employee to discuss the request for continued working if such is made, and to have a further meeting to hear any appeal against an adverse decision on the request. Unlike with the request to work part-time (see 2.4.1.3, above) no restriction was placed on the grounds for refusal.

[198] ERA 1996, s 98ZB(4) and (5), inserted by Age Regulations, Sch 8, para 23.

beyond it and that strict adherence to the lower limit is the only safe policy. Even where the retirement age survives justification or does not need it, the rules may still encourage the employer to be cautious in allowing employees to continue in employment, for the following reasons. Before the Age Regulations the situation was simply that the law of unfair dismissal ceased to operate once the employee reached the employer's normal retirement age (whenever that was set) or, in the absence of such an age, the age of 65.[199] No protection against unfair dismissal was thereafter provided. The government rightly took the view that such a provision was inconsistent with the Age Regulations and repealed it.[200] Had the government stopped there, it would have failed to implement its policy on the retention of mandatory retirement ages, at least on the conventional argument that the retirement of an employee is a dismissal for the purposes of the unfair dismissal legislation. Consequently, the unfair dismissal legislation had to be amended so as to provide that a 'retirement dismissal' may be regarded as unfair only if the employer has failed to comply with the request procedure outlined in the previous paragraph.[201] This will normally be done by means of the employer giving the employee notice of not less than six months nor more than one year of the intended date of retirement and of the employee's entitlement to make a request,[202] and then following the request procedure if it is invoked by the employee.

However, this still leaves open the question of whether any particular dismissal is a 'retirement dismissal', ie, whether retirement is the only or principal reason for the dismissal. Even in the case of dismissal at the mandatory retirement age this could be problematic if the employer did not routinely require employees to leave at that age. In the case of those who work beyond the retirement age, it will be necessary to distinguish between those who are dismissed on grounds of retirement and those dismissed for other reasons (such as competence or redundancy), who will now have a right to claim the protection of the unfair dismissal laws, whatever their age. This is likely to be a highly artificial exercise: there will often be no reason for an employer to dismiss an employee who is simply allowed to work on, except on one of the grounds which will allow access to the unfair dismissal protection. The Regulations seek to deal with this problem by deeming a dismissal a retirement dismissal if the employment is terminated on or after retirement age, and the employer gives the employee the six months to one year's notice mentioned in the previous paragraph.[203] Thus, where it is agreed that the employee will work beyond the normal retirement age or he or she is simply allowed to do so, the employee acquires, in effect, a minimum notice period of

---

[199] ERA 1996, s 109 and see *Secretary of State* v *Rutherford* [2006] ICR 785, HL.

[200] Age Regulations, Sch 8, para 25.

[201] ERA 1996, s 98ZG. In the case of a normal retirement age under 65 that age must also meet the justification test under the Age Regulations: s 98ZE(3)(4).

[202] Age Regulations, Sch 6, para 2.

[203] ERA 1996, s 98ZD(1)(2) and s 98ZE(4). S 98ZB makes equivalent provisions for the 'default' retirement age of 65 (ie, where the employer has no normal retirement age but the employee is in fact dismissed at age 65 or above).

six months.[204] It is unclear how employers will react to this increased formal-
isation of post-normal retirement working, where failure to follow the procedure
will at least leave the employer open to the claim that the reason for the dismissal
was something other than the retirement.[205] If employers become more reluctant
to agree to post-normal retirement working, this fact may add to pressures at the
time of the review to solve the problem by removing mandatory retirement ages
entirely.

In addition to disability and age discrimination laws, one could point to the
race relations legislation as continuing to operate so as to remove barriers to
work facing people from ethnic minorities. However, although significant
changes were made to the Race Relations Act 1976 by the Race Relations Act
1976 (Amendment) Regulations 2003, implementing in the UK Directive
2000/43/EC, those amendments were not particularly focused on access to
work. This may be because racial discrimination, conceived as an overall category, has a complex relationship with employment rates. Thus, for example,
whereas only 11% of white households were workless in Spring 2006 as against
twice that percentage for Pakistani/Bangladeshi households, the workless percentage for Indian households was just under 7%.[206]

4.4.3 'Family-friendly' policies

As we have seen, the third main group whose employment rate the government
wished to increase was that of lone parents or, in fact, lone mothers, because lone
fathers are only a very small proportion of lone parents and their employment rate
was not significantly different from that of 'partnered' fathers.[207] However, the
government took relatively limited steps to extend the law in our period so as to
increase the demand for such workers. The category of being a lone mother (or
even parent) was not one that appealed to the legislature, whether national or
European, as an explicit protected category within discrimination law. To some
considerable extent this did not matter. Most forms of employment discrimination against lone mothers would be caught by at least the indirect discrimination
provisions of the Sex Discrimination Act 1975. More importantly, the growing
range of rights for pregnant workers, whether lone or partnered, notably the right
to paid maternity leave and to return to work,[208] helped some single women
already in work not to drop out of the labour market upon pregnancy.

[204] Unless the initial discussions at retirement age produce agreement on continued working for a
period of less than six months: sch 6, para 3(2).   [205] ERA 1996, s 98ZD(5) and 98ZF.
[206] National Statistical Office, n 75 above, Table 2(iv). The Amendment Regulations are discussed
at 2.4.2 above.
[207] *Empowering people to work*, n 17 above, 52–53. Only 170,000 of 1.8 million lone parents are
fathers and their employment rate is 70%, compared to 57% for lone mothers (2005 figures).
[208] See 2.4 above. By 2006 the government had committed itself to extending the period of maternity leave and pay to nine months in 2007 and to a year by the end of the Parliament: Work and
Families Act 2006, s 1, amending Social Security and Contributions Benefits Act 1992, s 165(1).

However, it seems clear that these extensions to the rights of pregnant mothers and parents were driven by a desire to re-balance the demands of work and family life for all workers, not just lone parents.[209] In fact, some potentially useful innovations by the government were drafted in such a way as to reduce their utility for lone mothers seeking work. Thus, a most useful right would have been one which put pressure on the employer to offer work in a form which would be attractive to a lone mother, notably in a part-time form. However, the Part-Time Regulations, as their full title suggests,[210] were confined to attacking less favourable treatment by employers of part-time workers already employed by them, rather than requiring employers to have good reasons for refusing to offer part-time work to applicants. The second main theme of the Directive,[211] which triggered the Regulations, namely, the encouragement of part-time work, was implemented through 'best practice guidance' only.[212] Nor could this defect, from the point of view of the lone parent applicant, be overcome by using the right created by the Employment Act 2002 to ask for a change in hours, or indeed other working conditions, in order to carry out child care responsibilities.[213] That right is confined to those already in employment with the relevant employer for at least 26 weeks,[214] as well as applying to only the first five years of a child's life.[215]

Thus, the government's family-friendly policies seem to have been more focused on retaining mothers in employment rather than in facilitating the move of lone parents into employment. It seems likely that the government did not regard lack of demand from employers for employees to work part-time as a significant restriction on the ability of lone mothers to move into employment. Rather it took the view that supply-side restrictions were more important, notably the lack of high-quality and affordable child care, which restricted the willingness of mothers to enter the labour market. A particular advantage to the government of tackling the issue from the supply side was that better and affordable child care might encourage mothers (whether lone parents or not) into full-time as well as part-time

---

[209] See HM Treasury, DfEE, DWP, and DTI, *Choice for parents, the best start for children: a ten year strategy for childcare*, December 2004, which devotes very little space to the particular needs of lone parents but rather focuses on families in general.

[210] Part-time Workers (Prevention of Less Favourable Treatment) Regulations 2000, SI 2000/1551.   [211] Council Directive 97/81/EC, Annex, clause 5.

[212] DTI, *Part-time workers. The law and best practice—a detailed guide for employers and part-timers* (URN 02/1710). Some more imaginative steps to increase the supply of high-status part-time work, though still without any element of compulsion, were put forward by the Women and Work Commission, *Shaping a Fairer Future*, February 2006 (URN 06/697), 37–38.

[213] Now in ERA 1996, s 80F.

[214] Flexible Working (Eligibility, Complaints and Remedies) Regulations 2002, SI 2002/3236, reg 3.

[215] S 80F(3)—unless the child is disabled, in which case the upper age is 18. There is the potential to raise claims to work part-time under the indirect discrimination provisions of the SDA 1975, but experience with such claims has been patchy. See S Deakin and G Morris, *Labour Law* (4th edn, Oxford: Hart Publishing, 2005) 604–606. The authors comment that 'the notion of indirect discrimination is too open-ended and subject to tribunal discretion in its application for one to be confident' of success in such claims. It is interesting too that all the reported cases involved claims by workers already in employment.

employment, one of the particular characteristics of the British pattern of work by mothers being a relatively high rate of part-time employment, compared with other similar countries.[216]

4.5 Training

We have noticed above that the government had developed an analysis of globalisation which led to the conclusion that those with only low skill levels would find it increasingly difficult to find work in the British labour market of the future. We have seen as well that the various New Deal initiatives contained some minimum training or at least 'confidence-boosting' measures for those in the target categories. The Budget Report for 2004 sought to formalise some of these initiatives under the banner of a 'New Deal for Skills'. Trials were to be conducted with a 'Skills Coaching service', to be offered on a voluntary basis to those on Jobseeker's Allowance with the lowest skill levels, to help claimants identify the training opportunities which might be of most use to them in seeking work. More significantly, there were to be trials of a 'Learning Option' for the longterm unemployed and those on inactive benefits where lack of skill was a significant barrier to employment. Here the motivational mechanism was to be the carrot rather than the stick, ie, an entitlement to £10 per week on top of existing benefits for those who took up the offer of the free training. In the usual way, this additional benefit was to be conditional upon signing a 'Learning Agreement' with the Jobcentre Plus Personal Adviser, and upon active participation in the training recommended by the adviser. However, the stick was not very far away, so that:

... from April 2004, Jobcentre Plus has been testing the effectiveness of applying sanctions in those cases where jobseekers have been identified with a basic skills need but have proved unwilling to take up and complete training to tackle that need. The impact of this approach will be measured against the voluntary approach being used elsewhere in England. [By the same token,] we do not want to undermine the principle that people on benefits should go straight into jobs as soon as an appropriate opportunity arises, because the evidence shows that getting a job is the most effective way of helping them. So training must not become an excuse for delaying a move into suitable employment.[217]

In spite of these moves in relation to those without work, a government concerned with raising the skill level of the workforce cannot focus only on the skill levels of those out of work. However, in relation to the skills of those in employment

---

[216] *Ten year child care strategy*, n 209 above, Chart 2.2. Having children also had a bigger (adverse) impact upon the employment rate of women in the UK than in many other countries: Chart 2.1.

[217] DfES, DTI, DWP, HM Treasury, *Skills: getting on in business, getting on at work*, Cm 6483, March 2005, Pt 2, paras 195 and 196 (hereafter *Getting on*). Chapter 4 of this document describes the New Deal for Skills in some detail. At the time of writing these proposals were still under development in terms of national application.

governmental policy has gone through an almost complete turn-around over the past half century. When in the 1960s government at last convinced itself that training was too important to be left to employers, it embarked on a strongly inter-ventionist policy, designed to influence employers' demand for skilled workers, but it implemented this policy in close collaboration with unions and employers. Thus, the Industrial Training Act 1964[218] provided for the establishment of industry-by-industry industrial training boards, established on a tripartite basis, with the power, subject to Parliamentary approval, to levy employers compul-sorily to fund the training the board thought necessary for the industry in question. The training boards thus performed a coordinating function among employers which in some other countries is performed by employers' organisations, either alone or in conjunction with trade unions, but which had never proved possible in Britain because of the increasingly atomised nature of collective bargaining in the post-war period.[219] At a strategic national level training policy was one of the matters within the remit, first, of the tripartite National Economic Development Council and, later, of the Manpower Services Commission. These institutions were badly damaged in the deregulatory onslaught of the 1980s. Neither the NEDC nor the MSC survived,[220] whilst the industrial training boards shrivelled in number when the Employment and Training Act 1981[221] gave the relevant Minister the unilateral right to abolish the boards. Today, only two still function: in the areas of general and engineering construction, where the problems of employer coordination are particularly acute.[222]

The result was what we referred to in the first volume of this history as 'employer-led training',[223] ie, the quantity and quality of training for those in work was left to individual employers, who nevertheless had access, under certain conditions, to a substantial state training budget. The first question logically facing the Labour government was whether it would reverse the deference shown to employers' training decisions by the previous Conservative governments by seek-ing to develop a mechanism—perhaps a revived industrial training board system, perhaps something different—which could influence the demand side of the training equation. The market-failure argument for doing so remained as it always had been: that in the UK the atomised system of collective bargaining (if there was collective bargaining at all), and the limited powers of employers' organisations, meant that the sum of the training decisions by individual employers was likely to be less than the socially optimal level. This was because there was no system in place by which any individual employer could be sure to capture the full benefits of its expenditure on training (a trained employee might be poached by a compet-ing employer who did not spend money on training, for example) or, alternatively,

---

[218] LLPP, 4.2(a).   [219] See 3.5 above.   [220] LLPP, 439 and 607–612.
[221] Ibid, 601.
[222] See the Industrial Training Levy (Construction Board) Order 2006, SI 2006/334 and the Industrial Training Levy (Engineering Construction Board) Order 2006, SI 2006/335.
[223] LLPP, 612–615.

whereby the costs of training could be spread across all employers in the industry in some equitable way.

The first and crucial decision which the government took (or failed to take) meant that the system of deference to employers continued. In fact, it took some time for the government to focus on the training of those in work, its early attention being directed at school and post-school education. However, in 2003 it produced *21st Century Skills*,[224] leading to *Getting on in business, getting on at work*, two years later,[225] and the appointment of the Leach Review[226] to work out which skills it was crucial for the a modern British economy to obtain and retain. The proposals resulting from these documents seemed to leave employers in the driving seat: 'Our goal was to ensure that the design and delivery of publicly-funded training put employer needs centre stage.'[227] Nevertheless, the policy also aimed to encourage a higher level of employer commitment to training, whilst falling short of mandatory measures. The main expression of this policy was the National Employer Training Programme (to be available nationally only from the 2007/8 financial year). Training 'brokers', paid for by public funds, would take the initiative and approach employers with a proposal to assess their training needs and to put them in touch with trainers who could meet those needs. Employers would not be under any compulsion to respond to the broker's approach or accept his or her proposals, reliance being placed on the employer's self-interest in raising the skill level of its employees. There would be the carrot that public funding would pay for training up to 'Level 2',[228] regarded as the goal for all leavers from the school system, but beyond that employers would be expected to pay for most of the training, with some public subsidy being made available. Brokers would not be confined to recommending public sector training providers, and so the new system might have a major impact on the funding of further education colleges, which had previously received funding directly from the Learning and Skills Council but would now have to obtain at least a proportion of that funding from broker-advised employers and compete with private providers for those funds.[229] Whether this scheme of encouragement will have a substantial impact by way

---

[224] DfES, HM Treasury, DTI, DWP, *21st Century Skills—Realising our Potential—Individuals, Employers, Nation*, Cm 5810, 2003. [225] n 217 above.

[226] Which at the time of writing had produced only an interim report.

[227] *Getting on*, n 217 above, Pt 2, para 9.

[228] Equivalent to five GCSEs at grade A–C. As a result of the Teaching and Higher Education Act 1998, s 32, 16- and 17-year olds at work who have not obtained this level of education have a right to 'reasonable' time off with pay in order to reach this level: see ERA 1996, ss 63A–C and the Right to Time Off for Study or Training Regulations 2001, SI 2001/2801 (SI 1999/1058 for Scotland).

[229] *Getting on*, n 217 above, Pt 2, paras 11–27. As Ewart Keep has pointed out, this was part of a more general development whereby central government occupied the area which it regarded as appropriate for public initiative, to the detriment of other public sector training providers which had previously had an important role in this area, for example, local authorities: E Keep, 'State Control of the English Education and Training System—Playing with the Biggest Trainset in the World' (2006) 58 Journal of Vocational Education and Training 47.

of increasing the quality and quantity of the training of those in work remains to be seen.

As for tripartism, this was revived only in a very modified form. In 2003 a 'Skills Alliance', of which the TUC and CBI are members, was established to superintend the delivery of the government's new Skills Strategy. It meets four times a year but, as Keep has observed, 'it does not create policy itself, sets no budgets or targets and does not appear to be asked to approve new policy developments'.[230] In other words, its aim appears to be to facilitate the implementation of policies decided by central government; it is not the MSC by another name. Potentially more significant was the creation at the same time of Sector Skills Councils (SSCs), under the aegis of a Sector Skills Development Agency (SSDA). By 2005 there were twenty-five SSCs in existence. The overall purpose of the SSCs, in the language of *Getting on*, is 'to give employers in each sector a means of collectively analysing sector skills needs and linking these to the main drivers of productivity',[231] though unions and union learning representatives (see below) are also members of SSCs. Moving from analysis to action, however, is to be on the basis of agreement, not compulsion. Thus, the 'main mechanism through which SSCs will address employer skill needs is Sector Skills Agreements (SSAs). SSAs are designed to engage employers at the highest level in systematic analysis and action planning to address the skills required to raise performance.'[232] Besides reliance on the incentive of self-interest to promote these exercises in employer coordination, the government holds out the possibility that SSAs will influence the way the state spends its funds in related areas. Besides the funding by the SSDA of the initial analytical and developmental work, a SSC which reached an SSA was offered the prospect of the Learning and Skills Council (and even the Higher Education Funding Council) adapting their expenditures so as to promote the goals of the SSA.[233] On the other hand, if the SSC failed to reach an SSA, or one which the government regarded as ineffective, the SSDA could ultimate get rid of it and start again with a new body, for each SSC is licensed by the SSDA for periods of five years and has three-year 'contracts' with the SSDA governing its operations.[234] Overall, the SSCs represent a rather weak form of tripartism: they are perhaps more accurately characterised as mechanisms of government-driven employer coordination, with limited input from worker representatives.

In addition to this modest revival of tripartism outside the enterprise, the government took two limited steps to give training a higher profile in relations between employers and unions within the enterprise. First, the Employment Relations Act introduced an obligation on employers to consult unions recognised under the statutory procedure analysed in chapter 3 on their training policies, plans, and provision.[235] However, this obligation arises only where the CAC

---

[230] Ibid, 50.   [231] n 217 above, para 67.
[232] Ibid, para 80. However, in the film industry a levy system to fund training has been agreed and the government will give it statutory backing by creating an industrial training board: paras 82 and 85.
[233] Ibid, para 85.   [234] Ibid, para 78.
[235] S 5 of the 1999 Act, introducing ss 70B and C into TULRECA 1992.

has not only issued a recognition order against the employer but has also gone on to specify a method of bargaining for the parties, because they have been unable to agree one themselves,[236] and the parties have not subsequently agreed to modify that specified procedure. Since the CAC has specified a method in only thirteen cases to date (generally the parties manage to agree a method of bargaining),[237] the impact of this provision has probably been slight.[238]

More significant have been the provisions on 'union learning representatives' (ULRs) introduced by the Employment Act 2002.[239] The statutory provision is in fact confined in scope, dealing with the representatives' rights to time off as against their employer rather than their relationship with the union or its members. A ULR is entitled to reasonable time off for the purpose of analysing the training needs of the union members he or she represents, providing them with information and advice about training matters, arranging training for or promoting it to them; consulting with the employer about these activities; and for the purpose of undergoing training in relation to these activities. A ULR must have been identified as such to the employer by the union; the union must certify to the employer that the proposed ULR has undergone, or is about to undergo, training to fit him or her to act as a ULR; and the union must be one recognised, voluntarily or under the statutory procedure, for the purposes of collective bargaining, and the employees in relation to whom the ULR acts must be covered by the recognition arrangements. Thus, the ULR provisions cannot be used by a union to undermine recognition arrangements in place with another union. What is clear is that this legislation, being confined to the right to time off, does not create a system of ULRs but rather endorses an existing, socially-created system and encourages its development through the time-off right. The government estimated that there were about 3,000 ULRs in existence prior to the legislation,[240] and by 2005 it stated that there were 8,000 ULRs, who (in 2004) helped 60,000 workers with training, including 9,000 to gain basic literacy and numeracy skills.[241] These are relatively small numbers and will remain so even if the government achieves its goal of increasing the number of ULRs to 22,000 by 2010.[242] Nevertheless, the ULR provisions remain an interesting, if minor, example of legislative endorsement of an exclusively union mechanism for presence in the workplace. There is no provision for workforce-elected LRs, in the absence of a ULR; rather, the pattern is that of the original provisions for consultation over redundancies and transfers of business, ie, no union recognition, no learning representative.[243]

---

[236] See 3.3.2.2 above.

[237] CAC, *Annual Report 2005–2006*, June 2006, 19.

[238] It is conceivable that this provision has influenced the content of agreed methods of bargaining, but it is unclear whether and how far this is the case.

[239] S 43, introducing s 168A into TULRECA 1992.

[240] DTI, *Regulatory Impact Assessment: Placing Union Learning Representatives on a Statutory Footing*, 2002.   [241] *Getting on*, n 217 above, para 60.

[242] Ibid, para 63—it is not quite clear how the government by itself can have a target for something which is dependent upon union initiative.   [243] See 3.4.4.1 above.

Despite these two statutory innovations, and despite the skills policies adopted from 2003 onwards, the overwhelming emphasis of the government's active labour market policies since 1997 has been on those without work rather than on up-grading the skills of those in work. In the latter area, uncoordinated employers have been left to make most of the running, at least until very recently, with consequently little improvement overall in the skill levels of the workforce.

4.6 Migrant workers

If the level of skill in the domestic labour force is inadequate, one 'quick fix' towards alleviating that situation could be to encourage workers from other countries with the relevant skills to move to the UK for the purpose of taking up employment. As we shall see below, government policy in recent years towards migrant workers has increasingly moved in that direction. Encouragement of immigration, however, was something which the government found difficult to sell politically, and it became increasingly strident in its efforts to distinguish its positive policies towards skilled migrant workers from its negative ones towards asylum-seekers or illegal immigrants.

There are many ways in which people, not previously settled in the UK, may enter the country and take up work. They may be EU (or rather EEA) citizens with a Community law entitlement to enter the UK for the purpose of seeking or taking up work; they may seek and be granted asylum in the UK on the grounds that they have a well-grounded fear of persecution because of their political or religious beliefs in the country they have just left; they may be close family members of British citizens or of others already entitled to permanent residence in the UK; they may be students doing work incidental to their main purpose for being in the UK; they may be returning British citizens previously living in another country; or, of course, they may have entered or remained in the country illegally. However, our concern is not principally with any of these groups of migrant workers but with the government's policy towards those who openly seek permission to enter the UK for the purpose of taking up employment, having no entitlement to do so, sometimes referred to as the system of 'managed migration'. It is in relation to this group that the government's policy on the relationship between migrant workers and the labour market shows itself most clearly. This means that we are not concerned principally with the most controversial areas of the government's immigration policies, although these areas, as we shall see, can also have an impact on the functioning of the labour market.[244]

---

[244] The relevant domestic law is contained in Immigration Rules made under s 3(2) of the Immigration Act 1971. These are then supplemented by formal 'Instructions' to case-workers, made and published by the Immigration and Nationality Directorate of the Home Office, which are often the most illuminating about actual practice. The *Instructions* are available on: <http://www.ind.homeoffice.gov.uk/lawandpolicy/policyinstructions/idis/>.

It is possible to make an argument for a policy of unrestricted cross-border flows of labour, akin to the one which underlies the system of world trade in goods and services. However, given the extent to which a territorial attachment is central to people's self-identification, substantial flows of people from one country to another are likely to be accompanied by significant social costs for both those who move and those who are joined, costs which do not attach to the free movement of, say, steel bars. This perhaps goes some way to explain why completely free movement of persons has been implemented so far only within relatively homogenous regional areas (such as the EU) and not on a global basis. Nevertheless, even within this restricted policy framework, it is possible to make an argument in favour of a relatively liberal policy on migrant workers. Once one rejects the 'lump of labour' fallacy (ie, that the number of jobs in the economy is fixed),[245] it can be argued that an addition to the supply of qualified workers available to employers will foster the creation or growth of businesses and thus expand the number of jobs on offer. Thus both migrants and those already here will benefit from the higher level of economic growth thus generated. This may be particularly important for the host state if, as in the UK, the birth rate is below the replacement rate and, in consequence, there is a demographic shift within the existing population away from persons of working age and towards retirees. On this argument, the admission of foreign workers with skills appropriate to the UK economy should be freely offered, subject only to controls needed to mitigate the social costs which might arise out of large and sudden influxes of workers. It is true that workers already present in the UK may suffer a cost from the arrival of new workers, even if the argument that the migrants take jobs away from those already here is largely misplaced. That cost is reduced labour market power for the workers already here, who, in the absence of the migrants, might have been able to bid up the price of their labour but who will now find that the increased labour market competition prevents them from doing so—and in extreme cases the competition might exert a downward pressure on their wages.

Finally, there is the narrowest rationale for admitting migrant workers. This is that, in the current state of the economy, there are jobs for which sufficient domestic applicants cannot be found and migrants should be admitted to take up those specific jobs. On this analysis, migrant workers are admitted not so much for the contribution they can make to the future growth of the economy but, essentially, to permit it to continue to function in its current mode. It is, in other words, a static rather than a dynamic analysis of the role of migrant workers in the economy. The jobs in question may be unskilled and low-paid but need not be. Shortages of domestic labour could exist for relatively skilled workers who are not low-paid in the sense of being on or near the minimum wage but for

---

[245] See above, text attached to n 21, where we saw this argument was used to support policies seeking to raise the employment rate.

whom alternative, better-paying work is available.[246] Up until the 1990s the dominant policy of government towards migrant workers seeking employment in this country had been this third rationale. Slowly, however, the Labour governments engaged in cautious moves towards the second rationale, without ever adopting it wholeheartedly. Four main examples of this development can be identified: relaxation of the terms of the work permit scheme; introduction of the Highly Skilled Migrant Programme in 2002; the UK's treatment of workers from the countries which acceded to the European Union in 2004; and, finally, proposals made in 2006 for the introduction of a general 'points-based' system for migrant workers.

The main mechanism[247] for a migrant worker (not from an EEA state) to obtain permission to work in the UK is the work permit scheme, introduced shortly after the First World War but applying to Commonwealth citizens only in the 1960s. Our interest is in the most common form of work permit, the Business and Commercial permit. Two features of it demonstrate its attachment to the third model. First, only employers can apply for a work permit and then only in relation to a particular job; secondly, the government (in the shape of, formerly, the Overseas Labour Directorate and, now, Work Permits (UK)) will normally grant the permit only if there is no suitable EEA worker available. Lack of suitable domestic workers will be presumed in known shortage areas (and in certain other cases), but only where the worker in question has a skill at NVQ3 level or above.[248] In short, there must be an identified existing vacancy and the migrant worker is eligible to be considered for it only after domestic possibilities have been exhausted. As soon as elected to office, the Labour government instituted a review of the scheme with the aim of making it more responsive to changes in the labour market.[249] More important for future policy was the Highly Skilled Migrant Programme, introduced in 2002. The crucial difference from the main work permit scheme is that permits under the HSMP are applied for by the worker him- or herself, who therefore does not need to have a job before entering the UK and can switch freely from

---

[246] This is a not uncommon situation in the public sector, for example, teachers in London. Government, which is virtually a monopsony employer, has a policy of keeping wages down, in order to help the public finances. In this case the benefits of immigration are captured by the taxpayer. In the absence of migrant workers, the government would either have to tolerate a lower level of public service or revise its wage policy—or adopt some combination of the two.

[247] There are also small-scale permit schemes for certain specific groups but without the work permit restrictions (eg, seasonal agricultural workers or the Sectors Based Scheme (now confined to food manufacturing but previously embracing hospitality)) and certain permit-free schemes (eg, for working holidaymakers or Commonwealth citizens with a grandparent born in the UK). In fact, in 2005 it was said that there were some 50 legitimate ways of entering the UK for the purpose of work or study, which provided a main ground for the 'points-based' simplification discussed below: Home Office, *Selective Admission: Making Migration Work for Britain*, Consultation Document, 2005, Annex.

[248] In more traditional academic terms this is the equivalent of A-level. The job must also be offered on terms no less favourable than those available to domestic workers, in order to ensure the migrant is admitted to fill a genuine gap in the labour market and not one created by undercutting established terms and conditions of employment.

[249] The changes were announced in HM Treasury, *Budget 2000: Report*, para 3.77.

job to job once in the country. This represents a significant shift towards the view that it is beneficial to the future growth of the economy to have migrant workers enter the UK, but this view is restricted by the qualification that the migrants must be 'highly skilled'. This scheme saw the introduction in the UK of an open points-scoring system which was clearly aimed at singling out for admission the most advantageous of the migrant worker applicants. Points are scored for educational achievement, work experience, *past* earnings (as indicating labour market value), achievements in the chosen field (into which calculus may be brought the achievements of any partner of the applicant), and age.[250] Despite its significance for future policy the HSMP remains a small programme: in 2005 fewer than 25,000 applications were received under it, of which just under 15,000 were approved.[251]

The third significant step on the part of the government was its treatment of workers from eight countries which acceded to the EU in May 2004. Although, normally, workers from Member States have freedom of access to other Member States for the purpose of seeking and taking up work, as on some previous occasions that right was subjected by the relevant Accession Treaties to a transitional period in the case of the 'A8' countries,[252] which in varying forms could last up to seven years.[253] However, Member States are not required to take advantage of the transitional arrangements and three countries (Sweden, Ireland, and the UK) did not do so. The original intention of the government seems to have been to give workers from A8 countries exactly the same rights as those from the existing Member States, as Sweden and Ireland did. However, as so often with UK immigration policy, political controversy caused the government to qualify its policy in two ways. First, it required workers from the A8 countries to register with the British authorities (something which workers from the existing EU countries could not be required to do).[254] This was essentially a monitoring mechanism (so that the government would be in possession of hard data to use in the anticipated

---

[250] 'A young person's assessment has been introduced into HSMP in recognition of the greater potential that young highly skilled individuals have to be active in the labour market for a longer period'. Immigration and Nationality Directorate of the Home Office, *Immigration Directorates [sic] Instructions*, Chapter 5, Section 11, para 4.1. All applicants are expected to give an undertaking of willingness to make the UK their main home: para 3.3.

[251] Statement made by the Home Office, 1 December 2005 in response to a request made under the Freedom of Information Act, available on <http.//www.homeoffice.gov.uk/about-us/freedom-of-information/released-information/foi-4205-hsmp-applications?version=1>. The figures appear to relate to the first 10 months of the year. The country with the highest number of successful applicants was India, to whose nationals just over 8,000 permits were granted under the scheme from its inception to October 2005 (about 35% of the total).

[252] In fact, ten countries joined the EU in May 2004, but the transitional period did not apply to Malta or Cyprus, presumably because the threat to the labour markets of the existing EU countries from those countries was not thought to be significant.

[253] The complexities of the transitional arrangements are set out in EC Commission, *Report on the Functioning of the Transitional Arrangements set out in the 2003 Accession Treaty (period 1 May 2004–30 April 2006)*, COM (2006) 48 final.

[254] The Accession (Immigration and Worker Registration) Regulations 2004, SI 2004/1219.

public debate). Registration was not a pre-condition for entry into the British labour market, but was something required within the first month of any employment during the first year of residence in the UK; and registration was something which was granted virtually as of right.²⁵⁵ Between May 2004 and March 2006 some 329,000 registrations were effected.²⁵⁶ More controversial was the government's decision not to confer on workers from the A8 countries any entitlement to social security benefits during their first year working in the UK. This was effected by the introduction of an apparently general new condition for entitlement to benefit—that of a right to reside in the UK.²⁵⁷ This requirement supplemented the 'habitually resident' test, which itself had been introduced in 1994,²⁵⁸ replacing the previous 'resident' test, in order to deter 'benefit tourists'. The SSAC criticised the additional test, not so much on grounds of its impact on A8 workers, as for the unknown consequences of introducing this new and formally general requirement on other groups of worker.²⁵⁹ More importantly, it has been suggested that the UK was in breach of EU law in limiting A8 workers' access to benefits, ie, that the Accession Treaties permit Member States to exclude A8 workers but, if they admit them, require Member States to treat them in the same way as domestic workers in terms of access to benefits.²⁶⁰ In 2006 the sensitivity of the issue of migrant workers from accession countries was demonstrated when the government seemed minded to yield to public pressure and move towards some sort of restriction on workers from Bulgaria and Romania when those countries joined the Community.

Thus, by 2004 the government had taken three steps to liberalise its 'managed migration' policies: somewhat relaxing the rules of the traditional work permit scheme; introducing a Highly Qualified Migrant Programme; and allowing A8 citizens into the UK ahead of their Community law entitlement to take up work in the UK. In 2005, responding to the constant political pressures it had been under, especially in relation to asylum-seekers, the government announced a five-year review of the whole immigration system in *Controlling Our Borders: Making Migration Work for Britain, Five Year Strategy for Asylum and Immigration.*²⁶¹ The managed migration part of this review was taken forward in a Consultation Document, *Selective Admission: Making Migration Work for Britain,*²⁶² later in

²⁵⁵ Regs 7 and 8—though the migrant worker would have to stump up an application fee of £50 on each occasion. If the migrant worker did not change employment during the first year in the UK, then registration would be a one-off event.

²⁵⁶ *A Points-Based Migration System for Britain,* Cm 6741, March 2006, para 115. Later official figures suggested the figure was some 100,000 larger.

²⁵⁷ A result achieved through a combination of the Social Security (Habitual Residence) Amendment Regulations 2004, SI 2004/1232 and of regs 4(2) and 5(4) of the Accession (Immigration and Worker Registration) Regulations.

²⁵⁸ Income-Related Benefit Schemes (Miscellaneous Amendments) (No 3) Regulations 1994, SI 1994/1807.   ²⁵⁹ SSAC, *Seventeenth Report August 2003—July 2004,* para 4.1.

²⁶⁰ See P Larkin, Note (2005) 68 MLR 435, noting the ECJ's decision in Case C-138/02, *Collins v Secretary of State for Work and Pensions* [2005] ICR 37, though that case did not involve A8 workers. If this view is correct, the result is somewhat perverse, since it encourages Member States not to give A8 workers any access to their labour markets.   ²⁶¹ CM 6472, February 2005.

²⁶² n 247 above.

2005, and then to a set of formal proposals in a White Paper in March 2006, *A Points-Based Migration System for Britain*.[263] From our point of view, the importance of this exercise is that it underscored benefit to the domestic labour market as the rationale for the government's managed immigration policies (whilst also pursuing goals such as transparency, administrative simplification, and putting greater responsibilities on employers using migrant workers, now to be known as 'sponsors'). Thus, the Consultation Document stated that 'the purpose of the reform is to admit people selectively in order to maximise the economic benefit of migration to the UK'.[264] However, the document havered uncertainly between the second and third economic rationales outlined above for encouraging migration. In its Introduction it relied heavily on the argument that 'we cannot fill many job vacancies from the domestic labour market alone', thus invoking the third, static, and narrowest rationale for migration. By chapter 3, however, it was being argued that migration 'has contributed to some of the Government's core economic objectives around growth, productivity and stability', suggesting the broader second rationale. Either way, the document was concerned to combat the popular notion that migrant workers 'come and take our jobs'.

Although the proposals for reform were very much based around the existing work permit and HSMP schemes (into which as many as possible of the other entry methods were proposed to be folded), the 'contribution to the economy' argument was to be implemented by an even stronger emphasis on the skills of the migrant workers. Thus, highly skilled migrants were not only to be permitted to enter to take up work but positively sought after in an international competition among countries for their skills. By contrast, unskilled workers from outside the EEA would find their chances of securing anything other than temporary admission to the UK more restricted than under the present schemes. The proposals put migrants into five 'tiers', though only the first three interest us as being concerned with admission to take up work. The Tier 1 proposal[265] was based rather closely on the existing HSMP, ie, the admission of highly skilled workers on their own application. The points-based criteria for admission were very much the same, though somewhat more sophisticated and perhaps slightly easier to satisfy. Tier 2[266] was based on the business and commercial work permit scheme, ie, employer application to take on someone to fill an existing vacancy. However, Tier 2 was to be explicitly confined to workers who had achieved at least a medium level of skill, even in areas of recognised shortage. In those areas, which were to be identified by the SSDA (see above), it would not be necessary specifically to show that the migrant was not displacing a domestic worker; otherwise, that would be required, most obviously by showing that advertisement through Jobcentre Plus had not produced appropriate applicants. Both Tier 1 and Tier 2 migrants would be eligible to apply for permanent residence in the UK, in the case of Tier 2 workers after

---

[263] n 256 above. [264] n 247 above, para 1.3. [265] White Paper, n 256 above, 21 ff.
[266] Ibid, 25 ff.

five years, in the case of Tier 1 possibly after only two years. Unskilled workers from outside the EEA would fall within Tier 3[267] and would be at a considerable disadvantage compared to those in Tiers 1 and 2. They would be eligible only for temporary admission (for up to 12 months), without dependants, subject to a quota, and only if migrants from countries to which the UK could effectively return them at the end of the period of temporary admission.[268] This proposal was greeted with opposition by some of the traditional large users of unskilled migrant workers (for example, in the agricultural and hospitality industries), but the government's two main responses, which were somewhat in tension with one another, were that in relation to unskilled workers the labour market threat from migrant workers to the domestic workforce was the greatest and, on the other, that there were plenty of unskilled workers with a Community right to come to the UK to seek and take up work, as a result of the recent enlargement of the Community, without the need to create a further source of unskilled migrant labour.

Although the above account concerns government policy towards those, without a right to work in the UK, who apply in the proper manner for permission to enter the country to seek or take up work, the issue of illegal migration or of those who enter lawfully but overstay cannot be ignored in this analysis. Partly, this is because the policy towards those who apply in the proper form is at risk of being undone if it is possible for significant numbers of people to obtain and retain work whilst being in the country illegally—and certainly the government is at risk of political embarrassment in such a case, even if the number of illegal workers is small. Within employment law the obvious regulatory response was to apply sanctions to employers who took on workers without checking the entitlement of those workers to employment in the UK. Such a policy had been adopted by the Major government in section 8 of the Asylum and Immigration Act 1996.[269] However, the policy was strengthened in the Asylum, Immigration and Nationality Act 2006, which increased the severity of the sentences for the criminal offence involved[270] and, more importantly, introduced a system of civil penalties to supplement the rarely used criminal sanctions. In this way, the government could impose penalties on employers it thought had employed migrants working

---

[267] Ibid, 29 ff.

[268] This means that the country in question should be willing to take its workers back and that there should be no human rights objections in the UK to the compulsory return to that country of workers whose permission to be in the UK had expired.

[269] On which see Bernard Ryan, (1997) 26 ILJ 136. Such a policy is also recommended by the European Community: see 'Recommendation on combating the illegal employment of third-country nationals' (OJ C 304/1, 14 October 1996). In 1999 (Immigration and Asylum Act 1999, s 22) the Labour government added s 8A, requiring the Secretary of State to produce a Code of Practice showing how employers could comply with their obligations under s 8 and at the same time avoid breaches of the Race Relations legislation. See now s 23 of the 2006 Act.

[270] However, the government seems to have doubted whether the increased sentences would be enough and a Home Office minister was reported as encouraging the courts to use the Proceeds of Crime Act 2002 'to confiscate the earnings and possessions of people who were deliberately employing illegal immigrants' (*Financial Times* (UK Edition) 14 June 2006, p 1).

illegally without going through the proper checks, which penalties could be recovered by the government unless the employer appealed to a court, a procedure which neatly put the onus of taking action to defend itself on the employer.[271] Further, the issue of illegal immigration raises questions of employment protection, since those working illegally are in a peculiarly vulnerable position as against their employer and open to high levels of abuse, as we have seen in our discussion of the gangmasters' legislation.[272]

4.7 International setting and conclusions

We noted at the beginning of this chapter the US influences on the 'welfare to work' policies adopted by the British government. However, it would be wrong to conclude that the policy focus on the employment rate and on supply-side techniques for addressing that issue are purely Anglo-American phenomena. On the contrary, these policies have been a growing feature of all developed economies over the past two decades. The intellectual foundations for at least a good part of the policies subsequently adopted were in fact provided by the Organisation for Economic Cooperation and Development, whose *Jobs Study* of 1994, leading to an OECD Jobs Strategy, was highly influential in promoting supply-side reforms within an overall framework of stable macro-economic management.[273] Of more direct importance was the fact that this approach eventually came to dominate the European Community's policies in this area and, in so doing, to spawn a new method of Community interaction with the Member States, known as the 'open method of co-ordination'. However, that transfer of ideas to the EC was not an uncontested one. In 1993 the European Commission's White Paper, *Growth, Competitiveness and Employment*,[274] although reflecting some of the ideas later to be proposed in the OECD *Jobs Study*, nevertheless proposed an ECU400 billion Community expenditure on infrastructure projects to create jobs. This idea was thrown out summarily by the Member States at the Essen Council in 1994, no doubt as a result of a mixture of scepticism about whether such an old-fashioned demand-side mechanism would be effective, and an unwillingness to expand the Community's financial competence to such a large extent. Nor were the Member States willing to make the adoption of policies combating unemployment part of

---

[271] Such civil penalties are an increasingly common regulatory tool, to be found, for example, throughout the Financial Services and Markets Act 2000.   [272] See 2.4.1 above.

[273] OECD, *The OECD Jobs Study: Evidence and Explanations* and *Facts, Analysis, Strategies* (Paris, 1994). On this see D Ashiagbor, *The European Employment Strategy* (Oxford: OUP, 2005), on which we have drawn heavily in this section. The recommendations from the *Jobs Study* were up-dated in 2006, so as to shift the emphasis further from unemployment rates to employment rates: OECD, *Boosting Jobs and Incomes: Policy Lessons from Reassessing the Jobs Strategy*, 2006. Apart from the final section, on 'policy packages', this document could have been written within HM Treasury.

[274] COM (93) 700 final, 1993.

the 'Stability and Growth Pact' which accompanied the creation of a single currency (the euro).[275]

Nevertheless, the Essen Council did mark acceptance by the Member States that the Community should have a competence in the area of 'employment policy' (the phrase used to refer to Community policies aimed at unemployment or 'worklessness'). It was also clear that, despite the addition of what became the Social Chapter of the EC Treaty in 1992, that chapter was constructed so as to restrict the Community's competence in most of the areas which would be crucial to the development of an effective employment policy. Thus, unanimous consent of the Member States was required for Directives in the area of social security and the social protection of workers[276] and the chapter gave the Commission no power at all to propose Directives in the areas of combating social exclusion and the modernisation of social protection systems.[277] Of course, the Social Chapter could simply have had its scope extended, but the Member States were unwilling to give the Community Directive-making powers in such central and sensitive areas of national policy. Instead, a new Employment chapter[278] was added to the EC Treaty by the Treaty of Amsterdam in 1997.

In essence, the Community acquired a competence to take action in this sensitive new area, but only by accepting that its competence would not extend to top-down, 'hard' law measures (such as Directives) but would be limited to promoting co-ordination of Member States' employment policies via 'soft' law. In essence, though the exact procedures have been varied from time to time, the co-ordination takes the form of the Commission drawing up, in consultation with the Member States and the social partners, a set of guidelines for Member States to follow in implementing their national employment policies, which identifies areas of 'best practice' in the Member States. If and insofar these proposals are adopted by the Council, each Member State is required to draw up a National Reform Plan (NRP—originally a National Action Plan (NAP)) on how they will take the Community's guidelines into account and the Commission yearly assesses the NRPs and obtains other evidence about each Member State's implementation of the guidelines. The Commission and the Council then produce a Joint Employment Report, which assesses both the overall employment situation in the Community and may make recommendations to the Member States as to how they should carry out the policies enshrined in the guidelines (which are themselves refined from time to time). Thus, the European Employment Strategy and the 'open method of co-ordination' came into existence.[279]

---

[275] Ashiagbor, n 273 above, 102–103. The criteria which were included are set out in Art 121 EC. Given the subsequent chequered history of the stability and growth pact, the exclusion of employment criteria perhaps turned out to be less important than it seemed at the time.

[276] Art 137(1)(c) and (4), as it now is.   [277] Art 137(1)(j) and (k), and (2).

[278] Now Title VIII of Chapter III of the EC Treaty (arts 125–129).

[279] Since the Member States did not wait for the ratification of the Amsterdam Treaty before implementing the EES (itself an indication of the lack of 'hard' law in the process), but rather decided

Four points can be made about the EES. First, it focuses on supply-side measures or, where it does turn to the demand side, it does so in a way which is facilitative, rather than regulatory, of business, and so it can be said to mark the success of the philosophy advanced in the OECD *Jobs Study*. Thus, the four 'pillars' for action under the EES were defined in 1997 as: improving employability, developing entrepreneurship (a demand-side policy), encouraging adaptability (on the part of workers and legal structures), and strengthening equal opportunities between men and women.[280] Secondly, as can be seen from the description in the previous paragraph, the EES does not contain 'command and control' law of the type traditionally associated with the Community's social policy. Rather, the incentives towards compliance with the guidelines are, on the one hand, the positive incentive that the process may lead a Member State to discover from its interactions with the Commission and other Member States a particularly relevant policy or technique which it had not previously considered. The fact that the EES is an iterative process on an annual basis is particularly relevant here. On the other hand, the Member State risks reputational loss (through 'naming and shaming') if it fails to make adequate progress in pursuing the goals laid down at Community level. Thirdly, it is particularly difficult to assess the impact of the EES. As Moser and Trubek have suggested,[281] it seems probable that its impact depends heavily on the constellation of political forces in a particular Member State. In effect, the EES supports those who want to modernise existing social welfare systems, in contrast to those who either simply want to roll them back through deregulatory policies or, on the other hand, keep them unchanged. The EES is likely to strengthen the hand of the moderate reformers as against the radical reformers or the conservatives, where the moderate reformers are an already significant domestic force.

Finally, the relationship between the British government and the EES has been much smoother than its relationship with the EC's social policy. Since the coming into force of the Single European Act in 1987, and, even more so, of the changes to the Treaty agreed at Maastricht, the EC's social policy has presented the threat to the government that it might be required from time to time to legislate in areas where it would much rather not do so. Classic examples of this threat materialising in practice are the Working Time Directive[282] and the general framework

at the European Council in Luxembourg in 1997 to go ahead immediately, the EES is sometimes referred to as the 'Luxembourg process'.

[280] Council Resolution of 15 December 1997 on the 1998 Employment Guidelines (OJ C 30/98, 28 January 1998). See Ashiagbor, n 273 above, 132–133. The more detailed guidelines can be found in their current form in Council Decision of 12 July 2005 on Guidelines for the employment policies of the Member States (OJ L205/21, 6 August 2005). They are now referred to as 'integrated guidelines' because they are integrated with the Broad Economic Policy Guidelines emanating from the Growth and Stability Pact, though the EES is still not part of that Pact.

[281] James Mosher and David Trubek, 'Alternative Approaches to Governance in the EU: EU Social Policy and the European Employment Strategy' (2003) 41 JCMS 63 at 82–83 (this article is a very valuable analysis of the first phase of development of the EES).   [282] See 2.4.1 above.

Directive on employee consultation,[283] both of which, for good path-dependent reasons, were extremely difficult to integrate into the domestic culture of the UK. The EES simply does not generate this level of threat: provided the Member State is prepared to face the reputational loss, it can carry on with its own domestic priorities.[284] In fact, however, the British government did not need to accept the reputational penalties which non-compliance with the EES might have entailed, because, in fact, there was a very high degree of coincidence between the goals of the EES and the goals of the government under its 'welfare to work' policies, the two sets of policies even having their official starting points at the same time.[285] Not only were the goals of the government and the Community in this sphere congruent, but the British government's implementation strategies kept the UK comfortably in the front group of Member States whose performance measured best against the guidelines. Thus, the Member States, having initially been reluctant to set targets at EU level within the EES, eventually adopted an overall employment rate of 70% to be achieved by 2010, a rate which, as we have seen, the UK already comfortably exceeded. Consequently, the government was more likely to be in receipt of bouquets than brickbats from the Community in the employment policy area, which it may well have regarded as a pleasant change. Thus, the comments addressed to the UK in 2004 contained the sentence: 'The UK exceeds all the employment rate targets including those for women and for older workers.'[286]

Overall, the 'Welfare to Work' set of policies can be said to have been the Labour governments' response to the twin threats to the welfare state which became increasingly strong in the late 1980s and 1990s. On the one hand, the forces of globalisation meant that developed economies, even when running only just below an inflation-inducing level, could no longer be relied upon naturally to generate jobs at a rate which would keep unemployment at a low level. On the other, the apparent inability of political parties to secure election on platforms which contained promises significantly to increase taxation (or to increase taxation at all), and the desire of the electorate to be satisfied that public money, raised from taxation, was being wisely spent, meant that the government became increasingly concerned with levels of employment, since those not in employment were non-contributors to the economy as well as being, often, the recipients of benefit. This was a problem

---

[283] See 3.4.4.3 above.

[284] Cf the example of Italy, discussed by Mosher and Trubek, n 281 above, 74, pointing out that the Italian government, at least in the first phase of the EES, simply rejected it as irrelevant to the Italian labour market.

[285] The Luxembourg guidelines were adopted at the end of 1997 (n 279 above); *A New Contract for Welfare* (n 1 above) was published in early 1998.

[286] Council Recommendation of 14 October 2004 on the implementation of Member States' employment policies (OJ L326/47, 29 October 2004), Annex, 'United Kingdom'. See also Joint Employment Report 2005/2006, Annex. This is not to say that the Community was uncritical: the 2004 recommendations also pointed to the prevalence of low skills amongst the workforce and the consequences of this for productivity levels.

not only of fiscal balance but also of increasingly embedded social exclusion. 'Welfare to work' was a genuinely middle way—though perhaps not a 'third way'— set of policies, though not one exclusive to the UK (the *Jobs Study* and the EES pursued similar goals). On the one hand, 'welfare to work' rejected the 'entitlement' view of social security which had dominated much academic thinking about social security since the 1960s in favour of an approach based on reciprocity.[287] The increased conditionality of benefits which this entailed was regretted by many brought up on a more traditionally liberal view of the social security system, especially as conditionality involved not just a greater chance of losing benefit but also much greater intrusion on the part of the state into the lives of those who wished to keep their benefit entitlements (for example, through so-called 'agreements' between claimants and their 'advisers'). On the other hand, 'welfare to work' also involved rejection of a de-regulatory approach to the welfare state, in which fiscal balance was secured by simply scaling back entitlements, without any investment of pubic resources in helping claimants out of their dependency on benefits. In fact, the 'welfare to work' policies were characterised, not by retreat, but by ever-increasing forms of—sometimes expensive—public intervention, involving constant testing of the effectiveness of existing programmes, piloting of new ones, and a general tinkering with the detail. Whether one prefers the policies in fact adopted or either of the rejected policies is largely a matter of political predilection. What can be said is that the government set out its choice very clearly at an early stage in *A New Contract for Welfare* (1998);[288] it pursued that policy choice with quite remarkable consistency over the succeeding years; and, despite some considerable headaches (most notably the overpayment and clawing back of tax credits),[289] its policies in the social security area seem to have carried greater conviction with the electorate than its policies in some adjacent areas of large domestic expenditure, for example, health.

---

[287] See 4. 1 above.   [288] n 1 above.   [289] See 4.3.2 above.

5

Conclusion—A New Way Found?

5.1 The contingent path to labour market regulation

The purpose of this work has been to carry forward the story of British labour legislation and public policy from the point at which our earlier work concluded in the early 1990s, and in particular to provide an analysis and critique of the changes in legislation and policy which have occurred under the New Labour administration which came into office in May 1997. In the Introduction, we set forth our methodology for that analysis and critique; it was constructed around a tentative suggestion or working hypothesis, which it would be the object of the substantive chapters to test out and explore. The working hypothesis was that the New Labour administration had intensified a shift in the policy discourse for labour legislation of which the beginnings were clearly perceptible during the 1980s and which had continued in the earlier 1990s. This was a shift from a policy discourse which was focused predominantly upon the regulation of employment relations with the general aim of correcting inequality of bargaining power between management and workers, towards a policy discourse rather differently focused predominantly upon labour market regulation in the interests of full employment and inclusion of the population within the active workforce.

This Conclusion will, first, confirm that our working hypothesis was in a general sense well-founded; that, of course, was predictable, and we hope that the substantive chapters have adequately carried the burden of bearing out our hypothesis in detail. But we shall also try to take our analysis and critique slightly further than that; this will consist of venturing some conclusions about the particular kind or genre of labour market regulation which British governments have espoused during and since the 1990s, and more especially since 1997. The drawing of such conclusions involves an attempt to answer a general evaluative question which may be put in these terms: how far have British governments since the 1990s, and especially since 1997, succeeded in devising a policy framework and a practice of labour market regulation capable of reconciling the generally intense political conflicts which have attended on British labour legislation since the 1960s both between and within British governments and between British governments and the institutions and policies of the European Union?

The making of that kind of assessment depends in our view upon developing our understanding of the policy choices which have been made by successive British governments in the sphere of labour legislation since the 1990s, in particular our understanding of what policy options and legislative outcomes could reasonably be regarded as *feasible* ones for the governments in question, and also in what sense and to what extent the choices which were actually made were *path dependent* or contingent ones, in the sense that they responded to particular local circumstances or factors in the political experience of those in government rather than to the general policy design or policy framework within which they were made. For this purpose it is important to have some sense of what were the prevailing or typical orientations of policy development in the European region in the period in question. Although there is no single set of benchmarks in this respect, it is quite useful and informative to begin by setting the evolution of the policy discourse of British governments into the broader context of international policy discourse as instantiated by the policy analyses in the sphere of employment which were developed and applied by the OECD and the European Union (as represented by the European Commission).

The policy analyses in the sphere of employment of those two supranational institutions have this special significance to our present discussion: that during the period under review in this work each of those organisations became intensely involved in producing its own particular set of prescriptions for labour market regulation, and its own preferred amalgam of employment policy with social policy.[1] This was a convergence from very different institutional roles and institutional perspectives. The OECD is essentially an official policy forum for economic development between thirty market democracies, originating in the Organisation for European Economic Co-operation (OEEC), which was set up in 1947 for the economic reconstruction of Europe after World War II. Since the early 1990s, it has been increasingly preoccupied with problems of unemployment and interested in promoting active labour market regulation to reduce unemployment, an interest pursued by the articulation of its Jobs Strategy in 1994 and the subsequent concentration of quite a lot of its institutional resources on the development of that strategy. In recent years, the identification and evaluation of the negative social consequences of different national strategies of active labour market regulation has become a more prominent, if still minor, aspect of its activities in the employment sphere.[2]

---

[1] As in its own way also did the ILO in the shape of the 'Decent Work Agenda' which was established by the *Report of the Director-General on Decent Work* to the 87th Session of the International Labour Conference of 1999 and which amounted to a subsuming of the standard-setting function into a set of equally ranking strategic objectives, the effect of which was to bring employment policy and the promotion of full employment much further to the fore than it had previously been in the policy and practice of the ILO.

[2] Compare, for example, *OECD Employment Outlook 2004*, Editorial—Reassessing the OECD Jobs Strategy, though that theme is perhaps slightly more muted in *OECD Employment Outlook 2006* and the accompanying policy document *Boosting Jobs and Incomes—Policy Lessons from Reassessing the OECD Jobs Strategy*.

From this source, and from the national experiences which the OECD both reports upon and seeks to influence, we can begin to construct a picture or paradigm of supranational and national regulatory policies for the employment sphere as tending to converge, during the period under review, upon a policy framework constructed upon a basis of labour market regulation in which the maximising of employment rates and employment opportunities is highly prioritised, and in which there is considerable consensus about the importance of active labour market policies, especially those aimed at combating social exclusion and discrimination against minorities and disadvantaged groups. In this paradigm, there is a marked tendency to enfold and contain social policy and the regulation of employment relations in the interests of worker protection within the discourse of labour market regulation, and also often to attempt by so doing to smooth out or suppress conflicts, which may be very acute ones, as to how far social policy and the regulation of employment relations in the interests of worker protection are compatible with labour market regulation which is efficient in its principal goal of maximising employment and economic growth. That attempt, however, is usually unsuccessful, and reveals the fault-lines or cracks which the whole policy construct is trying to close or paper over.

This construct, and the tensions to which it seems to be inherently subject, is perfectly instantiated by the development of the policy of the European Union, as represented by the European Commission, in the employment sphere during the period under review. In the Introduction to this work[3] we described the beginnings of this evolution in the early and middle 1990s, and its culmination in the formation in 2000 of the so-called 'Lisbon Strategy'.[4] The deliberations and policy pronouncements of the ensuing years displayed a continuing uncertainty as to how far and in what shapes and forms to develop EU social policy and the 'European Social Model' within that general discourse of labour market regulation. Two streams of policymaking can be discerned, and it is evident that they are in some degree of tension with each other. On the one hand, there is a set of policy formulations which is concerned with the intensification of the employment maximising element in the Lisbon Strategy;[5] and in 2005 that Strategy was 're-launched' with a further inclination in that direction.[6] On the other hand, another set of policy documents seeks to maintain a distinctive Social Policy

---

[3] At 13–14.

[4] The best source for which is the Commission document *The Lisbon European Council—An Agenda of Economic and Social Renewal for Europe—Contribution of the European Commission to the Special European Council in Lisbon 23–24th March 2000*, Doc/00/7, Brussels, 28 February 2000.

[5] This seems to be the purpose and effect of the task force reports *Jobs, Jobs, Jobs—Creating More Employment in Europe—Report of the Employment Taskforce chaired by Wim Kok* (November 2003), and *Facing the Challenge—the Lisbon Strategy for Growth and Employment—Report from the High Level Group chaired by Wim Kok* (November 2004)—the second of those is often referred to as 'the Kok Report'.

[6] The key policy document is *Working Together for Growth and Jobs—A new start for the Lisbon Strategy—European Commission Communication to the Spring European Council* (COM (2005) 24, Brussels, 2 February 2005).

Agenda within the overarching framework of the Lisbon Strategy.[7] The proponents of the distinctive Social Policy Agenda seem to have a struggle in securing
consensus for any measures of worker protection which do not fall squarely
within the rationales of maximising employment or combating social exclusion;
they seem increasingly to fall back upon the notion of 'flexicurity', in an attempt,
both rhetorical and practical, to reconcile the enhancement of 'security' by means
of social policy with the vindication of efficiency by means of 'flexibility'.[8]

Of course, one cannot make any direct or simple comparison between the policy stance of the European Union as represented by the European Commission
and that of successive British governments; the supra-national role of the former
is very different from the national role of the latter. Nevertheless, after all due
allowance for that difference of role, one can still note quite a marked difference
between the two respective policy discourses as they have evolved in recent years.
The European Union as represented by the European Commission, although
firmly launched into the discourse of labour market regulation, still seeks to maintain the rhetoric and practice of social policy, and hovers between positions represented by the OECD on the one hand and, on the other hand, by more welfarist
versions of the 'European Social Model'. By 2006, by contrast, the New Labour
administration seems completely to have shed any such lingering existential
doubts about the version of labour market regulation which it had espoused. The
DTI significantly gave the title *Success at Work*[9] to the 'policy statement for this
Parliament' for the employment sphere, which it issued in March 2006; and the
document leaves no room for doubt that the 'success' in question is that which the
government judged itself to have achieved in realising its particular vision of efficient labour market regulation.

Thus Mr Alan Johnson, during a brief tenure of the office of Secretary of State for
Trade and Industry,[10] introduced the policy document with the modest claim that:

Since 1997 we have created one of the most successful labour markets in the world with
more people in work than ever before and the highest employment rate in the G8. Our
approach has been based on combining social justice with economic prosperity so that
businesses grow and employment expands, delivering opportunity for all.[11]

The document is less interesting for its almost unremitting rhetoric of self-
congratulation and finality than for the evidence which it provides of the extent to

---

[7] The crucial documents are the Commission Communications on *Social Policy Agenda* COM
(2000) 379 final—Brussels 28 June 2000, and on *The Social Agenda* COM (2005) 33 final—Brussels
9 February 2005, and also the *Report of the High Level Group on the future of social policy in an enlarged
European Union* (May 2004). This report is subject to the disclaimer that 'The content of this report
reflects the opinion of the High Level Group only and does not necessarily reflect the opinion or position of the European Commission'; interestingly, there is no such disclaimer for the two reports cited
at n 5 above.
[8] At the time of writing, the Commission seems to be experiencing delay and difficulty in fulfilling
its commitment in *The Social Agenda* COM (2005) 33 final to 'adopt a Green Paper on the development of labour law' which will 'analyse current trends in new work patterns and the role of labour law
in tackling these developments' (para 2.1).
[9] In full, *Success at Work—Protecting Vulnerable Workers, Supporting Good Employers*.
[10] May 2005–May 2006.   [11] *Success at Work*, n 9 above, Foreword, para 1.

which the objectives of the New Labour administration in the sphere of employment had during its nearly nine years in office become defined in terms of labour market regulation in the interests of the growth and flexibility of businesses.

So powerfully does that document represent the labour legislation and public policy of those years in terms of a serene voyage to a virtual Utopia of successful labour market regulation, that it seems almost impertinent to analyse or criticise the course of navigation which was pursued. Nevertheless, we hope that the foregoing substantive chapters will have suggested a number of senses in which governments since 1997 have actually taken a very complex and contingent path towards a set of objectives significantly different from that which they might, at the time at which the New Labour administration was first elected, have been expected to pursue. In the remaining sections of this Conclusion, we seek to point up this observation in relation to the three main aspects of regulatory activity in the employment sphere, the post-1990 history of which we have considered in the three preceding chapters.

5.2 'Welfare to Work'

The link between government legislation and policy and the labour market appears very clearly in the preceding chapter, which we entitled 'Promoting Work'. The set of governmental initiatives discussed in that chapter focused particularly on the external labour market, ie, on the quantity and quality of workers presenting themselves for the jobs that employers had on offer. One notable feature of the initiatives consisted in the close alignment of instruments of social security and labour law to serve a common purpose; and the melding of social security and tax law. Thus, if social security and tax law obliged claimants actively to seek work, advised them how best to obtain it and subsidised their employment once it had been obtained, labour law too underpinned the in-work subsidy through the national minimum wage and reduced the barriers to work through the ever-spreading net of discrimination laws. This was a highly significant development for both labour lawyers and social security lawyers. This focus in governmental policy on obtaining a job (ie, on the exit from welfare) was symbolised by the virtual eradication of the term 'social security' from governmental language and by structural changes in the relevant governmental departments. The Department of Social Security, mainly concerned with collecting contributions and dispensing benefits, disappeared as its functions were transferred to the Inland Revenue, whilst the Department for Work and Pensions emerged, charged with the function of developing and administering the pro-work programmes of the New Labour government.[12]

---

[12] For interesting reflections on these changes see Social Security Advisory Committee, *Seventeenth Report 2004*, Chairman's Foreword. As he pointed out, the SSAC is one of the few governmental instances where the term 'social security' survives.

However, it would be wrong to think that, in promoting these policies, the government was solely concerned with the benefits to employers of better external labour markets. It conceived better external labour markets as contributing very substantially to the amelioration of social problems in the areas of social exclusion and child poverty. A job was seen as the most effective route out of poverty and the most effective way of promoting self-respect and improving social welfare. Thus, the situation was not one in which the goals of a (labour market-oriented) employment law came to dominate the law of social security but was as much one in which employment law was put at the service of the goals of a job-oriented social security (or social welfare) law. For example, the government was concerned to emphasise the labour market value of its anti-discrimination reforms as well as their civil rights credentials; whilst the NMW not only promoted fairness at work but also cut against opportunistic behaviour on the part of employers who might seek to take advantage of the system of tax credits when setting wage rates. A notable feature of the Labour governments' approach to the promotion of work was the thoroughness of the approach. On the one hand, there was what one commentator has termed the 'widening of groups for whom labour market presence has been seen to be appropriate'[13] (notably lone mothers and the disabled). On the other, there was a significant intensification over time in the application of compulsory mechanisms beyond the unemployed (or jobseekers, as they must now be called) to embrace these wider groups of claimants.

By contrast, the government's approach to equivalent issues arising in the internal labour market was much more tentative. Of course, by definition the central problem of getting a job was solved for those who were members of an internal labour market, but the issue of inadequate skill levels was common to both markets. However, employers were left in almost unfettered control of their training policies, despite general acceptance of the proposition that the skill levels of the workforce in the UK were lower than those of comparable countries, the market failure arguments in favour of governmental regulation arising out of the atomised structure of employing enterprises in the UK and a history of tougher forms of intervention in the shape of the Industrial Training Boards of the 1960s. As we suggest below, any proposal to resuscitate the ITBs or to design some alternative was likely to cut across the government's commitment to 'light' regulation.

The area of 'welfare to work' was one where the Labour governments could claim considerable success in comparison with both the domestic situation in the 1980s and the contemporaneous situation in other EU Member States, with an employment rate of about 75% and an unemployment rate of about 5% for much of the period after the millennium. Although rightly claimed, this success needs to be put in context. First, although a great improvement on the position in the UK in the 1980s, the above figures would have been regarded as representing no

---

[13] Lisa Harker, 'A 21st Century Welfare State' in N Pearce and W Paxton (eds), *Social Justice, Building a Fairer Britain* (London: IPPR and Politico's Publishing, 2005) 265.

more than moderate success in any period up until the middle of the 1970s, when unemployment rates of 4% or less were not uncommon, at similar levels of employment. In other words, the remarkable run of employment success from the mid-1990s onwards did not completely restore full employment as it had been conceived of in the decades immediately after the Second World War—nor did the government claim to have done so. Secondly, and more importantly, the upward trend in employment rates and the downward trend in unemployment rates in fact began during the Major administration, which put the appropriate macro-economic policies in place.[14] The Labour governments' claim to novelty in this area lay not in their decision to continue the previous governments' policy of macro-economic stability or to retain the 'actively seeking work' requirement, introduced in 1989, but in the decision to devote resources to the introduction of the New Deals, which helped the target groups to find work, on either a compulsory or a voluntary basis. This decision was symbolised by the transmogrification of the Jobcentre into Jobcentre Plus. As has been remarked, 'at the heart of Jobcentre Plus is the model of the personal adviser helping individuals to search more effectively for work and offering incentives and removing barriers to help ease the path into employment ... '.[15] In consequence, evaluation of the success of the Labour government's post-1997 policies turns largely on what the New Deals added to the favourable employment trends which were already in place. The New Deals cannot claim credit for the whole of the fall in unemployment and the rise in employment which occurred after 1997 since some of that would have occurred even without the New Deals. An authoritative analysis has concluded that 'the scale of the effects is to be measured in the tens of thousands rather than the hundreds of thousands, but ... these policies have definitely not been a waste of resources'.[16]

It is sometimes suggested that the type of job which has been created by the British economy over the last decade and a half has been of low quality and low skill. As a general criticism of the performance of the economy that seems a misplaced statement. In fact, most of the new jobs created have been at the top end of the income distribution, ie, high skill and high quality jobs. However, there has also been significant job creation at the bottom end of the distribution as well as job *reduction* in the middle of the distribution.[17] Two points can be made about this development. First, it goes some way to explain the growth in income inequality in the UK over the period, a growth which government seems to have been content to tolerate. Secondly, and of more immediate relevance to the concerns of this book, the targets of welfare to work are likely to have moved into the jobs at the bottom end of the income distribution. The claimed social benefits of

[14] Peter Robinson, 'The Economy: Achieving Full Employment' in Pearce and Paxton (n 13 above), 345, Figure 15.5.   [15] Ibid, 344.

[16] Ibid, 346.

[17] M Goos and A Manning, 'McJobs and MacJobs' in R Dickens et al (eds), *The Labour Market Under New Labour* (London: Palgrave, 2003).

work are likely to be maximised only if those workers, having obtained a hold on the bottom of the jobs ladder, are able to climb up it into better paying and higher skilled jobs. It is unclear to what extent this has occurred. Certainly, there is relatively little emphasis in the New Deals on sustaining people in work, once they have found a job, and, as we saw,[18] an unwillingness to let human capital improvement on the part of workless people be used as a reason for moderating the pressure on them to take a job which is available and which they could do, although of low quality. A further criticism which is sometimes advanced of the governments' policies is what a commentator, perhaps a little unkindly, termed 'the tendency to "fetish" paid work as the route to citizenship'[19] at the expense of care, voluntary, or community work. The government perhaps perceived these other forms of work as not having the same potential to combat social exclusion as paid work, especially in terms of the relief of poverty.

5.3 The role of the social partners

As far as collective labour law is concerned, perhaps the most remarkable aspects of the post-1997 policies concerned what was not done rather than what was. This was most obvious in relation to the law of industrial conflict: it was not restored to its pre-Thatcher position, and indeed only relatively minor changes were made to the scheme of industrial conflict laws which the Labour government inherited in 1997. The government was very clear that this was its policy and no-one could realistically claim to be in doubt about it. Less clearly flagged were the limitations on the governments' policies towards collective bargaining. We have argued that regulation of the labour market was the prime aim of the governments' post-1997 policies. However, the adoption of this goal does not, in the abstract, tell one very much about the policies likely to be adopted towards collective bargaining. One can think of types of labour market regulation where collective bargaining and the 'social partners' more generally play a significant role in the regulatory process. In its review of the Jobs Strategy the OECD pointed out that countries with different labour law systems had been successful in boosting employment rates, so that there could not be said to be a one-to-one relationship between high employment and a particular system of labour law. Significantly, the role of collective bargaining was identified by the OECD as one of the areas where equally successful countries (in employment terms) had adopted different policies. Thus, in some successful countries 'collective agreements play a limited role' whereas other successful countries are 'characterised by a strong emphasis on coordinated collective bargaining and social dialogue'.[20] It does not take much imagination to place the UK in the

---

[18] See 4.5 above.   [19] Harker, n 13 above, 273.
[20] OECD, *Boosting Jobs and Incomes—Policy Lessons from Reassessing the OECD's Job Strategy*, 2006, 19.

first group and countries such as Austria, Denmark, the Netherlands, and Sweden in the second. David Coats has pointed out that the Netherlands 'has a higher level of real wage flexibility than the UK' and argues that 'this can partly be explained by the centralised nature of Dutch collective bargaining, which allows negotiators to take macro-economic factors into account in the wage formation process'.[21]

However, it is one thing to argue that different systems of labour law are compatible with equal levels of success in employment terms, and another to argue that a particular country has a free choice as to which model it adopts. To argue in this latter way is to ignore the force of arguments based on 'path dependency', ie, that the most politically attractive or efficient set of policies to achieve a particular outcome depends in part on the ex ante institutional make-up of the country in question.[22] What were the characteristics of collective bargaining in the UK by the late 1990s which made it unattractive to government as a major plank in the new model labour law? Three points can be made. First, the coverage of collective bargaining, at least in the private sector, was very low.[23] An instrument which reached only one fifth of the workforce was not likely to be an efficient mechanism for flexibility. Secondly, British collective bargaining was highly decentralised, being conducted at single-employer level rather than at the level of the industry or the whole economy. This was a trend which had been growing during the previous half-century and was a very pronounced feature of British collective bargaining by the end of the twentieth century. It was not the result of Thatcherite pressures (though her governments endorsed the trend), but of more long term and deep-seated forces in industrial relations.[24] The co-ordination function of collective bargaining, identified by Coats, was likely to be much more difficult to achieve in a decentralised system. Indeed, there was substantial recent historical experience in the UK which suggested that the decentralised British collective bargaining system lacked the institutional mechanisms, on the part of both employers and trade unions, which would permit it to support centralised wage deals. No permanent system of centralised wage determination, exchanging wage restraint for other benefits to workers, had resulted from the incomes policies promoted by Labour governments in either the 1960s or the 1970s,[25] which might suggest that the

---

[21] David Coats, *Who's Afraid of Labour Market Flexibility?* (London: The Work Foundation, 2006) 27.

[22] Thus, the easiest or most efficient way to get from A to B depends not only on where B is but also on where A is; and a number of travellers all aiming to get to B will take different efficient routes if they are starting from different points (ie, have different As). This error is perhaps committed by Coats who, on the one hand, argues (correctly) that 'countries need to consider the appropriate policy mix given their specific circumstances' and, on the other, concludes after referring to the experience of the Nordic countries: 'it would *therefore* be possible to have somewhat tighter regulation in the UK and retain our highly prized flexibility'.

[23] 21% of employees' pay in the private sector was affected by collective bargaining in 2005, having been no more than a percentage point or so higher in any of the years from 1997 onwards: DTI, *Trade Union Membership 2005* (March 2006), Table 28.

[24] *Labour Legislation and Public Policy* (LLPP) chapter 6.   [25] LLPP, 4.3 and 8.5.

forces operating in favour of the autonomy of the decentralised bargainers were very strong in the UK. Finally, there was the risk that a rejuvenated collective bargaining system, lacking centralised co-ordination, might generate the high levels of industrial conflict or of inflation which had been seen in the late 1970s. Although those risks might seem remote in the circumstances of the turn of the century, it is important not to underestimate the impact which the events of the late 1970s had upon the Labour party's perceptions of where its electoral weaknesses lay.[26]

Taken together, these factors suggested that getting the parties' consent to a shift in the level and objectives of bargaining, which corporatist high-level bargaining required, would not be an easy matter and that the project was not one about whose success one could be confident in a British context. In the light of these points, the government may have thought that a policy for regulation of the labour market which depended upon transforming the structure and culture of British collective bargaining ran the risk that reform of the labour market would be very slow in implementation, might fail to achieve its goals, and might even generate undesirable side-effects. In any event, the government did not embark on any such policy. On the contrary, the statutory recognition procedure was designed so as to ratify the existing system of single-employer collective bargaining. Moreover, the outcome of a successful claim, if the parties could not agree, was the imposition of a method of bargaining which was highly unsophisticated and limited (though arguably for that reason easy to enforce legally), and which contained no features likely to encourage a change in bargaining culture.[27] Nor, in this respect, was the existing structure of industrial relations challenged by the framework Directive on information and consultation, since its design as well— this time at EU level—focused on the single employer, at either establishment or undertaking level, though it did seek to extend employee influence to a greater range of managerial decisions than was covered by the statutory recognition procedure.[28] We have also noted that the government resisted the temptation to promote the cross-employer effects of collective bargaining by reintroducing any 'extension' mechanism on the back of its NMW policy.[29] Finally, we saw that only rather weak forms of tripartism were put in place by the post-1997 governments, although these governments did consult employers and, especially, trade unions

[26] See 3.1 above.
[27] Outside the statutory recognition procedure there was some union pressure towards the resuscitation of multi-employer bargaining, but with little success. See, generally, Keith Ewing. 'The Functions of Trade Unions' (2005) 34 ILJ at 13–15, on the decline of the 'regulatory' function of trade unions and collective bargaining.
[28] The UK chose to implement at undertaking level, which it interpreted as equivalent to a single legal entity (DTI, *Guidance on the Information and Consultation of Employees Regulations 2004*, para 5). This led to complicated drafting to permit group-wide agreements to count as pre-existing agreements under the Regulations (Information and Consultation of Employees Regulations 2004, reg 9).
[29] See 4.3.1.1 above.

more readily than their predecessors.[30] All in all, the government's support for collective bargaining, and the role of the social partners more generally, did not take a form which was likely to give the employees significant voice in the high-level policy choices which the governments made in the implementation of their regulatory policies.

To the contrary, it seems that the decentralisation of collective bargaining and the decline in the coverage of collective agreements were not unwelcome to the government in the context of its labour market policies. In 2003 the Treasury concluded:

... the UK system of industrial relations is one that appears conducive to wage flexibility. The decentralised and uncoordinated nature of collective bargaining means that relative wages can adjust to conditions across industries, sectors and regions. The decline in collective bargaining over the last past two decades also supports aggregate wage flexibility.[31]

Thus, not only were there substantial risks associated with any suggested policy of reforming British collective bargaining so as to use it in a positive way as a basis for promoting labour market reform, but the government, or parts of it, took the view that an unreformed collective bargaining system already promoted wage flexibility, in the negative sense that it provided no obstacle to the process. The unreformed bargaining system supported wage flexibility both because of its decentralised nature and because of its limited coverage, at least in the private sector.

Thus, in the period under review in this book, collective bargaining in the UK remained as distinct from collective bargaining in the major continental European countries as it had been throughout modern history. When Kahn-Freund was analysing collective agreements in the immediate post-Second World War period, that distinction resided in the non-legally enforceable nature of British collective agreements, whether as contracts or as codes of terms and conditions of employment.[32] However, at the time he was developing his analysis British collective agreements were still predominantly multi-employer agreements. With the chronic decline of multi-employer collective bargaining in the UK from the 1950s onwards, a second dimension of difference between the UK and the typical continental system of collective bargaining was added, namely, that of the level of bargaining and the focus on the situation of individual enterprises in the UK.[33] However, despite the failure on the part of the Labour governments significantly

---

[30] Perhaps the only examples of important input by the social partners into governmental initiatives were through the Low Pay Commission (see 4.3.1 above) and in relation to the transposition of the Framework Directive on consultation of employees (see 3.4.4.3 above).

[31] HM Treasury, *EMU and Labour Market Flexibility*, 2003, para 4.72.

[32] O Kahn-Freund, 'Legal Framework' in A Flanders and H Clegg (eds), *The System of Industrial Relations in Great Britain* (Oxford: Blackwell Publishing, 1954).

[33] Continental multi-employer bargaining, however, is not immune to the pressures for decentralisation. See, for example, Wolfgang Ochel, 'Decentralising Wage Bargaining in Germany—A Way to Increase Employment?' (2005) 19 Labour 91.

to alter the law relating to industrial conflict, or to embark on a project of reforming the structure and functioning of collective bargaining in the UK, towards the end of our period there was a potentially highly important innovation in the mechanisms for giving employees a collective voice at work. The EU initiative requiring consultation with employee representatives over high-level policy matters likely to affect employment was one which not only government but also unions and employers approached with a high degree of uncertainty, not to say suspicion. These ambiguous attitudes, as expressed in the transposing domestic regulations and the attitudes towards the use of those regulations by workers and employers make it difficult to predict at this stage whether this innovation will move the British system of collective employee representation towards any of the continental arrangements or whether it will operate so as to maintain the separateness of the British system.

5.4 Individual employment relations, managerial flexibility, and labour market regulation

This part of the Conclusion seeks to link up several themes which have been developed in the course of this work, and especially in the context of individual or personal employment relations, that is to say in the territory covered by chapter 2. The first and most general of those themes identifies a change in the basic nature or kind of regulation in which successive governments have engaged or sought to engage during the period under review. This theme is to the effect that there has been a general movement during this period from regulation of employment relations in the interest of correction of inequality of bargaining power to labour market regulation in the interests of competitive flexibility both of the labour economy as a whole and of individual employing enterprises. This continues and probably intensifies a tendency the beginnings of which in the 1980s were observed in the concluding chapters of *Labour Legislation and Public Policy*.

A second theme, or perhaps more accurately a refinement of the first theme, is that during this period successive governments became increasingly interested not merely in labour market regulation, but in regulation designed to secure particular kinds of flexibility for employing enterprises between and within certain sectors of the labour market, or certain particular types of labour market. The relevant sections of the labour market or particular types of labour market were, first, internal labour markets, secondly, external labour markets, and, thirdly, markets in labour under externalised management. These three typologies refer respectively to the situations where, first, after initial career recruitment from outside the employing enterprise, labour is subsequently engaged primarily from within the enterprise by promotion or lateral movement (or possibly by demotion); secondly, labour is engaged from outside the employing enterprise; and, thirdly, labour is engaged via intermediaries which or who assume functions of employment or management of labour. This theme is that special importance has been attached to securing both intra-segmental flexibility and inter-segmental flexibility for employing enter-prises within and between those labour market sections or situations.

Our third theme explores the different extents to which, and ways in which, during the period under review, successive governments moved towards various possible kinds of labour market regulation or sought to devise their own modes of labour market regulation. For the Thatcher and Major administrations, the move was from regulation of employment relations in the interests of correction of inequality of bargaining power to a particularly neo-liberal version of labour market regulation in the interests of competitive flexibility. For the Blair admin-istration, the move from regulation of employment relations in the interests of correction of inequality of bargaining power to labour market regulation in the interests of competitive flexibility was maintained and continued, but in less egregiously neo-liberal forms, and with a greater emphasis on social and eco-nomic inclusion.

Our fourth and final theme concerns the ways in which these diverse approaches to labour market regulation correlated with the methodology of regulation. For the Thatcher and Major administrations, the move from regulation of employment relations in the interests of correction of inequality of bargaining power to a partic-ularly neo-liberal version of labour market regulation in the interests of competitive flexibility essentially involved de-regulation and hostility to any re-regulation. For the Blair administration, the move from regulation of employment relations in the interests of correction of inequality of bargaining power to a rather less neo-liberal version of labour market regulation in the interests of competitive flexibility involved a choice of instruments which were less blunt. To realise that less extreme version of labour market regulation, various forms of light or soft regulation were generally preferred. Those consisted of methodologies such as: ensuring that rights would be derogable rather than absolute; preferring rights to consideration over rights to specific outcomes; imposing pressures for ADR; ensuring that statutory rights were capable of modification by ministerial legislation; and ensuring that parity claims between groups of workers were circumscribed.

But this is not to suggest there was a simple contrast between Conservative de-regulation and New Labour light regulation. Our observation is that the New Labour administration has made complex correlations between its particular aims in labour market regulation, and the methodologies which have been employed. Successive New Labour governments seem to have engaged in relatively light regu-lation, that is to say, to have used the tools which alleviate regulation, especially where heavy regulation would be specially threatening to their general and particu-lar labour market objectives. This section will seek to make that set of links by going through the successive areas into which chapter 1 was divided. First, how-ever, it will be useful somewhat to refine and elaborate the foregoing analysis of regulatory aims and regulatory methodologies.

That refinement and elaboration consists of identifying more fully a set of methodologies of labour market regulation and relating them to the aims with which governments have engaged in labour market regulation during the period under review. These methodologies or modes of labour market regulation may be conceived of as moves around or away from a starting point or original position; that starting point or original position consists of a situation in which employment relations are highly regulated in the interests of correction of inequality of bargaining power, and in a welfarist or worker-protective way. The moves around or away from that starting point may be evaluated and grouped according to how much of a departure they represent towards a contrasting situation of labour market regulation strongly in the interests of a neo-liberal conception of competitive flexibility.

So we are envisaging a set of moves which fall along a broad spectrum from one extreme (X) of highly welfarist or worker-protective regulation of employment relations to a contrasting extreme (Y) of strongly neo-liberal labour market regulation, the moves being identified by reference to the former extreme X. This way of thinking to a certain extent reflects a usage which is already conventional; when we speak about 'de-regulation' in the sphere of employment relations, we usually mean, in a general sense, movement from extreme X towards extreme Y. But it also helps to reveal something deceptive about that conventional usage, for 'de-regulation' in that particular sense does not necessarily or even typically produce a low overall level of regulation. On the contrary, movement from extreme X to extreme Y may turn out to necessitate a higher level of regulation than before, in the sense that the rule-book may become fatter than ever and governmental normative activity more intense than before.

Developing this way of thinking, we can usefully identify six methodologies, which fall into three groups according to how far they move from extreme X towards extreme Y. In the first group are four methodologies which between them represent the furthest set of moves towards extreme Y. They consist of:

1 De-regulation—in the particular sense of abolition or scaling down of an existing worker-protective measure or regime;
2 Non-regulation—meaning refusal to take a worker-protective measure in the face of specific pressure to do so;
3 Minimal regulation—meaning minimal compliance with an obligation to take a worker-protective measure; and
4 Individualising and liberalising regulation—meaning the taking of measures to individualise and liberalise employment relations.

We could give this group as a whole the description of de-regulation and liberalisation. There are then two further groups to which we may give the general descriptions of:

5 Light regulation; and
6 Re-regulation.

Re-regulation consists of a return or progression to a higher level of worker protection. Light regulation is the interesting wild card or joker in the pack; it identifies modes of regulatory activity which seek to achieve an intermediate position between extremes X and Y; we have indicated above some of the particular methodologies of regulation which have been deployed to achieve that aim. This is the most specifically evaluative of the categories of regulation which we are deploying; the application of it to a measure or set of measures involves the judgment that, calibrated against an envisaged standard of worker protection, the measure or set of measures in question involves some kind of relaxation or softening of that standard in deference to some notion of managerial flexibility or adaptability. Using this elaborated analysis, we proceed to characterise the regulatory activity which actually occurred (or failed to occur) during the period under review.

If we use this system of classification or characterisation to produce a synoptic analysis of the measures taken and not taken in the sphere of personal employment relations during the period under review, some interesting conclusions present themselves. It is useful to begin with a chronological perspective and then to refine it by reference to the subject-matter of the particular measures or non-measures (using the latter term to signify decisions not to take measures). From the chronological perspective we can observe interesting contrasts and comparisons between the three phases into which we divided our review of developments in the sphere of personal employment relations. In particular, from this perspective we can see the significance of taking the developments of the early and middle 1990s as a baseline from which to assess the evolutions which occurred after 1997 when the New Labour administration came into power.

Analysed in this way, the first phase which we reviewed, that of the Major administration from 1990 to 1997, presents itself as one which is strongly characterised by de-regulation and liberalisation, with a minor degree of light regulation. Most of the measures and non-measures fall into the first group. To break this down further, we would suggest that there were the following measures or non-measures of:

1 De-regulation—the abolition of the remaining Wages Councils;[34]
2 Non-regulation— the opposition to the EU initiative for Working Time regulation and failure to implementing the Working Time Directive, and abstention from the 'Social Chapter' resulting in non-participation in the Parental Leave Directive;[35]
3 Minimal regulation—the minimal implementation by the 1993 Act of the Pregnant Workers Directive, the Health and Safety Directive, and the amendments to the Acquired Rights Directive;[36]
4 Individualising and liberalising regulation—the Ullswater Amendment to the 1993 Act, and the employment-affecting aspects of the Deregulation and Contracting Out Act and of the Next Steps Initiative, Citizen's Charter Programme, and Private Finance Initiative.[37]

[34] See 2.2.1 above.   [35] Ibid.   [36] Ibid.   [37] See 2.2.4 above.

We would place into the category of:

5 Light regulation—the Pensions Act 1995,[38] and the Disability Discrimination Act 1995.[39]

If we turn to consider the first phase of the New Labour administration, from 1997 to 2001, we find that this mode of analysis confirms the view or hypothesis that the contrast between the measures and non-measures of this period and those of the Major administration, although real and significant, is far from complete. Those who hoped for a decisive swing from the extreme of labour market regulation in the interests of competitive flexibility to the other extreme of regulation of employment relations in the interests of correction of inequality of bargaining power were duly disappointed. The prevailing characterisation was that of:

5 Light regulation—into which we would place The National Minimum Wage Act, the subscribing to the 'Social Chapter', the Working Time Regulations, the measures relating to the qualifying period for and compensation for unfair dismissal, the Maternity and Parental Leave Regulations 1999,[40] the provision in 1999 for Stakeholder Pensions,[41] the employment-affecting aspects of the Human Rights Act 1998 and of the Data Protection Act 1998, and of the Public Interest Disclosure Act 1998;[42] the extension of some legislation to the category of 'worker'; and the Part-time Workers Regulations,[43]

although some of those measures verge upon the character of:

6 Re-regulation, none of them deserves that description in an unqualified sense, and even the measure of that period which is most deserving of that characterisation, the Race Relations Amendment Act 2000, is qualified by its confinement to the public sector.[44]

On the other hand, there were a number of measures which in various senses fell into our first group, that of de-regulation and liberalisation, some of them manifesting specific continuity with the policies of the previous administration. Included in this group, we find measures of:

1 De-regulation—the Lawful Business Practice Regulations 2000,[45] and, quite conspicuously,
4 Individualising and liberalising regulation—the Miller Amendment to the 1999 Act, the continuation of the employment-affecting aspects of the Citizen's Charter programme and the Private Finance Initiative, and the introduction of Performance Management in Schools.[46]

---

[38] See 2.2.1 above.   [39] See 2.2.2 above.   [40] See 2.3.1 above for all those measures.
[41] See 2.4.1 above.   [42] See 2.3.2 above for all those measures.
[43] See 2.3.3 above for those measures.   [44] See 2.4.1 above.   [45] See 2.3.2 above.
[46] See 2.3.4 above.

A generally similar analysis may be made of the second phase of the New Labour administration from 2001 onwards; we have not found that there was any substantial change of policy direction between the first and second phases. Some of the major measures of this phase constitute set-pieces of:

5 Light regulation—the 'flexible working' provisions of the Employment Act 2002, the Pensions Act 2004, the Gangmasters Licensing legislation,[47] and the Age Discrimination legislation of 2006.[48]

That said, we can observe in a somewhat more marked way during this second phase a centrifugal tendency away from light regulation towards more extreme forms of de-regulation and liberalisation of the one hand, and re-regulation on the other. Thus, for example:

1 De-regulation—the tribunal reform and dispute resolution provisions of Parts 2 and 3 of the Employment Act 2002,[49] while presenting themselves as light regulation, deserve to be regarded as de-regulatory; the same could be said of the potentially employment-affecting provisions of the Regulatory Reform legislation;[50]
2 Non-regulation—there was a hardening of resistance to legislation about temporary agency work, and other incidents of dogs that did not bark in the night when pressure to enhance worker protection in the face of economic re-structuring was resisted;[51]
3 Minimal regulation—the Fixed-term Employees Regulations were more obviously minimalist than the Part-time Workers Regulations had been;[52]
4 Individualising and liberalising regulation—there was still an individualising and liberalising edge to the *Wilson and Palmer* provisions of the Employment Act 2004, and to the intensifying programme of reform of public services, as for example in the 'Agenda for Change' in the NHS.[53]

On the other hand, there was also rather more:

6 Re-regulation—the 'family-friendly' provisions of Part 1 of the Employment Act 2002,[54] the Sexual Orientation Regulations and Religion and Belief Regulations, the Disability Discrimination Act 2005,[55] the measures to avoid a two-tier workforce in public services, the TUPE Regulations 2006,[56] and the apparent acceptance at the time of writing of the recommendations of the

---

[47] See 2.4.1 above for all those measures.
[48] See 2.4.2 above. Though it should be observed that many other EU Member States have taken an at least equally 'light' approach to the implementation of the relevant requirements of the Employment Framework Directive; compare Colm O'Cinneide, *Age Discrimination and European Law* (Luxembourg: Office for Official Publications of the European Communities/European Commission, 2005) 1–57, available at <http://europa.eu.int/comm/employment_social/publications/2005/ke6805147_en.pdf>. [49] See 2.4.1 above.
[50] See 2.3.4 above. [51] See 2.4.3 above. [52] See 2.4.3 above.
[53] See 2.4.4 above for all those measures. [54] See 2.4.1 above for those measures.
[55] See 2.4.2 above for all those measures. [56] See 2.4.4 above for all those measures.

Pension Commission (although we have argued that the Pensions White Paper of 2006, in which that acceptance occurred, imports its own particular ingredients of 'light regulation' into the regulatory mixture[57]).

If we now slightly refine that analysis by reference to the subject-matter of those measures and non-measures, some further interesting conclusions offer themselves, which enable us more fully to aggregate the two phases of the New Labour administration and to compare and contrast them with the previous Major administration. In order to tease out those conclusions, it is useful to return to our first two themes, which identified the conceptions or visions of a flexible labour market which successive governments sought to realise by their regulatory interventions and policy in the employment sphere. The approach of the Major administration was in this respect a relatively uncomplicated one; its vision of the flexible labour market was a straightforwardly neo-liberal one, which it sought to realise by de-regulation and liberalisation across the whole scope of the subject-matter of regulation in the employment sphere, moving into light regulation on an occasional rather than a systematic basis under specific political pressures, as with the Pensions Act and the Disability Discrimination Act of 1995.

The New Labour administration, while similarly committed to labour market regulation in the interests of competitive flexibility, had a more nuanced vision of the labour market which it wished to secure and maintain. This was conceived of, not so much as a general free-for-all for employing enterprises, as one in which social and economic inclusion was prominent, and in which freedom of manoeuvre between the three types of labour market or labour market sectors which we have identified was specially protected. The preferred methodology to achieve these objectives was that of light regulation; there was a willingness to diverge from the path of light regulation, in the opposing directions of de-regulation and liberalisation or of re-regulation, but preferably only where that was necessary to realise some crucial feature of that labour market objective or some other policy objective which was central to their overall strategy of government.

Some of those digressions into de-regulation and liberalisation on the one hand, and re-regulation on the other, were proactive and controlled ones. Thus, there was a special disposition towards de-regulation and liberalisation where that was necessary to achieve reform of public services, and to maintain freedom of manoeuvre towards the third type of labour market, that of externalised management—hence, for example, the particular resistance to further regulation of temporary agency work. Thus, on the other hand there was a similar disposition towards family-friendly and anti-discrimination re-regulation, that being seen as compatible with or conducive to maximising the inclusiveness of the labour market.

However, it is also the case that as the duration of political administrations increases, their space for policy manoeuvre diminishes; in the second phase of the

[57] See 2.4.1 above.

New Labour administration the digressions into de-regulation and liberalisation on the one hand, and re-regulation on the other, perhaps took on a more reactive and less controlled character. Thus the de-regulatory provisions of Parts 2 and 3 of the 2002 Act[58] were a response to an increase in employment litigation seen as posing an urgent problem, while the re-regulatory measures associated with the Warwick Accord were, equally, seen as necessary to retain the support of the trade unions and the labour movement for the administration in the conflict created by the government's programme of reform of public services.[59] And it is fairly evident that the government's re-regulatory responses to the arguments or recommendations of the Turner Commission on Pensions have been engendered by a mounting sense of crisis in that sphere.[60] That is an appropriate point at which to broaden this discussion from the specific area of regulation of personal employment relations, and to move on to some larger conclusions from the whole sphere of discussion of the present work.

5.5 A critical task for employment law

This brings us finally to our concluding remarks. With what success have the Labour governments sought a new way in labour law? One could argue that, at a deep level, there is nothing new in the Labour governments' approach to employment law. Like the Thatcher and Major governments before them, the post-1997 governments have required that proposals for new, and the maintenance of existing, legislation in the world of work pass the test of the promotion of economic efficiency generally and of encouraging the development of effective labour markets in particular. For this reason, it might be said, it was possible for the post-1997 governments to accept many of the reforms made by their predecessors in the 1980s and 1990s, a feature of each of the three areas of law into which we have divided our analysis in this book. However, this would be to ignore the break which the post-1997 governments made from the equation of efficient regulation with deregulation, which its predecessors largely adopted. Thus we have been able to identify the ways in which the New Labour administration, even if it has been similarly committed to a calculus of economic efficiency in its regulation in the employment sphere as the Thatcher and Major administrations were, has nevertheless developed a much more nuanced approach to the working out of that regulatory calculus, involving a more sophisticated set of economic arguments in which the positive value of economic and social inclusion and the positive potential of the elevation of 'market-friendly' labour standards is recognised rather than denied. To take but two examples of this approach in operation, it is difficult to think of a period of time, at least since the middle 1970s, when there has been a more explosive growth of anti-discrimination laws, both in terms of the types of

---

[58] See 2.4.1 above.   [59] See 2.4.4 above.   [60] See 2.4.4 above.

discrimination aimed at and the variety of techniques deployed to combat them—and it would be quite wrong to see this as solely or even mainly a response to exogenous pressures from the European Commission and Community. Again, the various New Deals represented a significant step beyond the simple policy of making benefit conditional on active but unaided work-seeking by claimants.

The focus of the post-1997 governments on regulation of labour markets, albeit at a more sophisticated level, left those governments open to criticism from the perspective of those focused on correction of inequality of bargaining power. Critics of the New Labour administration from this perspective might identify problems with their policies and measures in a number of areas, such as: the controlling of the growth of precarious employment and of insecurity of income for large sections of the workforce or of the expansion of extreme inequalities of income between sections of the workforce; the limitation of the growth of under-regulated sectors of the labour market, such as that of temporary agency work, or that of employment by intermediaries such as gangmasters; the need for more effective restraint of a culture of long hours of work; the addressing of the problems of provision of income in retirement, aggravated by demographic factors; the ensuring of effective training for employment of young entrants to the workforce; and the prevention of undue intrusion upon the autonomy of unemployed persons by the 'welfare to work' system. From this same perspective, there was, in addition, the problem of the very significant omission on the part of the New Labour administration to construct or to reconstruct a strong institutional voice for trade unions in the regulation of employment relations.

Although such criticism has been well represented in the academic literature, its political impact has been limited. Whether by luck or judgment, the New Labour administration had by the time of writing in 2006 experienced not merely seven but nine good years in terms of labour market regulation according to the politically crucial measures of unemployment, wage inflation, and industrial conflict, which had all been at low levels throughout their period in office, judged by the standards of any time in the post-war period or, in the case of unemployment, by the standards of the previous two decades. These positive outcomes have encouraged a political confidence within the ranks of government and of their advisers that the gains in terms of successful labour market regulation justify, indeed demand, a robust approach to the criticisms. It is ultimately a matter of personal choice how far and in what sense one adapts one's critique to that perspective. However, our acknowledgement above of the genuine seeking, and also to some extent the successful finding, of a 'new way' on the part of New Labour may itself have some positive value in terms of a widening of the horizons of theorising about labour legislation and the associated body of public policy. Thus, it is perhaps appropriate for academic analysis of the labour legislation of the past decade to develop in new directions which follow the governments' objectives—without of course any automatic deference to them.

The evidence for success of regulation in the sphere of employment that has generally been proffered by New Labour governments has been very much cast in the discourse of labour market regulation; it has tended to consist of indications that their measures and policies have achieved high levels of employment and so reduced the extremes of poverty in employment, and have created the conditions for the labour market to function so as to maximise social and economic inclusion and entrepreneurial prosperity, while at the same time retaining an apparatus of labour standards and protection of workers which is both respectable in an absolute sense and in any event the best available apparatus which is compatible with those labour market goals. The promotion of social inclusion and the expansion of the productive economy are challenging goals for a system of labour law, even if by no means the whole of the burden of achieving these aims is carried by the legal system. In many ways they constitute a greater challenge to employment law than that posed by the ideology of collective laissez-faire, where the aim was the simpler one of establishing a mechanism for joint regulation by employers and unions of employment relations, whilst leaving the substantive outcomes of that process to the bargainers. Now nearly the whole of the burden lies on the law and governmental policy and administration, with the bargainers cast in a subordinate role. To what extent the laws adopted by governments since 1997 have maximised the law's contribution to these goals is not wholly clear. There is already an extensive literature, part of it generated by the government's own research and part independently, which seeks to evaluate those claims, and to some of which we have referred in this book. Pursuing rigorous investigation into the question of what part the law of employment has played so far and might play in the future in achieving these profoundly important social objectives would be no unworthy task for employment lawyers to set themselves.

Index